Freight Transport Regulation

MIT Press Series on the Regulation of Economic Activity

General Editor
Richard Schmalensee, MIT Sloan School of Management

Freight Transport Regulation
Equity, Efficiency, and Competition in the
Rail and Trucking Industries

Ann F. Friedlaender
Richard H. Spady

The MIT Press
Cambridge, Massachusetts, and London, England

Copyright © 1981 by
The Massachusetts Institute of Technology

This book was set in Times New Roman by Asco Trade Typesetting Ltd., Hong Kong, and printed and bound in the United States of America.

Library of Congress Cataloging in Publication Data

Friedlaender, Ann Fetter.
  Freight transport regulation.

  Bibliography: p.
  Includes index.
    1. Railroads—United States—Freight. 2. Transportation, Automotive—United States—Freight. 3. Transportation and state—United States. 4. Freight and freightage—United States. I. Spady, Richard H., 1952–   joint author. II. Title.
HE2355.F74   388′.044′0973   80-23879
ISBN 0-262-06072-8

Contents

List of Figures

List of Tables

Series Foreword

Government regulation of economic activity in the United States has grown dramatically in this century, radically transforming government–business relations. Economic regulation of prices and conditions of service was applied first to transportation and public utilities and recently has been extended to energy, health care, and other sectors. In the 1970s, explosive growth occurred in social regulation focusing on workplace safety, environmental preservation, consumer protection, and related goals. The expansion of regulation has not proceeded in silence. Critics have argued that many regulatory programs produce negative net benefits, while regulation's defenders have pointed to the sound rationales for, and potential gains from, many of the same programs.

The purpose of the MIT Press series, Regulation of Economic Activity, is to inform the ongoing debate on regulatory policy by making significant and relevant research available to both scholars and decision makers. The books in this series will present new insights into individual agencies, programs, and regulated sectors, as well as the important economic, political, and administrative aspects of the regulatory process that cut across these boundaries.

This study of freight transport regulation by Ann F. Friedlaender and Richard H. Spady, based on research performed in connection with MIT's Center for Transportation Studies, is a path-breaking economic analysis with important policy implications. Using powerful modern econometric tools and paying careful attention to the special attributes of the railroad and trucking industries, the authors construct a general equilibrium model of freight carriage by these two modes that permits analysis of impact of policy changes on regional incomes. This model is used to estimate the efficiency and equity effects of a number of alternative regulatory policy changes. An important finding is that deregulation of freight transport would produce very large real-income transfers, a potentially serious problem for policymakers. In terms of both research quality and importance for regulatory policy, this first volume in the series sets a high standard indeed for those to follow.

Richard Schmalensee

Preface

Work on this study was begun in 1975 when deregulation in the transportation industries was still viewed skeptically by most policymakers. In the past five years, however, the political climate toward deregulation has changed dramatically. Hearings by the Senate Judiciary Committee focused attention on the costs of air regulation and played a major role in the eventual passage of legislation in late 1978 that substantially deregulated the air industry. Similar hearings on the costs of trucking regulation, which also were held by the Senate Judiciary Committee, served to catalyze interest in deregulation in the trucking industry, and a trucking regulatory reform bill was signed by President Carter on July 1, 1980. Concurrently, led by Conrail, a number of railroads have pushed actively for deregulation in the railroad industry, and the passage of legislation providing major regulatory reform in the railroad industry now appears likely. Finally, with the appointment of Darius W. Gaskins as Chairman of the Interstate Commerce Commission and the appointment of a number of other commissioners who favor relaxation of regulatory restrictions, the ICC recently has been transformed from an institution primarily concerned with preserving the regulatory status quo to one encouraging the workings of the free market in the surface freight industries.

Thus for the first time in almost 100 years, allocation of resources in the surface freight industries by the free market appears to be a real possibility. This presents us with a unique opportunity to observe the evolution of the rail and trucking industries from highly regulated and noncompetitive market structures into structures that are shaped by competitive forces. Because this study was started in 1975 and based its analysis on data available at that time, it is necessarily somewhat out of date at the present time. Moreover, because its conclusions are based on evidence obtained from econometric methods, they are necessarily subject to the limitations associated with such analysis. In particular, data limitations often preclude as complete an analysis as one would desire. Nevertheless, by providing a detailed analysis of a competitive market allocation in the rail and trucking industries, it should provide a benchmark that can be used to evaluate the ultimate market structure that will be established in the rail and trucking industries. As such its publication should prove to be particularly timely.

Ann F. Friedlaender
Richard H. Spady
July 10, 1980

Acknowledgments

Work on this study was supported by the Department of Transportation, Office of University Research, Grant DOT-OS-50239, and the Transportation Systems Center, Grant DOT-TSC-1599.

Work on this project encompassed many dimensions, and we are grateful to the many individuals who provided counsel and support. Robert W. Simpson, James Kneafsey, James Sloss, and Richard de Neufville worked on various aspects of this project, and the final product reflects their intellectual contributions. The analysis of rail costs was aided by research assistance provided by Scott Nason and Ronald Niefield, while the analysis of trucking costs benefitted greatly from the help provided by Thomas Bailey, Harold Furchtgott, and Shaw-er Judy Wang Chiang. Rosanne Snow, Sharon Lowenheim, and Shaw-er Judy Wang Chiang provided invaluable research assistance on the demand analysis; Rosanne Snow helped write the computer program for estimating translog cost functions. The regional income model was developed and estimated by Janice Halpern and Anthony Rodrigues. Laurence P. Michaels developed the program and performed the simulation analysis of a competitive equilibrium. Finally, Marc Thorman typed innumerable memos, papers, and reports with remarkable speed and efficiency.

Freight Transport Regulation

Chapter 1

Regulation and Regulatory Reform: An Overview

1.1 Transport Regulation and Regulatory Analysis

Freight transportation historically has been one of the most heavily regulated sectors in the American econmy. The Interstate Commerce Act of 1887 introduced economic regulation as a policy tool and brought rail rates under extensive controls to limit discriminatory pricing practices concerning persons, localities, routes, and traffic. This structure was subsequently extended to for-hire motor carriers and barge operators so that the bulk of intercity freight transportation is presently regulated in accordance with the structure of the original Interstate Commerce Act.[1] Thus not only are rates, routes, entry, merger, and abandonments currently closely monitored in the rail, trucking, and barge industries, but also the existing regulatory restrictions have paralleled closely those of the initial act. Consequently, even though the Interstate Commerce Act has been extensively amended in the ninety-plus years since its initial passage, the form and intent of regulatory restrictions have remained remarkably consistent during this period.

The forces behind the passage of the initial act of 1887 and its subsequent application have been extensively explored, and there are a number of somewhat contradictory hypotheses concerning them.[2] Perhaps the most appealing of these is the hypothesis that at its initial inception, regulation jointly served the interests of the railroads on the one hand, which were suffering from excess capacity, rate wars, and highly unstable profits, and the interests of the expanding agricultural population on the other, which was suffering from discriminatory pricing practices and excessive rates. Consequently, the railroads accepted regulation to ensure stability and orderly growth, while the agricultural interests actively sought regulation to protect them from the monopolistic exploitation of the railroads.

The Interstate Commerce Act of 1887 specifically required rates to be "just and reasonable," while prohibiting undue preference between persons, localities, and types of services, and the practice of charging more for a long haul than a short haul over a common line. However, while prohibiting all forms of personal price discrimination the act made no mention of commodity price discrimination, and value-of-service pricing rapidly achieved official sanction from the Interstate Commerce Commission (ICC).[3] Thus the rate structure was such that railroads treated shippers more or less equally with respect to their size and location, while receiving relatively high margins on high-value manufactured commodities and relatively low margins on low-value bulk and agricultural commodities.

At its time of inception, this policy made sense. It served the agricultural and populist interests by ensuring that rates for their commodities would be kept low and ensuring that the farmers and homesteaders would not see any potential economic rent expropriated by the railroads. It served the interests of the railroads by ending the instabilities caused by the frequent rate wars and by ensuring relatively stable profit levels through the high returns received on high-value manufactured commodities. Indeed, subject to the restriction upon personal price discrimination imposed by the act, it is likely that the value-of-service rate structure was also the profit-maximizing rate structure for the railroads. Moreover, since the demand for manufactured commodities was quite inelastic at that time, relatively little resource misallocation should have resulted from this pricing structure.

While many changes have taken place in the structure of the Interstate Commerce Act since its passage in 1887, three aspects have remained essentially constant:

Prohibition of personal price discrimination.

Value-of-service pricing.

Maintenance of carrier profitability.

Of these, the prohibition of personal price discrimination is probably the least controversial since it meets generally held standards of fairness and equity. Insofar, however, as economies of large-volume shipment exist, the requirement that rates be the same to large and small shippers or the requirement that rates be the same on high-density routes as low-density routes may in fact reflect discrimination in favor of low-density, rural shippers. This, of course, is entirely consistent with the populist intent of the value-of-service rate structure.

The Hoch–Smith Resolution, passed by Congress in 1925, explicitly required the ICC to give consideration to the relationship between agricultural freight rates and agricultural incomes and has been interpreted as giving clear legislative sanction to the maintenance of the value-of-service rate structure.[4] Consequently, the response to pressures that might lead to a change in the freight rate structure has been to extend regulation. Thus when the railroads were faced with an erosion of their high-value traffic by trucks, regulation was extended to motor carriers in 1935. Similarly, when water competition threatened to reduce the profitability of low-value shipments and put pressures on the railroads to increase rates on their captive bulk traffic, regulation was extended to barges in 1940. Since World War II, the ICC has carefully monitored minimum rate levels on water-competitive traffic to ensure that rail profitability is maintained at sufficiently high levels to preclude upward pressures on the rates of captive bulk traffic.[5]

Finally, while perhaps less obvious, the maintenance of carrier profitability has played an important role in regulatory policy. It is not a coincidence that regulation was instituted during a period of extreme rail instability and rate wars or that regulation was extended to motor carriers during a period of "excessive" competition and bankruptcies during the Great Depression. When faced with considerable excess capacity and the associated pressures to price down to short-run marginal costs, firms tend to attempt cartelization to maintain industry stability. Since, however, the same pressures that lead to rate cutting and rate wars also make policing the cartel difficult, regulation presents an attractive alternative. Carriers accept a perhaps somewhat reduced expectation of long-run profits for a reduction of their variance, while society is willing to guarantee the carriers relatively stable profits in exchange for the maintenance of a rate structure that may not be entirely consistent with the profit-maximizing behavior of the carriers.

Thus over the past ninety years a rather symbiotic arrangement has evolved among small rural shippers, agricultural interests, railroads, and trucking firms, in which each has accepted certain costs in exchange for other benefits. The rural and agricultural interests have accepted higher freight rates and prices on manufactured commodities in exchange for relatively low rates on the commodities they ship. The railroads have accepted low freight rates on agricultural commodities in exchange for high rates on manufactured goods. Trucking firms have accepted relatively low rates to low-density rural areas in exchange for the umbrella provided by the value-of-service rate structure and the industry stability and profitability provided by regulation. Thus while no one group is a clear winner, on balance each feels that its real income is higher as a result of regulation than it would be in its absence.

Since the agricultural and rural interests were a formidable political force in the late nineteenth and early twentieth centuries, it is not surprising that the coalition between the carriers and these interests survived at that time. What is surprising, however, is that well into the last quarter of the twentieth century, transportation regulation has existed in a form and intent that is basically unchanged from its inception. In view of the basic changes that have taken place in American society over the past ninety years, it is certainly reasonable to ask whether social and political institutions that were applicable at the turn of the century are still applicable. To state the question baldly: Are the benefits conferred by regulation upon the carriers and the rural and agricultural interests sufficiently great to warrant the costs in terms of resource misallocation that are generated by regulation?

Over the past twenty years economists have become increasingly critical of transport regulation. The issue was first raised by John Meyer and his associates (1959), who argued that the value-of-service rate structure imposed considerable costs upon society by encouraging shipments to go by truck, which had a distinct service advantage, instead of by rail, which was prohibited from practicing price competition. In addition, since the common carrier obligations imposed upon railroads and trucks made them maintain sufficient capacity to meet the demands of low-density shippers, the carriers were not able to adjust their capacity in an optimal fashion and were thus forced to operate with an inefficiently large plant. In addition, it is often argued that regulation and the ensuing cartelization of the rail and trucking industries have tended to blunt innovative initiatives so that the productivity growth in the rail and trucking industries has been less than it otherwise might have been.[6] Finally, it is also argued that the cartelization of these industries has enabled labor to obtain higher wage settlements than those achieved in more competitive industries.[7] Thus it is claimed that the potential benefits of regulation that accrue to carrier management have at least partially been extended to labor, with a consequent broadening of support for continued regulation.

In recent years a voluminous literature has developed attempting to quantify the costs that transport regulation imposes upon society.[8] While the specific methodologies differ substantially, and the magnitudes of the estimated costs vary, the conventional wisdom is that these costs are substantial. Indeed, related exercises with respect to the air industry encouraged the recently passed air deregulation bill[9] and have considerably strengthened the case for deregulation in the surface freight industries.

Pressures for deregulation in the surface freight industries are particularly strong. A regulatory reform bill for the trucking industry was passed in the summer of 1980, and similar legislation is likely to be passed for the rail industry before the end of 1980. While the deregulation embodied in both the rail and trucking bills is relatively modest, it nevertheless marks a significant departure from existing restrictions upon rate freedom, entry, and abandonment and thus gives firms in these industries considerably more incentive to act in a competitive fashion than they previously have had.

The pressures for deregulation have come from several sources. The recent experience of the airlines suggests that deregulation does not necessarily lead to Armegeddon. In addition, the inability of the railroads to utilize fully the band of rate freedom legislated under the 4-R Act,[10] in conjunction with their increasing financial plight, has caused the railroads to look with increasing favor upon deregulation. Indeed, prominent rail spokesmen have pushed strenuously for relaxation of restrictions with respect to rates, mergers, and abandonments.[11] Finally, with a number of new appointments, the ICC recently has been transformed from a staunch supporter of the regulatory status quo to a leadership position with respect to regulatory reform.

Nevertheless, concerns about deregulation remain extremely strong. Motor carriers continue to believe that "destructive" competition would ensue in the advent of deregulation, and small rural shippers and agricultural interests feel that deregulation would lead to substantial rate increases and a consequent reduction in real income. Thus conventional wisdom holds that deregulation would impose substantial and specific costs upon the existing beneficiaries of regulation.

However, in considering the potential costs that deregulation might impose upon its presumed beneficiaries, it is important to note that the world is not static. Fundamental changes have occurred in the transportation industries in the twenty years since Meyer and his associates wrote their pioneering work that may substantially affect the magnitudes of the costs and benefits of continued transport regulation.

In particular, the virtual completion of the Interstate Highway System has meant that truck transportation presents a viable, if somewhat more expensive, alternative to rail transportation for agricultural commodities that were formerly considered as captive rail shipments. In addition, the Interstate Highway System has permitted trucks to utilize larger loads and achieve higher speeds and thus to become increasingly competitive with rail. Wyckoff and Maister (1977) have estimated that efficient truck-load operations are in fact no more costly than rail.

The growth of truckload trucking operations has also had an impact upon the trucking markets, which in fact are increasingly dichotomized between carriers of general commodities, which largely perform a consolidation service and concentrate on less-than-truckload (LTL) operations, and the carriers of specialized commodities, which perform platform-to-platform, full-truckload (TL) services. Since the markets and technologies of these two types of carriers are very different, it would clearly be a mistake to treat trucking as a homogeneous entity. Indeed, the implications of deregulation in the truckload and LTL markets are very different and must be analyzed accordingly.

1.2 Analyzing Regulatory Reform

In view of these fundamental changes that have taken place in the transportation markets in the past few years, it may be desirable to reassess the impact of regulation upon the carriers and shippers to see whether the allocational costs and distributional benefits are in fact as large as they are generally believed to be.

In this connection, however, it is important to realize that regulation is not a single policy, but is actually a number of specific policies concerning rates, routes, mergers, abandonments, etc., on the affected modes. Of these, the following are probably the most important:

The maintenance of the value-of-service rate structure.

Railroad abandonment and infrastructure maintenance.

The maintenance of common carrier trucking obligations to light-density rural areas.

Value-of-service pricing   The importance of the maintenance of the value-of-service rate structure should be clear from the preceding discussion. Indeed, one can argue that its maintenance has formed one of the principal cornerstones of regulatory policy and has been a prime determinant in ICC decisions concerning minimum rates, umbrella pricing, and market dominance. Thus the value-of-service rate structure has been a major topic of analysis by economists and others concerned with the implications of regulation, and most of the alleged costs and benefits of transport regulation can be attributed, either directly or indirectly, to the maintenance of this rate structure.[12]

If in fact, however, truckload operations are competitive with rail operations, and inland agricultural shippers have viable alternatives to rail, the potential resource misallocations resulting from the value-of-service pricing structure become considerably less, while the potential costs of

eliminating it also become considerably less. Thus it is entirely possible that the maintenance of the value-of-service pricing structure is a nonissue: if truckload operations are really competitive with rail for high-valued manufactured traffic, then the bulk of this traffic should probably go by truck, and the current traffic allocation may in fact be too heavily oriented to rail; if truckload operations are really competitive with rail for agricultural shipments, then the railroads have little latent monopoly power with respect to inland agricultural shippers, and few income losses should accrue to these shippers in the absence of regulation.

Consequently, to analyze the implications of the maintenance of the value-of-service rate structure, it is essential to focus upon truckload (TL) trucking operations instead of less-than-truckload trucking (LTL) operations. Although Wyckoff and Maister (1975, 1977) have highlighted the role of TL operations, their implications for rail–truck competition and resource allocation have not been fully explored. Indeed, once the full implications of this form of competition have been explored, it may be the case that efficiency requires further curtailment of rail operations rather than their expansion.

In addition, to the extent that truck competition has acted as a constraint upon the railroads with respect to their pricing of high-value manufactured goods, it may be that the value-of-service rate structure is no longer applicable in the sense that rates may actually be higher relative to marginal costs on bulk commodities than on manufactured goods. In this case the presumed cross subsidy from manufactured to bulk commodities would no longer exist. Indeed, in this case, abandonment of value-of-service pricing might actually favor shippers of bulk commodities more than shippers of manufactured goods.

Moreover, the analysis of rail–truck competition has usually been couched in terms of a partial equilibrium analysis, in which measures of traffic misallocation have been made at existing rate levels, rather than at the rate levels that would exist in a competitive equilibrium. If all trucking and rail operations took place at constant marginal costs, measures of misallocation based on existing rates and costs would be meaningful. Since, however, rail and trucking costs are not constant, the final competitive equilibrium may look quite different from that implied by existing rates and costs. This problem is compounded when one realizes that rail and trucking demands depend on rail and trucking rates and shipment characteristics, and that rail and trucking costs depend upon the composition of shipments. Thus, for example, changes in rail rates on manufactured goods will lead to shifts in trucking demand functions, and the

resulting output shifts in each mode will lead to further shifts in the marginal costs of each mode. Thus a partial equilibrium analysis will fail to capture the full nature of rail–truck competition and a general equilibrium analysis is required.

Finally, since the policymakers clearly weight carrier and shipper income losses fairly heavily in their decisionmaking process, rational discourse requires some effort to assess the income costs of policy changes. Thus analyses of deregulation must be able to translate rate changes into income changes that would affect shippers and carriers. Consequently, it is necessary to build models that relate rate changes to regional income changes as well as to changes in carrier profitability.

Consequently, the primary focus of this study will be to perform a full general equilibrium analysis of the competitive equilibrium that would exist between rail and truckload trucking operations with respect to bulk and manufactured commodities. By comparing this with the existing equilibrium, it should be possible to assess the efficiency costs of maintaining the existing rate structure as well as its impact upon carrier profitability and regional income levels.

Of course, it is important to stress that a competitive equilibrium is not necessarily the presumed outcome of deregulation and the abandonment of the value-of-service rate structure. Oligopoly and monopolistic competition are the structural norms of American industry, and it is likely that they would also characterize a deregulated transportation industry. Nevertheless, since competition is the relevant efficiency norm, it is useful to evaluate the value-of-service rate structure using it as a standard. Moreover, in establishing the nature of the competitive equilibrium it should also be possible to consider the forces that would tend to push the transportation industries toward it or away from it in the absence of the value-of-service rate structure.

Railroad abandonment and infrastructure maintenance While regulatory policy has traditionally focused upon the value-of-service rate structure, the increasing financial plight of the railroads and the increasing deterioration of their roadbeds have focused attention on the quality of the railroad infrastructure, the costs of its maintenance, and the potential cost savings that could accrue from abandonment of light-density lines.

Basically the problem is this. During the past decade the railroads have been increasingly pressed for revenues as high-value traffic has been diverted by truckload trucking operations. Since high-value traffic traditionally has had a high price–marginal cost ratio, the loss of this traffic has made it increasingly difficult to maintain adequate profit levels from

its remaining traffic. Since general rate increases on agricultural and related bulk traffic were neither politically viable (because of pressures to maintain the traditional rate structure), nor economically tenable (because of competitive pressures from water carriers or truckload operations),[13] the railroads have tended to turn to deferred maintenance to maintain their ostensible profit levels.

Deferred maintenance is an attractive means of maintaining profits over a short-term business cycle since it takes several years for the roadbed to deteriorate sufficiently for its impact to become apparent. Thus as long as revenues can be expected to grow sufficiently in the future to provide the funds for the rehabilitation of the roadbed, deferred maintenance is a rational policy for railroads to follow.

If, however, the reduction in revenues arises from long-term secular forces having to do with the growth of competitive trucking operations rather than from short-term cyclical swings, problems are clearly created as the roadbeds continue to be cannibalized to meet the short-term financial obligations of the railroads. With the deterioration of the roadbed comes reduced speeds, increased derailments, and a deterioration of service. Thus a vicious cycle becomes established under which the service deterioration diverts traffic to trucks, which causes a reduction in rail revenues, which causes further deferred maintenance and a concomitant deterioration in service.

The state of the rail roadbed has currently reached crisis proportions,[14] and a number of alternatives are being considered to solve this problem. Of these, the least drastic is probably giving subsidized government-guaranteed loans to the railroads to permit them to bring the roadbeds up to acceptable levels. Since this would correct a major imperfection in the capital markets facing the railroads, this proposal has considerable merit.[15] Its major drawback, however, is that the infrastructure requirements and the revenue declines may be too large to make a politically viable loan program also effective.[16] Thus, instead of a rather modest loan program, a major program of infrastructure finance may be required. Of course, whether Congress would accept such a program is highly problematical.[17]

In the absence of major infrastructure investments, attention has focused on the possible economies arising from abandonment of light-density lines. Keeler (1974) and Harris (1977b) have both argued that substantial economies can be obtained from permitting the railroads to divest themselves of lightly used lines and their associated maintenance and operating costs.

From a political viewpoint, this proposal has the decided liability that it is at ostensible odds with traditional policies to ensure cheap and adequate transportation to rural, agricultural shippers. If, however, truckload operations are really rail competitive, one can argue that these shippers should not suffer under hardship in the event of rail abandonment.

Common carrier trucking obligations   Although trucking was largely brought under regulation as a means of preserving the value-of-service rate structure, current questions raised by trucking deregulation deal with the possibility of destructive competition and the adequacy of service to small shippers in light-density rural areas.

Currently, all regulated trucking firms have a common carrier obligation to serve all shippers regardless of their location or size. Since, however, LTL shipments, short hauls, small loads, and small shipments are more costly to transport than large-load, long-haul, truckload shipments, service to small shippers in light-density rural areas is inherently more expensive than service to large shippers in high-density urban areas. However, it is generally believed that the rate structure does not fully reflect these cost differentials.[18] Hence the existence of a cross subsidy is widely perceived in which rates to light-density rural areas are held below their remunerative levels.[19] Consequently, trucking regulation is often defended on the grounds that its elimination would lead either to substantial rate increases to small rural shippers, or to abandonment of service, or to both.[20]

In addition, proponents of regulation argue that common carrier trucking is subject to substantial economies of scale, and point to the large number of trucking mergers that have taken place in recent years as supporting evidence. Thus, according to them, in the absence of regulation, large trucking firms would exploit their inherent cost advantages and undercut their smaller competitors. The eventual market structure would consequently be characterized by a few large carriers giving service on the high-density, low-cost routes, with a fringe of small carriers providing service to the low-density, high-cost routes. Thus, according to this scenario, deregulation would lead to substantial service reductions and increases in rates to small rural shippers, and a highly concentrated market structure (and presumed accompanying high rates) in the high-density urban areas. Consequently, everyone would lose with the exception of the large, efficient trucking firms.

While the present regulatory structure provides clear incentives to merge to acquire additional operating authorities, it is difficult to argue

that trucking is inherently subject to increasing returns to scale. While large firms may presently have lower costs, these costs are not lower because the firm is large per se, but because the firm is able to carry a broader range of commodities over a geographically dispersed area and thus utilize its fleet more efficiently. In the absence of regulatory restrictions on commodities and localities, however, there is little reason to believe that large firms would be inherently more efficient than small firms. Thus it is likely that any economies of scale that are currently observed are due to regulatory practices rather than to the technological structure of the trucking industry.[21]

Nevertheless, it does appear to be true that service to low-density rural shippers is inherently more costly to produce than service to large shippers in high-density urban areas. Thus to the extent that the current rate structure may not adequately reflect these cost differentials, small shippers in low-density rural areas could be expected to face increases in rates.

In view of the uncertainties concerning the structure of costs with respect to different types of services on the part of common carrier trucking and the implications of these cost differentials for the trucking rate structure, it is important to undertake a thorough analysis of the costs and technology of the LTL trucking market. Once these cost differentials have been fully analyzed and understood, the implications of marginal cost pricing or of monopolistic rate making can be explored to evaluate the impact of deregulation upon rural shippers. In addition, such an analysis of the costs of common carrier trucking should permit a better understanding of the question of the existence of economies of scale in the regulated trucking industry.

In conclusion, then, this book will focus on the issues of the value-of-service rate structure, railroad infrastructure and abandonment, and common carrier trucking obligations, and assess the allocational and distributional implications of a relaxation of regulatory restrictions in these areas. As an important by-product, this study should yield substantially improved cost functions and demand functions for the various modes over those that are currently available. Thus from the view of positive economic analysis, this study should improve our understanding of rail and trucking cost and demand functions. From the view of normative policy analysis, this study should yield quantitative measures of the allocational and distributional costs and benefits resulting from present policies or specific alternatives. Consequently, while hardly providing the definitive analysis of the subject, it is hoped that this book will provide important insights that have previously been lacking in the area of regulatory analysis and will provide a firm analytical foundation upon which regulatory policy can be evaluated.

This book takes the following form. Chapter 2 discusses the costs and demand of rail and truckload trucking operations to provide a general overview of the structure of these industries. Chapters 3, 4, and 5, respectively, provide an analysis of the implications of relaxing restrictions concerning the value-of-service rate structure, the maintenance of the railroad infrastructure and service abandonment to light-density areas, and the maintenance of common carrier trucking obligations. Chapter 6 provides a brief summary and conclusions. A series of technical appendixes presents the econometric analysis of the costs of the relevant modes, the model of regional income determination, and the simulation analysis used to derive the competitive equilibrium.

Notes

1. Privately owned intercity carriage and agricultural commodities carried by truck are exempt from regulation. Thus while all rail shipments are subject to regulation, somewhat less than half of all trucking shipments and one-fourth of all inland waterway shipments are subject to regulation.

2. See, for example, Buck (1965), Kolko (1965), Benson (1955), Tarbell (1904), MacAvoy (1965), and Friedlaender (1969).

3. For example, the first annual report of the ICC stated, "The public interest is best served when the rates are so apportioned ... by making value an important consideration and by placing upon the higher classes of freight some share of the burden that on a relatively equal apportionment ... would fall upon those of less value." [ICC (1887, p. 36)].

4. For a good discussion of the Hoch–Smith Resolution see Nelson and Greiner (1965).

5. The formation of Amtrak and the takeover of rail passenger service on the part of the federal government can also be interpreted as an effort to maintain rail profitability and thus foreclose efforts to alter the value-of-service rate structure.

6. See, for example, Gellman (1971).

7. For an interesting analysis of this point see Moore (1976).

8. Of these, the most important are Keeler (1972, 1974), Harbeson (1969), Friedlaender (1969), Moore (1975), Boyer (1977), and Levin (1978).

9. See, for example, Douglas and Miller (1975), Eads (1972), Jordan (1970), and Keeler (1972).

10. The 4-R Act gave the railroads the freedom to raise or lower rates by 7 percent, subject to the constraint that "market dominance" not be present. The commission has interpreted the existence of "market dominance" in a narrow fashion, however, and generally prevented rate increases in the case where only one railroad serves a given area, even though trucks may offer substantial competitive alternatives.

11. For example, John Snow, Vice-President of the Chessie System, told reporters at the Transportation Roundtable in the National Press Club on October 13, 1978, that railroads are considering proposing total deregulation of the railroads over a five-year span. See *Traffic World* (October 23, 1978), 19 and 27.

12. The current state of the debate can probably be summarized in the ICC's analysis of the costs and benefits of regulation (ICC, 1976).

13. In fact, the railroads have tried to cope with this situation by general rate increases, which have generally exceeded those of the trucking industry.

14. For a good recent discussion of this problem see Federal Railway Association (1978).

15. Because the railroad infrastructure is nontransferable, financial institutions have traditionally been unwilling to give loans for infrastructure improvements. This has led to distortion of rail capital in that railroads have tended to invest fairly heavily in equipment, for which they can obtain funds because of its transferable nature, at the expense of infrastructure.

16. It is precisely the feeling that the railroads' problems are due to factors other than the deterioration of the roadbed that has apparently encouraged the railroads to pursue deregulation.

17. Of course, highways and waterways have traditionally been financed by the federal government while the railroad infrastructure has been privately financed. Thus there may be considerable justification in a policy that would impose some priority to federal expenditures on railroad infrastructure.

18. For an elaboration of these views, see Friedlaender (1978b) and Spady and Friedlaender (1978).

19. The extent of this cross subsidy is a source of considerable controversy. Many trucking executives claim that their firms actually make losses on these shipments. Since, however, measures of average costs are essentially arbitrary in a multiproduct firm, these claims should probably be greeted with some skepticism. As a more meaningful measure, one can consider whether revenues cover incremental costs, which measure the differential costs associated with providing a specific service. While not always easy to measure in practice, these can be measured in principle by estimating all of the cost savings that could accrue to a firm from abandoning a particular type of service. These cost savings reflect the incremental costs associated with the service, and a cross subsidy can be said to exist if its revenues fail to cover its incremental costs.

20. For an interesting view of the regulatory debate in trucking see National Research Council (1978).

21. For an elaboration of these views see Friedlaender (1978b), and Spady and Friedlaender (1978).

Chapter 2

Rail–Truck Competition and the Structure of Costs and Demand

2.1 Introduction and Overview

Before we can fully assess the implications of policies aimed at rate regulation or infrastructure investments, it is essential to have a full understanding of the nature of the technology, costs, and demand facing the rail and trucking industries. Thus this chapter serves as a background for much of the subsequent discussion concerning transportation policy and discusses our estimates of rail and trucking cost and demand functions.

Although there have been many previous analyses of rail and trucking costs and rail and trucking demand functions, they have all suffered from various weaknesses of specification and estimation.[1] Consequently, considerable effort has gone into a careful specification and estimation of the cost and demand functions used in this analysis to ensure that they have firm theoretical foundations. Since, however, a full discussion of the technical aspects of these cost and demand functions would not be of interest to most readers, this chapter will serve as a summary of our general methodology and results. The reader who is interested in technical details is directed to the appendixes on the estimation of the relevant functions.

While the rail industry is relatively homogeneous in the sense that most railroads carry all types of traffic and face relatively similar markets, the trucking industry is quite segmented and different types of carriers face quite different markets. In this connection, the most significant distinction probably lies between common carriers of general commodities and common carriers of specialized commodities. The former carriers are characterized by a large proportion of less-than-truckload (LTL) shipments, small loads, and a high component of terminal and consolidation activities. In contrast, carriers of specialized commodities are characterized by full-truckload (TL) shipments, large loads, and relatively little, if any, terminal or consolidation activities. Since common carriers of general commodities are primarily engaged in the transportation of relatively small shipments, and since railroads have largely removed themselves from the less-than-carload traffic and attempted to focus on large-lot shipments,[2] there is relatively little area of competition between railroads and LTL carriers of general commodities. Thus the main area of rail–

truck competition lies between railroads and specialized commodity carriers, which in many instances are able to obtain costs that are comparable to those achieved by the railroads.[3] Consequently, in this chapter we will focus upon the cost and demand functions of railroads and carriers of specialized commodities. Chapter 5, which focuses on the policy problems associated with the general commodity carriers, will discuss the cost and demand functions of these carriers in some detail.

The present chapter takes the following form. Sections 2.2–2.4 are concerned with the estimated cost functions and discuss, respectively, the general specification of the transportation cost functions and the specific estimates of the rail and trucking industries. Section 2.5 then considers the estimated rail and trucking demand functions.

2.2 The Specification of Transportation Cost Functions

The validity of econometric estimates of the costs of the various transportation modes remains an issue surrounded by controversy. While there have been numerous econometric studies of rail, trucking, and airline costs,[4] no one has yet developed a costing methodology that has yielded results that are generally accepted as valid. This inability to obtain a consensus concerning costing methodology and/or the validity of the empirical results arises not so much from a lack of effort, but rather from the failure to specify the cost functions that appropriately characterize the structure of technology.

Specifically, there appear to be three fundamental problems that one must address in specifying and estimating cost functions for the transportation industries.

First, the output of a transportation firm, whatever the mode, is multidimensional by its very nature. Not only does the firm produce different types of transportation services for different users at different origins and destinations, but also at different levels of quality. Consequently, the mix of output and shipment characteristics can have a major impact upon the costs of any given firm. For example, railroads specializing in coal traffic have very different cost characteristics from those specializing in general manufactured commodities for a given density of line. Similarly, trucks specializing in short-haul, LTL traffic have different costs from those specializing in long-haul, truckload traffic.

Since the mix of output and the way in which it is produced affect the firm's costs, it is clearly inappropriate to estimate cost functions by using a single aggregate measure of output such as ton-miles or passenger-miles.

To the extent that the mix of traffic and quality levels affect costs, a vector of outputs and quality levels that characterize the range of activities undertaken by the firms in a given transportation mode should be incorporated into the analysis. While it is unlikely that the available data will permit the fully desired degree of output disaggregation, it is clear that considerably more disaggregation is possible than has been undertaken in existing studies of transportation costs.

Second, it is generally agreed that the activities of each of the transportation modes are characterized by joint and common costs, implying that their technology is characterized by joint production. Although Hall (1973) has shown that a separable technology will always imply joint production, he has also shown that the converse is not true. We cannot assume, therefore, that cost functions based on a separable Cobb–Douglas technology are good representations of reality.[5] Instead, a flexible form is needed that will permit the determination of the underlying structure of technology from its estimated coefficients.

Third, to the extent that regulatory or other constraints prevent the firms in each mode from making optimal adjustments in capacity, they are not generally in a position of long-run equilibrium operating along their long-run cost function. Consequently, efforts to estimate long-run cost functions directly from cross-sectional data may yield seriously biased coefficients and biased measures of marginal costs.

This implies that one should estimate short-run functions when one suspects that an industry may be in long-run disequilibrium with chronic excess capacity. Since the long-run cost function is merely the envelope of the short-run cost function, it is always possible to derive the unobserved long-run cost function from the observed short-run cost function.[6] Thus, to the extent that the short-run cost function has been correctly specified, and its coefficients are therefore unbiased, the coefficients of the derived long-run cost function will also be unbiased and the long-run marginal costs obtained from the derived long-run total cost curve will also be unbiased. In addition, if other technological factors, such as the nature of the route network, influence costs, then these factors should be incorporated in the cost function [e.g., McFadden (1978)].

These arguments suggest that in estimating cost functions for the transportation industries, one should specify a cost function that incorporates multiple outputs as well as shipment characteristics in a sufficiently flexible form to permit the testing of a number of hypotheses concerning the separability, homogeneity, and jointness of the underlying production function. Moreover, if there is reason to believe that regulatory or other institutional constraints prevent "optimal" capacity adjustment, one should estimate a short-run variable cost function, which can be used to derive the associated long-run cost function and the underlying production function. Finally, the cost function should incorporate technological factors that may also influence costs and that are not directly related to specific outputs.

This analysis uses a translog hedonic cost function that meets the objections raised with respect to most cost functions: it permits multiple outputs and quality levels; it is of a sufficiently flexible form to test hypotheses concerning the underlying structure of production; it incorporates general technological factors; and it can be used in either its short-run or long-run form.

Since the methodology we use to estimate cost functions is entirely general, we will apply it to all of the relevant modes. Moreover, since the short-run cost function is somewhat more general, we present it here. Nevertheless, in actual estimation, we also use the long-run cost function.

The short-run variable cost function takes the following general form[7]

$$\tilde{C} = \tilde{C}(\psi(y,q), x, \tilde{w}, t), \tag{2.1}$$

where:

$\tilde{C}$ = a short-run variable cost.

ψ = measure of effective ton-miles.[8]

y = a $(1 \times N)$ vector of outputs.

q = a $(1 \times R)$ vector of shipment attributes associated with each output.

x = a $(1 \times H)$ vector of fixed factors.

$\tilde{w}$ = a $(1 \times J)$ vector of prices of the variable factors.

t = a $(1 \times M)$ vector of technological variables.

In recent years, considerable effort has gone into analyzing the properties of a number of different approximations of a general functional form such as that given in (2.1).[9] It now seems to be generally agreed that the translog approximation offers the greatest flexibility and computational ease.[10] We therefore use the following functional form in estimating the costs of the relevant rail and trucking industries:

$$\ln \tilde{C}(\psi, x, \tilde{w}, t) = \alpha_0 + \sum_{i=1}^{N} \alpha_i \ln \psi_i + \sum_{h=1}^{H} \beta_h \ln x_h$$

$$+ \sum_{j=1}^{J} \gamma_j \ln \tilde{w}_j + \sum_{s=1}^{M} \delta_s \ln t_s$$

$$+ \frac{1}{2} \left[\sum_i^N \sum_k^N A_{ik} \ln \psi_i \ln \psi_k + \sum_h^H \sum_l^H B_{hl} \ln x_h \ln x_l \right.$$

$$+ \sum_j^J \sum_r^J C_{jr} \ln \tilde{w}_j \ln \tilde{w}_r + \sum_s^M \sum_r^M D_{sr} \ln t_s \ln t_r$$

$$+ \sum_i^N \sum_h^H E_{ih} \ln \psi_i \ln x_h + \sum_i^N \sum_j^J F_{ij} \ln \psi_i \ln \tilde{w}_j$$

$$+ \sum_i^N \sum_s^M G_{is} \ln \psi_i \ln t_s + \sum_h^H \sum_j^J K_{hj} \ln x_h \ln \tilde{w}_j$$

$$+ \left. \sum_h^H \sum_s^M L_{hs} \ln x_h \ln t_s + \sum_j^J \sum_s^M P_{js} \ln \tilde{w}_j \ln t_s \right].$$

$$(2.2)$$

The output measure ψ represents physical output adjusted for the operating characteristics of the firm. Since a ton-mile carried in large loads and long hauls clearly has different impacts upon costs than one characterized by small loads and short hauls, it is necessary to take these into account in estimating costs. We thus postulate that effective output is a function of physical output and the operating characteristics of the firm and write

$$\psi_i = \psi_i(y_i, q^i) \qquad (2.3)$$

where:

y_i = physical output of type i.

q^i = a vector of operating characteristics associated with output type i (e.g., length of haul).

This expression can be given empirical content by making the assumption that this function is separable in physical output and operating characteristics, so that

$$\psi_i = y_i \phi(q^i). \qquad (2.4)$$

Finally, by making the assumption that $\phi(q^i)$ can be approximated by a translog function, we obtain the following expression, which can be substituted into the cost function (2.2) as appropriate:

$$\ln \psi_i = \ln y_i + \sum \alpha_r \ln q_r^i + \frac{1}{2} \sum_r \sum_s A_{rs} \ln q_r^i \ln q_s^i, \tag{2.5}$$

where i ranges over the relevant types of output.[11]

As indicated in Spady (1979), by using this specification of the cost function and by imposing various restrictions on the coefficients, we can test for homogeneity in factor prices, homogeneity in outputs, separability, and jointness in production. Moreover, it is also possible to derive long-run total costs, long-run and short-run marginal costs, and long-run and short-run factor demands over the relevant range from (2.2). Finally, by adjusting the vector of outputs to reflect differences in the quality of service, we can take service differentials into account.

Because much of our analysis relies on the estimated marginal costs of the rail and the trucking industries, it is useful to indicate how they are obtained. Since

$$\frac{\partial \ln C}{\partial \ln \psi} \equiv \frac{\partial C}{\partial \psi} \frac{\psi}{C}, \tag{2.6}$$

it is readily apparent that the marginal costs with respect to any given output are given by the following expression:

$$\frac{\partial C}{\partial \psi_i} = \frac{\partial \ln C}{\partial \ln \psi_i} \frac{C}{\psi_i}. \tag{2.7}$$

Thus by exponentiating the estimated cost function and by differentiating it with respect to the relevant output variable, it is a straightforward task to obtain the marginal cost function for any type of output from the estimated total cost function. The specific application of this general approach to the rail and trucking industries will now be discussed.

2.3 The Costs of Railroad Operations

In this section, we first discuss the general specification of the railroad cost function and consider the sample and variables used in estimating rail costs. We then discuss the characteristics of the estimated costs and technology of the railroads included in the sample. The section closes with a discussion of the estimated marginal costs of rail operations for different types of commodities in different regions of the country.

2.3.1 Specification of a Railroad Cost Function

Although the econometric estimation of rail costs and production functions has a long history,[12] previous studies have generally been inadequate in two respects. First, they have failed to distinguish the effect of way-and-structures capital on costs from that of track or route-miles; and second, they have ignored the effect upon costs of such variables as traffic mix by commodity type, average length of haul, and low-density route-miles. Since way-and-structures capital enters costs as a factor of production, increases in way-and-structures capital should reduce expenditures on other factors, ceteris paribus. In contrast, since an increase in route-miles represents an increase in common carrier obligations, increases in this variable should be associated with increases in expenditures on other factors of production. Consequently, in the absence of distinct measures of way-and-structures capital and route structure, some estimated cost functions obtain the counterintuitive result that increases in track actually lead to increases in costs [e.g., Keeler (1974), Caves et al. (1980a)]. Similarly, since ton-miles are not homogeneous but differ according to type of commodity, length of haul, etc., failure to incorporate these variables into the cost function can lead to biased estimates of total and marginal costs.

In specifying a rail cost function, we will assume that way-and-structures capital is fixed in the short run so that firms minimize expenditures on the remaining factors given the exogenously determined quantity of the fixed factor, technological conditions, and outputs. It is appropriate to regard way-and-structures capital as fixed not only because its quantity is difficult to vary over short periods, but also because railroads are generally believed to have permitted this factor to decay rapidly in many instances. Since it is unlikely that the optimal adjustment of this factor can be obtained through such depreciation, it would be inappropriate to treat this factor as variable.

The technological conditions the firm faces are exogenous since route structure and branchline mileage are explicitly controlled by the ICC, and average length of haul and traffic mix are determined by the route structure and shipper demands along these routes. Since railroads are obligated by their status as common carriers to satisfy all shipper demands at fixed prices, both output and the technological conditions influenced by demand are exogenous.

Thus, (2.1) applied in the current context is appropriate:

$$C = C(\psi_P, \psi_F, x, w, t), \tag{2.8}$$

where ψ_P is passenger service output, ψ_F freight service output, x the quantity of way-and-structures captial, w a vector of prices of variable factors, and t a vector of technological conditions.

Passenger service output is measured by passenger-miles y_P adjusted for two qualities, passenger average travel length (PATL) and passenger-miles per passenger route-mile (PDENS). We thus define

$$\psi_P = y_P \, \phi(\text{PATL}, \text{PDENS}), \tag{2.9}$$

where ϕ is a translog function. One expects that increases in passenger density will decrease the cost of producing a given amount of passenger-miles not only because of economies of utilization of equipment and centralization of ancillary services (ticket offices, terminals, etc.) but also because passenger service requires that track be kept in better condition. The effect of passenger average travel length on passenger service, however, may be ambiguous. Handling fewer passengers per passenger-mile lowers the cost associated with ticketing and boarding passengers; but increases in passenger average travel length are also associated with a shift in the type of passenger service provided from commuter to inter-state. If the latter is more expensive than the former, we would expect $\partial \psi_P / \partial \text{PATL} < 0$ for larger values of PATL.

For freight service output, revenue ton-miles is used. Since average length of haul and traffic mix are liable to have a direct effect on factor shares, they have been included as technological conditions, which is a less restrictive condition than including them in an hedonic function altering ton-miles. While it would be desirable to disaggregate ton-miles by commodity type, there are data and specification limitations which prohibit this; these limitations are discussed in detail in appendix B.

The measure of way-and-structures capital employed is the reproduction cost of land, way, and structures estimated by R. A. Nelson (1974) for the American Association of Railroads (AAR). This study used the basic methodology employed by the ICC in constructing its 1963 *Elements of Value*, using railroad reports to the ICC and the AAR to estimate reproduction cost as of December 31, 1971.

The following five factors are treated as being variable in this study: equipment, general and maintenance labor, traffic and transportation labor (other than train), on-train labor, and fuel and materials. Each railroad's variable costs are the sum of its expenditures on these five variable factors. In terms of the ICC's accounting system, variable cost is operating cost net of way-and-structures and equipment depreciation, plus fringe benefits and labor taxes on employee compensation chargeable to operating expenses, plus net equipment rentals, plus imputed opportunity and depreciation costs on equipment capital.

Finally, the following four technological variables are included in the cost function: freight route-miles operated, low-density route-miles, average length of haul, and the ratio of ton-miles of manufactured commodities to ton-miles of other commodities. As explained above, the inclusion of the variables measuring total route-miles and low-density route-miles attempts to incorporate the impacts upon costs of the nature of the route network and the common carrier obligations. The inclusion of average length of haul attempts to reflect the economies associated with long lengths of haul. Finally, the traffic mix variable attempts to capture the impact of different types of commodities upon costs. A full discussion of all of the variables used in the cost function is given in appendix B.

Data were available for 26 railroad systems providing passenger service within the years 1968–1970.[13] Of these systems, one (the Burlington Northern) was formed in 1970; comparable data were not available for its constituent systems. A second system, the Texas and Pacific, apparently abandoned its passenger service (or at least a very large portion thereof) early in 1970.

This leaves 75 observations. In preliminary estimation, however, 6 railroads were consistent outliers for which important regularity conditions (such as positive marginal costs and a positive marginal product of way-and-structures capital) were violated. Upon investigation it was found that these 6 roads had the six highest relative coal traffic levels. Since the cost characteristics of these railroads appear to be different from those of the other railroads, they were excluded from the sample.[14]

Excluding the 6 coal railroads leaves a sample of 20 railroad systems and 57 observations. These 20 systems, however, account for over 70 percent of the US total of most measures of railroad size and activity, including capital stock, operating cost, revenues, passenger-miles, and route-miles. For ton-miles, the figure falls to 68 percent, since the coal railroads account for a disproportionate number of ton-miles relative to other activities, which is consistent with our finding that their technology differs significantly from other roads.

Our specification has five variable factors, one fixed factor, four technological conditions, and two outputs, yielding 91 coefficients to be estimated in a full translog functional form. However, a large number of these can be eliminated by imposing homogeneity of degree one on the factor prices in the cost function, and mild separability conditions between the technological conditions and passenger output. Thus the final estimating equation yielded 69 coefficients, of which 26 appear only in the cost function.[15]

2.3.2 Characteristics of the Railroads

Before considering the estimated marginal costs associated with rail operations, it is useful to discuss the system characteristics of the railroads included in the sample and some of the more important aspects of their estimated costs and technology. Table 2.1 presents data concerning the freight network characteristics for 1969, while table 2.2 presents passenger service data.[16] Table 2.3 presents cost and revenue data.

Table 2.1 has three notable aspects. The first is that while average length of haul generally increases with route-miles, there are small roads providing generally long-haul service (e.g., the Western Pacific) and large roads with comparatively short average hauls (e.g., the Penn Central). Second, way-and-structures capital per route-mile varies widely among the railroads, with a tendency for railroads in the East to have higher values which may or may not be explained by their nongeographic characteristics. Third, overall traffic density, as measured by ton-miles/route-mile, is not necessarily closely related to the percentage of route-miles in low-density service. (Compare, for example, the Erie-Lackawanna, with 46.5 percent low-density line and 5,367 ton-miles/route-mile, with the Chicago, Milwaukee, & St. Paul, with 32.5 percent low-density line and 1,639 ton-miles/route-mile.)

Table 2.2 shows that passenger service varies widely in both passenger average travel length and passenger-miles/route-mile. While commuter service is associated with higher-density service, there are important exceptions.

Table 2.3 presents the ICC's estimates of operating costs, our estimates of short-run or variable costs, and total revenues. While most railroads had revenues exceeding the ICC operating cost, most did not have revenues covering these estimated variable costs. This is, of course, an important indicator of the road's financial viability, since only the excess of revenues over the variable cost measure can be applied to nonlabor taxes in providing a return to way-and-structures investment. If revenues do not sufficiently exceed variable costs, owners of railroads will be "unwilling" providers of capital—that is, the reproduction value of the capital will be greater than the present discounted value of the profit stream. Under such circumstances, profit-maximizing behavior will consist of "consuming" the capital and investing the proceeds in nonrail enterprises. The firm's problem in this case is to realize the greatest

Table 2.1 Freight Network Characteristics, 1969[a]

	Route-miles	Estimated miles of B branchline	Ton-miles per ton (average length of haul)
Atchison, Topeka & Santa Fe Ry.	12,895	3,397.7	597.2
Boston & Maine Corp.	1,525	698.5	172.6
Burlington Northern Inc.	24,182	7,850.3	419.0
Central R.R. Co. of New Jersey	592	392.2	68.8
Chicago & North Western Trans.	11,509	4,017.3	278.1
Chicago, Milwaukee, & St. Paul	10,483	3,422.1	377.2
Chicago, Rock Island & Pacific	7,255	1,981.9	390.1
Delaware & Hudson Ry. Co.	734	71.2	210.1
Erie-Lackawanna Ry. Co.	2,889	1,344.1	340.9
Grand Trunk Western R.R. Co.	946	281.6	173.8
Gulf Mobile and Ohio R.R. Co.	2,704	410.8	301.1
Illinois Central R.R. Co.	6,780	1,030.2	294.0
Missouri Pacific R.R. Co.	8,943	2,249.8	344.9
Penn Central Transportation Co.	20,227	7,194.0	293.8
Seaboard Coast Line R.R. Co.	9,275	1,852.5	215.7
Southern Pacific Transportation	11,651	2,119.9	510.3
Southern Ry. Co.	6,060	1,137.4	237.7
Texas & Pacific Ry. Co.	1,944	521.0	223.3
Union Pacific R.R. Co.	9,480	2,763.0	646.5
Western Pacific R.R. Co.	1,176	80.3	513.1

	Way-and-structures investment per route-mile (12/31/71 dollars)	Revenue ton-miles per route-mile (thousands)
Atchison, Topeka & Santa Fe Ry.	190,472	3,672
Boston & Maine Corp.	364,814	1,916
Burlington Northern Inc.	205,166	2,355
Central R.R. Co. of New Jersey	483,590	2,963
Chicago & North Western Trans.	154,486	1,618
Chicago, Milwaukee, & St. Paul	178,134	1,639
Chicago, Rock Island & Pacific	175,815	2,702
Delaware & Hudson Ry. Co.	327,704	4,788
Erie-Lackawanna Ry. Co.	473,546	5,367
Grand Trunk Western R.R. Co.	289,091	3,117
Gulf Mobile and Ohio R.R. Co.	148,709	3,195
Illinois Central R.R. Co.	215,896	3,516

Table 2.1 (continued)

	Way-and-structures investment per route-mile (12/31/71 dollars)	Revenue ton-miles per route-mile (thousands)
Missouri Pacific R.R. Co.	159,530	2,972
Penn Central Transportation Co.	421,723	4,358
Seaboard Coast Line R.R. Co.	161,800	3,356
Southern Pacific Transportation	198,787	5,682
Southern Ry. Co.	183,578	4,224
Texas & Pacific Ry. Co.	162,449	2,892
Union Pacific R.R. Co.	196,231	4,903
Western Pacific R.R. Co.	309,467	4,155

a. Burlington Northern data are for 1970.

Table 2.2 Passenger Service Characteristics, 1969[a]

	Passenger-miles	Passenger-miles per passenger	Passenger-miles per passenger route-mile
Atchison, Topeka & Santa Fe Ry.	850,862,336	652.4	178,602.5
Boston & Maine Corp.	91,412,560	16.5	540,902.7
Burlington Northern Inc.	852,906,496	73.9	112,106.5
Central R.R. Co. of New Jersey	119,532,976	18.9	796,886.5
Chicago & North Western Trans.	618,075,392	23.4	679,203.7
Chicago, Milwaukee, & St. Paul	330,715,136	47.1	275,825.8
Chicago, Rock Island & Pacific	144,175,152	20.9	182,500.1
Delaware & Hudson Ry. Co.	16,192,015	169.3	83,035.9
Erie-Lackawanna Ry. Co.	331,727,616	21.6	233,118.4
Grand Trunk Western R.R. Co.	62,344,000	84.1	155,471.3
Gulf Mobile and Ohio R.R. Co.	56,183,408	143.3	199,231.9
Illinois Central R.R. Co.	844,285,184	35.9	442,265.6
Missouri Pacific R.R. Co.	63,095,616	320.2	48,535.0
Penn Central Transportation Co.	3,356,078,080	36.7	558,322.7
Seaboard Coast Line R.R. Co.	620,631,808	537.8	154,655.3
Southern Pacific Transportation	402,457,600	61.3	81,684.1
Southern Ry. Co.	140,016,576	339.3	135,543.6
Texas & Pacific Ry. Co.	8,713,061	117.5	22,002.6
Union Pacific R.R. Co.	487,329,536	677.3	104,847.1
Western Pacific R.R. Co.	59,295,152	701.7	64,591.6

a. Burlington Northern data are for 1970.

Table 2.3 Revenues and Costs, 1969[a]

	ICC operating costs	Short-run or variable costs	Revenues
Atchison, Topeka & Santa Fe Ry.	576,312,832	694,899,616	719,216,304
Boston & Maine Corp.	58,617,360	70,158,381	69,453,900
Burlington Northern Inc.	740,009,984	915,800,392	877,547,200
Central R.R. Co. of New Jersey	45,684,784	58,923,789	52,287,630
Chicago & North Western Trans.	251,587,328	324,249,364	285,981,400
Chicago, Milwaukee, & St. Paul	230,631,168	289,201,244	269,108,200
Chicago, Rock Island & Pacific	211,222,464	290,226,116	259,584,300
Delaware & Hudson Ry. Co.	34,416,336	41,450,502	45,026,479
Erie-Lackawanna Ry. Co.	199,661,344	248,399,610	251,261,248
Grand Trunk Western R.R. Co.	67,609,456	109,150,451	75,503,240
Gulf Mobile and Ohio R.R. Co.	74,481,968	92,913,703	99,688,190
Illinois Central R.R. Co.	255,608,176	319,080,372	322,700,200
Missouri Pacific R.R. Co.	261,886,080	334,933,560	351,632,100
Penn Central Transportation Co.	1,414,161,920	1,848,936,880	1,651,977,008
Seaboard Coast Line R.R. Co.	366,088,960	506,902,348	484,636,600
Southern Pacific Transportation	719,317,248	866,947,848	923,921,600
Southern Ry. Co.	264,663,536	354,287,040	378,360,500
Texas & Pacific Ry. Co.	65,024,848	92,883,315	85,845,440
Union Pacific R.R. Co.	477,072,384	545,440,152	630,406,904
Western Pacific R.R. Co.	62,531,904	75,169,813	67,764,250

a. Burlington Northern data are for 1970.

"payout" before bankruptcy. Given current institutional constraints (firms cannot simply sell their equipment and abandon their roadbeds) and the existence of a rental market in equipment, firms will cost minimize in equipment and other variable factors while deferring track maintenance. Thus roads whose revenues consistently fall short of our measure of variable costs will "consume" their way-and-structures capital, but will also avoid bankruptcy until (roughly speaking—the ICC measure of operating cost does not include net equipment rentals) revenues fall below their operating costs. It is important to note that once a railroad concludes that its business is unprofitable, bankruptcy will ensue even if revenues and factor prices stay constant since the fundamental mechanism increasing variable costs is the deliberate depletion of the way-and-structures capital stock.[17] From table 2.3 it is apparent that although many railroads were covering their operating costs as estimated by the ICC, they were not covering their true variable costs.

The parameters of the estimated cost functions and their economic interpretations are fully discussed in appendix B. Here we will briefly note that the estimated cost function appears to fit a neoclassical model of costs and technology extremely well. In particular, the elasticities of demand for the variable factors are all negative, with most factors acting as substitutes for each other. However, equipment and fuel and materials appear to be complements, as are traffic and general labor and transportation and general labor. Moreover, the estimated cost function indicates that way-and-structures capital, the technological conditions, and output significantly affect factor intensities and factor shares. Thus their inclusion in the cost function is not only required from a formal statistical point of view, but also yields important information concerning the interrelationships between factor usage and the technological conditions under which a given railroad operates.

It is also useful to summarize the impact of the technological conditions upon marginal costs and returns to scale. In particular, as network size increases, there is no notable effect on costs provided the number of low-density route-miles remains constant. The latter have substantial cost effects at the margin. Average length of haul also has a substantial effect on costs, though, strictly speaking, this is entirely independent of the issue of returns to scale with which it is often confused in the evaluation of merger benefits. Since our model distinguishes between track-miles and way-and-structures capital, we find, as neoclassical production theory would lead us to expect, that increases in capital decrease variable costs. Thus each road faces a neoclassical technology with joint production of freight and passenger services; our usual intuitions concerning such technologies continue to be applicable.

What is surprising, however, is that the railroads in our sample generally exhibit diminishing returns to scale in the short run at the existing levels of output. For a hypothetical firm facing the sample mean values of each variable, the elasticity of short-run or variable costs with respect to passenger service is estimated to be approximately 0.113, while the estimated elasticity of these costs with respect to ton-miles is 1.122.

A little reflection will indicate, however, that this result is not as surprising as it first appears. The conventional view of the railroads is that of an industry plagued with excess capacity, that is, track. In this situation, it is expected that increases in output will lead to reductions in average fixed costs and hence in average total costs. Thus given the simplistic view of the railroads one would expect to find rather marked short-run economies of scale.[18]

Table 2.4 Effect of Passenger Service on Variable Costs, by Railroad, 1969

	Elasticity of cost with respect to passenger service	Standard error	Marginal cost ($ per passenger service unit)
Atchison, Topeka & Santa Fe Ry.	0.0957	0.0414	0.1329
Boston & Maine Corp.	−0.0305	0.0667	−0.0829
Central R.R. Co. of New Jersey	0.0561	0.0633	0.0764
Chicago & North Western Trans.	0.0492	0.0528	0.0553
Chicago, Milwaukee, & St. Paul	0.0344	0.0597	0.0381
Chicago, Rock Island & Pacific	0.0121	0.0424	0.0509
Delaware & Hudson Ry. Co.	0.0803	0.0490	0.1609
Erie-Lackawanna Ry. Co.	0.0368	0.0411	0.0640
Grand Trunk Western R.R. Co.	0.1238	0.0626	0.1777
Gulf Mobile and Ohio R.R. Co.	0.1209	0.0453	0.1848
Illinois Central R.R. Co.	0.1307	0.0633	0.0802
Missouri Pacific R.R. Co.	0.0305	0.0357	0.1113
Penn Central Transportation Co.	0.0460	0.1033	0.0405
Seaboard Coast Line R.R. Co.	0.1288	0.0486	0.1585
Southern Pacific Transportation	0.1253	0.0436	0.2184
Southern Ry. Co.	0.0917	0.0266	0.2374
Texas & Pacific Ry. Co.	0.0734	0.0543	0.2851
Union Pacific R.R. Co.	0.1067	0.0328	0.1961
Western Pacific R.R. Co.	0.0876	0.0381	0.1379

The problem with this view, however, is that it neglects to consider the allocation of traffic over the network or to differentiate between way-and-structures capital and track. If, for example, a given railroad finds that its mainline track is heavily utilized but its light-density track is under-utilized, increases in mainline traffic may well cause marginal costs to rise. Moreover, if maintenance on all lines has been deferred, increases in traffic could lead to increases in marginal cost, whatever the distribution of the traffic over the network. Again, the problem arises because of the failure to distinguish way-and-structures capital from track per se. Even though the railroad may have considerable excess track in the sense of desiring abandonment of service, it may also have an insufficient capital stock if maintenance has been deferred sufficiently long. In this case, the problem with the excess track is not so much that it reflects a nonoptimal adjustment in the capital stock, but rather that it reflects unprofitable common carrier obligations.

In table 2.4 we present estimates of the elasticity of cost with respect to passenger service, the corresponding standard error, and the marginal cost of passenger service, by railroad, for 1969. From the estimated cost function, we obtain, at mean factor prices,

$$\frac{\partial \ln C}{\partial \ln \psi_1} = 0.1129 - 0.1417 \ln x + 0.0619 \ln \psi_1 + 0.0573 \ln \psi_2, \qquad (2.10)$$
$$\phantom{\frac{\partial \ln C}{\partial \ln \psi_1} =} (0.0548) \quad (0.0836) \qquad (0.0477) \qquad (0.0581)$$

where ψ_1 and ψ_2 are passenger and freight output, respectively, and x is the quantity of way-and-structures capital. Thus, the marginal cost curve for passenger service slopes upward at the point of approximation. For low levels of ψ_1 and ψ_2, however, $\partial \ln C/\partial \ln \psi_1$ may be less than zero. In table 2.4, one railroad (the Boston and Maine) has $\partial \ln C/\partial \ln \psi_1 < 0$, but the standard error of this estimate is comparatively large. A substantial number of roads have estimated values of $\partial \ln C/\partial \ln \psi_1$ which are smaller than their estimated standard errors, so that differences in estimated marginal costs should be interpreted cautiously. Nonetheless, these estimates are reasonably behaved in that they indicate upward sloping supply curves through almost all of the sample range.

Table 2.5 gives the estimates of the elasticity of costs with respect to freight output $\partial \ln C/\partial \ln \psi_2$, its standard error, and the estimated marginal costs, $\partial C/\partial \psi_2$ for each railroad in 1969. There are substantial differences among roads in both $\partial \ln C/\partial \ln \psi_2$ and $\partial C/\partial \psi_2$. At mean factor prices, we obtain from the estimated cost elasticity:

$$\frac{\partial \ln C}{\partial \ln \psi_2} = 1.1289 - 0.0346 \ln x + 0.1117 \ln t_1 - 0.0847 \ln t_2$$
$$\phantom{\frac{\partial \ln C}{\partial \ln \psi_2} =} (0.0833) \quad (0.3604) \qquad (0.1495) \qquad (0.1672)$$
$$- 0.0312 \ln t_3 - 0.03104 \ln t_4 + 0.0573 \ln \psi_1 + 0.1772 \ln \psi_2,$$
$$(0.1457) \qquad (0.0820) \qquad (0.0581) \qquad (0.2260)$$
$$(2.11)$$

where t_1 and t_2 are low-density and total route-miles, respectively, t_3 is average length of haul, and t_4 is the ratio of manufactured commodity ton-miles to bulk commodity ton-miles. Since the coefficients of (2.11) appear only in the cost equation, it is not surprising that they have large estimated standard errors. Nonetheless, table 2.5 estimates of $\partial \ln C/\partial \ln \psi_2$ seem to have sufficiently small estimated standard errors to justify the inference that large roads (in terms of ψ_2) have values of $\partial \ln C/\partial \ln \psi_2$ in excess of 1, while smaller roads often have much smaller values. Together with (2.11), this suggests that the main determinants of $\partial \ln C/\partial \ln \psi_2$ are

Table 2.5 Effect of Ton-Miles on Variable Costs, by Railroad, 1969

	Elasticity of cost with respect to ton-miles	Standard error	Marginal cost (mils per thousand ton-mile)
Atchison, Topeka & Santa Fe Ry.	1.2176	0.0941	17.3445
Boston & Maine Corp.	0.6592	0.1284	17.7217
Central R.R. Co. of New Jersey	0.6982	0.1464	23.4284
Chicago & North Western Trans.	1.1088	0.1014	18.3686
Chicago, Milwaukee, & St. Paul	1.0488	0.1067	17.8350
Chicago, Rock Island & Pacific	0.9781	0.0933	14.3268
Delaware & Hudson Ry. Co.	0.5332	0.1995	6.9784
Erie-Lackawanna Ry. Co.	0.9996	0.1329	17.1178
Grand Trunk Western R.R. Co.	0.6527	0.1723	22.3502
Gulf Mobile and Ohio R.R. Co.	0.8071	0.1607	8.9214
Illinois Central R.R. Co.	1.0784	0.1008	14.9486
Missouri Pacific R.R. Co.	1.0703	0.1026	13.4740
Penn Central Transportation Co.	1.4491	0.2538	31.0053
Seaboard Coast Line R.R. Co.	1.1778	0.1091	19.9624
Southern Pacific Transportation	1.2541	0.1129	16.8214
Southern Ry. Co.	1.0539	0.1285	14.2913
Texas & Pacific Ry. Co.	0.7391	0.1960	12.5630
Union Pacific R.R. Co.	1.2050	0.1315	14.8369
Western Pacific R.R. Co.	0.4967	0.2398	7.0115

ψ_1 and ψ_2. Indeed, since ψ_1 and ψ_2 are positively correlated in the sample ($r = 0.83$), it is difficult to distinguish the separate effects of ψ_1 and ψ_2 on $\partial \ln C/\partial \ln \psi_1$ and $\partial \ln C/\partial \ln \psi_2$.[19]

At the point of approximation short-run returns to scale ($\partial \ln C/\partial \ln \psi_1 + \partial \ln C/\partial \ln \psi_2$) are estimated to be 1.235 with an estimated standard error of 0.091. Thus a short-run marginal cost pricing would generate revenues exceeding variable costs by 23.5 percent.[20] Table 2.6 gives our estimates by road of ($\partial \ln C/\partial \ln \psi_1 + \partial \ln C/\partial \ln \psi_2$) for 1964, which indicates that a substantial number of railroads face short-run decreasing returns to scale. Since a number of analysts [e.g., Keeler (1974)], have found evidence that the railroads are subject to economies of scale, this result is apparently surprising. The two results can easily be reconciled, however, by recognizing that these measures of scale economies reflect short-run costs, while other measures of scale economies typically reflect long-run costs. Thus, if a firm is suffering from a short-run capital short-

Table 2.6 Short-Run Returns to Scale and the Ratio of Revenues to Variable Costs

	Short-run returns to scale	Revenues per variable cost
Atchison, Topeka & Santa Fe Ry.	1.3133	1.0350
Boston & Maine Corp.	0.6287	0.9900
Central R.R. Co. of New Jersey	0.7543	0.8874
Chicago & North Western Trans.	1.1581	0.8820
Chicago, Milwaukee, & St. Paul	1.0832	0.9305
Chicago, Rock Island & Pacific	0.9902	0.8944
Delaware & Hudson Ry. Co.	0.6135	1.0863
Erie-Lackawanna Ry. Co.	1.0364	1.0115
Grand Trunk Western R.R. Co.	0.7765	0.6917
Gulf Mobile and Ohio R.R. Co.	0.9281	1.0729
Illinois Central R.R. Co.	1.2091	1.0113
Missouri Pacific R.R. Co.	1.1008	1.0499
Penn Central Transportation Co.	1.4952	0.8935
Seaboard Coast Line R.R. Co.	1.3066	0.9561
Southern Pacific Transportation	1.3794	1.0657
Southern Ry. Co.	1.1456	1.0679
Texas & Pacific Ry. Co.	0.8126	0.9242
Union Pacific R.R. Co.	1.3117	1.1558
Western Pacific R.R. Co.	0.5843	0.9015

age, it is quite possible that it could face short-run diseconomies of scale, while still being subject to long-run economies of scale. Consequently, firms that have practiced extensive deferred maintenance and have failed to maintain their track and roadbed should experience short-run diseconomies of scale. This is corroborated by the Penn Central's estimated short-run returns to scale of 1.495.

Table 2.6 also gives our estimates of the revenue–variable cost ratio by road for 1969, which indicates that revenues generally failed to cover short-run variable costs. This indicates that railroads did not face prices near their short-run marginal costs. To examine this issue further we have calculated the ratio of average revenue to marginal cost for passenger and freight service separately; these ratios and other relevant data are reported in tables 2.7 and 2.8 respectively.

From table 2.7 it is apparent that roads providing commuter service—characterized by low values of PATL and high values of PDENS—have high ratios of passenger revenue to passenger service units. It is also apparent that the difference is due to the lower cost of producing com-

Table 2.7 Average Revenue and Short-Run Marginal Cost of Passenger Service, by Railroad, 1969

	PATL	PDENS	Revenue per passenger-mile
Atchison, Topeka & Santa Fe Ry.	652.4207	178,602.5059	0.0401
Boston & Maine Corp.	16.5931	540,902.7188	0.0943
Central R.R. Co. of New Jersey	18.9190	796,886.5078	0.0721
Chicago & North Western Trans.	23.4113	679,203.7266	0.0366
Chicago, Milwaukee, & St. Paul	47.1232	275,825.8008	0.0508
Chicago, Rock Island & Pacific	20.9097	182,500.1934	0.0495
Delaware & Hudson Ry. Co.	169.3283	83,035.9746	0.0632
Erie-Lackawanna Ry. Co.	21.6046	233,118.4941	0.0538
Grand Trunk Western R.R. Co.	84.1034	155,471.3223	0.0507
Gulf Mobile and Ohio R.R. Co.	143.3704	199,231.9434	0.0708
Illinois Central R.R. Co.	35.9633	442,265.6797	0.0316
Missouri Pacific R.R. Co.	320.2677	48,535.0894	0.0381
Penn Central Transportation Co.	36.7046	558,322.7578	0.0688
Seaboard Coast Line R.R. Co.	537.8148	154,655.3223	0.0494
Southern Pacific Transportation	61.3950	81,684.1084	0.0364
Southern Ry. Co.	339.3881	135,543.6367	0.0613
Texas & Pacific Ry. Co.	117.5217	22,002.6792	0.0593
Union Pacific R.R. Co.	677.3151	104,847.1465	0.0389
Western Pacific R.R. Co.	701.7095	64,591.6689	0.0399

	Revenue per passenger service unit	Short-run marginal cost ($ per passenger service unit)	AR/MC
Atchison, Topeka & Santa Fe Ry.	0.0702	0.1329	0.5283
Boston & Maine Corp.	0.2986	−0.0829	−3.6034
Central R.R. Co. of New Jersey	0.1996	0.0764	2.6119
Chicago & North Western Trans.	0.0825	0.0553	1.4907
Chicago, Milwaukee, & St. Paul	0.0636	0.0381	1.6692
Chicago, Rock Island & Pacific	0.1048	0.0509	2.0600
Delaware & Hudson Ry. Co.	0.0446	0.1609	0.2771
Erie-Lackawanna Ry. Co.	0.1167	0.0640	1.8251
Grand Trunk Western R.R. Co.	0.0449	0.1777	0.2526
Gulf Mobile and Ohio R.R. Co.	0.0637	0.1848	0.3446
Illinois Central R.R. Co.	0.0495	0.0802	0.6179
Missouri Pacific R.R. Co.	0.0262	0.1113	0.2356

Table 2.7 (continued)

	Revenue per passenger service unit	Short-run marginal cost ($ per passenger service unit)	AR/MC
Penn Central Transportation Co.	0.1077	0.0405	2.6572
Seaboard Coast Line R.R. Co.	0.0715	0.1585	0.4511
Southern Pacific Transportation	0.0288	0.2184	0.1319
Southern Ry. Co.	0.0639	0.2374	0.2694
Texas & Pacific Ry. Co.	0.0210	0.2851	0.0736
Union Pacific R.R. Co.	0.0609	0.1961	0.3105
Western Pacific R.R. Co.	0.0540	0.1379	0.3918

muter passenger-miles rather than higher revenues per passenger-mile. This revenue advantage is further increased by the lower marginal costs generally experienced by commuter roads. In fact it is possible to divide the roads into two very distinct classes. The first class, the commuter roads, has passenger average travel lengths ranging from 16 to 47 miles, generates from 180,000 to 800,000 passenger-miles per passenger route-mile, and has average revenue–marginal cost ratios generally exceeding 1.49. The second class, which provides interstate service, has PATLs of 60 to 700 miles, PDENS values of 22,000 to 190,000, and average revenue–marginal cost (AR–MC) ratios below 0.53. An exception to the AR–MC ratio rule for commuter roads is the Illinois Central, with a ratio of 0.62 (which still exceeds the maximum achieved by the interstate roads), while the Gulf Mobile and Ohio, an interstate road, slightly exceeds the Chicago, Rock Island and Pacific, a commuter road, in PDENS.

It does not follow from the AR–MC ratio of the commuter roads that passenger service is profitable in toto, but only that it is profitable at the margin. The unfavorable AR–MC ratios experienced by the interstate roads, in contrast, indicate that even at the margin interstate service is a losing proposition. This difference between the two classes of service suggests that different policy responses would be appropriate. For the commuter roads, programs to win ridership combined, if necessary, with local operating subsidies may make continued operation of this service by the private sector *possible*, since commuter roads will find that such increases in ridership generally will improve profits. The marginal incentives faced by interstate roads are so adverse that removing this service from the private sector would probably be the only hope of providing

Table 2.8 Average Revenue and Marginal Cost per Ton-Mile, by Railroad, 1969

	Revenue/ ton-mile (mils)	Short-run marginal cost (mils)	AR/MC	Elasticity of cost with respect to ton-miles
Atchison, Topeka & Santa Fe Ry.	14.4650	17.3445	0.8340	1.2176
Boston & Maine Corp.	20.8188	17.7217	1.1748	0.6592
Central R.R. Co. of New Jersey	24.8897	23.4284	1.0624	0.6982
Chicago & North Western Trans.	14.1396	18.3686	0.7698	1.1088
Chicago, Milwaukee, & St. Paul	14.6790	17.8350	0.8230	1.0488
Chicago, Rock Island & Pacific	12.8774	14.3268	0.8988	0.9781
Delaware & Hudson Ry. Co.	12.5202	6.9784	1.7941	0.5332
Erie-Lackawanna Ry. Co.	15.0537	17.1178	0.8794	0.9996
Grand Trunk Western R.R. Co.	24.5282	22.3502	1.0974	0.6527
Gulf Mobile and Ohio R.R. Co.	11.0760	8.9214	1.2415	0.8071
Illinois Central R.R. Co.	12.4152	14.9486	0.8305	1.0784
Missouri Pacific R.R. Co.	13.1382	13.4740	0.9751	1.0703
Penn Central Transportation Co.	16.1060	31.0053	0.5195	1.4491
Seaboard Coast Line R.R. Co.	14.5829	19.9624	0.7305	1.1778
Southern Pacific Transportation	13.7338	16.8214	0.8165	1.2541
Southern Ry. Co.	14.4443	14.2913	1.0107	1.0539
Texas & Pacific Ry. Co.	15.1767	12.5630	1.2080	0.7391
Union Pacific R.R. Co.	13.1543	14.8369	0.8866	1.2050
Western Pacific R.R. Co.	13.3813	7.0115	1.9085	0.4967

interstate service of reasonable quality. From this point of view, the formation of Amtrak was probably wise, but our estimates and subsequent experience give no reason to expect that nonsubsidized operation will be possible, particularly in the absence of drastic changes in passenger density.

Table 2.8 presents average revenues, marginal costs, and AR–MC ratios for freight service. As might be expected, the AR–MC ratio of freight service is closely related to $\partial \ln C / \partial \ln \psi_2$ ($r = -0.87$). That is, roads with small values of $\partial \ln C / \partial \ln \psi_2$ (and thus of $\Sigma \ \partial \ln C / \partial \ln \psi_i$) have high AR–MC ratios, and vice versa; this indicates that roads with short-run economies of scale face the most favorable AR–MC ratios in freight service. As we saw earlier, $\partial \ln C / \partial \ln \psi_2$ varies substantially among roads, with ton-miles being the primary cause of the variation. The general pattern that emerges is what one would expect: roads with high traffic levels face higher marginal costs, ceteris paribus, and therefore find additional traffic disadvantageous at the margin. This imples, of course, that marginal cost pricing would indicate traffic reductions and rate increases on much of their traffic. Indeed, the simulation results that are discussed in the next chapter indicate that this is precisely the policy that the Eastern railroads should follow.

Of course, it is important to stress that these costs represent short-run marginal costs for given infrastructure. In view of the railroads' chronic inability to raise funds for infrastructure capital [e.g., FRA (1978)], and the ICC's reluctance to permit the railroads to rationalize their capital stock through abandonments, it seems likely that short-run marginal costs are a better reflection of railroad cost structures than long-run marginal costs. Hence, we will base the ensuing discussion of rail marginal costs and pricing policies on these short-run costs. Since, however, economic efficiency dictates adjustments in the capital stock, we will also consider the relationship between prices and long-run marginal costs. Thus chapter 3 will discuss the competitive equilibrium that would result from pricing at short-run marginal cost, while chapter 4 will discuss the implications of capital stock adjustments and the competitive equilibrium that would result from pricing at long-run marginal cost.

2.3.3 Marginal Cost and Supply Functions

Having discussed the marginal costs of specific railroads at a specific point of output, it is now useful to discuss the marginal cost functions associated with different types of railroads and different types of output. This is particularly important for the analysis of the next chapter, which considers the implications of a competitive equilibrium in the rail and trucking industries. Thus the marginal cost or supply functions obtained here form one of the cornerstones of the equilibrium analysis used in the next chapter.

The marginal cost function for any given firm can be obtained from the estimated translog cost function by using the following relationships:

$$\frac{\partial C_f}{\partial \psi_{if}} = \frac{\partial \ln C_f(\psi_{fP}, \psi_{fM}, \psi_{fB}, w_f, x_f, t_f)}{\partial \ln \psi_{if}}$$
$$\times \frac{\hat{C}_f(\psi_{fP}, \psi_{fM}, \psi_{fB}, w_f, x_f, t_f)}{\psi_{if}}, \tag{2.12}$$

where ψ_{if} represents the output of type i (i = passenger P, manufactures M, and bulk B) by firm f, $\hat{C}_f$ the estimated costs of firm f, w_f the vector of factor prices facing firm f, x_f the way-and-structures capital available to firm f, and t_f the vector of technological characteristics available to firm f. Thus by holding all variables constant at their observed levels and by varying ψ_{if}, it is straightforward to obtain the firm's marginal cost or supply function for output type ψ_i.

As long as all firms face increasing costs, economic theory indicates that the industry's supply function can be obtained by a horizontal summation of all of the firms' marginal cost functions. But for industries in which firms face increasing returns to scale, the supply curve becomes undefined.

Although most of the railroads in the sample face decreasing returns to scale, a number of them exhibit increasing returns to scale over the relevant range. Thus a horizontal summation would attribute all of the output to these railroads, which is a highly unlikely outcome in view of their capacity constraints. Thus instead of deriving an industry supply curve by horizontally summing the marginal cost functions of the underlying firms, we derive an industry supply curve by using a weighted average of the relevant variables of the firms in the industry. Therefore the marginal cost function for the industry is estimated as

$$\frac{\partial C}{\partial \psi_i} = \frac{\partial \ln C(\tilde{\psi}_P, \tilde{\psi}_M, \tilde{\psi}_B, \tilde{w}, \tilde{x}, \tilde{t})}{\partial \ln \psi_i} \frac{\hat{C}(\tilde{\psi}_P, \tilde{\psi}_M, \tilde{\psi}_B, \tilde{w}, \tilde{x}, \tilde{t})}{\psi_i}, \tag{2.13}$$

where the variables have their previous meanings and the tilde indicates that all variables are measured as a weighted (by ton-miles) average of the firms in the sample.[21]

In terms of analyzing the implications of rail–truck competition, it would be desirable to utilize as much geographic and commodity disaggregation as possible. Since, however, the rail cost functions use bulk and manufactured commodities as output variables, we must limit our discussion to the marginal costs of these two broad commodity types. Similarly, although it would be possible to separate the railroads according to their ICC territory, limitations on trucking data necessitated dividing the trucking sample into two distinct regions: one corresponding to the ICC's Official Territory and one comprising the rest of the country. Hence we limit our analysis of marginal costs to two commodity types (bulk and manufactures) and two geographic areas (the Official Region and the South–West Region, the latter of which we use to denote the rest of the country).

The railroads in the sample included in the Official Territory are given as follows: the Boston and Maine; the Central of New Jersey; the Delaware and Hudson; the Erie-Lackwanna; the Grand Trunk Western; and the Penn Central. To obtain the marginal costs of manufactured commodities, we thus took a weighted average over these firms of the relevant

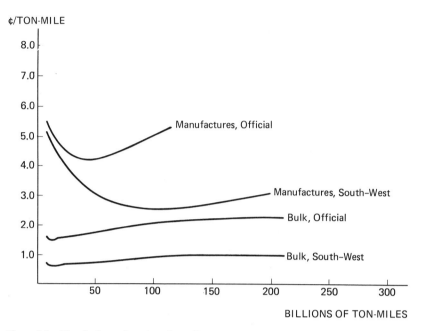

Figure 2.1 Marginal cost functions for rail operations, Official and South–West Regions, 1972.

variables and applied them to (2.13). By varying the amount of manufactured ton-miles, it was then straightforward to develop a marginal cost function at the existing values of the other variables for the railroads in the Official Region. A similar procedure was used to obtain the manufactured marginal cost functions for the remaining railroads in the sample, which comprise the South–West Region. Similar procedures were also followed to obtain the marginal cost functions for bulk commodities of the railroads in the Official and South–West Regions.[22] These cost curves were then scaled to reflect the size of the actual rail market. Thus the estimated marginal cost or supply curves are not true industry supply curves, but, rather, represent those that would result from an industry composed of identical firms, each of which had the characteristics obtained from a weighted average of all of the firms in the region. As such, they represent stylized supply curves and are indicative of the general behavior of the industry rather than of any particular firm.

Figure 2.1 presents these stylized marginal cost functions for bulk and manufactured commodities in the Official and South–West Regions.[23] These curves indicate considerable diversity in the behavior of rail costs.

Marginal costs in the Official Region are substantially greater than those in the South–West Region, while the marginal costs of hauling bulk commodities are considerably below those of hauling manufactured goods. These differences are not only due to regional differences in capital stock, and factor prices, but are also due to differences in average length of haul.

The short-run marginal costs of hauling manufactured goods in the Official Region appear to be particularly high. Not only do they reach their minimum at approximately 4.31¢/ton-mile, but they rise rapidly beyond that point. In contrast, the short-run marginal cost function for manufactured goods in the South–West Region reaches its minimum of 2.76¢/ton-mile at considerably higher output levels, and rises slowly beyond that point. Thus while the cost structure seems to limit the competitive ability of the railroads in the Official Region with respect to manufactured goods, the railroads in the South–West Region do not seem to be laboring under similar constraints.

Although the short-run marginal cost function associated with bulk commodities is substantially higher for the railroads in the Official Region that those in the South–West Region, the two marginal cost functions have quite similar characteristics and rise throughout the relevant range. Nevertheless, while the marginal costs of bulk carriage are generally around 2¢/ton-mile for the railroads in the Official Region, these costs are around 1¢/ton-mile for those in the South–West Region.

In conclusion then, this analysis corroborates the view that the marginal costs associated with manufactured goods is substantially greater than those associated with bulk commodities, and that the marginal costs of the railroads in the Northeast are substantially higher than those in the rest of the country. As we shall see in the next chapter, these cost differences will have important implications for policy and the allocation of traffic between rail and trucks.

2.4 The Costs of Trucking Operations

As we have mentioned, in analyzing the implications of rail–truck competition, it is important to analyze the segment of the trucking industry that competes directly with the railroads. In this regard, Wyckoff (1974) and Wyckoff and Maister (1975, 1977) have argued convincingly that the relevant trucking market is truckload carriers of specialized commodities rather than LTL carriers of general commodities. Since the former carriers concentrate on full-truckload carriage they are able to avoid the costs of consolidation and terminal handling associated with LTL carriage. Moreover, by making heavy use of owner-operators who tend to be nonunionized and accept a return on capital that is less than the general norm, these truckload carriers are able to utilize cheaper labor and capital inputs than are available to most LTL carriers.[24] Consequently, full-truckload carriage is considerably cheaper than LTL carriage and is, in fact, competitive with many rail operations for a wide range of commodities and types of shipments. Thus in this section we will focus upon the general specification and estimated marginal costs of the common carriers of specialized commodities.[25] The first two subsections of this section describe the general specification and estimated characteristics of these carriers, while the third discusses the nature of their estimated marginal cost functions.

2.4.1 Specification of Trucking Costs
A simple specification for a cost function for motor carriers would be the translog function applied to a general long-run cost function

$$C = C(y, w), \tag{2.14}$$

where C is costs, y output in thousands of ton-miles, and w is a vector of factor prices for, respectively, labor, fuel, capital, and purchased transportation. A major problem with this specification, however, is that ton-miles are not homogeneous: 10 tons taken 500 miles and 50 tons taken 100 miles are both 5,000 ton-miles, but there is no a priori reason to believe that the two combinations have the same input requirement sets. If all firms engaged in only a small number of similar activities, or if data were available on the number of ton-miles produced in each haul–load combination, then it might be feasible to expand the vector of outputs and specify a multiple-output cost function. But the typical common carrier will handle a wide range of length of haul–shipment size combinations, and no data, aside from certain firm averages, are available on these combinations.

The data related to the characteristics of firm output for carriers of specialized commodities are limited to the following: ton-miles, total tons, vehicle-miles, and number of shipments. In addition, data are available on insurance and loss and damage payments, which are used as a proxy for the composition of output; firms specializing in high-value commodities should have relatively large insurance payments, while those specializing in low-value commodities should have relatively low insurance payments.

From these variables, the following firm average of service characteristics can be constructed: average shipment size (total tons/number of shipments); average length of haul (ton-miles/total tons); average insurance payments (insurance/ton-miles); and average load per vehicle (ton-miles/total vehicle-miles). However, shipment size and average load are highly collinear because most shipments are in truckload lots. Consequently, we generally omit shipment size in the estimated cost functions.

Given the nature of the common carrier industry, it is realistic to regard these service characteristic variables as beyond the firm's determination. Since common carriers must serve the general public, these variables will be determined by the orders received by the firm and the firm's operating rights. The firm cannot change prices to discourage undesirable traffic, and the ICC ostensibly exerts pressure concerning the quality of service as measured by time in transit. (Unfortunately, no direct measure of this service dimension is available.) While firms may engage in sales efforts to encourage desirable traffic or petition the ICC for operating rights for potentially profitable traffic, their common carrier obligation to accept all customers at established rates also makes them vulnerable to undesirable traffic, particularly from nontransportation firms that operate their own truck fleets and "skim" what would be desirable traffic for their own fleet. Consequently, we will regard these variables as exogenous.

In terms of their impact upon costs, we would expect higher loads and longer hauls to be associated with lower costs. Although truckload carriers incur substantially lower handling and pickup and delivery costs than their LTL counterparts, the terminal component of the shipment is still significant. Thus to the extent that firms can spread these terminal costs over longer hauls, these costs per ton-mile will drop, causing total costs (e.g., terminal plus linehaul) per ton-mile to drop. Similarly, costs will be lower as firms can utilize equipment as fully as possible. Consequently, large average loads are generally associated with high equipment utilization and full backhauls, which lead to lower costs. It is important to note, however, that since operating rights may specifically forbid certain types of backhauls, low average loads may not only reflect unbalanced traffic flows but also specific operating right restrictions. Finally, since high-value goods generally require more careful handling and packing, we would expect costs to increase with average insurance payments.

If we view these variables as a measure of the services associated with each firm's ton-miles, a cost function of the form

$$C = C(\psi(y, q), w) \qquad (2.15)$$

would be appropriate, where q represents the four service characteristics, and $\psi(y, q) = y\phi(q)$ as in (2.4). In the technology corresponding to (2.14), factors are combined to make a level of effective output ψ which can be divided according to a subtechnology into any combination of ton-miles and service characteristics satisfying $\psi = y\phi(q)$.

This specification of "quality separability" may be excessively restrictive, however, since it implies that service characteristics have no direct effect on factor intensities. Thus it may be more suitable to view the service characteristics as technological conditions and specify

$$C = C(\psi, w, t), \tag{2.16}$$

where ψ is ton-miles[26] and t is the vector of service characteristics now, under the cirumstances of common carrier operations, being viewed as technological conditions determined by operating rights.

Estimation of the three different specifications of the trucking cost function indicated that the technological specification given in (2.15) was uniformly superior in terms of the usual statistical criteria. Hence the cost function and marginal costs discussed here are all based on a translog specification of (2.16).[27]

The data used to estimate the costs of truckload carriage were based on a sample of 362 common carriers of specialized commodities not elsewhere classified (nec), in 1972. All data came from *Trinc's Blue Book of the Trucking Industry* (1973), which summarizes the individual firm reports to the ICC. Since, however, preliminary analyses indicated regional differences in the cost functions, the sample was divided into two subsamples and cost functions for the carriers in the Official Territory and the carriers in the rest of the country, which we designate as the South–West Region, were estimated separately.[28] The sample for the Official Territory consists of 201 firms that operate primarily in the Northeast and Central States, which represent the older manufacturing areas in the country. The sample for the South–West Region consists of 161 firms operating in the South, Southwest, and Far West, which represent the newer centers of economic activity in the country.

Since the capital requirements associated with trucking operations are relatively low, it is likely that trucking firms are in a long-run equilibrium. Consequently, it is appropriate to estimate a long-run cost function for these firms. Therefore, to each firm's operating costs was added a 12-percent opportunity cost for capital, with capital measured as "carrier operating property—net." The firms' total costs were divided into labor costs, fuel expenditures and fuel taxes, purchased transportation, and other. "Other expenditures" consist mostly of the imputed opportunity cost of capital, depreciation, and maintenance of capital items (tires, etc.), and were assumed to be payments for capital services. Each firm's "carrier operating property—net" was taken as a measure of the quantity of capital (and thus of capital services), so that "other expenditures" divided by "carrier operating property—net" gave a firm-specific price of capital. A firm-specific price of labor was obtained by dividing labor expenditures by the average number of employees. Since direct quantity measures of purchased transportation and fuel were not available, regional prices for these inputs were estimated by a method whose assumptions and results are given in appendix C.

2.4.2 Characteristics of Trucking Costs and Technology
The estimated trucking cost functions for the Official and South–West Regions are given in appendix C, and we will briefly summarize the principal findings here. As was true of the estimated rail technology, the estimated trucking technology appears to meet the assumed neoclassical postulates remarkably well: the implied marginal product of each of the factors was positive; the estimated marginal costs of all of the observations in the samples were positive; the elasticities of demand for each factor were negative over the sample; and the Allen–Uzawa elasticities of substitution had reasonable signs and magnitudes. In particular, all factors appear to be substitutes for each other, except for fuel and capital, which appear to be complements. This result is reasonable, since equipment is the primary form of capital owned by specialized commodity carriers, and larger rigs require more fuel. In addition, the elasticities of substitution between purchased transportation and fuel and purchased transportation and capital are quite high, which indicates that these firms substitute relatively freely between using their own rig (capital) and hiring owner-operators (purchased transportation). Finally, the own price elasticity of fuel is relatively high, which is also consistent with the ability of these firms to use owner-operators instead of their own equipment.

In terms of rail competition, the most significant findings have to do with the estimated marginal costs and their behavior with the scale of output and operating characteristics. In this respect, it is interesting to note that the estimated marginal costs are on the order of 4.0¢/ton-mile for bulk commodities and 4.5–5.0¢/ton-mile for manufactured commodities in both regions, making them highly rail competitive. Moreover, these costs are quite sensitive to average load and average length of haul, indicating that substantial economies could be obtained if carriers of specialized commodities could obtain higher load factors and longer hauls.

Finally, and most important, the costs of these carriers exhibit distinct economies of scale, which are particularly marked in the Official Region. For example, at the point of approximation, the estimated elasticity of costs with respect to output in the Official Region is 0.7873 (with a standard error of 0.0280), while that in the South–West Region is 0.9362 (with a standard error of 0.0563). Moreover, in the Official Region these economies of scale at the mean extend over an extremely broad range of output and only disappear at output levels that are far beyond the mean output level. Indeed, the estimated marginal costs imply that one or two trucking firms could in principle supply the Official Region and obtain marginal costs on the order of 2.5¢/ton-mile.[29] In contrast, the region of scale economies in the South–West Region is relatively small, and scale economies are exhausted at output levels relatively near the mean.

Since the cost function displays distinct nonhomotheticities and significant interactions among output levels, factor prices, and operating characteristics, generalizations from the behavior of the cost function at the mean are somewhat misleading. Nevertheless, the estimated characteristics of the cost function are such that virtually every firm in the Official Region sample displays evidence of economies of scale, and a significant number of those in the South–West Region also display evidence of economies of scale. This implies, of course, that even though the railroads currently face substantial competition from carriers of specialized commodities, the competition would be considerably greater in a deregulated environment.

The finding of economies of scale in the carriage of specialized commodities is extremely surprising. Conventional wisdom holds that since these carriers perform relatively few terminal services and consolidations, they have virtually no capital costs associated with pickup and delivery activities. In addition, since many of these firms rely heavily upon owner-operators, the capital requirements associated with the linehaul portion of the trip are also relatively low. Hence, one would expect this industry to be characterized by constant costs and many small firms operating on the minimum portion of their average cost curve. However, the finding of economies of scale was extremely robust and persisted when the samples were stratified by length of haul, average load, and revenue per ton-mile in an effort to control for potential differences in technology arising from firms that specialize in different types of commodities and carriage.

Nevertheless, it is admittedly difficult to reconcile these findings of economies of scale with one's intuition concerning the nature of this segment of the industry.[30] A possible explanation for this surprising result may lie in the distinction between regulatory economies of scale and technological economies of scale. Technological economies of scale refer to the basic technology of the industry and imply that the structure of costs and production is such that marginal and average costs fall as output expands. In contrast, regulatory economies of scale refer to institutional conditions that make it possible for large firms to achieve economies of utilization that are unavailable to smaller firms.

In view of the small capital requirements associated with truckload trucking operations, it is extremely difficult to believe that carriers of specialized commodities would be subject to technological economies of scale. However, in view of the rigid commodity restrictions imposed upon these firms by the ICC and the difficulties associated with obtaining new operating authorities, it is quite easy to imagine that these firms would be subject to substantial regulatory economies of scale.

In particular, although carriers of specialized commodities have quite general operating authorities with respect to geographic area, they have extremely narrow operating authorities with respect to commodity. Thus, unless carriers have a wide range of commodity operating authorities, they are subject to empty backhauls or empty hauls as the van travels widely to pick up approved commodities. However, the commission has traditionally made it rather difficult to obtain operating authorities, requiring expensive and time-consuming hearings.[31] Since large firms tend to be large because they have substantial operating authorities and since large firms have the financial resources to obtain more operating authorities, it is quite likely that carriers of specialized commodities are subject to rather substantial regulatory economies of scale. Because large firms are able to achieve higher loads, carry shipments for longer hauls, and obtain better equipment utilization and fewer empty backhauls, they are able to produce ton-miles of service at considerably less costs than their smaller counterparts. Consequently, we observe apparent economies of scale. Nevertheless, to the extent that these economies are due to advantages provided by operating authorities rather than due to technological factors per se, these cost advantages should disappear in a deregulated environment. Hence it is likely that the observed economies of scale and cost savings afforded by large size are somewhat overstated.

Nevertheless, it is important to note that whether economies of scale exist or not, the costs of truckload carriers of specialized commodities are quite low in absolute terms and highly competitive with those of many rail shipments. Thus the comparative advantage of rail lies in the relatively narrow area of large, mutiple, or bulk shipments, while truckload trucking operations provide an increasingly viable alternative to rail for the transportation of a wide range of manufactured commodities.

2.4.3 Marginal Cost and Supply Functions

The statements concerning trucking costs can be better understood by considering the industry marginal cost or supply functions derived from the estimated trucking cost functions. As was true in the case of the railroads, we estimate these functions using the weighted means of the observations in the sample. Thus

$$\frac{\partial C}{\partial y_i} = \frac{\partial \ln C(\tilde{y}_M + \tilde{y}_B, \tilde{w}, \tilde{q}^i)}{\partial \ln y_i} \frac{\hat{C}(\tilde{y}_M + \tilde{y}_B, \tilde{w}, \tilde{q}^i)}{y_i}, \tag{2.17}$$

where i ranges over manufactured and bulk goods (M and B), w represents the vector of factor prices, q^i represents the vector of shipment characteristics associated with commodity type i, and the tildes indicate that all variables are measured at the weighted sample mean. Note that the regional superscripts have been omitted for notational simplicity.

Since the variables are measured at the weighted sample mean, the resulting marginal cost function represents that of a stylized firm, which has the characteristics of the firms in the sample. This is then scaled upward to reflect the size of the market.[32] Hence, the supply functions used in this analysis in effect assume that the industry is composed of identical firms, each of which has the characteristics of the stylized firm, whose factor prices and shipment characteristics are given by a weighted mean of the firms in the sample.

Figure 2.2 presents the estimated industry marginal cost or supply function for carriers of specialized commodities in the Official and South–West Regions. Consistent with our previous discussion, the marginal cost functions in the Official Region exhibit marked and persistent economies of scale. For manufactured commodities, the marginal trucking costs in the Official Region reach levels of 4¢/ton-mile; for bulk commodities, the marginal costs approach 3¢/ton-mile. The difference in these costs is due solely to differences in shipment characteristics, and reflects the economies obtainable due to size of load and length of haul.

Although trucking firms in the South–West Region exhibited economies of scale at the mean values of factor prices and shipment characteristics, these economies are not global and disappear for many firms as interactions among output levels, shipment characteristics, and factor prices are taken into account. Thus when the marginal costs are evaluated at the weighted mean of factor prices and shipment characteristics, the

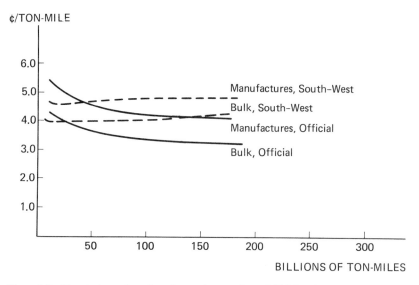

Figure 2.2   Marginal cost functions for truck operations, Official and South–West Regions, 1972.

range of economies of scale become rather narrow. Marginal costs of both manufactured and bulk commodities fall until output levels of approximately 20 billion ton-miles are reached for the industry as a whole, and then rise slowly. At their minimum, the marginal costs of manufactured goods are about 4.5¢/ton-mile, while those of bulk commodities are approximately 4.0¢/ton-mile. Again, the larger loads and lengths of haul associated with bulk commodities account for the differentials in the marginal costs associated with carrying bulk and manufactured commodities.

2.5 The Demand for Rail and Trucking Services

In this section we discuss the general specification of the demand function used in this analysis and then consider the nature of the estimated demand functions.

2.5.1 Specification of Freight Demand Functions
In analyzing the demand for freight transportation, it is important to realize that it is used as a factor of production. Consequently, the specified demand function should be able to be related to the underlying cost and production functions. In addition, because transportation reflects goods

in transit, freight rates do not reflect the true cost of transportation, which also includes inventory components. Thus the demand for freight transportation will not only be affected by the rates themselves, but also by the shipment characteristics, which affect inventory costs.

While the specification of a derived demand function for transportation is conceptually straightforward, the treatment of shipment characteristics is less so. In particular, it is not clear whether shipment characteristics should enter the demand function as direct arguments, components of an inventory function, or in both capacities. The implication of each approach can be seen as follows.

For the sake of simplicity, let us assume that a given firm uses a composite transportation input τ and a composite other input x to produce an aggregate output y, and that the firm is in long-run equilibrium. Furthermore, let us assume that the price of the composite input x reflects its full costs, but that the price of the transportation input τ does not, and that, in particular, costs are affected by the characteristics of the goods shipped.

If the shipment characteristics actually affect the technology employed,[33] they should enter the cost function directly. If, however, they reflect only inventory costs, they should be incorporated into an inventory cost function. In the first case, the underlying cost function and its associated transportation demand function can be written as

$$C = C(P_\tau, q, P_x, y), \tag{2.18a}$$

$$\tau = \frac{\partial C(P_\tau, q, P_x, y)}{\partial P_\tau}, \tag{2.18b}$$

where P_τ represents the rate for transport service, q shipment characteristics, P_x the price of nontransport inputs, y output, C total costs, and τ the demand for the composite transport input. This specification indicates that shipment characteristics affect costs independently of their impact on rates. If, however, shipment characteristics solely affect rates and inventory costs, the underlying cost function and its associated transport demand function can be written as

$$C = (\gamma[P_\tau(q), q], P_x, y), \tag{2.19a}$$

$$\tau = \frac{\partial C(\gamma[P_\tau(q), q], P_x, y)}{\partial \gamma}. \tag{2.19b}$$

Finally, if shipment characteristics affect both the technology and inventory costs, the underlying cost function and its associated transport demand function can be written as

$$C = C(\gamma[P_\tau(q), q], q, P_x, y), \tag{2.20a}$$

$$\tau = \frac{\partial C(\gamma[P_\tau(q), q], q, P_x, y)}{\partial \gamma}. \tag{2.20b}$$

Although (2.20a) is clearly the most general formulation, in practice it cannot be identified.[34] Thus the choice really comes down to whether shipment characteristics are treated as part of an inventory cost function (2.19a) or as direct parameters in the demand function (2.18a).

If the demand functions are estimated over relatively heterogeneous outputs, it seems reasonable to assume that shipment characteristics will be related to the technology employed and thus to utilize a specification related to (2.18a). If, however, the demand functions are estimated over relatively homogeneous outputs, it is reasonable to assume that shipment characteristics only enter the demand function through the effective price of transportation and to use the specification implied by (2.19a). Since the demand functions used to estimate the relationships between rail and TL trucking utilize data ranging over a wide range of commodity types, we employed a specification related to (2.18a) in estimating the demand for rail and truckload service.[35]

Since firms typically cannot adjust factor usage in an optimal fashion, it is likely that they are operating along an inefficient short-run cost function instead of an efficient long-run cost function. Thus, estimates of long-run cost functions are often subject to bias because firms are not in long-run equilibrium. This suggests that whenever there is some suspicion that firms may not be in long-run equilibrium, it is desirable to specify and estimate a short-run cost function. If in fact firms cannot make optimal adjustments in factor utilization, the short-run cost function is clearly the appropriate specification. Moreover, even if firms are in fact in long-run equilibrium, no bias will exist if we specify and estimate a short-run cost function; the short-run cost function will merely indicate that optimal amounts of the fixed factor are used.[36] Thus, it is in general preferable to specify a short-run cost function and its associated factor demand equations instead of a long-run cost function and its factor demand equations.

In terms of the present analysis, we assume that the transport-using firm faces a technology that can be described by the following short-run cost function:

$$C_s = C_s(P_R, P_T, q_R, q_T, X, y), \tag{2.21}$$

where P_R and P_T represent (respectively) rail and trucking rates, q_R and q_T

vectors of shipments attributes associated with (respectively) rail and trucking activities, X a vector of fixed factors (capital, labor, materials, etc.), and y an aggregate output measure of the firm.

This specification assumes that the firm has already decided upon its cost-minimizing levels of capital, labor, and materials and chooses its usage of rail and truck transportation to minimize its transportation costs.[37] This view is also consistent with treating the shipment attributes as arguments of the cost function rather than as arguments of an inventory function. In particular, once a firm has chosen its optimal level of capital, labor, and materials, it also has made many of the logistics decisions concerning length of haul, size of shipment, commodity value, density, etc. Hence these shipment characteristics enter the cost function as explicit technical arguments, and the firm's problem reduces to choosing the cost-minimizing amount of rail and trucking services to employ, given the freight rates.

As long as the firm is a price taker, differentiation of the cost function will yield a factor demand function for transport services. Thus in general terms, we can write the rail or trucking demand function as

$$\frac{\partial C_s}{\partial P_i} = \frac{\partial C_s(P_T, P_R, q, x, y)}{\partial P_i}, \qquad i = T, R, \tag{2.22}$$

where the variables are as previously defined.

To estimate the rail and trucking demand function we assume that the firm's underlying technology can be described by the following translog function:

$$\ln C = \alpha_0 + \sum_i \alpha_i \ln P_i + \sum_j \beta_j \ln q_j + \sum_h \gamma_h \ln x_h + \delta y \ln y$$

$$+ \frac{1}{2} \sum_i \sum_l A_{il} \ln P_i \ln P_l + \sum_i \sum_j B_{ij} \ln P_i \ln q_j$$

$$+ \sum_i \sum_h C_{ih} \ln P_i \ln x_h + \sum_i D_{iy} \ln P_i \ln y$$

$$+ \frac{1}{2} \sum_j \sum_r E_{jr} \ln q_j \ln q_r + \sum_j \sum_h F_{jh} \ln q_j \ln x_h$$

$$+ \sum_j G_{jy} \ln q_j \ln y + \frac{1}{2} \sum_h \sum_s H_{hs} \ln x_h \ln x_s$$

$$+ \sum_h I_{hy} \ln x_h \ln y + \frac{1}{2} J_{yy} (\ln y)^2. \tag{2.23}$$

Differentiation of this expression with respect to the price of the ith transportation input yields the following factor share equation for the ith mode:

$$S_i \equiv \frac{P_i \tau_i}{C_s} = \frac{\partial \ln C}{\partial \ln P_i}$$
$$= \alpha_i + \sum_l A_{il} \ln P_l + \sum_j B_{ij} \ln q_j + \sum_h C_{ih} \ln x_h + D_y \ln y, \qquad i = R, T,$$

$$(2.24)$$

where S_i represents the share of each mode and the subscript i represents the traffic carried by each mode.

In terms of estimation, there are two problems associated with (2.24). First, data are not generally available to relate the fixed factors to the transportation shares; and second, this formulation assumes that all industries in all regions have the same technology. Fortunately, neither of these problems is insoluble. If we assume that the underlying technology is such that production is separable between transportation and the fixed factors, then $C_{ih} = 0$ for all i, h, and the terms in the fixed factors drop out. While moderately restrictive, this assumption does not appear unreasonable since it permits transport shares to vary with the scale of output but not with factor utilization per se. Moreover, if we assume that changes in factor shares with respect to changes in factor prices and regions are the same across industries and regions, the introduction of intercept dummy variables will capture the relevant technological differences. This assumption is not too restrictive since it permits the elasticity of substitution to be variable and to vary among industries and regions.[38]

Thus the final estimating equation takes the following form:

$$S_i = \alpha_i + \sum \beta_j \mathrm{Dum}_j + \sum A_{il} \ln P_l + \sum B_{ij} \ln q_j + D_{iy} \ln y, \qquad i = R, T,$$

$$(2.25)$$

where Dum_j represents a commodity or regional dummy variable, and the other variables were previously defined. Thus the expenditure share on one mode can be expressed as a function of rail and trucking rates, shipment characteristics associated with each mode, aggregate industry output, and a number of zero–one dummy variables for the relevant regions and commodities.

Since (2.25) represents a factor share equation instead of an explicit demand function, we cannot obtain estimates of the elasticity of demand for rail and truck services directly from this equation. However, Berndt and Wood (1975) have shown that we can derive the relevant price elasticities as follows:[39]

$$E_{ii} = A_{ii}/S_i + S_i - 1, \qquad i, j = T, R, \tag{2.26a}$$

$$E_{ij} = A_{ij}/S_i + S_j, \qquad i, j = T, R, \tag{2.26b}$$

where E_{ii} and E_{ij} represent respectively the partial own price elasticity and the partial cross price elasticity of demand,[40] A_{ii} and A_{ij} the relevant coefficients of the factor share equation, and S_i and S_j the estimated cost shares.

Because the shipment characteristics enter directly into the cost function, it is desirable to derive expressions for the elasticity of demand with respect to these characteristics. Since $S_R = P_R R/C_s$ and $S_T = P_T T/C_s$, by solving for R and T, differentiating, and transforming the resulting expression into elasticities, we obtain

$$\mu_{qj}^i = (\partial S_i/\partial \ln q_j)(1/S_i) + \partial \ln C_s/\partial \ln q_j, \qquad i = T, R, \tag{2.27}$$

where μ_{qj}^i represents the elasticity of demand for mode i with respect to the jth shipment characteristic. The first term can be derived directly from the estimated factor share equation, while the second term requires a knowledge of the cost function. If, however, we assume that shippers always compensate for change in shipment characteristics so as to keep transportation costs constant, this term drops out. We thus calculate

$$\mu_{qj}^i = (\partial S_i/\partial \ln q_j)(1/S_i), \tag{2.28}$$

which represents the compensated elasticity of demand for mode i with respect to the jth shipment characteristic.

Finally, the transport demand functions for mode i can thus be obtained from this by using the following expression:

$$\tau_i = \frac{\hat{S}_i}{P_i} C_s. \tag{2.29}$$

Since transportation is assumed to be the only variable factor in this formulation, C_s represents the sum of transport expenditures, and the factor demand equation can be readily determined from the factor share equation.[41]

2.5.2 The Structure of Rail and Trucking Demand
In order to estimate the rail and trucking demand functions, we must give (2.25) empirical content and specify the shipment characteristics, the

regions, and the commodities that were used in our analysis. Since shipment characteristics are postulated to affect production costs directly, it would be desirable to include such variables as frequency of delivery, shipment size, reliability, and so forth. Unfortunately, however, data were only available for the following variables: average length of haul for rail and truck; average load for rail and truck; and commodity value.

In terms of regions, we utilized the three broad geographical areas utilized by the ICC in its rail classification: The Official Territory; the Southern Region; and the Western Region (which includes the Southwestern Region, the Western Trunk Line, and the Mountain–Pacific Regions). Thus this analysis only permits relatively broad regional variation.

With respect to commodities, our initial intention was to utilize the following broad commodity types, which are representative of the major commodity types carried by rail and truck: durable manufactures; nondurable manufactures; field crops (grains, corn, cotton, etc.); livestock, fruit, vegetables, and other agricultural commodities; petroleum and petroleum products; coal; and other bulk commodities (minerals, chemicals, and other). However, when the model was estimated using all of these commodity types, the results were unsatisfactory when field crops, other agricultural products, and coal were included in the sample. Since agricultural products are typically carried by exempt carriers, and since there is virtually no trucking of coal, the truck shares for these commodity types were too low to permit reasonable estimation of these commodities. The problem arises, of course, because the relevant substitutes to rail are exempt motor carriage and barge for agricultural products and barge for coal. Unfortunately, however, data are unavailable to enable us to estimate their demand. Hence, field crops, other agricultural, and coal were dropped from the sample, which was estimated over the remaining commodities.

Because there are only two variable factors, rail and truck, the estimation of one factor share equation is sufficient to permit the estimation of the coefficients of both the rail and trucking share equations.[42] We thus estimated the following trucking share equation,[43]

$$S_T = \alpha_T + A_{TT}\ln(P_T/P_R) + B_{T1}\ln q_1 + B_{T2}\ln q_2 + B_{T3}\ln q_3$$
$$+ B_{T4}\ln q_4 + B_{T5}\ln q_5 + C_{Ty}\ln y + \sum_{i=2}^{3}\text{RDUM}_i$$
$$+ \sum_{i=2}^{4}\text{CDUM}_i, \tag{2.30}$$

where:

S_T = the trucking share, defined as truck revenues divided by the sum of rail and trucking revenues.

P_T = truck revenue per ton-mile.

P_R = rail revenue per ton-mile.

q_1 = truck-tons per vehicle.

q_2 = truck average length of haul.

q_3 = value of commodity.

q_4 = rail-tons per car.

q_5 = rail average length of haul.

y = wage and salary payments. This was used as a proxy for output, which was not available on a region and commodity basis.

$RDUM_2$ = dummy variable for Southern region: 1 if observation was from the South, 0 otherwise.

$RDUM_3$ = dummy variable for Western region: 1 if observation was from the West, 0 otherwise.

$CDUM_2$ = commodity dummy variable for nondurable manufactures; 1 if observation was a nondurable manufactured commodity, 0 otherwise.

$CDUM_3$ = commodity dummy variable for petroleum and petroleum products: 1 if observation from petroleum or petroleum products, 0 otherwise.

$CDUM_4$ = commodity dummy variable for other bulk commodities (mineral, chemicals, and other): 1 if observation from other bulk commodities, 0 otherwise.[44]

To estimate the factor share equations for rail and trucking services, we used a combination of cross-sectional and time-series data for these four broad commodity types and three regions for the five-year period 1968–1972. Thus there were a total of sixty observations in the sample.[45]

Table 2.9 presents the estimated trucking share equation. The coefficients are generally significant and of the expected sign. In particular, the dummy variables indicate that the trucking share of nondurables, petroleum, and minerals–chemicals is higher than the trucking share for durable manufactures, although this difference is not generally significant. The regional dummies indicate that the trucking share is significantly

Table 2.9 Trucking Share Equation

Variable	Coefficient	Standard error
Constant	0.3212	0.1422
CDUM2	0.1129	0.1404
CDUM3	0.5757	0.3957
CDUM4	0.1597	0.2646
RDUM2	−0.0762	0.0205
RDUM3	−0.2348	0.0365
$\ln P_T/P_R$	−0.1672	0.0845
$\ln \text{LOAD}_T$	−0.2631	0.1756
$\ln \text{ALH}_T$	−0.0257	0.0864
$\ln \text{VAL}$	0.0800	0.1238
$\ln \text{LOAD}_R$	0.0911	0.1137
$\ln \text{ALH}_R$	0.1295	0.0989
$\ln y$	0.0067	0.0094

$R^2 = 0.463$
SSR $= 0.04015$
$F = 69.0782$

Table 2.10 Own Price Elasticities and Cross Price Elasticities, by Region and Commodity, 1972

	Own price elasticity		Cross price elasticity	
	Truck	Rail	Truck–rail	Rail–truck
Durable manufactures				
Official Territory	−0.8262	−0.8428	0.1638	0.1671
South	−0.9906	−0.6989	0.1820	0.0848
West	−1.2385	−0.5480	0.1480	0.0655
Nondurable manufactures				
Official Territory	−0.9863	−0.7022	0.1820	0.1260
South	−1.0701	−0.6432	0.1791	0.1076
West	−1.3823	−0.4864	0.0972	0.0342
Petroleum & related				
Official Territory	−0.5867	−1.1638	0.0836	0.1659
South	−0.6620	−1.0420	0.1150	0.1810
West	−0.8318	−0.8373	0.1650	0.1660
Mineral, chemical & other				
Official Territory	−1.1592	−0.5893	0.1667	0.0848
South	−1.3780	−0.4879	0.0989	0.0350
West	−1.8183	−0.3707	0.1569	0.0320

lower in the South and West, with substantially less trucking being used in the West than in the Official Territory. The price coefficient indicates that increases in truck rates relative to rail rates will cause a substitution away from trucking, while the coefficients on the shipment characteristics indicate that increases in truck load or length of haul will cause a substitution away from trucks and that an increase in value will cause a substitution in favor of trucks. Similarly, an increase in rail length of haul and average load will cause a substitution away from rail. Finally, an increase in economic activity will increase trucking's share of demand, but by an insignificant amount.

Table 2.10 presents the own price elasticities and the cross price elasticities associated with these estimates. The own price elasticity of demand for trucking is close to unity for both types of manufactured commodities, substantially less than unity for petroleum products, and greater than unity for minerals, chemicals, and other bulk commodities. Interestingly, the trucking demand appears to be the most sensitive to rate changes in the Official Territory. The own price elasticity of demand for rail service is less than unity for manufactured goods, approximately unity for petroleum and related products, and substantially less than unity for minerals, chemicals, and other commodities. Moreover, rail demand appears to be the most sensitive to prices in the Official Territory and the least sensitive in the West. The cross price elasticities of demand are positive, but uniformly low. This indicates, of course, that a rise in rates on either mode will encourage some substitution toward the other mode; however, the shift will be relatively small. For example, a 10-percent increase in trucking rates on durable manufactures will reduce trucking demand by 8.3 percent in the Official Territory, and increase rail demand by 1.7 percent. Similarly, an increase in rail rates of 10 percent in the Official Territory will reduce rail demand by 8.4 percent, and increase truck demand by 1.6 percent.

Since the elasticities of each mode are generally less than one, increases in rates should lead to increases in revenues. This of course, does much to explain the observed behavior of the rail and trucking industries to ask for across-the-board rate increases to raise revenues. Moreover, since the elasticity of rail demand appears to be substantially lower than that of truck, this also explains why the railroads tend to apply for more blanket rate increases than the trucking industry.

Additional insight into the nature of the rail and trucking demand functions can be obtained by applying (2.29) to the estimated factor share equation and plotting the resulting demand functions. Note that since our

Table 2.11 Elasticity of Demand for Trucking Services with Respect to Shipment Characteristics

	Shipment characteristics				
	$LOAD_T$	ALH_T	$LOAD_R$	ALH_R	VAL
Durable manufactures					
Official Territory	−0.5211	−0.0509	0.1804	0.2566	0.1585
South	−0.6360	−0.0622	0.2202	0.3132	0.1935
West	−0.8578	−0.0839	0.2969	0.4224	0.2609
Nondurable manufactures					
Official Territory	−0.6327	−0.0619	0.2190	0.3116	0.1925
South	−0.7009	−0.0686	0.2426	0.3452	0.2132
West	−1.0109	−0.0998	0.3499	0.4979	0.3075
Petroleum & related					
Official Territory	−0.3958	−0.0387	0.1370	0.1949	0.1204
South	−0.4304	−0.0421	0.1489	0.2119	0.1309
West	−0.5245	−0.0513	0.1816	0.2583	0.1596
Mineral, chemical, & other					
Official Territory	−0.7807	−0.0763	0.2703	0.3845	0.2375
South	−1.0064	−0.0984	0.3484	0.4956	0.3061
West	−1.5538	−0.1519	0.5378	0.7652	0.4767

analysis is limited to bulk and manufactured commodities and the Official and South–West Regions, we take a weighted average over commodities and regions and aggregate accordingly.

Figure 2.3 plots the rail demand function for bulk and manufactured commodities in the Official and South–West Regions, all of which exhibit the same general shape: they are concave to the origin and hence relatively inelastic at high rates and relatively elastic at low rates. However, for any given rate, the rail demand function for manufactured goods in the South–West Region exhibits the greatest elasticity, while that for bulk commodities in the Official Region exhibits the least.

Figure 2.4 plots the demand functions facing the trucking industry, which indicate the same general shape as those facing the rail industry. However, the concavity of the trucking demand functions appears to be somewhat greater than that of the rail demand functions. Hence at high rates (e.g., in excess of 4¢/ton-mile), the trucking demand functions are somewhat less elastic than their rail counterparts. The converse is true for low rates (e.g., less than 2¢/ton-mile). In addition, for any given rate,

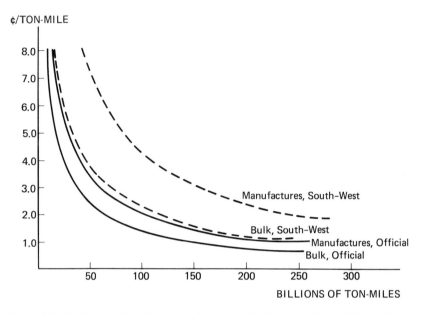

Figure 2.3   Rail demand functions, manufactures and bulk commodities, Official and South–West Regions, 1972.

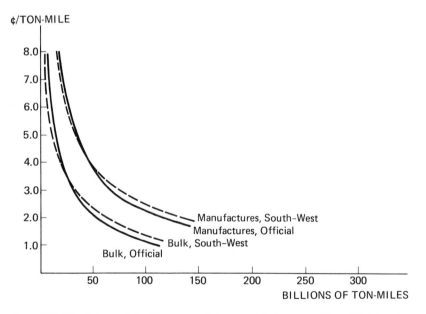

Figure 2.4   Truck demand functions, manufactures and bulk commodities, Official and South–West Regions, 1972.

Table 2.12 Elasticities of Demand for Rail Services with Respect to Shipment Characteristics

	$LOAD_T$	ALH_T	$LOAD_R$	ALH_R	VAL
Durable manufactures					
Official Territory	0.5315	0.0520	−0.1840	−0.2618	−0.1617
South	0.4488	0.0439	−0.1553	−0.2210	−0.1352
West	0.3795	0.0371	−0.1314	−0.1869	−0.1155
Nondurable manufactures					
Official Territory	0.4504	0.0440	−0.1559	−0.2218	−0.1370
South	0.4213	0.0412	−0.1458	−0.2074	−0.1281
West	0.3557	0.0348	−0.1232	−0.1752	−0.1082
Petroleum & related					
Official Territory	0.7851	0.0768	−0.2717	−0.3866	−0.2388
South	0.6773	0.0662	−0.2344	−0.3335	−0.2060
West	0.5280	0.0516	−0.1828	−0.2600	−0.1606
Mineral, chemical, & other					
Official Territory	0.3969	0.0388	−0.1374	−0.1955	−0.1207
South	0.3563	0.0662	−0.1233	−0.1755	−0.1084
West	0.3168	0.0310	−0.1096	−0.1560	--0.0964

the trucking manufacturing demand function appears to be somewhat more elastic than the bulk demand functions.

It is important to note that these demand functions are portrayed for given shipment characteristics. Since, however, demand is sensitive to shipment characteristics, it is useful to analyze how it responds to changes in shipment characteristics across commodities and regions. Table 2.11 presents the elasticities of demand for trucking service with respect to shipment quality, while Table 2.12 presents comparable elasticities for the rail industry. Both tables indicate that each mode is sensitive to increases in the characteristics of the goods it carries.

Truck demand appears to be quite sensitive to the average load of truck shipments, but quite insensitive to its average length of haul. Increases in the average length of haul and average load of rail shipments have only a modest impact on truck demand, while the value of the shipment is positively related to trucking demand. These figures indicate that as average load increases, there is a definite substitution away from trucks, and that this substitution is greatest for minerals, chemicals, and other, and smallest for petroleum products. These results are not surprising, since minerals, chemicals, and other tend to be relatively low-value com-modities, and hence particularly well suited for rail transportation.

The elasticities of demand for rail also indicate considerable substitutability between rail and truck service with respect to shipment character-istics. Thus increase in rail average load or average length of haul will tend to reduce rail traffic, while increases in truck average load or average length of haul will increase rail traffic. However, the elasticity of rail demand with respect to its own shipment characteristics is considerably less than the elasticity of truck demand with respect to its shipment characteristics, indicating that large shipments and long hauls on rail have less possibilities for substitution than large shipments and long hauls on truck. Increases in the size of the truck shipment appear to have a substantial impact on rail demand, while increases in the average length of haul of truck shipments appear to have very little. Although both tables indicate that increases in the average load of trucking shipments will induce considerable substitution to rail, the elasticities of rail demand with respect to truck load are considerably less than the elasticity of demand of truck demand with respect to truck load. This indicates that relatively more large shipments go by rail than by truck, and is entirely consistent with observed shipper behavior.

2.6 Summary and Conclusions

Perhaps the most significant information to come from this analysis of rail and trucking costs is the wide disparity in the behavior of costs across regions and commodities. While the latter is not surprising since different commodity types have different shipment characteristics and thus a dif-ferential impact upon costs, the observed regional cost differentials in both the rail and trucking industries were somewhat surprising. While the Eastern railroads have long maintained that their costs are higher, this analysis indicates that for levels of manufacturing output beyond 50 billion ton-miles, these differentials are on the order of 75 percent, with costs in the Official Region being approximately 4.5¢/ton-mile and those in the South–West Region being approximately 2.4¢/ton-mile. Similarly, while railroads in the South–West Region can carry bulk commodities at costs that are on the order of 1¢/ton-mile, railroads in the Official Region can only carry these commodities at costs of approximately 2¢/ton-mile. Thus the costs of the Eastern railroads are almost twice those of their Western and Southern counterparts.

While the trucking cost differentials between the Official and the South–

West Regions are not as striking, the difference in the structure of costs is. Since the trucking industry in the Official Region continues to enjoy economies of scale at high levels of output and since the trucking industry in the South–West Region exhausts these economies of scale at relatively low levels of output, at industry outputs beyond 50 billion ton-miles, Eastern trucking firms appear to enjoy clear cost advantages over their counterparts in the South and West. Moreover, these differentials increase as the scale of output grows, indicating that Eastern trucking firms are increasingly competitive with rail as their output increases.

Since the railroads in the Official Territory appear to be characterized by inherently high costs, and since trucking firms in the Official Territory appear to be characterized by inherently low costs,[46] this indicates that, ceteris paribus, an efficient allocation of resources would utilize more trucking in the Official Region than elsewhere in the nation.

Of course, resources cannot be allocated on the basis of costs alone, since demand must also affect the nature of the competitive equilibrium. Moreover, since the marginal cost and demand functions are all inter-dependent, a simple extrapolation of the existing cost or supply function and the demand functions will not indicate the final general equilibrium solution to an abandonment of value-of-service pricing and the establishment of competitive pricing. A full analysis of the implications of abandoning value-of-service pricing must necessarily be of a general equilibrium nature and must also include distributional as well as efficiency considerations. Having laid the groundwork for such an analysis in this chapter, let us now turn to an analysis of the implications of a competitive pricing solution in the rail and trucking industries.

Notes

1. See Friedlaender (1978a) for a full review of the literature and the weaknesses associated with existing estimates of transport cost and demand functions.

2. In recent years freight forwarders have taken over the consolidation of LCL shipments into full carload lots, which they then send by conventional boxcar or by trailers-on-flatcars (TOFC). For an interesting discussion of the role of the freight forwarders see Sloss and Harrington (1978).

3. For an interesting discussion of the nature of the trucking industry see Wyckoff (1974), Wyckoff and Maister (1975, 1977), and Taff (1976a, b).

4. For a review of the literature, see Kneafsey (1975) for rail, Oramas (1975) for truck, and Douglas and Miller (1975) for air.

5. See, for example, Keeler (1974), Kneafsey (1975), and Eads et al. (1969).

6. This approach has been utilized by Keeler (1974) and Kneafsey (1975) in the railroad industry and by Eads et al. (1969) in the airline industry.

7. The specific form of this function will be discussed in more detail in the cost appendices.

8. In addition, in some cases, we treat shipment characteristics as technological variables. For a full discussion of the costing methodology, see appendixes A, B, and C. While it is often convenient to treat the fixed factors as technological variables, we treat them separately to distinguish between the short-run and long-run cost functions.

9. See, for example, Hall (1973), Diewert (1971), Christensen et al., (1973), and Denny (1974).

10. For a full discussion of the properties of the translog function see appendix A and Lau (1974b).

11. See appendix A for a full discussion of the use of this generic output function. It is useful to note that in some cases the operating characteristics are treated as technological variables instead of as arguments in a hedonic output function. See Spady (1979) for a full discussion of the relationship between the hedonic specification and the technological specification.

12. See Klein (1947, 1953), Borts (1952, 1960), Keeler (1974), Griliches (1972), Hasenkamp (1976a, b), and Caves and Christensen (1976).

13. Actually, data were collected for 44 class I linehaul railroads for the years 1968–1972. For the other railroads in the United States, the *Carload Waybill Statistics* sample was clearly inadequate; for the years preceding 1968 mergers made much of the B branchline and capital data useless, and other data were difficult to obtain, particularly in machine-readable form. The years 1971 and 1972 were not used due to Amtrak operations.

14. It is possible to include the observations for four of these roads—the Denver and Rio Grande, the Louisville and Nashville, the Norfolk and Western, and the Reading—with the observations for the other 20 roads and obtain results which generally satisfy the regularity conditions but which have somewhat different implications from those obtained using the 20 noncoal roads alone. Using the estimates presented in appendix B, for which the sample consisted of 19 noncoal roads, a prediction interval test permits rejection of the hypothesis that coal and noncoal roads have the same technology at the 0.005 level. For a full discussion of this point see Spady (1979).

15. For a full discussion of the final estimating equation see appendix B. Note that in terms of degrees of freedom, the parameters that appear only in the cost function are relevant since the factor share equations introduce additional degrees of freedom. Appendix B also discusses the treatment of the autoregressive structure of the disturbances.

16. Because of the merger, the Burlington Northern data are for 1970.

17. It is of further interest to note that in the period immediately preceding bankruptcy firms will rent rather than purchase equipment, since the distress sale at bankruptcy—or operation under trusteeship—of the equipment will not realize its market value. Thus, ceteris paribus, one would realistically expect equipment shortages to arise in periods preceeding major bankruptcies.

18. This view has received considerable support from Keeler's work (1974), which indicated that efficiency requires the abandonment of substantial quantities of track.

19. An interesting side point here is that at the point of approximation the isocontour of ψ_1 and ψ_2 is quite nearly a straight line, though it is, as other studies have found, convex. But the standard errors of the relevant coefficients are such that concavity could almost assuredly not be rejected.

20. Since $\Sigma(\partial \ln C/\partial \ln \psi_i) = (1/C)(\partial C/\partial \psi_i)\psi_i$, and $P_i = \partial C/\partial \psi_i$ under marginal cost pricing, $\Sigma(\partial \ln C/\partial \ln \psi_i) = (\Sigma P_i\psi_i)/C$, the ratio of revenues to costs.

21. See appendix E for a full discussion of the derivation of the marginal cost functions.

22. However, these marginal cost functions take the volume of coal and agricultural commodities as given. As explained below, efforts to obtain meaningful demand functions for coal and agricultural commodities proved futile, precluding an analysis of a competitive equilibrium for these commodities. Thus we took their volumes as being exogenously determined, and obtained marginal cost functions for the remaining bulk commodities.

23. Note that since these marginal cost functions are jointly determined, it is only possible to draw the marginal cost curve for one type of output on the assumption that the other output is held constant. We thus draw the marginal cost curve for each commodity type on the assumption that the output of the other commodity type is held constant at its existing output levels.

24. Wyckoff and Maister (1975) have an interesting analysis of owner-operators and the role they play in the trucking industry.

25. The ICC lists a number of types of carriers of specific commodities including household goods carriers, automobile carriers, refrigerated goods carriers, and carriers of general commodities not elsewhere classified (nec.) Since the nec carriers transport a wide range of rail-competitive traffic, it was felt that their costs would be the most representative of the rail-competitive trucking market. Chapter 5 contains a full description of the costs of the LTL trucking market.

26. Since (2.14) is a special case of (2.15) in which q is identically one, we will now use ψ to denote output for simplicity. It should be clear from the context whether the appropriate notion of output coincides with generic ton-miles.

27. Furchtgott (1978) has a discussion of the properties of the three models estimated for truckload trucking. Appendix C gives a full discussion of estimated cost functions and the definitions of the variables used.

28. Although it would have been desirable to estimate cost functions for more disaggregate regions, data limitations precluded this. The sample of the Official Territory included firms is the following five ICC trucking regions: Central States East, Central States West, Middle Atlantic, North Middle Atlantic, and New England. The South–West Region included the remaining ICC trucking regions.

29. The implications of this finding will be discussed in detail in chapter 3, where we consider the nature of the competitive equilibrium.

30. In a recent study, Chow (1978) finds some evidence of economies of scale in the LTL carriers of general commodities but no evidence of economies of scale in the truckload carriers.

31. In recent months the commission appears to have relaxed its stand on operating authorities substantially, and is now granting them to most applicants without lengthy hearings or delay.

32. See appendix E for a full discussion of the derivation of the marginal cost and supply functions.

33. That is, if the different shipment characteristics affect the production possibility sets the firm faces.

34. The difficulty, of course, comes from distinguishing q's effect on γ from q's direct effect on C without arbitrarily assigning different functional characteristics for each.

35. In fact, we also estimated the demand function using the specification implied by (2.19a), but found that it did not perform as well as that implied by (2.18a).

36. In long-run equilibrium, the value of the long-run cost function must equal the sum of the factor payments to each factor at its optimal level. Thus

$$C(y, w) = \sum w_i x_i^*$$

where w_i represents the price of factor i, and x_i^* represents the cost-minimizing amount of that factor. Let us assume that we treat the first factor as fixed. Thus

$$C_s = C(y, w) - w_1 x_1^* = \sum_{i=2} w_i x_i^*.$$

But the left-hand side of this equation is merely the short-run variable cost function

$$C_s = C(y, w, x_1^*).$$

If we estimate the short-run variable cost function and use it to derive the optimal amount of x_1, we will find that the observed amount of x_1 will equal the optimal amount x_1^*. Hence, no bias will occur if we specify a factor as being fixed that is actually variable.

37. Note that no bias will exist if we specify a factor as fixed that is actually variable since the amount of the factor employed will represent the cost-minimizing amount.

38. We present the argument for the long-run cost function for notational simplicity. Thus suppose the underlying cost function for the hth industry in the dth region to be given by

$$\ln C^{hd} = \alpha_0^{hd} + \sum_i \alpha_i^{hd} \ln P_i + B_y^{hd} \ln Y + \frac{1}{2} \sum_i \sum_j A_{ij}^{hd} \ln P_i \ln P_j + \sum_i B_{iy}^{hd} \ln P_i \ln Y.$$

The factor share equation for the ith factor is thus given by

$$S_i^{hd} = \frac{\partial \ln C^{hd}}{\partial \ln P_i} = \alpha_i^{hd} + \sum_j A_{ij}^{hd} \ln P_j + B_{iy}^{hd} \ln Y.$$

If we utilize a cross-sectional analysis, this suggests that we should employ industry and regional dummy variables in the constant, price, and output terms. If, however, $A_{ij}^{hd} = A_{ij}^{lo}$ and $B_{iy}^{hd} = B_{iy}^{lo}$ for all industries h and l, all regions d and o, and all factors i and j, intercept dummies will capture the relevant differences in technology. Since $\partial S_i^{hd}/\partial \ln P_j = A_{ij}^{hd}$ and $\partial S_i^{hd}/\partial \ln Y = B_{iy}^{hd}$, the assumption that $A_{ij}^{hd} = A_{ij}^{lo}$ is equivalent to the assumption that factor shares respond to changes in factor prices in an identical fashion across industries and regions, while the assumption that $B_{iy}^{hd} = B_{iy}^{ol}$ is equivalent to the assumption that factor shares respond to changes in output identically across industries and regions.

39. Uzawa (1962) has shown that the elasticity of substitution between two factors can be given by $\sigma_{ij} = CC_{ij}/C_i C_j$, where C_i and C_j represent the first derivatives of the cost function with respect to the price of the ith and jth factors, respectively, and C_{ij} represents the second derivative of the cost function with respect to the relevant factor price. Using the translog cost function and performing the relevant differentiation yields $\sigma_{ij} = (A_{ij} + S_i S_j)/S_i S_j$ and $\sigma_{ii} = (A_{ij} + S_i^2 - S_i)/S_i^2$. Allen (1956) has shown that the conventional demand elasticities can be related to the elasticities by the following expression: $E_{ii} = S_i \sigma_{ii}$ and $E_{ij} = S_j \sigma_{ij}$. Performing the relevant substitution yields (2.26a) and (2.26b).

40. These are partial price elasticities because they neglect the price effect caused by changes in the price of the commodity. Allen (1956) has also shown that the full own price elasticity E_{ii} of demand and the full cross elasticity of demand E_{ij} are given, respectively, by $E_{ii} = S_i(\sigma_{ii} - \eta)$ and $E_{ij} = S_j(\sigma_{ij} - \eta)$, $i, j = T, R$, where η represents the elasticity of demand of the commodity with respect to its own price. The price elasticity of the produced commodity enters because increases in the price of any factor not only cause a substitution among factors, but also cause the price of the commodity to rise, inducing a substitution away from the commodity. Thus, the own price elasticity of demand for the commodity η plays a role that is similar to the income effect in consumer theory.

41. Note that in this formulation we assume that C_s is constant and hence that the aggregate elasticity for transport services is unity.

42. Since we postulate that firms are cost minimizers, we must impose the constraint that the cost function is homogeneous of degree one in factor prices, and thus require that

$A_{TT} + A_{TR} = 0$.

In addition, we impose the symmetry condition that $A_{TR} = A_{RT}$.

43. Note that since we constrain $A_{TT} + A_{TR} = 0$, we can incorporate the prices in ratio form. It should also be noted that all variables are estimated as deviations from the sample mean.

44. See Friedlaender (1978a) for a full discussion of the data used in this anslysis.

45. The dummy variables were standardized on the Official Territory and on durable manufactures.

46. However, it is important to voice a word of caution with respect to the inherent economies associated with the trucking firms in the Official Region since the observed economies of scale may well be of a regulatory rather than a technological nature.

Chapter 3

Rail–Truck Competition and Value-of-Service Pricing

3.1 Introduction and Overview

The value-of-service rate structure has long been held up as an example of the inefficiencies caused by regulation in the surface freight industries.[1] Conventional wisdom contends that rail transportation enjoys a clear cost advantage over truck transportation for all shipments of a carload size (e.g., over 15 tons), except those with short haul (e.g., less than 200 miles), or very high value (e.g., computer parts).[2] Since, however, the value-of-service rate structure has traditionally maintained high rail rates on manufactured goods and has prevented railroads from pricing these goods competitively, shippers have had a clear incentive to use trucks, which provide superior service with respect to transit time, shipment size, etc. Thus most of the critics of transport regulation feel that the value-of-service rate structure creates a substantial misallocation of resources by encouraging the use of high-cost trucking operations instead of low-cost rail operations. Therefore, according to them, in the absence of regulation, rail rates on manufactured commodities would fall and there would be a shift in freight shipments away from truck and toward rail.

In recent years, however, a revisionist view has evolved, which holds that the inefficiencies caused by value-of-service rate making may be considerably less than generally believed.[3] Basically this view holds that trucking costs of manufactured goods are considerably lower than generally believed, while rail costs are considerably higher. Thus the competitive advantage that rail operations enjoy over trucking operations is actually quite limited and efficient resource allocation requires increased use of trucks for the carriage of manufactured goods.

Adherents of this view point to two major pieces of evidence. First, Wyckoff (1974) and Wyckoff and Maister (1975) have analyzed the trucking industry extensively and argued that the true source of rail competition comes from full-truckload carriers of specialized commodities instead of from LTL carriers of general freight.[4] Since truckload carriage does not incur costs of consolidation and terminal handling, the cost of truckload trucking operations are considerably lower than the costs of LTL operations and are in fact competitive with rail. Second, the railroads have consistently attempted to raise rates on manufactured goods rather than lower them, arguing that the rates on boxcar operations fail to cover costs. Indeed, the rail industry is presently lobbying for reduced regulation to permit it to raise rates and/or abandon service selectively on a wide range of manufactured commodities.[5] Thus, according to many railroad sources, not only does the value-of-service rate structure fail to permit the railroads to earn sufficient revenue on much of their manufactured traffic and permit them to maintain low rates on bulk and agricultural traffic, but it also may engender losses on much of their manufactured traffic. Consequently, instead of leading to reduction in rates of manufactured commodities, rational pricing may actually require an increase in these rates.

The findings of this chapter strongly support the revisionist view with respect to rail rates and indicate that not only are the price–marginal cost ratios higher for bulk than for manufactured commodities, but also that rates on manufactured goods are less than marginal costs. Thus economic efficiency would dictate increases in rail rates on manufactured goods and a reallocation of this traffic in favor of trucks. Nevertheless, it is important to note that because of the wide geographical variation that exists in rail and trucking costs, it is not appropriate to make sweeping generalizations about the economic effects of moving from the existing rate structure to one that would reflect competitive pricing.

With respect to the Official Territory, our research indicates that railroads carry manufactured goods at rates considerably below marginal cost and carry bulk commodities at rates slightly greater than marginal cost. In contrast, trucks carry both types of goods at rates in excess of marginal cost, with the price–marginal cost ratio for bulk commodities considerably higher than that of manufactured goods. Thus, contrary to the conventional wisdom, the rate structure appears to favor manufactured goods rather than bulk commodities on both modes. Since rail rates on manufactured commodities are currently below marginal costs, while truck rates on manufactured commodities are above marginal costs, a move toward competitive pricing on these commodities would lead to substantial increases in rail rates, reduction in trucking rates, and, because trucking costs are highly competitive with rail costs, a substantial modal shift from rail to trucking shipments. In contrast, since both rail and trucking rates are greater than marginal cost for bulk commodities, a move toward competitive pricing would reduce rates on both modes, with relatively greater reductions in truck than in rail shipments. Nevertheless, because of the inherent advantage of railroads with respect to shipping bulk commodities, there would still be a shift in the modal split in favor of railroads on this traffic.

Within the South–West Region, rail rates are slightly below marginal costs for manufactured commodities and considerably in excess of marginal costs for bulk commodities; truck rates are substantially above marginal costs for manufactured commodities, but slightly below marginal costs for bulk commodities. Thus the value-of-service rate structure seems to apply to trucking rates, while the revisionist view of the rate structure seems to apply to rail rates. Consequently a move toward competitive pricing would imply an increase in rail rates and a reduction in trucking rates for manufactured commodities, and a reduction in rail rates and an increase in trucking rates for bulk commodities. In terms of modal splits, a competitive pricing structure would lead to a reallocation of manufactured traffic in favor of truck and a reallocation of bulk commodities in favor of rail.

Thus within both regions, a competitive equilibrium in the rail and trucking industries would be characterized by a mode split in favor of truck for manufactured goods and a mode split in favor of rail for bulk commodities. In terms of each mode, railroads would carry substantially more bulk commodities than manufactured goods while trucks would carry more manufactured commodities than bulk commodities. This scenario implies that railroads would largely perform a wholesaling function, carrying commodities between major traffic centers, while trucks would largely perform a retailing function, carrying commodities in truckload shipments from these major traffic centers to more geographically dispersed areas.

Of course, the notion that railroads should concentrate upon wholesale or linehaul operations that require relatively little switching and consolidation is not new and is widely held by transportation analysts.[6] What is startling, however, is the finding that the present railroad rate structure not only yields a substantially lower price–marginal cost ratio on manufactured than bulk commodities, but also that it yields a price–marginal cost ratio of less than unity for manufactured goods and greater than unity for bulk commodities. Thus if any cross subsidy exists in the railroad rate structure, it appears to go from shippers of bulk commodities to shippers of manufactured goods.

The distributional implications of these findings are interesting and indicate that the heavy losers from an abandonment of value-of-service pricing would be trucking firms, railroads in the South–West Region, shippers of manufactured goods, and workers in the manufacturing industries. Conversely, the gainers would be the railroads in the Official Territory and shippers of bulk commodities. Thus not only must the gainers and losers be weighed against each other, but the efficiency gains that would result from competitive pricing policies must be weighed against the rather sizable income losses that would occur to certain groups of carriers, shippers, and industries.

This chapter takes the following form. Section 3.2 outlines the analytical framework used to assess the impact of changes in pricing policy while Sections 3.3 and 3.4, respectively, quantify the efficiency and distributional impacts of substituting competitive pricing for the existing rate structure. Section 3.5 provides a brief summary and conclusion.

3.2 Analytical Foundations for Evaluating Transport Policy

A basic theme of this analysis is that comprehensive evaluation of any transportation policy requires an assessment of its distributional and allocational impacts within a general equilibrium setting. Thus in addition to analyzing changes in rates and modal splits in a ceteris paribus setting, it is important to recognize and incorporate the interdependencies that exist among modes and between the transport sector and the rest of the economy. For example, since the demand for trucking services depends upon rail rates (and vice versa), and since rail and trucking costs depend upon their respective traffic mixes, a given change in rail rates on manufactured goods will generate shifts in the trucking demand functions as well as shifts in the marginal costs of carrying the relevant commodities for each mode. These shifts in turn engender further shifts in the cost and demand functions until a full general equilibrium is reached with respect to traffic levels, rates, and costs, for all commodity types in each mode. Because these interdependencies may be substantial, it is likely that the ultimate general equilibrium effects of any change may be substantially different from the proximate partial equilibrium effects. This implies, of course, that policymakers concerned with the distributional impact of policy changes should also focus upon the general equilibrium changes in income since an initial income loss may be offset or reinforced by further general equilibrium responses within the transportation sector.

Finally, since the demand for transportation services is closely tied to regional incomes and output levels, it is important to incorporate the linkages between freight rates and traffic volumes on the one hand and regional income and output levels on the other. Thus a full general equilibrium analysis recognizes the entire range of interdependencies among modes, traffic volumes, rates, costs, regional incomes, and regional output.

Of course, each transportation mode carries an enormous range of commodities over an enormous range of origins and destinations, and an analysis that incorporates the full complexity of the transportation industries and their interrelationships would be an impossible undertaking. Since, however, these general equilibrium effects have not been dealt with previously, an initial effort in this direction should yield important dividends by highlighting the nature of the problem and quantifying the magnitudes of the differences between the partial equilibrium effects of a policy change and its general equilibrium effects.

Consequently, this chapter will focus upon the interrelationships between rail and regulated truck transportation with respect to modes and between bulk and manufactured commodities with respect to outputs. While we clearly recognize that water, pipeline, and exempt and private carriage transport a considerable portion of freight traffic, data limitations required that the analysis be limited to these two modes. Similarly, while we also recognize that manufactured and bulk commodities are aggregates of many different commodities, each of which has diverse shipment characteristics and transportation requirements, data limitations and analytical tractability required that the analysis be limited to these two generic commodity types. Finally, in keeping with the relatively aggregate framework of the analysis, we limit the regional analysis to two broad regions: the Official Territory, and the South–West Region, the latter of which encompasses the rest of the ICC regions.

The basic structure of the analysis is presented in figure 3.1, which depicts two linked models:

A regional transportation model that determines for each region the marginal costs, revenues, outputs, and rates for manufactured and bulk commodities by rail and truck and the total levels of rail and truck profits, costs, and factor demands.

A regional income model that determines for each region incomes, outputs, and employment levels by broad commodity type.

Thus the regional transportation model simultaneously solves for the equilibrium levels of rates, output, marginal costs, and revenues for rail and truck and bulk and manufactured commodities, and the modal levels of costs, revenues, profits, and factor utilization. Similarly, the regional income model determines the equilibrium levels of income, employment, and output by industry and by region. Although the transportation

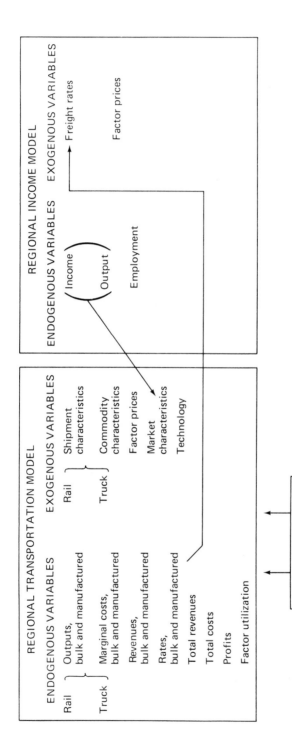

Figure 3.1 Transportation policy model.

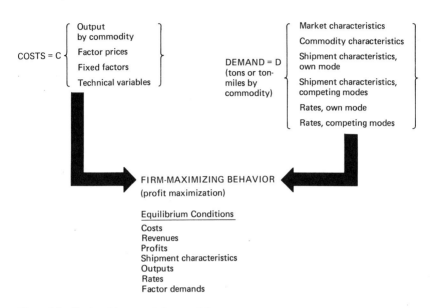

Figure 3.2   Regional transportation model.

models for each region and the regional income model are in principle fully interdependent, in practice the linkages between changes in regional income and transport demand are quite weak. Hence, the model used in this analysis is effectively recursive rather than simultaneous; changes in freight rates affect regional income levels, but changes in regional incomes do not have a significant impact upon freight rates.

Since an understanding of the analytical structure of both of these models is essential to the ensuing policy analysis, this subsection outlines the basic structure of these models. The next subsection therefore discusses the structure of the regional transportation model, and the following subsection discusses the structure of the regional income model. The interactions of these two models will be explicitly considered in .the analysis, and policy simulation will be discussed in the ensuing sections of this chapter.

3.2.1 The Regional Transportation Model

The heart of the analysis lies in the model of the regional transportation market. Conceptually, this is quite straightforward, and is illustrated in figure 3.2. We postulate that for any given mode, there is a known industry or firm cost function, which relates costs to outputs, factor prices, and various technological factors. Similarly, we assume that there is a known firm or industry demand function relating shipments to market characteristics, commodity characteristics, shipment characteristics of own and competing modes, and rates of own and competing modes. Given these cost and demand functions for each mode, and assuming profit-maximizing behavior on the part of the firms in the industry, we can determine the equilibrium level of rates, shipments, profits, costs, revenues, shipment characteristics, and factor demand in the short run and in the long run across all modes and all commodity types.

Although the analytical framework is quite general and could be used to determine the profit-maximizing rate structure in each mode or the joint profit-maximizing rate structure across both modes, in this analysis we are specifically interested in determining the competitive equilibrium across modes and commodities that would result from marginal cost pricing. In stressing the competitive equilibrium, we are primarily motivated by the familiar concepts of economic efficiency and Pareto optimality, which state that if prices are equal to marginal cost everywhere in the economy, the resulting equilibrium will be efficient, in this sense: no increase in output of one commodity is possible without reducing that of another; and no increase in the consumption of one individual is possible without reducing that of another.

While the normative significance of the equality of prices and marginal costs has a long history in the economics literature, it is important to stress that its desirability is based on a number of very strong assumptions. In particular, the normative significance of setting price equal to marginal cost in any one sector can only be demonstrated unambiguously if the following conditions are met: income is distributed in an optimal fashion; there are no economies of scale; and price equals marginal cost in all other sectors. Unfortunately, none of these conditions is likely to be met in the US economy. While the optimal distribution of income is not known, it is unlikely that the current income distribution could be viewed as optimal in any sense; there is some evidence of economies of scale in both the rail and trucking industries; and prices almost certainly deviate from marginal cost throughout the economy. Thus instead of being in a "first-best" world in which the equality of price and marginal cost can be shown to be optimal, we live in a "second-best" world in which systematic deviations from marginal cost may be desirable.[7]

Nevertheless, an analysis of a competitive equilibrium is useful for several reasons, First, in spite of the caveats that must be associated with the normative aspects of marginal cost pricing, it is generally agreed that competition is preferable to monopoly. Second, since marginal cost pricing provides a measure of the opportunity costs of the resources used, it is useful for a determination of an efficient resource allocation. Third, an analysis of a competitive equilibrium provides a useful benchmark with respect to the characteristics of the outcome of the competitive process. Fourth, it provides a measure of carrier profits in a competitive environment and hence indicates whether competition could or could not be sustained in the transportation industries. Consequently, although considerable caution must be used in attributing normative significance to a competitive equilibrium, it seems desirable to provide a comparison of the existing equilibrium with one that would result from a competitive environment in which price would equal marginal cost.

As explained above in analyzing the competitive equilibrium in the transportation markets, we have limited our discussion to two modes (rail and truck) and two commodities (bulk and manufactures) in each region. Although the cost and demand functions are interrelated within each region, we assume that they are not interrelated between regions.[8] Hence we omit regional superscripts for notational simplicity.

The basic structure of the model can be seen in the following marginal cost and demand functions for each mode and each commodity:

$$\text{MC}_{TM} = \text{MC}_{TM}((y_{TM} + y_{TB}), w_T, Q_{TM}); \tag{3.1}$$

$$\text{MC}_{TB} = \text{MC}_{TB}((y_{TM} + y_{TB}), w_T, Q_{TB}); \tag{3.2}$$

$$\text{MC}_{RM} = \text{MC}_{RM}((y_{RM} + y_{RB}), w_R, Q_{RM}, t_R, y_{RM}/y_{RB}); \tag{3.3}$$

$$\text{MC}_{RB} = \text{MC}_{RB}((y_{RM} + y_{RB}), w_R, Q_{RB}, t_R, y_{RM}/y_{RB}); \tag{3.4}$$

$$y_{TM} = y_{TM}(P_{TM}, P_{RM}, Q_{TM}, Q_{RM}, X_{TM}); \tag{3.5}$$

$$y_{TB} = y_{TB}(P_{TB}, P_{RB}, Q_{TB}, Q_{RB}, X_{TB}); \tag{3.6}$$

$$y_{RM} = y_{RM}(P_{TM}, P_{RM}, Q_{TM}, Q_{RM}, X_{RM}); \tag{3.7}$$

$$y_{RB} = y_{RB}(P_{TB}, P_{RB}, Q_{TB}, Q_{RB}, X_{RB}). \tag{3.8}$$

Here the y's represent physical output levels, the w's factor prices, the Q's shipment attributes, the t's exogenously determined technological factors, the X's exogenously determined market factors, the subscripts R and T refer (respectively) to the rail and trucking modes and the subscripts M and B refer (respectively) to manufactured and bulk commodities.

Although the specific arguments of marginal cost and demand functions will be discussed in more detail below, it is useful to discuss the general nature of these arguments and consider whether they are exogenously or endogenously determined.

Equations (3.1) and (3.2) represent the marginal cost functions for trucking manufactured and bulk commodities and indicate that the marginal costs of each commodity depend on the volume of manufactured and bulk commodities carried ($y_{TM} + y_{TB}$), the vector of factor prices facing the trucking firm (w_T), and the shipment characteristics associated with each commodity type (Q_{TM}, Q_{TB}).

The marginal costs of rail transport are given by (3.3) and (3.4) and differ from the trucking marginal cost function by the inclusion of a number of variables representing rail technology (t_R) and a variable representing traffic mix (y_{RM}/y_{RB}). Although this latter variable is treated analytically as a technological variable, it plays an important role in the marginal cost function since it is clearly endogenous rather than exogenous, as the other technological variables are assumed to be. In addition, it is important to note that the technological variables include way-and-structures capital, which is assumed to be fixed in the short run. Thus, while the trucking marginal cost functions reflect long-run marginal costs, the rail marginal cost functions reflect short-run marginal costs.

Finally, (3.5)–(3.8) represent the demand function for each mode and each commodity. They all take an identical form and postulate that demand for each commodity on each mode is a function of the modal rate for the commodity and the competing mode's rate for the commodity ($P_{TM}, P_{TB}, P_{RM}, P_{RB}$), the modal shipment attributes of the commodity and the competing mode's shipment attributes of the commodity ($Q_{TM}, Q_{TB}, Q_{RM}, Q_{RB}$), and the market characteristics for the relevant mode and commodity ($X_{TM}, X_{TB}, X_{RM}, X_{RB}$).

Thus the interdependencies arise because the marginal costs for each commodity on any given mode depend on the amount of each commodity carried by that mode, and because the demand for each commodity on any given mode depends upon the rates charged for that commodity for each mode. Thus if all other variables are exogenously given, the system of eight equations can be used to solve for the equilibrium prices and outputs in each mode ($P_{ij}, y_{ij}, i = T, R, j = M, B$).[9]

Let us consider first the determination of the initial equilibrium. In this case, rates are taken as exogenously determined by regulatory practices. Given rail and truck rates for each commodity, the shipment attributes of each commodity, and the market characteristics facing each mode, (3.5)–(3.8) determine the output levels of each commodity and mode. We then substitute these values into each of the marginal cost functions to obtain the marginal costs for each commodity on each mode, given the relevant vector of shipment attributes, factor prices, and technology. Thus as long as prices bear no relationship to marginal costs, the system can be solved independently.

In a competitive equilibrium, however, price equals marginal cost. Hence we substitute prices for marginal costs in (3.1)–(3.4) and obtain a system of eight equations in eight unknowns: the four outputs (y_{ij}, $i = T, R, j = M, B$), and the four prices ($P_{ij}, i = T, R, j = M, B$). Simple inspection of these equations clearly indicates their simultaneous nature and also indicates their sensitivity to the endogenous variables. In particular, changes in output levels of any given commodity will change the marginal costs associated with that commodity. But if price equals marginal cost, this will also affect the demand functions. Thus a partial equilibrium analysis is not possible.

The difficulties with a partial equilibrium analysis can clearly be seen by considering the subproblem of determining the competitive equilibrium for manufactured goods. In this case, we would take bulk output and prices as given (i.e., we use $\overline{P_{TB}}, \overline{P_{RB}}, \overline{y_{TB}}, \overline{y_{RB}}$ at their observed values). However, since the traffic mix is a variable in the railroad marginal cost function, changes in the amount of manufactured commodities carried by the railroads will lead to shifts in both the marginal cost functions for rail and manufactured commodities. This should then engender changes in the equilibrium traffic levels of bulk commodities under marginal cost pricing. But these changes in bulk traffic levels would affect all of the marginal cost functions. Thus the partial equilibrium analysis of the manufacturing traffic alone would fail to capture the cost and demand interrelationships between the bulk and manufacturing traffic and hence fail to give a true picture of the general equilibrium effects of competition. Similar problems arise with partial equilibrium analyses of traffic allocations on each mode or traffic allocations of bulk commodities.

Because factor prices, shipment characteristics, and rail technology are treated as exogenous variables, it is also possible to undertake comparative static analyses of the general equilibrium response of the system to changes in any of these variables. In the context of the status quo, these comparative static experiments will indicate the changes in total costs or revenues that could arise from a change in any of the variables. In the context of the competitive equilibrium, changes in the variables will not only engender direct changes in the marginal cost or demand functions, but also secondary changes in these functions due to the changes in the equilibrium levels of rates and outputs. It is interesting to note, however, that the direct comparative static effects are generally greater than the indirect general equilibrium effects. Moreover, the changes introduced by moving from the initial equilibrium to the competitive equilibrium tend to swamp those occasioned by comparative static changes in the exogenous variables. This indicates, of course, that the existing equilibrium is far removed from the competitive equilibrium.

Finally, because the railroads' way-and-structures capital is assumed to be fixed, it is important to note that the estimated competitive equilibrium represents a short-run, rather than a long-run, equilibrium. Since institutional and regulatory constraints have traditionally prevented the railroads from adjusting their infrastructure capital in an optimal fashion [e.g., FRA (1978)], it is likely that the short-run equilibrium is more relevant for pricing policies than the long-run equilibrium. Because, however, substantial resource misallocations may exist from the failure to adjust the railroads' way-and-structures capital in an optimal fashion, it is important to determine the long-run competitive equilibrium. This will be done in chapter 4, which discusses the implications of adjustments in the railroads' infrastructure.

3.2.2 The Regional Income Model

Most regional models are concerned with estimating the income and employment levels of a state or a standard metropolitan statistical area (SMSA) and therefore make the small-country assumption that national prices and income levels are exogenous to the region.[10] Since, however, national economic activity is the summation of the economic activity that takes place throughout the nation, this assumption is clearly not correct. Nevertheless, most regions are sufficiently small relative to the total level of economic activity that relatively few biases result from such an approach.

In the case of the present analysis, however, which divides the nation into two large regions, the Official and the South–West, such an assumption is clearly unwarranted and the interregional linkages have to be explicitly considered. Hence the regional income model adopts a relatively simple framework in terms of income determination to enable these interregional linkages to be captured.

The framework of the model is illustrated in figure 3.3. Commodity shipments between any origin–destination pair are postulated to be a function of production costs, transport costs or freight rates, and regional income levels. Regional output is simply the sum of all regional shipments. Employment in any region is postulated to be a function of regional

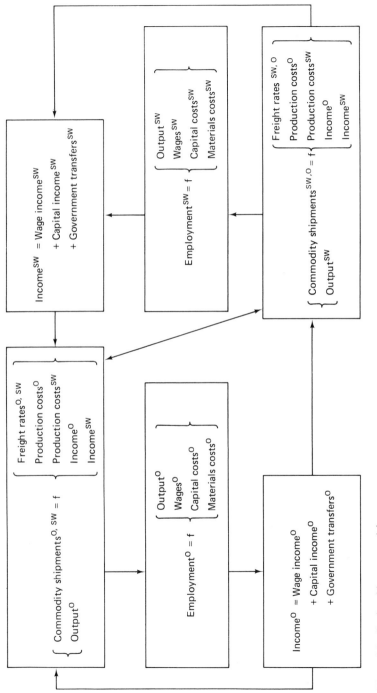

Figure 3.3 Regional income model.

output and factor prices, while regional income is simply the sum of wage payments, capital payments, and government transfers.

Although the structure of the model is quite simple, figure 3.3 makes clear that there are a number of interregional linkages. In particular, changes in freight rates will not only affect the delivered prices between any two points of origin and destination, but will also affect the delivered prices at any destination point from any other point of origin. Hence changes in freight rates will alter the relative price configuration of delivered prices among regions and hence change regional output levels, which in turn will change regional employment and income levels. In principle these changes in regional income levels should affect transportation demand, which should then lead to further adjustments in freight rates and hence in regional income levels. In practice, however, these second-round effects were quantitatively quite small. Hence in estimating the regional income effects, we treated the model as being effectively recursive with changes in freight rates leading to changes in regional income.

3.3 A Competitive Equilibrium in the Rail and Trucking Industries

Having discussed the properties of the underlying marginal cost and demand functions, and the structure of a competitive general equilibrium solution in the rail and trucking industries, we are now in a position to discuss the equilibrium that would result if value-of-service pricing were abandoned and a competitive equilibrium resulted. This section will focus upon the efficiency aspects of such a change, while the following section will discuss its distributional implications.

The discussions of the underlying cost and demand functions in the preceding chapter indicated that trucking and rail costs and demands display considerable geographical differences. Consequently, we will discuss separately the implications of a competitive equilibrium in the Offical and the South–West Regions.

3.3.1 Competitive Equilibrium in the Official Territory
The Official Territory comprises the bulk of the older, industrialized centers in the country and includes New England, the Mid-Atlantic States, and the East-Central States.[11] As such, it represents an area marked by high population densities, a megalopolis extending along the Atlantic seaboard, and fairly geographically dispersed centers of economic activity throughout the area. Thus while the region is admittedly charac-

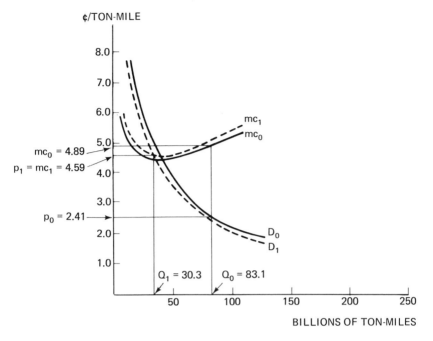

Figure 3.4   Rail, manufactures, initial and competitive equilibria, Official Region, 1972.

terized by large urban centers, it is also characterized by a fairly dense network of economic activity throughout. This relatively uniform dispersion of economic activity has particular implications for rail costs and intermodal competition.

Because of the dispersed nature of economic activity, rail operations in the Official Territory involve a relatively high degree of retailing activities in which the railroads perform much of the pickup and delivery operations as well as the linehaul journey. Their traffic is characterized by relatively short hauls with a disproportionately large number of single- or double-boxcar movements. Consequently, within the Official Region railroads devote a disproportionate amount of resources to expensive switching and consolidation operations instead of to the relatively inexpensive linehaul journey. The high-cost nature of these rail operations was discussed in the previous chapter, which indicated that the costs of railroad operations in the Official Territory were at least 50 percent more than those of railroads in the rest of the country.

While the railroad rate structure makes considerable allowance for shippers' needs, it makes relatively little allowance for cost differentials

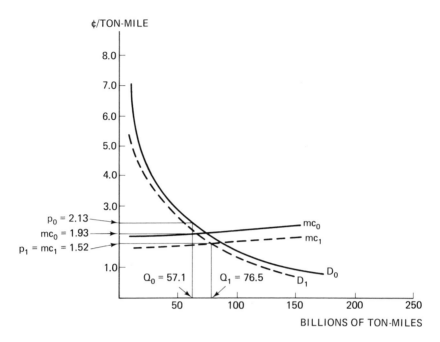

Figure 3.5   Rail, bulk, initial and competitive equilibria, Official Region, 1972.

among railroads and treats the rail industry as being fairly homogeneous. Consequently, although the rate structure reflects considerable variability with regard to commodity types, it does not reflect much geographical variability with regard to carrier costs. Thus even though manufactured commodities are traditionally carried at high rates relative to those of bulk commodities, the rail costs in the Official Territory are sufficiently high that the railroads in this region actually carry these commodities at rates that are substantially below marginal costs.[12]

This can be clearly seen in figures 3.4 and 3.5 which plot the existing industry demand and marginal cost curves for the railroads in the Official Territory[13] for manufactured and bulk commodities, respectively. The solid lines marked D_0 and mc_0 in each figure represent the existing demand and marginal cost curves facing the railroads, while the points P_0 and Q_0 represent the existing rates and volume levels. These figures are somewhat surprising, and indicate that while railroads in the Official Territory carry bulk commodities at rates that are somewhat above marginal costs, they carry manufactured commodities at rates that are substantially below marginal costs. In particular, at the existing equilibrium, rail rates and marginal costs are respectively estimated to be 2.405¢/ton-mile and

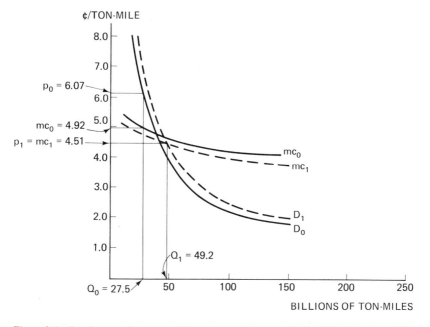

Figure 3.6   Truck, manufactures, initial and competitive equilibria, Official Region, 1972.

4.892¢/ton-mile for manufactured goods and 2.125¢/ton-mile and 1.931¢/ton-mile for bulk commodities. Thus the price-marginal cost ratio is somewhat above unity for bulk commodities, but substantially less than unity for manufactured commodities.

The relationship between rates and marginal costs clearly indicates that the railroads are not maximizing profits in the Official Territory. Moreover, the relationship between rates and marginal costs for manufactured commodities clearly indicates that the railroads devote excessive resources to the carriage of manufactured goods. Thus at least in the Official Territory, efficiency dictates a reduction of rail carriage and an increase of rates on manufactured commodities.[14]

Because the railroads jointly produce transportation of bulk and manufactured commodities, it is not meaningful to discuss the average costs of either of these commodities. However, the relationship between the rates on manufactured commodities and their marginal costs would lead us to expect that the railroads in the Official Region would experience substantial losses. This is corroborated by the figures in table 3.1, which indicate that the Eastern roads suffered losses of $251 million in excess

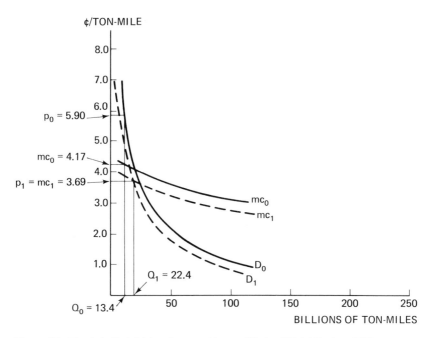

¢/TON-MILE

$p_0 = 5.90$

$mc_0 = 4.17$

$p_1 = mc_1 = 3.69$

mc_0

mc_1

D_0

D_1

$Q_1 = 22.4$

$Q_0 = 13.4$

BILLIONS OF TON-MILES

Figure 3.7   Truck, bulk, initial and competitive equilibria, Official Region, 1972.

of variable costs in 1972. Of course, these figures are consistent with the situation of these roads before their reorganization into Conrail.

Figures 3.6 and 3.7 present the existing situation in the trucking industry in the Official Region. In contrast to the railroads, which price at marginal cost or below it, the special commodity carriers appear to enjoy rates that are substantially greater than marginal costs in both the bulk and manufactured goods markets. Specifically, at the existing equilibrium, rates and marginal costs for manufactured commodities are estimated to be respectively 6.067¢/ton-mile and 4.922¢/ton-mile, while those of bulk commodities are estimated to be respectively 5.901¢/ton-mile and 4.169¢/ton-mile. Although the price–marginal cost ratios are rather high, it is interesting to note that the estimated profits accruing to trucking operations only totaled $110 million. This arises because marginal costs are less than average costs at the existing equilibrium. Thus even though the price–marginal cost ratio is relatively high, the revenue–cost ratio is relatively low. This indicates that even though these trucking firms may be exercising some monopoly power in setting their rates collectively, the ICC acts as a restraining force and keeps rates below their monopoly levels.

Table 3.1 Market Characteristics, Initial and Competitive Equilibria, Official Region, 1972

	Price (¢/ton-mile)	Marginal cost (¢/ton-mile)	Output (bill. ton-miles)	Costs ($bill.)	Revenues ($bill.)	Profits ($bill.)	DWL[a] ($mill.)
Initial equilibrium							
Rail							
Manufactured	2.405	4.892	83.083	–	1.993	–	566.8
Bulk	2.125	1.931	57.116	–	1.214	–	25.4
Total[b]	–	–	–	4.543	4.292[c]	−0.251	592.2
Truck							
Manufactures	6.067	4.922	27.512	–	1.669	–	50.7
Bulk	5.901	4.169	13.373	–	0.789	–	71.6
Total[b]	–	–	–	2.348	2.458	0.110	122.3
Competitive equilibrium							
Rail							
Manufactured	4.590	4.590	30.284	–	1.390	–	683.8
Bulk	1.522	1.522	76.469	–	1.164	–	62.2
Total[b]	–	–	–	2.440	3.636[c]	1.196	746.0
Truck							
Manufactured	4.505	4.505	49.206	–	2.217	–	141.2
Bulk	3.693	3.693	22.428	–	0.828	–	95.1
Total[b]	–	–	–	3.654	3.045	−0.609	236.3

a. Deadweight loss evaluated at existing rates and at competitive equilibrium.
b. Rail costs reflect total variable costs. Truck costs reflect total costs.
c. Includes revenues of $1.082 billion for coal, agricultural, and passenger traffic.

Thus table 3.1 and figures 3.4–3.7 present a picture of the rail and trucking industries in the Official Territory that is far from a competitive equilibrium. Specifically, if not actually maximizing profits, the trucking firms appear to earn some monopoly profits and to price substantially above marginal costs. In contrast, the railroads price at levels close to or below marginal costs, and appear to subsidize shippers of manufactured commodities. Thus instead of acting as monopolists, railroads apparently act as a regulated public utility, providing subsidized service to certain groups of users.

The general nature of a competitive equilibrium in the rail and trucking industry in the Official Region should be clear from figures 3.4–3.7; rail rates on manufactured commodities would rise, truck rates on manufactured and bulk commodities would fall, and outputs would contract or expand accordingly. Because, however, the marginal cost and demand functions are all interrelated, changes in any of these rates would lead to shifts in the cost and demand curves. Thus the competitive equilibrium cannot be determined directly from figures 3.4–3.7, but must be determined jointly and the resulting shifts in the demand and cost functions taken into account.[15]

The lines in figures 3.4–3.7 marked D_1 and mc_1 give, respectively, the marginal cost and demand functions that would exist at the new equilibrium. With respect to manufactured commodities, the increase in rail rates and reduction in trucking rates cause the rail demand function to shift in, and the trucking demand function to shift out. The increase in output levels causes the trucking cost function to shift in, while the increase in rail output of bulk commodities causes the rail marginal cost function to shift up.[16] Similarly, the fall in trucking and rail rates on bulk commodities causes both of the bulk demand functions to shift in, while the increase in trucking output of manufactured commodities and the reduction of rail output of manufactured commodities causes both rail and trucking marginal cost functions to shift down.

The net result of these shifts and a determination of a competitive equilibrium is an increase in rail rates and a reduction of rail carriage of manufactured goods, a reduction of rail rates and an increase in rail carriage of bulk commodities, and a reduction of trucking rates and an increase in trucking carriage of both manufactured and bulk commodities. Moreover, at the competitive equilibrium railroads are now earning profits of $1.196 billion relative to variable costs, while trucks are suffering losses of $609 million.

While the estimated railroad profitability that would exist under a competitive equilibrium is a considerable improvement over the actual losses that accrue in the existing equilibrium, it is important to note that this only represents a net return of 3.44 percent on the estimated capital stock of $17.997 billion. Since this figure is considerably below the opportunity cost of capital of 9 percent, this implies that railroads will not earn a normal return in a short-run competitive equilibrium and that some form of government subsidy will still be required to enable the railroads to maintain their infrastructure at adequate levels.

Although the carriers of specialized commodities are estimated to lose some $600 million in a competitive equilibrium, these figures should be viewed with considerable skepticism in view of the questions concerning the economies of scale that apparently exist among these carriers. Nevertheless, the differences in profitability between the existing equilibrium and the competitive equilibrium are sufficiently great that we can reasonably infer that these carriers would lose in the advent of competition.

In view of the existing divergence from marginal cost pricing, it seems clear that substantial changes in consumers' and producers' surplus should result from moving from the existing equilibrium to a competitive equilibrium. Since, however, some of the gains in consumers' surplus accruing to shippers resulting from rate reductions also reflect losses in producers' surplus accruing to carriers, the efficiency loss accruing to society from noncompetitive pricing is given by the difference between the change in consumers' surplus and the change in producers' surplus. This is called the deadweight loss (DWL), which measures the net losses in consumers' and producers' surplus for which there is no potential compensation.

In assessing the DWL associated with current pricing policies, it is not clear whether they should be evaluated at the existing equilibrium, using the existing demand and marginal cost functions, or evaluated at the competitive equilibrium, using the demand and marginal cost functions that would obtain in a competitive equilibrium. We have consequently estimated the DWL that would obtain in each market using the demand functions and marginal cost functions associated with both the existing and competitive equilibria. These figures are given in table 3.1 under the column DWL, and indicate that if the DWL is measured in terms of the existing relationships it totals $700 million, while if it is measured in terms of the competitive equilibrium relationships it totals $1 billion, with the major source of the loss being in the rail carriage of manufactured commodities. Thus in the Official Region, current pricing policies appear to lead to an efficiency loss of $700 million to $1 billion.

3.3.2 Competitive Equilibrium in the South–West Region
Although the railroad rate structure in the South–West Region is similar to that of the Official Territory in that manufactured goods are priced at levels below marginal cost and the price–marginal cost ratio of bulk commodities is substantially greater than that of manufactured goods, it differs from that in the Official Territory in that the absolute levels of the price–marginal cost ratios on both types of goods are considerably greater than those in the Official Territory. Consequently, although the railroads in the Official Territory fail to cover variable costs, the railroads in the South–West Region earn substantial profits in excess of variable costs in the initial equilibrium. Thus a movement to a competitive equilibrium in the South–West Region would lead to a modest increase in

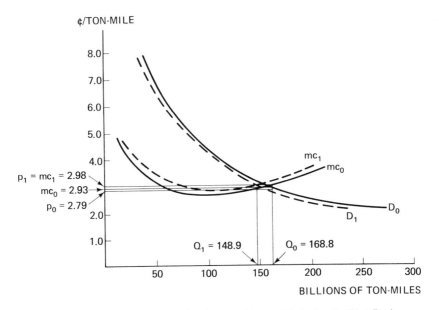

Figure 3.8   Rail, manufactures, initial and competitive equilibria, South–West Region, 1972.

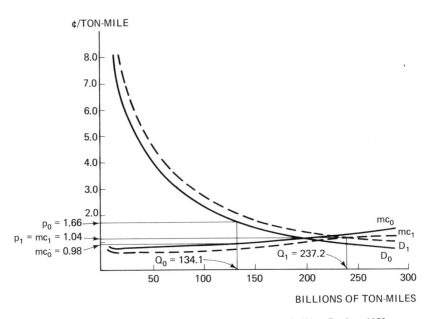

Figure 3.9   Rail, bulk, initial and competitive equilibria, South–West Region, 1972.

Table 3.2 Market Characteristics, Initial and Competitive Equilibria, South–West Region, 1972

	Price (¢/ton-mile)	Marginal cost (¢/ton-mile)	Output (bill. ton-miles)	Costs ($bill.)	Revenues ($bill.)	Profits ($bill.)	DWL[a] ($mill.)
Initial equilibrium							
Rail							
Manufactures	2.790	2.925	168.839	–	4.711	–	55.9
Bulk	1.664	0.981	134.080	–	2.230	–	332.2
Total[b]	–	–	302.910	6.099	8.223[c]	2.123	338.1
Truck							
Manufactures	5.454	4.602	31.777	–	1.733	–	38.1
Bulk	3.965	3.972	22.166	–	0.879	–	0.0
Total	–	–	53.943	2.467	2.612	0.145	38.1
Competitive equilibrium							
Rail							
Manufactures	2.979	2.979	148.932	–	4.437	–	21.8
Bulk	1.043	1.043	237.234	–	2.475	–	356.4
Total[b]	–	–	386.166	6.567	8.194	1.627	377.7
Truck							
Manufactures	4.610	4.610	42.122	–	1.942	–	44.3
Bulk	3.975	3.975	16.002	–	0.636	–	0.6
Total	–	–	58.124	2.712	2.578	−0.134	44.9

a. DWL evaluated at existing rates and competitive equilibrium.
b. Rail costs represent total variable costs. Truck costs represent total costs.
c. Includes $1,282 billion of revenues from coal, agricultural, and passenger traffic.

rail rates and traffic reduction for manufactured commodities and a substantial rate reduction and traffic increase for bulk commodities. Hence a competitive equilibrium in the South–West Region would be characterized by increased railroad specialization in bulk commodities, and a reduction in overall profitability.

Figures 3.8 and 3.9 and table 3.2 illustrate these points. The lines in the figures marked D_0 and mc_0 represent, respectively, the demand and marginal cost functions that exist under the current rate structure and show that rail rates are somewhat below marginal cost for manufactured goods and considerably above marginal cost for bulk commodities. In particular, table 3.2 indicates that in 1972 the rail rates on manufactured and bulk commodities in the South–West Region were, respectively,

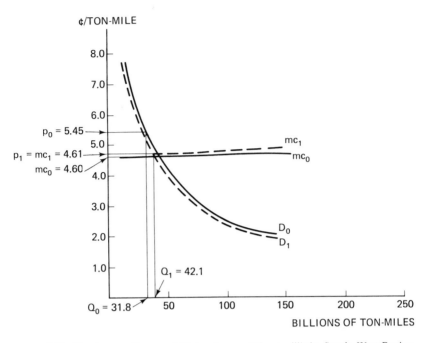

Figure 3.10   Truck, manufactures, initial and competitive equilibria, South–West Region, 1972.

2.790¢/ton-mile and 1.664¢/ton-mile, and their marginal costs were, respectively, 2.925¢/ton-mile and 0.981¢/ton-mile. Thus the price–marginal cost ratio on manufactured goods was 0.95 and that on bulk commodities was 1.70. In view of the high profitability of bulk traffic, we would expect the railroads in this region to be earning substantial profits, and table 3.2 indicates that their estimated profits over variable costs are on the order of $2.123 billion, which represents a net rate of return of 7.97 percent.

In contrast to the carriers of specialized commodities in the Official Region that were earning rates substantially in excess of marginal cost on both bulk and manufactured commodities, in the South–West Region these carriers earn a relatively modest return on their carriage of manufactured goods and actually carry bulk commodities at rates that are slightly less than marginal cost. Thus while specialized commodity carriers in the Official Region appeared to act more like monopolists than regulated common carriers, the specialized commodity carriers in the South–West Region appear to operate under more effective regulatory constraints.

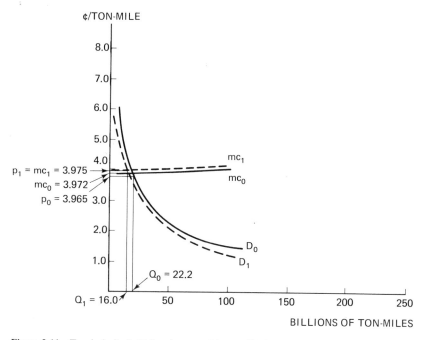

Figure 3.11   Truck, bulk, initial and competitive equilibria, South–West Region, 1972.

Figures 3.10 and 3.11 and table 3.2 illustrate these points. The lines marked D_0 and mc_0 represent, respectively, the demand and cost functions at the existing rate levels and show that while trucking rates are in excess of marginal costs on manufactured goods, they are virtually at marginal cost on bulk commodities. In particular, the rates on manufactured and bulk commodities are estimated to be, respectively, 5.454¢/ton-mile and 3.965¢/ton-mile, while the marginal costs on manufactured and bulk commodities are estimated to be, respectively, 4.406¢/ton-mile and 3.972¢/ton-mile. Thus the price–marginal cost ratios on each type of commodity are, respectively, 1.185 and 0.998. Carriers in this industry consequently earn profits of $145 million.[17]

As was true in the Official Region, changes in rates will lead to shifts in all of the demand and cost functions, making it impossible to obtain the competitive equilibrium directly from the existing demand and marginal cost functions. In particular, the fall in trucking rates and the rise in rail rates for manufactured commodities will tend to shift the trucking demand function out and the rail demand function in. With respect to costs, as long as firms are operating on the increasing portion of their cost curves, increases in the output of one commodity will cause the marginal costs of the other commodity to rise, while reduction in the output of one commodity will cause the marginal costs of the other commodity to fall. Even though trucking output of manufactured goods rises while that of bulk commodities falls, both marginal cost curves rise, indicating that trucks must be operating around their region of decreasing costs with respect to bulk commodities. Similarly, since rail output of manufactured commodities falls while that of bulk commodities rises, these output effects will cause an upward shift in the manufactured marginal cost function and a downward shift in the bulk marginal cost function. However, the output mix also affects rail costs, and increases in the share of bulk commodities causes reductions in rail marginal costs, ceteris paribus. Since the share of bulk commodities rises, the commodity mix effect reinforces the output effect, causing bulk marginal costs to shift downward. Although the commodity mix effect has an opposite effect on manufactured marginal costs from the output effect, the output effect is somewhat stronger, leading to an upward shift in the rail marginal cost function for manufactured commodities.

The lines marked D_1 and mc_1 in figures 3.8–3.11 show, respectively, the general equilibrium demand and marginal cost curves that are obtained in each market at the competitive equilibrium. Thus competitive pricing in the South–West Region would lead to a substantial expansion of rail service in bulk commodities, and a curtailment of rail traffic in manufactured goods. Thus, as was true in the Official Territory, competitive pricing would lead to a modal split in favor of rail for bulk commodities and in favor of truck for manufactured goods.

Table 3.2 quantifies these effects and indicates that rail rates on manufactured commodities in the South–West Region would rise by 6.8 percent while those on bulk commodities would fall by 37.3 percent, reaching levels of 2.979¢/ton-mile and 1.043¢/ton-mile, respectively. In contrast, trucking rates on manufactured goods and bulk commodities would remain essentially constant, although increasing slightly. In terms of profitability, rail profits would fall considerably, from $2.123 billion to $1.627 billion, which represents a fall in the net rate of return to capital stock from 7.97 percent to 5.36 percent. Since this is below the opportunity cost of capital, it appears that the short-run returns to scale are such that the railroads cannot sustain a normal return to capital in a competitive equilibrium. This raises the question whether adjustments in output or capital stock could be made that would enable the railroads to be competitive with other sectors of the private market, and we will consider this question in some detail in the next chapter. Finally, table 3.2

also indicates that trucking firms would suffer actual losses of $134 million in a competitive equilibrium.[18]

In terms of the efficiency gains that would result from competitive pricing, our analysis has indicated that rail and trucking rates deviate from marginal costs in the South–West region, and thus that DWL results from existing pricing policies. Unlike the Official Region, however, where the efficiency losses were concentrated in rail carriage of manufactured goods and truck carriage of manufactured and bulk commodities, in the South–West Region the efficiency losses are concentrated in rail carriage of bulk commodities. Moreover, these losses are relatively modest in comparison to those of the Official Region and total no more than $400 million, whether evaluated at the existing or competitive equilibrium. Since approximately $350 million of these arise from rail carriage of bulk commodities, it is clear that the pricing distortion that appears in the other markets is relatively modest.

In conclusion, then, this analysis indicates that the value-of-service rate structure may no longer be an adequate description of existing regulatory practices. With respect to the railroads, not only are the markups relative to marginal costs on bulk commodities higher than those on manufactured commodities, but rail rates are also less than marginal costs for manufactured commodities in both the Official and South–West Regions. In addition, although both commodity types are currently priced above marginal cost for trucking shipments in the Official Territory, the markup relative to marginal costs is also higher on bulk commodities than on manufactured goods. Thus only trucking rates in the South–West Region can currently be characterized as having a strong value-of-service element.

In terms of efficient traffic allocation, these relative rate differentials among manufactured and bulk commodities indicate that a movement from the existing rate structure toward competitive pricing would be characterized by a substantial reduction in rail traffic of manufactured goods and substantial increase in rail traffic of bulk commodities. Trucking shipments would change accordingly, leading to a traffic allocation in which trucks concentrate on the carriage of manufactured commodities while railroads concentrated upon the carriage of bulk commodities. Thus contrary to the conventional wisdom, which holds that much trucking traffic could be carried more efficiently by rail, this analysis indicates that economic efficiency would be served by substituting trucking for rail service on a substantial portion of manufactured traffic and increasing rail specialization in the carriage of bulk commodities. This analysis supports the view, therefore, that the railroads' inherent advantage lies in large-volume wholesaling activities while that of trucks lies in the carriage of manufactured goods. In this connection it is important to stress that the current traffic misallocations do not arise because the railroads carry too few manufactured commodities, but because they still carry too many.

3.3.3 General Equilibrium Effects of Selected Policy Changes

Having analyzed the nature of the competitive equilibrium that would exist in the rail and trucking industries, it is now useful to consider how this equilibrium would be altered under a number of policy changes that would affect the marginal cost and/or demand functions of the carriers in the bulk or manufactured goods markets. Of these, the most relevant appear to be changes in fuel prices, changes in the characteristics of the trucking shipments, changes in the size of the transport market, and changes in the size of trucking firms. While changes in the railroad infrastructure are clearly also relevant, they will be considered in chapter 4, which focuses on the problem of railroad costs and railroad capital.

We thus now perform a number of comparative static experiments in which certain variables are changed in the relevant cost or demand functions to reflect specific policy changes or exogenous changes that affect the transportation industries, assuming competitive behavior. The resulting equilibria with respect to rates and outputs are given in table 3.3, and those with respect to costs, revenues, and profits are given in table 3.4. Note, however, that since changes in any rate will lead to shifts in all of the functions, it is difficult to attribute any general equilibrium change to the shift in any given exogenous variable. It is useful, therefore, to analyze the comparative static response of the system in two steps: first, the shift in the demand and/or cost curve that results from the initial change in the exogenous variable; and second, the general equilibrium response of the system to the initial change. That is, at marginal cost pricing a shift in any function must necessarily cause the equilibrium price and output in that market to change. These price and output changes will, however, engender changes in all of the other demand and cost functions. Thus any change in an exogenous variable will lead to an initial partial equilibrium shift in the affected function and a full general equilibrium shift in all of the functions. Consequently, in assessing the impact of changes in any of the exogenous variables, it is useful to dis-

Table 3.3 Comparative Static Equilibria, Official and South–West Regions, 1972

| | Manufactured commodities | | | | Bulk commodities | | | |
| | Rail | | Truck | | Rail | | Truck | |
	Rate (¢/ton-mile)	Output (bill. tons)	Rate (¢/ton-mile)	Output (bill. tons)	Rate (¢/ton-mile)	Output (bill. tons)	Rate (¢/ton-mile)	Output (bill. tons)
Official								
Initial conditions	2.405	83.083	6.067	27.512	2.125	57.116	5.901	13.373
Competitive equilibrium	4.590	30.284	4.505	49.206	1.522	76.469	3.693	22.428
10% truck fuel rise	4.589	30.336	4.521	48.989	1.523	76.482	3.703	22.349
10% rail fuel rise	4.708	29.159	4.500	49.609	1.547	74.804	3.686	22.607
10% rise in truck load	4.577	29.161	3.924	59.374	1.501	74.873	3.242	26.719
10% rise in demand	4.624	32.617	4.420	55.557	1.563	80.444	3.596	25.817
Monopoly truck	4.449	25.505	2.938	83.261	1.422	63.898	1.741	58.949
South–West								
Initial conditions	2.790	168.830	5.454	31.774	1.664	134.080	3.965	22.166
Competitive equilibrium	2.979	148.932	4.610	42.122	1.043	237.234	3.975	16.002
10% truck fuel rise	2.979	149.086	4.630	41.851	1.043	237.352	3.900	15.895
10% rail fuel rise	3.056	144.233	4.611	42.597	1.067	230.891	3.976	16.288
15% rise in truck load	2.973	147.213	4.324	46.695	1.039	234.205	3.717	17.452
10% rise in demand	3.014	161.496	4.622	46.411	1.067	253.953	3.983	17.867

Table 3.4 Revenue, Costs, and Profitability, Initial Equilibrium, Competitive Equilibrium, and Equilibria under Specified Scenarios, Official and South–West Regions, 1972 ($Billions)

	Rail					Truck				
	Revenues[a]			Costs[b] ($bill.)	Profits ($bill.)	Revenues			Costs ($bill.)	Profits ($bill.)
	Manuf. ($bill.)	Bulk ($bill.)	Total ($bill.)			Manuf. ($bill.)	Bulk ($bill.)	Total ($bill.)		
Official										
Initial equilibrium	1.998	1.214	4.292	4.543	−0.251	1.669	0.789	2.458	2.348	0.110
Competitive equilibrium	1.390	1.164	3.634	2.440	1.194	2.217	0.828	3.045	3.654	−0.609
10% truck fuel rise	1.392	1.165	3.637	2.442	1.195	2.215	0.828	3.042	3.655	−0.613
10% rail fuel rise	1.372	1.157	3.609	2.434	1.175	2.232	0.883	3.066	3.678	−0.612
10% rise in truck load	1.335	1.124	3.539	2.364	1.175	2.330	0.866	3.196	3.902	−0.706
10% rise in demand	1.510	1.257	3.848	2.608	1.239	2.456	0.928	3.384	4.040	−0.656
Monopoly truck	1.135	0.909	3.124	2.038	1.086	2.447	1.026	3.473	3.353	0.120
South–West										
Initial equilibrium	4.710	2.230	8.222	6.099	2.123	1.733	0.879	2.612	2.469	0.143
Competitive equilibrium	4.437	2.475	8.194	6.567	1.627	1.942	0.636	2.578	2.712	−0.134
10% truck fuel rise	4.442	2.477	8.201	6.573	1.628	1.938	0.634	2.572	2.710	−0.140
10% rail fuel rise	4.408	2.463	8.153	6.564	1.589	1.964	0.648	2.612	2.744	−0.162
10% rise in truck load	4.377	2.434	8.093	6.484	1.609	2.019	0.649	2.668	2.792	−0.124
10% rise in demand	4.868	2.710	8.860	7.120	1.740	2.145	0.712	2.857	2.976	−0.119

a. Revenues include $1.080 billion from agricultural commodities, coal, and passenger traffic in the Official Region and $1.282 billion from agricultural commodities, coal, and passenger traffic in the South–West Region.
b. Rail costs reflect total variable costs, while truck costs reflect total costs.

tinguish between the initial partial equilibrium effect and the final general equilibrium effect. These are presented in table 3.5.

Fuel Price Increases   In view of the increases in fuel prices that have occurred since the Arab oil embargo of 1973, it is useful to assess the relative impacts of a 10-percent increase in trucking and rail fuel costs upon the competitive equilibrium. Since railroads are generally believed to be more energy efficient than trucks, one would expect such an increase to raise trucking costs more than rail costs and to lead to greater general equilibrium impact in the case of trucking fuel price increases than in the case of rail fuel price increases. It is interesting to note, however, that the opposite appears to be the case. In particular, table 3.5 indicates that a 10-percent increase in truck fuel prices would lead to initial increases in the trucking marginal cost function of 0.3–0.4 percent, while comparable rail fuel price increases would increase the rail marginal cost function on the order of 2–3 percent. The resulting general equilibrium changes are of comparable magnitudes, with trucking fuel price increases having no discernible impact on the equilibrium demand or cost functions or upon the final competitive equilibrium levels of rates, outputs, costs, profits, etc. In contrast, while the comparable changes engendered by an increase in rail fuel prices are admittedly small, they are nevertheless quantifiable and imply a slight but significant shift of traffic in favor of trucks.

This result with respect to increases of fuel prices is somewhat puzzling and doubtless reflects the behavior of the underlying cost functions. The railroad cost function exhibited very little elasticity of substitution among fuel and other factors, while the trucking cost function indicated substantial substitutability between fuel and purchased transportation. Hence increases in rail fuel costs tend to be translated into increases in marginal costs, while increases in trucking fuel prices tend to encourage substitution of owner-operators, and hence relatively little change in the observed marginal cost function. Of course, since owner-operators would face similar fuel price increases, it is likely that their prices would also increase, leading to less substitution than would otherwise be expected. Nevertheless, as long as the price of purchased transportation does not increase as much as fuel prices, there would still be some substitution of purchased transportation for fuel, which would tend to offset the impact of the trucking price increase. Therefore, while the figures used in this analysis doubtless underestimate the cost increases that would accrue from an increase in trucking fuel prices, they are probably qualitatively

Table 3.5 Values of Demand and Marginal Cost Curves at Selected Points, by Alternative Scenario, Official and South–West Regions, 1972[a]

| | Manufactured commodities | | | | Bulk commodities | | | |
| | Rail | | Truck | | Rail | | Truck | |
	$Q = 30.0$ MC	$p = 4.5$ Q	$Q = 50.0$ MC	$p = 4.5$ Q	$Q = 76.0$ MC	$p = 1.5$ Q	$Q = 22.0$ MC	$p = 4.5$ Q
Official								
Absolute values								
Initial conditions	4.304	35.431	4.590	40.944	2.018	89.590	3.999	19.280
Competitive equilibrium	4.593	31.171	4.498	49.276	1.521	77.940	3.697	17.130
10% truck fuel rise	–	–	4.511	–	–	–	3.704	–
Final	4.593	31.221	4.511	49.275	1.522	78.008	3.706	17.134
10% rail fuel rise	4.725	–	–	–	1.538	–	–	–
Final	4.699	31.154	4.500	49.604	1.549	77.898	3.693	17.234
10% rise in truck load	–	31.781	4.038	49.946	–	78.072	3.385	17.107
Final	4.568	29.894	3.999	49.909	1.504	74.981	3.283	17.016
10% rise in demand	–	34.288	–	54.204	–	85.735	–	18.843
Final	4.653	33.990	4.467	54.323	1.555	85.005	3.631	19.036
Monopoly truck	–	–	2.990	–	–	–	1.907	–
Final	4.404	25.054	2.950	48.875	1.444	59.259	1.782	16.944
Percentage change								
Base = initial equilibrium								
Competitive equilibrium	6.71	–12.02	–2.00	20.35	–24.63	–13.00	–7.55	–11.15

Table 3.5 (continued)

	Manufactured commodities				Bulk commodities			
	Rail		Truck		Rail		Truck	
	$Q = 30.0$ MC	$p = 4.5$ Q	$Q = 50.0$ MC	$p = 4.5$ Q	$Q = 76.0$ MC	$p = 1.5$ Q	$Q = 22.0$ MC	$p = 4.5$ Q
Base = competitive equilibrium								
10% truck fuel rise	–	–	0.29	–	–	–	0.19	–
Final	0.0	0.16	0.29	0.0	0.07	0.09	0.24	0.02
10% rail fuel rise	2.87	–	–	–	1.12	–	–	–
Final	2.31	–0.05	0.04	0.67	1.84	–0.05	–0.11	0.61
10% rise in truck load	–	1.96	–10.23	1.36	–	0.18	–8.44	–0.13
Final	–0.54	–4.10	–11.09	1.28	–1.12	–3.74	–11.20	–0.67
10% rise in demand	–	10.00	–	10.00	–	10.00	–	10.00
Final	1.31	9.04	–0.69	10.24	2.24	9.06	–1.79	11.13
Monopoly truck	–	–	–33.52	–	–	–	–48.42	–
Final	–4.11	–19.62	–34.42	–0.81	–5.06	–23.97	–51.80	–1.09
South–West								
Absolute values								
Initial equilibrium	2.874	154.159	4.618	42.330	1.069	249.550	3.969	21.864
Competitive equilibrium	2.980	147.625	4.607	43.632	1.044	249.665	3.975	15.823
10% truck fuel rise	–	–	4.628	–	–	–	3.991	–
Final	2.980	147.798	4.628	43.634	1.045	249.883	3.991	15.827
10% rail fuel rise	3.071	–	–	–	1.078	–	–	–
Final	3.062	147.636	4.607	44.136	1.071	249.696	3.976	16.113

Table 3.5 (continued)

	Manufactured commodities				Bulk commodities			
	Rail		Truck		Rail		Truck	
	$Q = 150.0$ MC	$p = 3.0$ Q	$Q = 40.0$ MC	$p = 4.5$ Q	$Q = 240.0$ MC	$p = 1.0$ Q	$Q = 16.0$ MC	$p = 4.0$ Q
10% rise in truck load	–	147.960	4.312	44.060	–	248.783	3.712	15.228
Final	2.976	145.563	4.314	44.017	1.042	245.403	3.716	15.177
10% rise in demand	–	162.387	–	47.995	–	274.653	–	17.406
Final	3.003	162.497	4.610	48.254	1.061	274.763	3.980	17.730
Percentage change								
Base = initial equilibrium								
Competitive equilibrium	3.69	–4.24	–0.24	3.08	–2.34	0.05	0.15	–27.63
Base = competitive equilibrium								
10% truck fuel rise	0.0	–	0.46	–	0.09	–	0.40	–
Final	0.0	0.12	0.46	0.0	0.09	0.08	0.40	0.03
10% rail fuel rise	3.05	–	–	–	3.26	–	–	–
Final	2.75	0.01	0.0	1.16	3.26	0.0	0.03	1.83
10% rise in truck load	–	0.23	–6.40	0.98	–	–0.36	–6.62	–3.76
Final	–0.13	–1.40	–6.36	0.88	–0.19	–1.71	–6.52	–4.08
10% rise in demand	–	10.00	0.65	10.00	–	10.00	–	10.00
Final	0.77	10.07	0.65	10.59	1.63	10.04	0.13	12.05

a. Outputs Q measured in billion ton-miles; marginal costs MC and prices p measured in ¢/ton-mile.

correct in indicating that the increase in trucking costs is probably less than generally believed, since some of the burden may be borne by owner-operators.

Increases in Truck Average Load   Current regulatory practices require trucking firms to obtain certificates of operating authority for the transportation of all nonagricultural commodities. For carriers of specialized commodities, these operating authorities are extremely narrowly defined,[19] forcing carriers to obtain large numbers of distinct operating authorities to maintain full equipment utilization.

However, the average loads of most of the trucking firms in the sample are well below those of the capacity of the trucks utilized by these carriers. This indicates that these firms have difficulty maintaining full truckloads during all of their hauls and that the trucks are moving at less than capacity during a significant proportion of the journey. This suggests that if restrictions on commodities carried were relaxed, these trucking firms could increase their average load and capacity utilization.

To assess the impact of relaxed regulatory restrictions on an operating authority we consequently analyze the impact of an increase in average load of 10 percent. This change has direct effects upon both the marginal cost functions and the demand functions. Since trucking firms are able to obtain substantial economies of capacity utilization, a 10-percent increase in the average load has a substantial impact upon the marginal costs of trucking operations, reducing them by approximately 10 percent in the Official Region and by approximately 6.5 percent in the South–West Region.[20] However, increases in average load also affect the demand function through changes in shipment characteristics. Nevertheless, these effects are relatively small, indicating that the primary impact of increases in trucking load come about through the efficiencies of greater equipment utilization rather than through the impact of operating characteristics upon demand.[21]

Since trucking marginal cost functions fall relatively more than trucking demand functions rise, the net effect is a reduction in trucking rates. This in turn leads to an inward shift in rail demand functions and hence a shift in the rail commodity mix and the rail marginal cost function. Thus the full general equilibrium effects of a 10-percent change in the average trucking load is a fall in trucking marginal costs and reduction in trucking rates of 10–12 percent; inward shifts in rail demand function and a fall in rail rates of approximately 1.5 percent; and a modal shift in favor of truck traffic.

Increases in the Size of Trucking Firms   As explained in the previous chapter, the marginal costs of trucking operations were developed on the assumption that the size of the average trucking firm did not change. It thus envisioned the maintenance of the status quo, in which entry into the trucking industry is tightly regulated and in which the size and number of trucking firms does not change dramatically. This raises the question, however, of what would happen if entry restrictions were relaxed.

The trucking cost functions in the South–West Region indicated the existence of very modest economies of scale, with firms operating on the rising portion of their marginal cost curves, but on the falling portion of their average cost curves at a competitive equilibrium. However, the competitive equilibrium in the South–West Region is sufficiently close to the point of minimum average cost, and the estimated returns to scale are sufficiently small, that it is likely that free entry would have no discernible effect upon the equilibrium in the trucking industry in the South–West Region. Stated alternatively, carriers of specialized commodities in the South–West Region display cost characteristics that are sufficiently close to the competitive norm that it is likely that free entry and deregulation would lead to a long-run competitive equilibrium that is quite close to the postulated short-run competitive equilibrium.

Since, however, the estimated trucking cost functions exhibited rather dramatic economies of scale in the Official Region, it is likely that the long-run competitive equilibrium would be quite different from its short-run counterpart. In particular, at the short-run competitive equilibrium, trucking firms were producing on the falling portion of their average and marginal cost curves, indicating that firms would attempt to exploit these economies of scale if permitted. Consequently, we developed a marginal cost function based on two or three firms that had exhausted their economies of scale. Each of these firms was enormous by present standards, producing outputs on the order of 20 billion ton-miles and having marginal costs of the order of 2.94¢/ton-mile. Since these costs are well below rail marginal costs for manufactured commodities and only slightly above rail marginal costs for bulk commodities, this suggests that such a change would lead to a substantial shift of traffic from rail to trucks. Indeed, in this scenario, railroads carry approximately 25 percent of manufactured goods and approximately 55 percent of bulk commodities as opposed to the projected short-run competitive equilibrium, in which railroads are projected to carry approximately 33 percent of manufactured commodities and 75 percent of bulk commodities.[22]

Of course, this scenario should be viewed with considerable skepticism since it is based on the assumption that the observed trucking economies of scale are of a technological nature. We have previously argued, however, that they are probably of a regulatory nature and in fact reflect size-related advantages that accrue to firms arising from operating authorities and equipment utilization rather than from size per se. Consequently, if the trucking industry were deregulated and requirements for operating authorities were abolished, it is unlikely that we would still observe economies of scale in the trucking industry. This scenario probably best describes, therefore, a situation in which restrictions on operating authority were maintained, but for which the commission imposed no checks on acquisitions or the size of firms. As such it describes a possible outcome in a quasi-regulated environment. While useful as a polar case, it is important to stress that it yields relatively little information about the probable outcome of deregulation in the trucking industry.

Increase in Transport Demand   Since transportation is sensitive to the behavior of the national economy, it is useful to analyze the possible outcome of a 10-percent increase in the demand for transportation services. This can be taken to yield measures of the elasticity of the response of the rail and trucking industries with respect to the demand for transportation services and can be used to analyze the effects of changes in aggregate demand upon the transportation industries.

As explained above, a shift in the transport demand functions will yield initial price and output changes, which will then induce further changes in the underlying marginal cost and demand functions. These secondary changes are relatively modest, however, leading to further shifts in the marginal cost and demand functions of less than 3 percent. Thus the final shift in the rail and trucking demand functions is slightly more than 10 percent for both commodities in both regions. In terms of the equilibrium prices and quantities, trucking output rises by somewhat more than 10 percent while rail output rises by somewhat less than 10 percent; rates in both the trucking and rail industries rise by less than 2 percent, which is consistent with the relative magnitudes of the shifts in the demand and marginal cost functions and the relatively constant nature of marginal costs over the relevant range.

While the general equilibrium effects of the changes outlined above are certainly not trivial, it is important to note that they are relatively modest in comparison with the general equilibrium effects of moving from the status quo to a policy of marginal cost pricing. In terms of transportation policy, therefore, it appears that the major innovation would be an abandonment of the existing rate structure and the determination of a competitive equilibrium. While policies to relax entry and operating restrictions would doubtless have an important impact, they appear to be of a second order of magnitude relative to those occasioned by marginal cost pricing. Thus in terms of rates, outputs, and traffic allocation, it appears that the major changes in the transportation industries would come from competitive pricing policies rather than from policies that lead to changes in fuel prices, trucking loads or firm size, or transport demand.

3.4 Distributional Impact of a Competitive Equilibrium

Up to this point we have concentrated upon the efficiency gains and losses arising from moving from the status quo to a competitive equilibrium. Since, however, any change in rates must necessarily affect shippers and consumers of transportation services, we will now analyze the income gains and losses that could be expected to accrue from such a change. In this connection, it is useful to distinguish between direct and indirect effects. The direct income effects come from the rate changes themselves and reflect the revenue gains or losses accruing to shippers or carriers, while the indirect effects come from the changes in economic activity that arise from the rate changes.

In a world with an ideal income distribution, all individuals have identical social welfare weights and these gains and losses would cancel out, leaving us with measures of the DWL arising from inefficient pricing policies. In the real world, however, income is not distributed in an optimal fashion and there is little reason to believe that shippers and carriers have the same social welfare weights. Consequently, it is desirable to quantify the revenue gains and losses accruing to each group.

In addition to these direct income gains and losses, it is important to realize that regional economic activity depends upon freight rates. Therefore, changes in transport rates will affect relative manufacturing costs and hence levels of regional output and employment. Since these indirect effects may be sizable, it is also useful to quantify the income gains or losses that accrue to the other sectors of the economy as a result of the change in freight rates.

3.4.1 Direct Income Effects
The direct income effects can be measured by the gain or loss in consumers' surplus and carrier profits arising from a movement from the

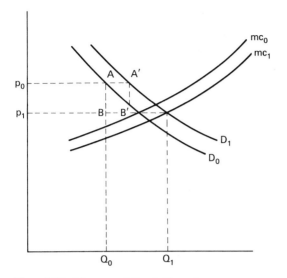

Figure 3.12 Measures of direct shipper loss.

status quo to a competitive equilibrium. Insofar as prices are initially above marginal cost, competitive pricing will lead to gains in the consumers' surplus of shippers; and conversely, it will lead to losses if prices are below marginal costs.

The measure of these gains and losses can be seen in figure 3.12, which illustrates the initial equilibrium and the competitive equilibrium. As explained above, since a movement to a competitive equilibrium will generally lead to shifts in the demand and marginal cost functions, the demand and marginal cost curves that describe a comeptitive equilibrium will differ from those that describe the status quo. Hence the lines D_0 and mc_0 depict, respectively, the demand and marginal cost functions associated with the initial equilibrium, while the lines marked D_1 and mc_1 depict, respectively, those associated with the competitive equilibrium.

Since prices are generally above marginal cost, let us depict the initial equilibrium by a price equal to P_0 and an output equal to Q_0. As drawn in figure 3.12, we assume that a competitive equilibrium leads to an outward shift in the demand function and reduction in the marginal cost function and a new equilibrium at P_1 and Q_1.[23] Hence, measures of consumers' or producers' surplus will differ depending upon whether the initial or equilibrium demand and cost functions are used. For example, figure 3.12 indicates that if the initial demand function is used, the gains to the *existing* shippers of moving to a competitive equilibrium would be given by the area P_0ABP_1, while if the equilibrium demand function were used, then gains would be given by the area $P_0A'B'P_1$.

In the case of shifting demand curves, it is not clear whether the initial or the equilibrium demand function presents the appropriate measure of the change in consumers' surplus. The initial demand function indicates how much shippers would gain or lose as a result of a ceteris paribus rate change, while the equilibrium demand function indicates how much shippers would gain or lose after all the general equilibrium effects had worked their way through the system. Thus, using the initial demand curve will set an inner measure of the gain in consumers' surplus if the demand curve shifts out, and will set an outer measure of the gain in consumers' surplus if the demand curve shifts in. Similarly, using the equilibrium demand curve will set an outer measure of the gain in consumers' surplus if the demand curve shifts out, and will set an inner measure of the gain if the demand curve shifts in. Consequently, it seems reasonable to take a simple average of the gains in consumers' surplus using the initial and equilibrium demand curves, and we measure the gain or loss in consumers' surplus to existing shippers as $0.5(P_0 - P_1) \times (Q_0 + Q_1)$.[24]

Table 3.6 indicates that these direct income gains and losses are quite large. In the Official Region, rail rates on manufactured goods are substantially below marginal cost, and a movement to marginal cost pricing would lead to losses in consumers' surplus of some $1.238 billion. Counteracting this, however, are the reduction on rates on bulk commodities carried by rail and truck, and on manufactured commodities carried by truck. It follows that existing rail shippers of bulk commodities would enjoy increases in consumers' surplus of $402 million, while existing shippers using trucks would enjoy gains of $600 million on manufactured goods and $395 million on bulk commodities. Clearly, however, the existing rail shippers of manufactured goods in the Official Region would experience losses of a sufficient magnitude to indicate that they are currently enjoying a substantial subsidy that is marginally less than the potential benefits that would accrue to other shippers as a result of deregulation.

In the South–West Region, rail rates for manufactured commodities are also below marginal cost, and competitive pricing would lead to losses to existing shippers of $300 million. In the other markets, prices are generally above marginal costs, and marginal cost pricing would lead to rate reduction and gains in consumers' surplus to existing shippers. In this case, the largest gainers are current rail users of bulk commodities,

Table 3.6 Direct Income Gains and Losses Accruing to Shippers and Carriers Resulting from a Competitive Equilibrium, Official and South–West Regions, 1972

	Price change (¢/ton-mile)	Initial output (bill. tons)	Competitive output (bill. tons)	Consumers' surplus ($bill.)	Initial profits ($bill.)	Competitive profits ($bill.)	Profit change ($bill.)
Official							
Rail							
Manufactures	2.185	83.083	30.284	−1.238	–	–	–
Bulk	−0.603	57.116	76.469	0.402	–	–	
Total	–	–	–	−0.836	−0.251	1.194	1.445
Truck							
Manufactures	−1.562	21.512	49.206	0.600	–	–	–
Bulk	−2.208	13.373	22.428	0.395	–	–	–
Total	–	–	–	0.995	0.110	−0.609	−0.719
South–West							
Rail							
Manufactures	0.189	168.830	168.839	−0.300	–	–	–
Bulk	−0.021	134.080	134.080	1.155	–	–	–
Total	–	–	–	0.853	2.213	1.627	−0.496
Truck							
Manufactures	−0.844	31.777	31.777	0.311	–	–	–
Bulk	0.010	22.166	22.166	−0.002	–	–	–
Total	–	–	–	0.309	0.143	−0.134	−0.277

who would receive increases in consumers' surplus of $1.155 billion, followed by current truck users of manufactured commodities, who would receive increases in consumers' surplus of $311 million.

In terms of the present rate structure relative to a competitive equilibrium, therefore, it appears that the primary beneficiaries are the existing rail shippers of manufactured goods, while the primary losers are the existing rail shippers of bulk commodities. Thus, contrary to the conventional wisdom concerning value-of-service rate making, there does not appear to be a cross subsidy from manufactured goods to bulk commodities in the railroad rate structure. Indeed, a cross subsidy appears to exist in precisely the opposite direction. In the case of trucking, however, the conventional wisdom appears to hold in that shippers of bulk commodities currently enjoy relatively lower rates than those of manufactured goods. In the event of competitive pricing, then, trucking shippers of manufactured goods would receive larger direct income gains than those of bulk commodities.

In addition to affecting shippers directly, it is important to realize that moving from the status quo to a competitive equilibrium would have important effects upon carriers. In particular, table 3.6 indicates that the railroads in the Official Region would be the largest gainers, while trucking firms in the Official Region would be the largest losers. In addition, both rail and trucking firms in the South–West Region would lose substantially.

Under present policies railroads in both regions carry a substantial number of manufactured goods at rates considerably below marginal cost. Thus marginal cost pricing should increase their profitability on this traffic. Because, however, they currently carry bulk commodities at rates considerably in excess of marginal costs, competitive pricing should also lead to reduction in profits on this traffic. For the railroads in the Official Region, the gains from competitive pricing of manufactured commodities outweigh the losses from competitive pricing of bulk commodities, and total profits would increase by $1.445 billion as a result of competitive pricing. In contrast, for the railroads in the South–West Region the losses from competitive pricing of bulk commodities are greater than the gains of competitive pricing of manufactured goods, leading to a reduction in profits of $496 million. Thus at a competitive equilibrium railroads in the Official Region would earn profits of $1.194 billion, while those in the South–West Region would earn profits of $1.627 billion, representing, respectively, net returns to capital of 3.44 percent and 5.37 percent. Since these figures are below the opportunity cost of capital, this implies that some subsidies would be needed for roadbed investment and maintenance if the railroads were not going to deplete their capital stock.

Of course, it is important to stress that this analysis is based on the determination of a short-run competitive equilibrium in which the existing capital stock is taken as given. Thus it may be the case that if the railroads are able to achieve an optimal capital stock, they could earn a normal return to capital. Consequently, in addition to changes in pricing policies, it is likely that the ICC should encourage infrastructure changes that would enable the railroads to achieve long-run marginal costs, and the nature of these changes will be discussed at length in the next chapter.

The situation in the trucking industry is interesting. Since prices are presently above marginal costs, carriers of special commodities are currently earning profits. Because, however, these carriers are apparently subject to economies of scale, marginal cost pricing would lead to losses. In the Official Region these losses are fairly large, totalling $600 million, while they are a more modest sum of $134 million in the South–West Region. Thus not only would marginal cost pricing remove the economic rents currently earned by these carriers, but it would also lead to losses and require subsidies to be granted. Of course, the statement that marginal cost pricing would lead to losses is a direct result of the estimated returns to scale in these industries, and if these economies are of a regulatory nature rather than a technological nature, it is likely that they would not materialize. However, it is unlikely that these carriers are subject to increasing costs, indicating that marginal cost pricing would end the economic rents currently obtained by these carriers. Thus it appears that in addition to the rail shippers of manufactured commodities in the Official Region, trucking firms in the Official and South–West Regions and railroads in the South–West Region are the main beneficiaries of current pricing policies.

3.4.2 Indirect Effects

Since freight rates affect delivered goods prices, changes in freight rates should lead to changes in the costs of materials inputs and hence in regional production costs. Since production is not generally tied to any one region, however, increases in production costs in any one region should cause firms to move to areas where production costs are lower. Hence changes in freight rates should lead to output and employment adjustments and hence to changes in regional income. In this section, therefore, we briefly discuss the model used to analyze these income changes and quantify those that could be expected to result from a movement to a competitive equilibrium from the status quo.

Modeling Regional Income   Since appendix D gives a full discussion of the regional income model that is used to assess the indirect income effects associated with changes in freight rates, in this section we will briefly summarize the model used and our estimates of the income and employment effects resulting from the establishment of a competitive equilibrium.

Because we are interested in assessing how changes in freight rates in any given region affect production decisions in all regions, we have developed a framework that takes regional linkages concerning economic activity explicitly into account.[25] In this analysis, this linkage comes through equations that attempt to explain the flow of goods between regions as a function of market prices, freight rates, and income.

The basic assumption we make is that, ceteris paribus, a region A will import more from another region B if the price of the good produced in B falls for consumers in A. This can occur if costs of production fall in region B or if the cost of transporting the commodity from region B to A decreases. Similarly, if incomes rise in region A, and if the good is a normal good, more should be imported into A, not only from B but from all other regions.

Unfortunately, adequate data are not available to permit the estimation of a full set of equations that have as the dependent variable the flow of a good from each region to every other region. Thus let Y_K^{OD} be the flow of good K from region O to region D, where O indexes the region of origin and D indexes the region of destination of the flow. Since this analysis utilizes the five ICC regions, $O = 1, \ldots, 5$, and $D = 1, \ldots, 5$.[26] Then we hypothesize that Y_K^{OD} is a function of its own price, prices of substitute commodities, and the level of income in the importing region:

$$Y_K^{OD} = Y(I^D, P_K^{OD}, \tilde{P}_K^{OD}, \tilde{P}_{SK}^{OD}), \tag{3.9}$$

where:

P_K^{OD} is the price of Y_K^{OD}.

$\tilde{P}_K^{OD}$ is a vector of prices of good K if it were imported from another region. For example, $\tilde{P}_K^{12} = (\tilde{P}_K^{22}, \tilde{P}_K^{32}, \tilde{P}_K^{42}, \tilde{P}_K^{52})$.

$\tilde{P}_{SK}^{OD}$ is a vector of prices of substitute commodities. For example, if Y_K is coal, $\tilde{P}_{SK}^{OD}$ might be a vector of prices of competing fuels such as oil and gas.

I^D is the income in the region of destination.

Equation (3.9) is really the reduced form of two structural equations that describe two distinct but simultaneous decisions. The first is the decision as to how much of good K, say machinery, to consume in region D, and the second is where in the country to purchase that total amount of machinery. The first decision depends on the aggregate price level of the commodity, the price of other goods that substitute for it in consumption, and regional income. The second decision depends on the price of the commodity and transportation costs. Thus (3.9) expresses both of these decisions in a reduced form, single equation.

Total output of commodity K in region O is then simply given as the sum of all of its shipments from that region:

$$Y_K^O = \sum_{D=1}^{5} Y_K^{OD}. \tag{3.10}$$

Once we have obtained estimates of regional output by commodity type, it is necessary to determine how employment is related to that output. This can be done in a fashion analogous to that used in obtaining the transport demand function by postulating a general industry cost function and using Shephard's lemma to obtain its associated labor demand equation.

We thus postulate that regional technology can be described by the following general cost function:

$$C = C(Y, w_L, w_K, w_E, t), \tag{3.11}$$

where Y is an output measure, w_L, w_K, and w_E are (respectively) the prices of labor, capital, and energy services, and t represents time. The time index t is introduced to capture technical change over time and is used because this function must be estimated using a time series.

Since any cost function can be approximated by the translog, we employ the following specific functional form:

$$\ln C = \alpha_0 + \sum_i \alpha_i \ln w_i + \alpha_y \ln y + \alpha_2 \ln t$$
$$+ \frac{1}{2} \sum_i \sum_j B_{ij} \ln w_i \ln w_j + \frac{1}{2} B_{tt} (\ln t)^2 + B_{yt} \ln y \ln t$$
$$+ \frac{1}{2} B_{yy} (\ln y)^2 + \sum_i B_{iy} \ln w_i \ln y + \sum B_{it} \ln w_i \ln t, \quad i = L, K, E. \tag{3.12}$$

The derived factor share equation for labor is

$$S_L = \frac{\partial \ln C}{\partial \ln w_L}$$
$$= \alpha_L + B_{LL} \ln w_L + B_{LK} \ln w_K + B_{LE} \ln w_E + B_{Lt} \ln t$$
$$+ B_{Ly} \ln y. \tag{3.13}$$

This factor share equation can be used to obtain the required labor demand.

The basic causality in this analysis goes from regional output to regional employment and then to regional income. Thus regional output is assumed to depend upon regional production costs (inclusive of transportation costs) relative to those in other regions, while regional employment depends upon regional output and factor prices (which are assumed to be exogenously given). With given factor prices, regional income is simply the sum of factor payments in each industry plus transfers.

In particular, regional income is the sum of wage payments, proprietors' income, property income, and transfers less taxes. For our purposes, however, it is permissible to concentrate on labor income, since the other components of regional income are almost certainly determined independently of freight rates. Moreover, since we assume that wages are determined exogenously, once we have determined the change in labor demand occasioned by a change in output, which is in turn occasioned by a change in freight rates, we should have captured the bulk of the change in regional income due to a change in the rate structure. Thus once we have derived the elasticity of labor demand with respect to a change in output, it is a straightforward task to translate this into a change in regional income.

The Impact of Changing Freight Rates Upon Regional Income Since appendix D gives a full discussion of the derivation of the regional income model, we will give a brief summary of the results in this section and indicate by how much regional income could be expected to change in response to competitive pricing in the transportation industries.

Ideally, we would like to encompass all forms of economic activity in this analysis. Unfortunately, however, data limitations forced us to focus on the manufacturing sector. Hence this analysis will yield measures of the income losses accruing to the manufacturing sectors as a result of competitive pricing. Since other sectors would also be affected, this is clearly an underestimate of the total income changes that would result from freight rate changes. Nevertheless, it should be indicative of the orders of magnitude involved.

Before discussing the impact of changing freight rates upon manufacturing activity, however, it may be useful to discuss briefly the nature of the sample used in the analysis. In particular, although we separated the United States into two major regions in the efficiency analysis, in this section we will consider the five ICC regions separately: The Official Territory; the Southern Region; the South–Western Region; the Western Trunk Line; and the Mountain–Pacific Region. Thus we disaggregate the South–West Region into its four component parts. In addition, since the commodity flow equations were estimated over the five ICC regions for two time periods, 1967 and 1972, yielding a maximum of fifty observations, missing observations precluded the estimation of commodity flow equations for all but nine industries. Since, however, these nine industries include a wide range of durable and nondurable industries, it is likely that their aggregate behavior is representative of that of the manufacturing industry as a whole.

We thus estimate (3.9) in a linear form to obtain measures of the elasticity of shipments from region of origin O to region of destination D for industry type i, denoted by E_i^{OD}. These elasticities can then be aggregated with respect to region and industry type to yield a weighted elasticity of output in a given region of origin with respect to changes in freight rates in that and all other regions (cf. appendix D).

From the labor demand equation (3.13) we then obtain an elasticity of labor with respect to output. Since wage income is identically equal to the product of employment and wages, as long as wages remain constant, the percentage change in income must equal the percentage change in employment. Once we have estimated, therefore, the percentage change in freight rates arising from the determination of the competitive equilibrium, we can estimate the percentage change in output, the percentage change in employment, and the percentage change in income arising in each region.

To obtain the actual changes in income and employment arising from the postulated change in freight rates resulting from a competitive equilibrium, we first calculate the weighted change in freight rates that would obtain in each region, which are given in table 3.7. Note that we assume that these changes in each region of origin are assumed to hold in each region of destination. Moreover, since the South–West Region encompasses all of the ICC regions other than the Official Territory, we assume that the rate change that occurs in the South–West Region also occurs in each of the ICC regions with the exception of the Official Territory. We then apply these to the output elasticities to obtain the percentage change

Table 3.7 Estimated Changes in Regional Manufacturing Employment and Income Arising from Competitive Equilibrium, by Region of Origin, 1972

	Official	Southern	Western Trunk Line	South–Western	Mountain–Pacific	Total South–West[a]
Percentage change in freight rates arising from competitive equilibrium	15.17	−0.14	−0.14	−0.14	−0.14	−0.14
Elasticities of employment with respect to freight rates	−0.03931	−0.12272	−0.09097	−0.01029	−0.49833	na
Percentage change in employment	−0.5963	0.0176	0.0131	0.0015	0.0718	na
Actual change in employment (thous.)	−35.387	0.704	0.157	0.019	1.701	2.581
Actual change in income ($ mill.)	−591.380	5.274	1.427	0.152	16.541	23.394

a. Sum of Southern, Western Trunk Line, South–Western, and Mountain–Pacific.

in output that results from these rate changes. These changes in outputs are then applied to the employment elasticities to yield estimates of the changes in employment and income in each region that result from the movement from the status quo to a competitive equilibrium in the rail and trucking markets.

Table 3.7 clearly indicates that the pattern of indirect income changes parallels that of the direct income changes. In particular, freight rates on manufactured goods are postulated to rise by some 15.2 percent in the Official Territory and to fall by a negligible amount (-0.14 percent) in the rest of the country as a result of marginal cost pricing.[27] This leads to a loss of some 35,000 manufacturing jobs in the Official Territory and a gain of some 2,500 manufacturing jobs in the South–West Region. The associated income changes are a reduction of some $590 million in manufacturing income in the Official Territory and an increase of some $23 million in the South–West Region. Note, moreover, that since the Mountain–Pacific Region appears to be the most sensitive to changes in freight rates, most of the income gains within the South–West Region are concentrated in the far West.

3.5 Policy Implications

This analysis indicates that changes in the value-of-service pricing to permit the attainment of a competitive equilibrium are not entirely costless. In terms of economic efficiency per se, such a change is clearly desirable and would eliminate an aggregate deadweight burden that presently exists in excess of $1 billion. Moreover, the analysis of the distributional effects of such a change clearly indicates that the potential gainers could compensate the losers, while still leaving considerable funds remaining. Thus in terms of the usual criteria used to evaluate policy changes, such a change would clearly be said to be desirable.

But the inescapable fact remains that the income losses associated with such a change are substantial. Rail shippers of manufactured goods in the Official Territory would face increased transport expenditures in excess of $1.2 billion. Those in the South–West Region would face increases of $300 million. In addition, the income losses to workers employed in the manufacturing industries in the Official Region would also total approximately $600 million. Moreover, trucking firms would face reduction in profits of approximately $1 billion, while the railroads in the South–West Region would face reductions in profits of approximately $500 million. The total income losses to affected shippers, carriers, and factors, therefore, is approximately $3.5 billion. Counteracting this, of course, are reductions in shippers' expenditures on bulk commodities in excess of $1.5 billion, gains to the railroads in the Official Territory of approximately $1.5 billion, and gains to the trucking shippers of bulk and manufactured commodities of approximately $1 billion. The direct and indirect income gains clearly exceed the comparable income losses. Nevertheless, unless some means are found to compensate the losers, it is clear that political pressures will make such a change difficult to achieve. In particular, this analysis indicates that manufacturing activities in the Official Territory are receiving substantial implicit subsidies in the form of rail rates that are considerably below marginal cost. While rail rates on manufactured goods in the South–West Region are also below marginal cost, the differentials are considerably less than those in the Official Territory. Hence a movement toward competitive pricing would increase rail rates on manufactured goods in the Official Region relative to those in the rest of the country. However, the focus of manufacturing activities has steadily moved away from the older, industrialized Northeast, and efforts to rationalize the rate structure would clearly exacerbate the problems of adjustment caused by a long-term secular movement of manufacturing activity away from the Northeast. Hence while the South and West would clearly gain on balance from a change in the rate structure and the establishment of a competitive equilibrium, the Northeast and Central States would doubtless lose. In view of the rather precarious situation of these urban and state economies, it is certainly legitimate to question whether such a change makes social or political sense, or, alternatively, whether we can make these changes without developing some new and innovative means of establishing transitional subsidies that will make the movement from the status quo to a competitive equilibrium politically and socially tolerable.

In this connection, it seems clear that the present policy of making the railroads bear the subsidy is clearly wrong. While the railroads are presently suffering the losses due to pricing below marginal cost, it is clear that they are not the recipients of the benefits of such a subsidy. Indeed, bankruptcy was the reward conferred upon the Northeast railroads for their endeavors, and since the reorganization of these railroads into Conrail, its reward for continued subsidies to shippers is political battles over the size and probable duration of its legislated operating subsidies. The problem, however, is not primarily one of the efficiency or inefficiency of Conrail or its predecessors, but whether its shippers of manufactured commodities will pay the full costs of rail service in the

Northeast. Thus although the Eastern railroads are the apparent problem, they really are not. If rates covered costs, the Eastern roads could earn a modest return on capital. However, this return would still be less than the opportunity cost of capital, indicating that long-term subsidies and/or changes in the capital stock would be required if the railroads were to offer attractive alternatives to investments in other industries in the private sector.

Nevertheless, it is clear that the primary problem among the Eastern railroads is the subsidy to rail shippers of manufactured goods via the railroad rate structure. When viewed in this light, the railroad rate structure appears to be a particularly clumsy vehicle for this subsidy. In particular, if the continued levels of manufacturing activities in the Official Region appear to be sufficiently meritorious to warrant a subsidy in excess of $1 billion, let this subsidy be paid directly to the manufacturing concerns in the form of a direct wage or employment subsidy instead of an indirect subsidy through the rail rate structure. This would have the effect of removing the railroads from the political domain and making the nature of the political problem clear, namely, the viability of certain manufacturing industries in the Northeast instead of the viability of the Northeast railroads.

In conclusion, while the establishment of a competitive equilibrium in the transportation industries would have clear efficiency gains, it is by no means costless or unambiguously desirable in the absence of mechanisms designed to compensate the losers who would be hurt by such a move. Since, however, the primary losers would be manufacturing activities in the Northeast, it is certainly reasonable to ask whether the railroad rate structure is the proper vehicle to maintain income transfers to these activities. If the answer is affirmative, then society should be willing to subsidize the Northeast railroads, which are merely acting as a conduit for a subsidy that ultimately accrues to the manufacturing industries using these railroads. If, however, the answer is negative, then society should probably bite the bullet and let competitive pricing prevail and develop alternative means of subsidizing Northeast manufacturing activity.

Since this analysis indicates that present pricing policies impose a clear deadweight burden on society, and since the estimated income gains are considerably in excess of the estimated income losses, society would on balance benefit from the abandonment of value-of-service pricing. Thus the focus of policy should not be how to prop up an inefficient and probably ultimately unviable pricing structure in the transportation industries, but rather how to introduce direct subsidies that are thought to be politically necessary in a politically viable way. Since it is almost certain that preferable alternatives exist, let us concentrate, therefore, on their development instead of tying ourselves to an outmoded and inefficient pricing structure that neither fully serves the needs of the railroads, the shippers, nor society at large.

Notes

1. This argument was first put forth by John Meyer et al. (1959) and has been extended in recent years by Harbeson (1969), Friedlaender (1969), and Moore (1972).

2. Of course, piggybacking could provide an alternative to truck for shipments of a smaller size, shorter haul, and higher value than those afforded by conventional rail operations.

3. See, for example, Boyer (1977) and Levin (1978).

4. In particular, in addition to listing fifteen specific truckload commodity categories (e.g., household goods, automobiles, and refrigerated products), the commission has one category of specific commodities not otherwise grouped. In recent years, trucking firms have expanded their operating rights in this area and can carry a broad range of manufactured commodities under truckload rates.

5. For a discussion of this point, see *Traffic World* (October 23, 1978), 19.

6. See, for example, Meyer et al., (1959) and Morton (1969).

7. In recent years, a large literature has arisen on the question of the optimal relationship between prices and marginal costs in the presence of constraints and distortions that prevent society from achieving its "first-best" social optimum. See Baumol (1979), Diamond and Mirrlees (1971), and Lipsey and Lancaster (1956).

8. The failure to consider regional interrelationships arises from data limitations and is an admitted limitation of the analysis. Some effort to correct this deficiency is made in the analysis of freight rates and regional incomes that is undertaken in section 3.4 of this chapter.

9. Although we treat shipment characteristics as exogenously determined, this may be a shortcoming in the analysis. In particular, under current regulatory practices it is probably reasonable to treat variables such as average length of haul and average shipment size as exogenously determined since carriers have a common carrier obligation to carry all shipments. Thus the nature of their traffic is largely determined by shipper demand. In an unregulated environment, however, it is quite possible that firms would treat these shipment characteristics as control variables in the profit-maximization process. In this case, they should be treated as endogenous and the analysis altered accordingly. In this analysis, however, we will treat them as exogenously determined, although we will perform some comparative static experiments with these variables.

10. See. for example, Adams et al. (1975) and Friedlaender et al. (1975).

11. This grouping of states is bounded on the west by Illinois and on the south by the Ohio River, West Virginia, and the Potomac River.

12. It is important to note that these marginal costs and rates are based on commodity averages and do not indicate that every commodity is carried at rates below marginal cost.

13. These were taken from figures 2.1 and 2.3 in the previous chapter.

14. It is interesting to note that Conrail, which is composed of most of the railroads in this sample, has recently proposed increases on rates on a wide range of manufactured commodities, claiming that it carries these commodities at a substantial loss. Thus this analysis corroborates Conrail's position.

15. For a full discussion of the methodology used to determine this new equilibrium see Michaels (1978).

16. Note that trucking marginal costs are a function of total output, while the rail marginal costs are a function of total output and the ratio of bulk to manufactured commodities. Since truck marginal costs fall with total output, increases in bulk carriage will cause a downward shift in the trucking marginal cost function, for any level of manufactured output. Similarly, since rail marginal costs are rising, an increase in bulk commodity carriage will lead to an upward shift in the marginal cost function for manufactured goods at any level of output. Since, however, the rail marginal cost function also contains the ratio of bulk to manufactured goods as an argument, increases in this ratio will tend to shift the function downward. Nevertheless, at least at the estimated competitive equilibrium, the output effect appears to outweigh the commodity mix effect for rail carriage of manufactured goods. Finally, note that since rail output of manufactured goods falls, the commodity mix effect and the output effect work together in the rail marginal cost function for manufactured goods.

17. It is interesting to note that the trucking firms in the South–West Region earn profits that are greater than those earned by trucking firms in the Official Region. This arises because trucking firms in the South–West Region are operating on the rising portion of their marginal cost curve, so that marginal costs are close to or above average costs.

18. Since trucking firms appear to be operating on the rising portion of their marginal cost function, this result is somewhat puzzling. However, even though marginal costs are rising, equilibrium output levels are still sufficiently close to the minimum marginal costs that they lie below average costs. Hence total costs are greater than revenues at competitive pricing levels. This result is, of course, consistent with the finding of modest economies of scale in this trucking sector.

19. For example, Fulda (1961) cites cases in which "iron and steel and articles made thereof" do not include tractors, tractor engines, or used foundry machinery or cases in which "liquid petroleum products" do not include crude oil. Although the commission has been somewhat more flexible in granting operating authorities in the past year of two, during the period of analysis its attitudes were consistent with those described by Fulda (1961). Nelson (1965) also has an interesting discussion of the commission's attitude toward the granting of new operating authorities.

20. These regional discrepancies can be explained by regional differences in economies of scale and lend support to the hypothesis that the observed economies of scale in the Official Territory are largely due to economies of capacity utilization rather than to size per se.

21. It is interesting to note that these demand effects are positive for manufactured goods and negative for bulk commodities. To the extent that average load reflects inventory costs, one would expect increases in average load to serve to reduce demand. For manufactured goods, however, the average loads are typically quite low relative to truckload capacity. Hence increases in average load may induce improved service and hence actually lead to reduction in inventory costs. Since bulk commodity loads are closer to truckload capacity, the increase in average load tends to reflect a direct increase in shipper inventory costs that are not offset by service improvements.

22. Note that even though trucking costs are estimated to be less than rail costs for manufactured goods, trucks do not carry all of these commodities because the demand for these goods is not infinitely elastic.

23. This generally describes the case in the trucking industry. The principles of measurement do not depend upon the nature of the shift.

24. Of course, when price is initially below marginal cost, the appropriate measure is $0.5(P_1 - P_0)(Q_0 + Q_1)$.

25. In this respect, this model differs from most regional models, which assume that changes in income in a given region do not affect aggregate income or income levels in other regions. For examples of the usual approach to modeling regional income see Friedlaender et al. (1975), Adams et al. (1975), and Glickman (1971).

26. Although we divided the country into two regions for the general equilibrium analysis of transport pricing, in the analysis of regional income determination it is useful to disaggregate the country into the five ICC regions: Official; Southern; South–Western; Grand Trunk Line; and Mountain–Pacific. The Official Region is identical in both analyses, while the other four regions will be aggregated to obtain the regional income effects from changes in freight rates in the South–West Region.

27. These percentage changes in freight rates were calculated from a Divisia index of the rail and trucking rates before and after the establishment of the competitive equilibrium.

Chapter 4

Rail Costs, Profitability, and Infrastructure

4.1 Introduction and Overview

The preceding chapter argued that since most railroads operate under short-run decreasing returns to scale, the railroad industry could approach financial viability under a competitive solution in which price equalled short-run marginal cost. However, the changes in rates and traffic allocation that would result from this solution are of a sufficiently large order of magnitude that one must classify this policy change as being a somewhat draconian measure. Not only would there be substantial income transfers between different groups of shippers, but there would also be substantial income transfers between carriers, with trucking firms possibly suffering losses at the competitive equilibrium. Consequently, even though a competitive equilibrium would substantially improve economic efficiency and railroad profitability, the political feasibility of such a solution must be questioned in the absence of compensation being paid to the losers.

In considering the nature of the competitive equilibrium, however, it is important to remember that the solution discussed in the previous chapter was based on short-run marginal costs for the existing stock of railroad way-and-structures capital. Since the railroads have practiced deferred maintenance for a number of years, however, it is highly unlikely that the actual capital stock approaches the optimal one. This suggests that rail costs might be reduced and efficiency improved, and that the potential income losses to shippers might be reduced by policies aimed at rationalizing the railroad infrastructure. Thus this chapter will explore the impact upon railroad costs and profitability of a number of policies that would affect both the quality and nature of the railroad infrastructure.

Section 4.2 discusses the impact of various changes in the railroad infrastructure upon rail costs and profitability under the existing equilibrium and under a competitive equilibrium. Section 4.3 then considers the nature of the long-run marginal costs and policies that could be implemented to achieve long-run competitive equilibrium. Section 4.4 provides a summary and evaluates the implications of policies aimed at rationalizing the railroad infrastructure as opposed to policies aimed at achieving competitive pricing in the rail and trucking industries.

4.2 Rail Costs, Profitability, and Infrastructure Changes

As we indicated previously, existing analyses of railroad costs tend to have two fundamental weaknesses. First, they generally fail to differentiate between way-and-structures capital, which is a measure of the quantity and quality of the capital utilized in the roadbed, and track, which in addition to being a proxy for the roadbed capital is also a measure of common carrier obligations to haul commodities. Second, they generally fail to take the route network into account and differentiate between high-density, fully utilized track and light-density, underutilized track.[1]

Consequently, some studies have reached the counterintuitive conclusion that the marginal product of capital is negative since increases in track lead to increased expenditures on other factors, ceteris paribus.[2] The problem, however, is not that capital has a negative marginal product, but that track is a poor proxy for capital. Indeed, because of the high variability of maintenance expenditures, it is quite possible to reduce track while increasing the total amount of way-and-structures capital. Thus, while track is clearly related to way-and-structures capital, it also is a useful measure of the common carrier obligations of the firm. When viewed in this light, the estimated impact of track upon costs is eminently reasonable since track reduction is also associated with reduction in trains, crews, etc.

Similarly, by failing to differentiate between low-density track and high-density track, many studies overstate the potential savings arising from track reduction.[3] While reduction in low-density track could doubtless lead to substantial cost savings and increased profitability by reducing costs without concomitant traffic reductions, reduction in mainline track would not necessarily lead to cost reduction if the existing traffic were routed over less efficient lines or to increased profits if traffic were also reduced substantially. In addition to considering the total track, therefore, it is important to consider the distribution of traffic over the rail network.[4]

While this study certainly does not fully incorporate all of the dimensions of railroad capital or networks, it makes an initial attempt in that direction by distinguishing among three elements of the railroad infrastructure: way-and-structures (WS) capital, total track, and low-density track. Way-and-structures capital is a measure of the capital utilized in the roadbed and as such should be treated as a conventional factor of production. In contrast, track and low-density route-miles should be treated as technological variables that affect the costs of the railroad firm in a way that is not necessarily associated with conventional production theory. For example, while an increase in the fixed factor, WS capital, should lead to reduction in other factors and hence reduction in variable costs, an increase in low-density route-miles or total track may increase costs by increasing common carrier obligations.

Clearly, however, the three measures are not unrelated. A ceteris paribus reduction in WS capital will reduce the quality of the existing track and hence lead to cost increases by requiring increased amounts of variable factors, because more money must be spent on equipment maintenance and train crews as the quality of the roadbed deteriorates and speeds are reduced. Similarly, a ceteris paribus reduction in track will not only lead to reduction in common carrier obligations and improvements in the quality of the existing track, but will also lead to increases in the utilization of the existing track. The first two considerations will tend to reduce costs, while the latter considerations will tend to increase them, making the impact of reduced track somewhat ambiguous. Reduction in low-density track will reduce common carrier obligations and their associated costs and will therefore tend to generate cost savings.

This analysis will therefore attempt to quantify the impact of changing these three infrastructure measures upon rail costs to assess the possible savings that could accrue from policies aimed at changing any of these variables. In doing this, the analysis will take place in three different contexts. We will begin by discussing the impact of the infrastructure variables upon short-run variable costs, and factor utilization for the railroads used in this sample. We will then analyze the impact upon costs and profitability under two different scenarios: the status quo, under which existing rates and output levels are held constant; and a short-run competitive equilibrium, in which all goods are priced at marginal cost. In the first scenario we therefore attempt to assess the cost savings that could accrue to the railroads at current output levels, while under the second scenario we attempt to assess the response of the short-run competitive equilibrium to changes in the stock and nature of rail capital and technological variables.

4.2.1 Railroad Costs and Infrastructure Variables

Just as we can calculate the marginal cost of rail operations with respect to output, we can also calculate the marginal cost of rail operations with respect to the technological variables. Within the translog framework, these are estimated to be

Table 4.1 Marginal Cost Effects of Capital, Route-Mileage, and Output at Sample Mean

Variable	$\partial C/\partial z$ at sample mean (dollars)
x = way and structures capital	-0.1099[a]
t_1 = low-density route miles	63,291.8
t_2 = route-miles	5,169.18

a. To convert this to a rate of return, the asset prices as of 12/31/71 must be converted to a weighted mean of the asset prices over the sample. This yields an estimated rate of return of 13.083 percent before depreciation.

Table 4.2 Elasticities of Cost and Factor Demands with Respect to Way-and-Structures Capital and Technological Conditions at the Point of Approximation[a]

	Elasticity of cost	Equipment	General labor	Yard & switching labor (traffic & trans.)	On-train labor	Fuel & materials
x = way & structures capital	-0.42678	-1.065 (0.142)	-0.306 (0.131)	-0.289 (0.137)	-0.194 (0.118)	-0.058 (0.304)
t_1 = low-density route-miles	0.29108	0.311 (0.083)	0.310 (0.071)	0.442 (0.072)	0.412 (0.065)	0.078 (0.119)
t_2 = route-miles	0.08641	0.485 (0.127)	-0.153 (0.100)	-0.212 (0.100)	-0.261 (0.083)	0.358 (0.105)

a. Figures in parentheses represent standard errors.

$$\frac{\partial C}{\partial t_i} = \frac{\partial \ln C}{\partial \ln t_i} \frac{\hat{C}}{t_i}, \tag{4.1}$$

where $\hat{C}$ represents the fitted value of costs in dollars and t_i the relevant technological variables.[5] Table 4.1 presents these estimated marginal costs at the sample mean and indicates that for a hypothetical firm facing mean values of all of the variables, the marginal cost of a mile of low-density track is \$63,292, while the marginal cost of an average mile of track is \$5,170. Note, however, that since low-density route-miles are included in total route-miles, the total cost of adding a low-density route-mile is \$68,462. Table 4.1 also indicates that an additional 12/31/71 dollar of WS capital lowers variable costs by 10.99¢, or, equivalently, yields a return on capital of 13.08 percent.

Although the infrastructure variables affect costs, these effects largely come about through factor substitutions and changes in factor intensities. Thus it is useful to analyze the impact of changes in the infrastructure variables upon costs to determine the way in which changes in these variables affect marginal costs.

Table 4.2 presents the elasticities of costs and factor demands with respect to the infrastructure variables. The first column gives the elasticity of cost with respect to the appropriate argument, which can be viewed as being the weighted sum of the factor demand elasticities of the remaining five columns, with the weights being the estimated factor shares at the point of approximation.

Thus, for example, the 4.3-percent decrease in variable cost brought about by a 10-percent increase in WS capital can be seen to consist of 10.6-percent savings in equipment usage, a 3.1-percent decrease in general labor, a 2.9-percent decrease in yard and switching labor, a 1.9-percent decrease in on-train labor, and a 0.6-percent savings in fuel and materials. The main effect of an increase in WS capital is thus seen to be a decrease in equipment requirements with somewhat lesser savings in the labor categories. This confirms the intuition that the savings in variable costs that result from an increase in WS capital have increased train speeds as their source. If this is so, then the observed disparity between the on-train labor demand elasticity (-0.194) with those of the other two labor categories (-0.306, -0.289) might be explained by work rules that require train crews to be paid by distance rather than by actual hours worked.

Table 4.2 also indicates that a reduction of low-density route-mileage of 10 percent would reduce total variable costs by 2.9 percent. This comes about by reducing yard and switching labor by somewhat over 4 percent, reducing general labor and equipment expenditures by somewhat over 3 percent, and by reducing fuel and materials expenditures by somewhat less than 1 percent. Thus the primary savings arising from abandonment of low-density line are concentrated in transportation and switching categories associated with moving trains over lightly utilized track.

A 10-percent reduction in general track or route-miles only leads to a reduction of total costs of 0.86 percent. In terms of factor utilization, reductions in general route-miles lead to sizable reductions in equipment and materials expenditures, but increases in labor expenditures. Thus as the same volume of traffic is moved over a smaller network, increased expenditures on labor and switching are required, while savings on fuel and equipment are achieved.

In evaluating the effects of changing route-mileage, however, it is important to note that a 10-percent change in total track or route-miles changes both general route-miles and low-density route-miles by 10 percent. Thus the impact of a uniform change in network size is obtained by adding the second and third rows of table 4.2. Conversely, a ceteris paribus 10-percent change in total route-miles is not only a shift in overall traffic density (since ton-miles/route-miles changes) but also a shift in the distribution of rail line densities (since low-density route-miles do not change) and capital per route-mile (since WS capital does not change). Consequently, an increase in route-miles is not only a change in network size but also implicitly a change in the type of service provided over that network.

Keeping in mind these considerations, the appropriate interpretation of the elasticities with respect to route-miles contained in table 4.2 is that a change in general track or route-miles without a concomitant change in low-density route-miles has a small impact on variable costs, but a significant effect on factor intensities; the factor shares of equipment and fuel and materials rise in response to a reduction in general route-miles, while those of the labor factors decrease. In fact, this type of network expansion, which can be viewed as an overall density decrease combined with a move toward a more uniform distribution of densities over rail lines, actually decreases the demand for labor. In contrast, a uniform reduction in network size increases the demand for every factor, with the labor factor share declining and those of equipment and fuel and materials rising. Thus the second and third rows of table 4.2 taken together make it clear that what distinguishes the provision of low-density service from that of general network expansion is the greater labor intensity of the former.

In addition to analyzing the elasticities of cost with respect to the technological conditions for a hypothetical railroad facing mean factor prices, output levels, technological conditions, and operating characteristics, it is useful to consider the values of these elasticities for each firm in the sample to determine which firms might be the most sensitive to changes in their infrastructure. Estimates of the elasticity of costs with respect to WS capital and its standard error evaluated at the points corresponding to the nineteen sample railroads in 1969 are presented in the first two columns of table 4.3.[6] The third column presents estimates of the effect (in 1969 dollars) on the variable cost of increasing WS capital by one 1969 dollar, that is, $\partial C / \partial x$, where x reflects WS capital, with capital measured in 1969 dollars rather than 12/31/71 dollars. We will refer to (minus) this value as the gross rate of return to investment in WS capital, but it should be noted that this corresponds to a profit concept of rate of return at the margin $[\partial(\text{profits}) / \partial x]$ only when bankruptcy and perverse regulatory conditions (such as those which set prices based on "operating" rather than economic costs) can be ignored. The net rate of return is the gross rate adjusted for depreciation. Since the

Table 4.3 Effect of Way-and-Structures Capital on Variable Costs, by Railroad, 1969:
Restricted Model

	Elasticity of cost with respect to capital	Standard error	Gross rate of return
Atchison, Topeka & Santa Fe Ry.	−0.4228	0.1273	−0.1416
Boston & Maine Corp.	−0.1707	0.0717	−0.0291
Central R.R. Co. of New Jersey	−0.2326	0.1065	−0.0580
Chicago & North Western Trans.	−0.3975	0.0961	−0.0843
Chicago, Milwaukee, & St. Paul	−0.4029	0.0900	−0.0759
Chicago, Rock Island & Pacific	−0.2343	0.1182	−0.0639
Delaware & Hudson Ry. Co.	−0.1591	0.0618	−0.0367
Erie-Lackawanna Ry. Co.	−0.3463	0.0869	−0.0820
Grand Trunk Western R.R. Co.	−0.2775	0.0885	−0.1241
Gulf Mobile & Ohio R.R. Co.	−0.2440	0.0695	−0.0709
Illinois Central R.R. Co.	−0.4756	0.1060	−0.1303
Missouri Pacific R.R. Co.	−0.2627	0.1289	−0.0752
Penn Central Transportation Co.	−0.6067	0.1603	−0.1632
Seaboard Coast Line R.R. Co.	−0.4397	0.1074	−0.1890
Southern Pacific Transportation	−0.4463	0.1498	−0.2066
Southern Ry. Co.	−0.3039	0.1153	−0.1142
Texas & Pacific Ry. Co.	−0.1461	0.0674	−0.0533
Union Pacific R.R. Co.	−0.3693	0.1348	−0.1376
Western Pacific R.R. Co.	−0.1929	0.0632	−0.0446

law of diminishing returns ($\partial^2 C/\partial x^2 > 0$) holds for every sample point,
a firm whose net rate of return is less than its opportunity cost of investment is overinvested from a cost-minimization point of view.

Since overinvested firms have a net rate of return that is less than the
opportunity cost of capital, table 4.3 enables us to determine which
railroads were overinvested or underinvested in 1969. The range of
yields on railroad bonds in 1969 was roughly 7–9 percent. Using a
2-percent depreciation rate yields a range of 9–11 percent for gross
returns, so that the net rate equals the bond rate. Extending this range
by 1 percent on either side to allow for errors in estimating depreciation
and opportunity costs indicates that every railroad whose gross rate of
return falls within 8–12 percent can be said to have an approximately
optimal level of investment. Table 4.3 indicates, however, that only four
railroads with a total of 21,404 route-miles met this criterion: the Chicago
and North Western; the Erie-Lackawanna; the Southern; and the Grand

Trunk Western. In contrast, nine railroads with 35,356 total route-miles appear to have been overinvested and earned rates of return below 9 percent: the Boston and Maine; the Central of New Jersey; the Chicago, Milwaukee, and St. Paul; the Chicago, Rock Island, and Pacific; the Delaware and Hudson; the Gulf, Mobile, and Ohio; the Missouri Pacific; the Texas and Pacific; and the Western Pacific. Since these railroads apparently had excessive investments in WS capital, a policy of deferring maintenance to reduce their capital stock would appear to have been a rational policy for these roads to pursue. Finally, there are six large roads with a total of 70,308 route-miles that appear to have been underinvested: the Atchison, Topeka and Santa Fe; the Illinois Central; the Penn Central; the Seaboard Coast Lines; the Southern Pacific; and the Union Pacific. Instead of excessive capital, the problem facing these railroads was insufficient WS investment. Apparently, the railroads had already experienced excessive deferred maintenance.

One interpretation of these results is that overinvested roads generally have track and structures whose value and condition exceed those required for cost-minimizing service, given their technological conditions and level of output. Conversely, the WS of the underinvested roads has deteriorated beyond the optimal level. Beyond the usual caution required for the interpretation of statistical estimates, it should be remembered that railroads do not generally operate under competitive conditions in their output markets. Thus, for example, if it is possible to discourage traffic on low-density lines by allowing low-density track (and thus low-density service) to deteriorate, the firm may find it profitable to allow this track to deteriorate to a condition worse than that which would minimize costs in the short run. For this and other reasons (such as expected bankruptcy) it may not be correct to conclude from net rate of return–opportunity cost gaps that firms are not pursuing long-run profit maximization. The strongest conclusion that would seem warranted is that, if opportunity costs represent social costs, the socially optimal method of providing the required services is not being employed.

The marginal cost of low-density service is estimated in table 4.4. Since t_2 (route-miles) includes the miles counted in t_1 (low-density route-miles), $\partial C / \partial t_1$ is the marginal cost of moving 1 route-mile from general service to low-density service. As such, it does measure the concept most relevant to the policy question of low-density line abandonment—the additional costs of providing low-density service that are due to the fact that the line is low-density—but it does so by using a somewhat arbitrary dichotomous classification. Since the costs of low-density

Table 4.4 Effect of Low-Density Route-Miles on Variable Costs, by Railroad, 1969:
Restricted Model

	Elasticity of cost with respect to low-density route-miles	Standard error	Corresponding marginal costs ($)
Atchison, Topeka & Santa Fe Ry.	0.3852	0.0728	76,764
Boston & Maine Corp.	0.1762	0.0694	19,666
Central R.R. Co. of New Jersey	0.1374	0.0834	20,593
Chicago & North Western Trans.	0.3106	0.0536	24,004
Chicago, Milwaukee, & St. Paul	0.3056	0.0526	25,871
Chicago, Rock Island & Pacific	0.3173	0.0542	45,856
Delaware & Hudson Ry. Co.	0.1853	0.0651	118,683
Erie Lackawanna Ry. Co.	0.2975	0.0517	59,055
Grand Trunk Western R.R. Co.	0.1769	0.0690	63,217
Gulf Mobile & Ohio R.R. Co.	0.2542	0.0507	59,473
Illinois Central R.R. Co.	0.3295	0.0575	105,540
Missouri Pacific R.R. Co.	0.3374	0.0596	50,441
Penn Central Transportation Co.	0.4272	0.0910	112,179
Seaboard Coast Line R.R. Co.	0.3491	0.0629	100,042
Southern Pacific Transportation	0.4083	0.0823	169,981
Southern Ry. Co.	0.3339	0.0588	100,981
Texas & Pacific Ry. Co.	0.2239	0.0555	40,783
Union Pacific R.R. Co.	0.3843	0.0723	79,366
Western Pacific R.R. Co.	0.2197	0.0576	189,296

service vary with the particular traffic density, our estimates, which ignore this fact, must be interpreted with appropriate caution.[8]

Nonetheless, as table 4.4 shows, the estimates of the marginal cost of low-density service for those roads with a small number of low-density miles fall within the range of those estimated for other roads. Moreover, estimates of $\partial \ln C / \partial \ln t_2$, that is, the marginal cost of an extension of the route network (and thus of a lowering of overall density), are insignificant (the ratio of the estimate to its standard error is less than 1.25) for both the original and restricted model. Thus, aside from the effects due to (very) low-density route-miles, there are no apparent effects of density on cost (as opposed to factor shares).

One inadequacy of our approach is that it provides no estimate of the savings that would be available if low-density service were eliminated. There are two reasons for this. The first, to which any regression approach is subject, is that the abandonment of a substantial portion of B branch-lines might substantially alter railroad technology. In this case, a simulation approach which incorporates more specific data concerning branch-line operation would be appropriate. An example of such an approach can be found in Harris (1977a). The second reason that a total estimate is not available is that the translog functional form is not well behaved as one of its arguments approaches zero.

In conclusion then, it appears that rail costs are quite sensitive to changes in WS capital and to changes in light-density route-miles, but not to changes in general route-miles. Thus efforts to adjust amounts of WS capital through roadbed maintenance or efforts to abandon light-density lines are likely to have a rather large impact on costs, while the abandonment of general track per se will lead to relatively few economies.

4.2.2 Infrastructure Changes and Aggregate Cost Savings

Another view of the impact of changes in the infrastructure upon rail costs and profitability can be seen by extending the analysis of the previous chapter to incorporate infrastructure effects. In this connection, it is useful to perform two different conceptual experiments, one dealing with the existing equilibrium and the other dealing with the short-run competitive equilibrium. In the first case, we hold rates and outputs at their existing levels and consider the cost savings that would accrue from changes in the route structure. In the second case we analyze how the short-run competitive equilibrium would respond to similar changes in the infrastructure. Thus the first analysis can be characterized by an unchanged regulatory policy in conjunction with a policy aimed at changing the railroad infrastructure; the second analysis can be viewed as a combination of regulatory changes in rate making and changes in abandonment and investment policies. Since, however, this second analysis still deals with relatively marginal changes in the capital stock, it should not be confused with the establishment of a long-run competitive equilibrium, which reflects an optimal adjustment in the railroad infrastructure as well as adjustments in rates and outputs. This long-run analysis will be considered below, when we analyze the nature of the railroads' long-run marginal costs.

Cost Savings at the Initial Equilibrium   The previous section indicated that rail costs were quite sensitive to changes in light-density route-miles or WS capital, but were relatively insensitive to changes in general track.

This section reaches similar conclusions by analyzing the impact of various infrastructure changes upon marginal costs and total costs of the stylized railroads in the Official and South–West Regions that we developed in the previous chapter.

Our analysis permits three different infrastructure variables to change: the amount of WS capital; the amount of general track; and the amount of low-density track. Ceteris paribus increases in WS capital will raise the amount of capital embodied in each mile of track and thus will lead to reductions in variable cost. Similarly, ceteris paribus reductions in light-density track will increase the amount of capital embodied per mile of track while reducing the proportion of low-density mileage; both of these factors should lead to cost reductions. In contrast, ceteris paribus reductions in general track will not only lead to increases in capital embodied per mile of track but will also lead to increases in the proportion of low-density track. While the first factor should tend to reduce costs, the second should tend to increase them.

Obviously, ceteris paribus changes in track are difficult to achieve since reductions in track are usually accompanied by the removal of the capital associated with the track. It is therefore useful to consider the impact of simultaneous changes in track mileage and WS capital to reflect the scrapping of the capital in conjunction with the scrapping of the track.

We consequently analyze six different cases, representing a number of different policies that could be followed with respect to route abandonment and roadbed investments:

A ceteris paribus 10-percent increase in WS capital. This reflects an investment of $1.798 billion in the Official Region and of $1.900 billion in the South–West Region.

A ceteris paribus 10-percent reduction in low-density route-miles. This reflects a reduction of 1,592 low-density miles in the Official Region and of 2,714 low-density miles in the South–West Region.

A ceteris paribus 10-percent reduction in general route-miles. This represents a reduction of 4,445 route-miles in the Official Region and of 10,022 route-miles in the South–West Region, while leaving the low-density route-miles in each region unchanged.

A 10-percent reduction in low-density route-miles and general route-miles in each region.

A 10-percent reduction in low-density route-miles accompanied by a concomitant reduction in WS capital. If we assume that WS capital is equally distributed among general and light-density track, this leads to a reduction in WS capital of 2.7 percent in the South–West Region and of 3.6 percent in the Official Region. Of course, since it is likely that low-density track has a lower level of capital embodied in it, this experiment will somewhat overstate the reduction in capital that could be expected to accompany the abandonment of light-density track.

A 10-percent reduction in general track accompanied by a 10-percent reduction in WS capital. Since this experiment implicitly leaves low-density track intact, it implicitly assumes that the capital in low-density track has been fully depreciated in terms of its useful life and that all capital is embodied in ordinary track. As such, it also probably over-estimates the capital reduction that would result from an abandonment of mainline track.[9]

Table 4.5 shows the levels of marginal costs and total costs that were estimated for the stylized railroads in the Official and South–West Regions under the status quo and under each of the postulated infrastructure changes. Note that these represent a new steady-state equilibrium and hence do not reflect the time path required to obtain these changes.

A 10-percent increase in WS capital leads to aggregate cost reduction in the Official Region of $193 million and of $163 million in the South–West Region. Since these cost savings reflect the steady-state equilibrium that would result from increases in WS capital if there were no further adjustments in rates or outputs, they can be used to yield an outer limit estimate of the returns to roadbed investment. By neglecting the time path of the returns, we implicitly evaluate these investments at a zero rate of discount and obtain yields net of depreciation and property taxes of 7.80 percent in the Official Region and of 5.37 percent in the South–West Region.[10]

Since these figures ignore the time path that is required to reach the steady-state equilibrium, they considerably overstate the gross returns to infrastructure investment. Thus the estimated return of 5.37 percent in the South–West Region clearly indicates that infrastructure investment is not an attractive venture to the railroads in this region. While the figure of 7.53 percent in the Official Region is somewhat higher, it is still below the opportunity cost of capital of 9.0 percent and indicates that infrastructure investment is also not attractive in the Official Region. Thus these figures are consistent with the conventional wisdom that the railroad infrastructure will not be supported by the private capital market. Moreover, their differentials are consistent with the view that the railroads in the East are more undercapitalized than those in the West. Hence, the returns to increases in WS capital are somewhat higher in the Official Region than in the rest of the country.

Table 4.5 also reflects the clear differentials that can be obtained from

Table 4.5 Total Costs and Marginal Costs under Specified Infrastructure Investments, by Official and South–West Regions, 1972

	Official			South–West		
	Total cost ($bill.)	Marginal cost Manuf. (¢/ton-mile)	Bulk (¢/ton-mile)	Total cost ($bill.)	Marginal cost Manuf. (¢/ton-mile)	Bulk (¢/ton-mile)
Absolute values						
Initial equilibrium	4.543	4.845	1.936	6.099	2.929	0.982
10% rise in WS capital	4.350	4.644	1.859	5.936	2.854	0.960
10% reduction in low-density route-miles	4.348	4.613	1.836	5.854	2.799	0.931
10% reduction in general route-miles	4.494	4.783	1.904	6.054	2.899	0.968
10% reduction in total route-miles	4.303	4.562	1.806	5.811	2.772	0.917
10% reduction in low-density route-miles + WS capital[a]	4.422	4.698	1.865	5.900	2.820	0.938
10% reduction in general route-miles + WS capital[b]	4.715	5.012	1.992	6.327	2.983	0.993
Percentage change						
10% rise in WS capital	−4.25	−4.15	−3.98	−2.67	−2.56	−2.24
10% reduction in low-density route-miles	−4.29	−4.79	−5.17	−4.02	−4.44	−5.19
10% reduction in general route-miles	−1.08	−1.28	−1.65	−0.74	−1.02	−1.43
10% reduction in total route-miles	−5.28	−5.84	−6.71	−4.72	−5.36	−6.62
10% reduction in low-density route-miles + WS capital[a]	−2.66	−3.03	−3.67	−3.26	−3.72	−4.48
10% reduction in general route-miles + WS capital[b]	3.78	3.45	2.89	2.26	1.84	1.12

a. Way-and-structures (WS) capital reduced by 3.6% in Official and 2.7% in South–West Region.
b. Way-and-structures capital reduced by 10% in both regions.

abandoning low-density track as opposed to abandoning general track. Thus a 10-percent reduction in low-density track will lead to a cost savings of $195 million in the Official Region and of $245 million in the South–West Region, while similar reductions in general track will lead to cost reductions of $49 million in the Official Region and of $45 million in the South–West Region.[11] Viewed alternatively, reduction in low-density track leads to cost reductions of $122,518 per mile in the Official Region and of $90,259 per mile in the South–West Region.[12] In contrast, elimination of mainline track leads to cost savings of $11,024 per mile in the Official Region and $4,490 per mile of track in the South–West Region.

These figures indicate that railroads in the Official Region have relatively more low-density track than their counterparts in the rest of the country.[13] Since railroads in the Official Region are characterized by a relatively uniform traffic network, reduction in low-density lines increases the traffic volumes and efficiencies of the remaining lines. In contrast, since railroads in the South and West are characterized by a number of major high-density corridors and a number of low-density feeder routes, reduction in these feeder routes leads to relatively few cost savings. These differentials in the economies associated with light-density lines also explain the estimated differentials associated with general track abandonment.

Of course, reductions in general track while holding the infrastructure constant will lead to increases in the capital embodied in the remaining track, which will tend to reduce costs. Since, however, track abandonment must generally be accompanied by reduction in WS capital, a more likely result for general track reduction is increased costs, rather than reduced costs. Indeed, a 10-percent reduction in general track accompanied by a 10-percent reduction in WS capital leads to increases in total costs of $228 million in the South–West Region and of $172 million in the Official Region. Since these figures can be viewed as the cost increases occasioned by changes in network configuration, the differentials between these cost increases and the cost changes occasioned by a ceteris paribus reduction in general track can be viewed as alternative measures of the productivity of roadbed capital.[14]

The importance of the capital embodied in the track can also be seen by comparing the cost savings accruing to a ceteris paribus reduction in low-density track and similar reductions accompanied by reduction in WS capital. Thus table 4.5 indicates that if capital is allocated evenly among general track and light-density track, a 10-percent reduction in light-density track and its accompanying capital will lead to respective cost savings of $121 million and $199 million in the Official and South–West Regions, reflecting cost savings per mile of track of $76,024 and $73,313 in the Official Region and the South–West Regions, respectively. These savings are somewhat less than those estimated in the case in which low-density track is reduced without a concomitant reduction in captial.

Table 4.5 also gives the short-run marginal costs associated with these various infrastructure changes. As was true in the case of total costs, these changes are relatively large for changes in WS capital or low-density route-miles, but relatively modest for changes in general track. At the initial point of equilibrium, these changes in marginal costs get translated into changes in total costs and hence in profitability. In a competitive environment, however, these changes would get translated into shifts in equilibrium rates and outputs, which would then lead to further shifts in the affected demand and marginal cost curves. Hence the general equilibrium results of these infrastructure changes should be rather different from the partial equilibrium changes that we have just analyzed.

General Equilibrium Effects of Infrastructure Changes   In the previous chapter we analyzed how rates, outputs, costs, profits, and the demand and cost functions shifted in response to changes in various exogenous policy variables. We do the same analysis here, focusing upon changes in the six infrastructure variables that we have discussed.

We analyze these general equilibrium effects by considering the changes in the competitive equilibrium that would result from the introduction of these infrastructure changes. We thus use the estimated competitive equilibrium, which was derived in the previous chapter as a benchmark, and then analyze the changes in rates, outputs, profits, etc., that would result from changing the capital or track that is in the rail system. Thus while the benchmark in the partial equilibrium analysis was the existing equilibrium, the benchmark in the general equilibrium analysis is the competitive equilibrium.

An intuitive understanding of the general equilibrium effects of these infrastructure changes can be given as follows. The key factor is the change in the marginal costs of rail shipments that results from reducing various types of track or changing the levels of roadbed capital. By lowering rail marginal costs, these changes should lead to increases in outputs and reduced rates in competitive rail markets. These reduced rail rates should then cause the demand function for trucking services to shift in, which results in reduced trucking rates and output. Since, however, output levels and mixes have changed in each mode as a result of these initial shifts in the demand and cost curves, further shifts in the marginal cost curves are likely to result. Nevertheless, these secondary changes should be small, and the net effect of changing the level and quality of the rail infrastructure should be increased rail output, reduced rail rates, reduced trucking output, and reduced truck rates.

Table 4.6 gives the equilibrium rates and output that would result in each of the rail and trucking markets under the specified track or capital changes. As was true in the partial equilibrium analysis, the greatest changes result from a 10-percent reduction in low-density track, followed by a 10-percent increase in WS capital. Relatively little change results from reduction in general route-miles, and reductions in general route-miles accompanied by a reduction in WS capital act perversely and actually lead to rail rate increases and traffic reductions.

Table 4.7 shows how these general equilibrium effects are divided among the proximate effects caused by the infrastructure change directly, and the second-order effects caused by the general equilibrium response of the system. Thus, for example, table 4.7 indicates that the marginal rail costs of shipping manufactured goods in the Official Region shifts from 4.593¢/ton-mile to 4.399¢/ton-mile as a result of increasing WS capital by 10 percent.[15] This increase in WS capital also directly reduces rail marginal costs of bulk commodities from 1.521¢/ton-mile to 1.495¢/ton-mile. These reductions in the marginal cost schedule lead to ceteris paribus reductions in rail rates and subsequent shifts in the demand and marginal cost curves throughout the system. The shifts that occur at the final equilibrium are given in the row marked Final. Thus the changes in output levels and mixes that result from the general equilibrium effects cause the marginal rail costs of manufactured goods to rise from 4.399¢/ton-mile to 4.432¢/ton-mile and lead to similar shifts in the rail marginal cost schedule for bulk commodities. However, these secondary shifts are quite minor compared to the initial shift. Similarly, the shift in the trucking demand function occasioned by the fall in rail rates is relatively modest and the subsequent shifts in rail demand function and trucking marginal cost function are negligible.

Thus the simulation analysis is consistent with economic intuition: reduction in rail marginal costs leads to reduction in competitive rail rates, which causes inward shifts in trucking demand functions of a lesser order of magnitude.

Since output levels and rates change in a general equilibrium setting,

Table 4.6 Comparative Static Equilibrium Specified Infrastructure Changes, Official and South–West Regions, 1972

	Manufactured commodities				Bulk commodities			
	Rail		Truck		Rail		Truck	
	¢/ton-mile	bill. ton-miles	¢/ton-mile	bill. ton-miles	¢/ton-mile	bill. ton-miles	¢/ton-mile	bill. ton-miles
Official								
Competitive equilibrium	4.590	30.284	4.505	49.206	1.521	76.469	3.693	22.248
10% rise in WS capital	4.413	32.095	4.513	48.589	1.490	78.707	3.702	22.184
10% reduction in low-density route-miles	4.416	32.063	4.514	48.589	1.478	79.554	3.703	22.115
10% reduction in general route-miles	4.548	30.697	4.507	49.057	1.508	77.442	3.695	22.332
10% reduction in total route-miles	4.377	32.501	4.516	48.439	1.464	80.584	3.706	22.018
10% reduction in low-density route-miles + WS capital	4.484	31.355	4.510	48.827	1.490	78.672	3.699	22.209
10% reduction in general route-miles + WS capital	4.755	28.730	4.498	49.756	1.543	75.039	3.685	22.600
South–West								
Competitive equilibrium	2.979	148.932	4.610	42.122	1.043	237.234	3.975	16.002
10% rise in WS capital	2.915	153.097	4.609	41.712	1.026	241.916	3.975	15.796
10% reduction in low-density route-miles	2.866	156.358	4.608	41.401	1.004	248.608	3.974	15.506
10% reduction in general route-miles	2.954	150.548	4.610	41.963	1.032	240.485	3.975	15.858
10% reduction in total route-miles	2.841	158.090	4.607	41.238	0.992	252.069	3.974	15.359
10% reduction in low-density route-miles + WS capital	2.884	155.123	4.609	41.519	1.008	247.216	3.974	15.566
10% reduction in general route-miles + WS capital	3.027	145.979	4.610	42.421	1.050	235.326	3.976	16.086

Table 4.7 Value of Demand and Marginal Cost Curves at Selected Points, by Mode, Commodity and Selected Infrastructure Changes, Official and South–West Regions, 1972[a]

	Manufactured commodities				Bulk commodities			
	Rail		Truck		Rail		Truck	
	$Q = 30.0$ MC	$p = 4.5$ Q	$Q = 50.0$ MC	$p = 4.5$ Q	$Q = 76.0$ MC	$p = 1.5$ Q	$Q = 22.0$ MC	$p = 4.5$ Q
Official Region								
Absolute value								
Competitive equilibrium	4.593	31.171	4.498	49.276	1.521	77.940	3.697	17.130
10% rise in WS capital	4.399	–	–	–	1.495	–	–	–
Final	4.432	31.197	4.450	48.771	1.485	78.004	3.704	16.994
10% fall in low-density route-miles	4.392	–	–	–	1.446	–	–	–
Final	4.436	31.200	4.501	48.701	1.471	78.009	3.704	16.941
10% fall in general track	4.541	–	–	–	1.499	–	–	–
Final	4.555	31.178	4.499	49.159	1.505	77.959	3.699	17.070
10% fall in total track	4.342	–	–	–	1.426	–	–	–
Final	4.400	31.207	4.502	48.662	1.456	78.028	3.708	16.880
10% fall in low-density track + WS capital	4.465	–	–	–	1.470	–	–	–
Final	4.497	31.189	4.500	48.975	1.485	77.984	3.701	16.994
10% fall in general track + WS capital	4.762	–	–	–	1.569	–	–	–
Final	4.740	31.149	4.496	49.733	1.545	77.888	3.691	17.219

Table 4.7 (continued)

| | Manufactured commodities | | | | Bulk commodities | | | |
| | Rail | | Truck | | Rail | | Truck | |
	$Q = 30.0$ MC	$p = 4.5$ Q	$Q = 50.0$ MC	$p = 4.5$ Q	$Q = 76.0$ MC	$p = 1.5$ Q	$Q = 22.0$ MC	$p = 4.5$ Q
Percentage change								
Base = competitive equilibrium								
10% rise in WS capital	−4.23	–	–	–	−1.71	–	–	–
Final	−3.51	0.08	−1.07	−1.15	−2.37	0.03	0.19	−0.79
10% fall in low-density route-miles	−4.38	–	–	–	−4.93	–	–	–
Final	−3.42	0.06	0.07	−1.16	−3.29	0.09	0.19	−1.10
10% fall in general track	−1.13	–	–	–	−1.45	–	–	–
Final	−0.83	0.02	0.02	−0.24	−1.05	0.02	0.05	−0.35
10% fall in total track	−5.47	–	–	–	−6.27	–	–	–
Final	−4.20	0.12	0.04	−1.25	−4.27	0.11	0.30	−1.46
10% fall in low-density track + WS capital	−2.79	–	–	–	−3.35	–	–	–
Final	−2.09	0.06	0.04	−0.61	−2.37	0.06	0.11	−0.79
10% fall in general track + WS capital	3.68	–	–	–	3.16	–	–	–
Final	3.20	−0.07	−0.04	0.93	1.58	−0.07	−0.16	0.52

Table 4.7 (continued)

| | Manufactured commodities | | | | Bulk commodities | | | |
| | Rail | | Truck | | Rail | | Truck | |
	$Q = 150.0$ MC	$p = 3.0$ Q	$Q = 40.0$ MC	$p = 4.5$ Q	$Q = 240.0$ MC	$p = 1.0$ Q	$Q = 16.0$ MC	$p = 4.0$ Q
South–West Region								
Absolute values								
Competitive equilibrium	2.980	147.625	4.607	43.612	1.044	249.685	3.975	15.823
10% rise in WS capital	2.905	–	–	–	1.020	–	–	–
Final	2.911	147.616	4.606	43.197	1.026	249.677	3.975	15.614
10% fall in low-density route-miles	2.846	–	–	–	0.991	–	–	–
Final	2.861	147.608	4.606	42.865	1.000	249.669	3.975	15.322
10% fall in general track	2.949	–	–	–	1.029	–	–	–
Final	2.953	147.620	4.606	43.462	1.031	249.681	3.975	15.678
10% fall in total track	2.816	–	–	–	0.976	–	–	–
Final	2.835	147.603	4.606	42.691	0.987	249.665	3.975	15.174
10% fall in low-density track + WS capital	2.867	–	–	–	0.997	–	–	–
Final	2.880	147.610	4.606	42.990	1.005	249.671	3.975	15.382
10% fall in general track + WS capital	3.033	–	–	–	1.056	–	–	–
Final	3.031	147.631	4.607	43.947	1.052	249.690	3.976	15.910

Table 4.7 (continued)

	Manufactured commodities				Bulk commodities			
	Rail		Truck		Rail		Truck	
	$Q = 150.0$ $p = 3.0$ MC Q		$Q = 40.0$ $p = 4.5$ MC Q		$Q = 240.0$ $p = 1.0$ MC Q		$Q = 16.0$ $p = 4.0$ MC Q	
	MC	Q	MC	Q	MC	Q	MC	Q
Percentage change								
10% rise in WS capital	−2.52	—	—	—	−2.30	—	—	—
Final	−2.32	−0.01	−0.02	−0.95	−1.72	−0.01	0.0	−1.32
10% fall in low-density route-miles	−4.50	—	—	—	−5.08	—	—	—
Final	−3.99	−0.01	−0.02	−1.72	−4.21	−0.01	0.0	−3.71
10% fall in general track	−1.04	—	—	—	−1.44	—	—	—
Final	−0.91	−0.0	−0.02	−0.34	−1.25	0.0	0.0	−0.92
10% fall in total track	−5.50	—	—	—	−6.51	—	—	—
Final	−4.87	−0.01	−0.02	−2.11	−5.46	−0.01	−0.03	−4.10
10% fall in low-density track + WS capital	−3.79	—	—	—	−4.50	—	—	—
Final	−3.36	−0.01	−0.02	−1.43	−3.74	−0.01	0.0	−2.79
10% fall in general track + WS capital	1.78	—	—	—	1.17	—	—	—
Final	1.71	0.0	0.0	0.77	0.77	0.0	0.03	0.55

a. All outputs (Q) measured in billions of ton-miles; price (p) and marginal costs (MC) measured in ¢/ton-mile.

it is no longer possible to infer profitability changes from changes in costs alone. Hence table 4.8 gives the costs, revenues, and profit levels that would result in each market under the specified changes in routes or capital. Consistent with our earlier analysis, reduction in low-density route-miles and increases in WS capital lead to the greatest increases in profitability, while a reduction in general route-miles has relatively little impact on profitability.

A comparison of tables 4.5 and 4.8 indicates the danger of partial equilibrium analysis, however. The previous analysis assumed that rate levels and outputs would remain constant and merely estimated the cost savings that would accrue to the railroads as a result of reducing track or increasing roadbed capital. Once it is recognized that output levels and rates will change in response to the competitive structure of the system, however, it is clear that the results of the partial equilibrium analysis are highly misleading. For example, table 4.8 indicates that total rail costs may actually rise as a result of reducing low-density track because of the increase in output generated by cost savings.[16]

If demand is sufficiently elastic, and the inward shifts in the rail demand function are slight, then rate reductions will lead to revenue increases. Table 4.8 indicates that these increases are relatively modest, however, so that the net increase in profitability is quite small. For example, the 10-percent reduction in low-density route-miles only increases rail profits by $16 million in the Official Region and by $12 million in the South–West Region, representing respective savings per low-density route-miles of $10,052 and $4,420 in each region. Similarly, increasing WS capital by 10 percent increases profits by $28 million in the Official Region and by $36 million in the South–West Region. If we evaluate these increases at the steady state and impose an implicit zero rate of discount, we find that these returns represent a negative net return to capital in both regions (-1.65 percent in the Official Region and -1.31 percent in the South–West Region). Thus once general equilibrium effects in rates and output levels are taken into account, the profitability of infrastructure investments appears to be reduced considerably.

Of course, the present situation is clearly far removed from a competitive equilibrium, and it may well be the case that the cost savings given by the partial equilibrium analysis may be more relevant for short-run policy purposes than the profitability increases given by the general equilibrium analysis. Nevertheless, even in the absence of regulatory rate reform, it is true that markets and rates are not stable. Hence the general equilibrium changes probably give a more realistic measure

Table 4.8 Revenues, Costs, and Profits by Mode and Region under Specified Rail Infrastructure Changes, 1972

	Rail					Truck				
	Revenues			Costs[b] ($bill.)	Profits ($bill.)	Revenues			Costs[b] ($bill.)	Profits ($bill.)
	Manuf. ($bill.)	Bulk ($bill.)	Total[a] ($bill.)			Manuf. ($bill.)	Bulk ($bill.)	Total ($bill.)		
Official										
Competitive equilibrium	1.390	1.164	3.634	2.449	1.194	2.217	0.828	3.045	3.654	−0.609
10% rise in WS capital	1.416	1.173	3.669	2.447	1.222	2.193	0.821	3.014	3.619	−0.605
10% fall in low-density route-miles	1.416	1.176	3.672	2.462	1.210	2.193	0.819	3.012	3.617	−0.605
10% fall in general route-miles	1.396	1.168	3.644	2.449	1.195	2.211	0.825	3.036	3.644	−0.608
10% fall in total route-miles	1.422	1.180	3.682	2.472	1.210	2.188	0.816	3.004	3.607	−0.603
10% fall in low-density route-miles + WS capital	1.406	1.172	3.658	2.459	1.199	2.202	0.822	3.024	3.630	−0.606
10% fall in general route-miles + WS capital	1.366	1.158	3.604	2.440	1.164	2.238	0.833	3.071	3.684	−0.613
South–West										
Competitive equilibrium	4.437	2.475	8.194	6.546	1.627	1.942	0.636	2.578	2.712	−0.134
10% rise in WS capital	4.462	2.483	8.227	6.564	1.663	1.923	0.628	2.550	2.685	−0.135
10% fall in low-density route-miles	4.481	2.495	8.258	4.619	1.639	1.908	0.616	2.524	2.661	−0.137
10% fall in general route-miles	4.445	2.481	8.208	6.594	1.614	1.934	0.630	2.565	2.699	−0.134
10% fall in total route-miles	4.491	2.501	8.274	6.647	1.627	1.900	0.610	2.510	2.648	−0.138
10% fall in low-density route-miles + WS capital	4.474	2.492	8.248	6.620	1.628	1.913	0.618	2.532	2.668	−0.136
10% fall in general route-miles + WS capital	4.419	2.471	8.172	6.597	1.575	1.956	0.640	2.596	2.723	−0.127

a. Revenues include $1.080 billion from agricultural commodities, coal and passenger traffic in the Official Region and $1.282 billion from agricultural commodities, coal, and passenger traffic in the South–West Region.

b. Rail costs represent total variable costs; truck costs represent total costs.

of the ultimate returns to infrastructure investments and abandonments than those offered by the partial equilibrium changes. Thus it might be reasonable to view the partial equilibrium analysis as representing the short-term effects of infrastructure changes, with the general equilibrium analysis representing the longer-term effects of these changes, when competitive pricing forces are given a chance to operate.

4.3 Infrastructure Changes and Long-Run Marginal Costs

The previous section analyzed a number of specified changes in roadbed capital and network density upon the total costs and marginal costs of the stylized railroads in the Official and South–West Regions. As was discussed in the initial section of this chapter, however, there are wide divergences in the capitalization of the railroads in the sample, and hence wide divergences in the changes in the capital stock needed to enable the railroads to reach points of long-run equilibrium and hence attain long-run marginal costs. Thus this section explores the characteristics of the long-run cost functions of the railroads in the sample and the changes in the infrastructure implied by the attainment of these long-run costs. We thus first discuss the relationship between long-run returns to scale and short-run returns to scale and show how the latter can be obtained from the former. We then discuss the situation of the railroads with respect to long-run returns to scale and consider the levels of the optimal capital stock. We close by analyzing a number of alternative infrastructure policies designed to foster a private solution to the railroad problem.

4.3.1 Calculations of Long-Run Returns to Scale
Panzar and Willig (1977) have shown that multiple-output production displays (local) long-run returns to scale if and only if

$$\sum \frac{\partial \ln C^l}{\partial \ln \psi_i} < 1, \tag{4.2}$$

where C^l is a neoclassical long-run cost function. Short-run returns to scale are defined analogously with C^s, the short-run cost function, replacing C^l in (4.2).

The relation between long-run and short-run returns to scale can be seen as follows. At a long-run equilibrium, long-run total costs equal short-run total costs, that is,

$$C^l(\psi, w, t) = C^s(\psi, x_F^*, w_V, t) + w_F x_F^*, \tag{4.3}$$

where the subscripts F and V correspond to fixed and variable factors, respectively, and $w = [w_V, w_F]$, etc. Moreover, at the point of long-run equilibrium, the change in short-run costs with respect to the fixed factor must equal the (negative) value of the returns to that factor; thus

$$\frac{\partial C^s}{\partial x_F^*} = -w_F. \tag{4.4}$$

Finally, at long-run equilibrium, short-run marginal costs with respect to output must equal long-run marginal costs:

$$\frac{\partial C^s}{\partial \psi} = \frac{\partial C^l}{\partial \psi}. \tag{4.5}$$

It is then a matter of direct calculation [using $\Sigma \, \partial \ln C^l / \partial \ln \psi_i = 1/C^l \Sigma (\partial C^l / \partial \psi_i) \psi_i$] to show

$$\Sigma \frac{\partial \ln C^l}{\partial \ln \psi_i} = \frac{1}{1 - \Sigma(\partial \ln C^s / \partial \ln x_F^*)} \Sigma \frac{\partial \ln C^s}{\partial \ln \psi_i}. \tag{4.6}$$

This equation allows one to estimate long-run returns to scale, and thus the feasibility of marginal cost pricing, from an estimated short-run cost function provided one knows a point of long-run equilibrium.

4.3.2 Returns to Scale and the Historical Position of US Railroads, 1968–1970

In calculating (4.6), it is necessary to use a point of long-run equilibrium —one in which (4.4) holds. We have previously calculated that at the point of approximation a $1 increase in WS capital decreases variable costs by about 13.1¢. This is what we have called a gross rate of return of 13.1 percent. Allowing 1.2 percent for land-based taxes (see below) and 2 percent for depreciation, the hypothetical firm, represented by the point of approximation, would be in long-run equilibrium if it faced an opportunity cost of capital of 9.9 percent. Thus it is not unreasonable to assume that the point of approximation is also a point of long-run equilibrium in view of the bond range of 7–9 percent and the fact that equity capital commands a higher rate of return than capital raised through the issuance of debt.

Calculating (4.5) at the point of approximation gives a value for the long-run elasticity of cost with respect to output of 0.8655 with an estimated standard error of 0.0809. Thus it appears that for such a firm there are increasing returns to scale, although the hypothesis of constant returns to scale cannot be decisively rejected.

Before extending the analysis to specific roads in our sample, it is useful to examine the implications of this calculation at the point of approximation in detail. A policy of long-run marginal cost pricing would yield revenues exceeding variable costs by 23.5 percent; this corresponds to $95,048,000. Against this, taxes on profits and property (which are not included in variable cost), depreciation on WS capital, and a return to WS capital must be paid. Since most of the taxes to be paid are land based, an extrapolation of the ratio of these taxes to the value of WS capital on a national basis to our hypothetical road yields a tax bill of $16,241,000. This leaves a "profit" to the road of $78,807,000. Since the value of the WS capital in dollars for our hypothetical road is $1,319,200,000, this yields a rate of return (profit) before depreciation of 5.974 percent. Subtracting 2 percent for depreciation, this leaves a net return on WS capital of 3.974 percent.

The gap between the assumed 9.9-percent opportunity cost of capital and the 4.0-percent profit rate realized under marginal cost pricing is precisely what the estimate of 0.8655 as $\Sigma(\partial \ln C^l / \partial \ln \psi_i)$ indicates concerning returns to scale and the feasibility of marginal cost pricing. Since there are increasing returns to scale, the funds left over after paying other factors are not sufficient to compensate for the opportunity costs of capital.

Equation (4.6) indicates that as long as the elasticity of costs with respect to the fixed factor, WS capital, is negative (i.e., $\partial \ln C^s / \partial \ln x_F < 0$), the elasticity of long-run costs with respect to output will be less than the short-run elasticity of costs. Since all firms in our sample have a positive marginal product of capital (i.e., $\partial \ln C^s / \partial \ln x_F < 0$), those firms whose short-run cost elasticity of less than one will also have a long-run cost elasticity less than one. Hence only the larger firms are possible candidates for long-run marginal cost pricing. In table 4.9 we calculate the long-run returns to scale by assuming that 1969 was a point of long-run equilibrium and list the gross rates of return (of depreciation and taxes) that this assumes. We find one road has an estimated $\Sigma \partial \ln C^l / \partial \ln \psi_i$ that equals one, but that several other larger roads have values that fall very close to one. Given the standard error of our estimate even at the point of approximation, and the arbitrary opportunity costs assumed in these calculations, it seems possible that for the larger roads in the sample, unsubsidized marginal cost pricing would be feasible at

Table 4.9 Short-Run and Long-Run Economies of Scale, by Railroad, 1969

	Short-run returns to scale $(\Sigma \partial \ln C^s / \partial \ln \psi_i)$	Estimated gross rate of return	Long-run returns to scale $(\Sigma \partial \ln C^l / \partial \ln \psi_i)$
Atchison, Topeka & Santa Fe Ry.	1.3133	−0.1234	0.9588
Boston & Maine Corp.	0.6287	−0.0318	0.5304
Central R.R. Co. of New Jersey	0.7543	−0.0982	0.5415
Chicago & North Western Trans.	1.1581	−0.0678	0.8764
Chicago, Milwaukee, & St. Paul	1.0832	−0.0573	0.8325
Chicago, Rock Island & Pacific	0.9902	−0.0405	0.8625
Delaware & Hudson Ry. Co.	0.6135	−0.0370	0.5292
Erie-Lackawanna Ry. Co.	1.0364	−0.0906	0.7488
Grand Trunk Western R.R. Co.	0.7765	−0.1429	0.5889
Gulf Mobile & Ohio R.R. Co.	0.9281	−0.0617	0.7647
Illinois Central R.R. Co.	1.2091	−0.1106	0.8616
Missouri Pacific R.R. Co.	1.1008	−0.0537	0.9263
Penn Central Transportation Co.	1.4952	−0.1467	0.9670
Seaboard Coast Line R.R. Co.	1.3066	−0.1615	0.9481
Southern Pacific Transportation	1.3794	−0.1773	0.9990
Southern Ry. Co.	1.1456	−0.0952	0.9156
Texas & Pacific Ry. Co.	0.8126	−0.0525	0.7110
Union Pacific R.R. Co.	1.3117	−0.1358	0.9622
Western Pacific R.R. Co.	0.5843	−0.0272	0.5227

slightly higher traffic levels. In the next section, we analyze this possibility under the assumption of opportunity costs of capital of 9 percent and 4 percent.

4.3.3 Optimal WS Capital Stock and Long-Run Returns to Scale under Alternative Assumptions

To obtain the optimal capital stock, we solve (4.4) for the optimal amount of WS capital x_F^* at a given long-run return to capital w_F. In table 4.10 we thus present the actual 1969 capital stock (measured in 12/31/71 dollars) along with the capital stocks that would have been optimal (i.e., that minimized total cost) under the assumptions of 9-percent and 4-percent opportunity costs for capital at 1969 levels of input. The 9-percent opportunity cost represents an approximate value of the actual opportunity cost in 1969; 4 percent represents an opportunity cost that might obtain under a program of government-subsidized loans for WS

Table 4.10 Way-and-Structures Capital under Alternative Assumptions, by Railroad, 1969

	Actual 1969 capital stock ($)	Optimal stock—9-percent opportunity cost ($)	Optimal stock—4-percent opportunity cost ($)
Atchison, Topeka & Santa Fe Ry.	2,456,142,944	2,475,809,728	3,567,587,040
Boston & Maine Corp.	556,342,344	204,556,036	302,444,308
Central R.R. Co. of New Jersey	286,285,852	246,903,632	353,686,924
Chicago & North Western Trans.	1,777,987,904	1,173,499,568	1,703,280,400
Chicago, Milwaukee, & St. Paul	1,867,388,128	1,088,922,896	1,584,922,816
Chicago, Rock Island & Pacific	1,275,541,776	559,772,888	830,283,536
Delaware & Hudson Ry. Co.	240,534,884	98,655,374	146,230,940
Erie-Lackawanna Ry. Co.	1,368,074,544	1,115,932,976	1,601,103,696
Grand Trunk Western R.R. Co.	273,480,176	305,982,592	445,570,168
Gulf Mobile & Ohio R.R. Co.	402,110,944	242,593,232	358,505,340
Illinois Central R.R. Co.	1,463,778,720	1,369,939,728	1,960,008,112
Missouri Pacific R.R. Co.	1,426,682,688	773,845,184	1,145,149,264
Penn Central Transportation Co.	8,530,201,280	9,574,752,128	13,333,691,904
Seaboard Coast Line R.R. Co.	1,500,704,128	1,819,743,696	2,620,893,920
Southern Pacific Transportation	2,316,068,800	2,996,214,912	4,311,076,096
Southern Ry. Co.	1,112,486,176	927,891,456	1,365,158,000
Texas & Pacific Ry. Co.	315,801,132	168,415,378	249,385,334
Union Pacific R.R. Co.	1,860,276,128	2,003,867,504	2,892,163,936
Western Pacific R.R. Co.	363,934,248	119,531,114	176,896,296

rehabilitation. In both cases, we have assumed a depreciation rate of 2 percent and a taxation rate of 1.2 percent. Since, as noted earlier, the marginal product of WS capital is positive and obeys the law of diminishing returns throughout the sample range, use of this factor increases as its price decreases. As table 4.10 shows, the optimal amount of WS capital varies considerably with opportunity cost.

This does not mean, however, that total economic costs are very responsive to the opportunity cost of WS capital. In table 4.11 we calculate the total cost of each railroad's services in 1969 using the actual and optimal capital stocks and a 9-percent opportunity cost for capital. For a surprising number of roads the efficiency losses due to a nonoptimal capital stock are quite small; in the aggregate, these losses are estimated to be about $180 million. While this loss is, of course, a deadweight burden, it is not clear how much of it is avoidable, in that it is difficult to vary WS capital in response to short-run fluctuations in the traffic

Table 4.11 Total Costs Assuming a 9-Percent Opportunity Cost for Way-and-Structures Capital, 1969

	Costs with actual capital stock ($)	Costs with optimal capital stock ($)	Losses due to a nonoptimal capital stock ($)
Atchison, Topeka & Santa Fe Ry.	921,311,208	921,168,528	142,679
Boston & Maine Corp.	134,421,840	116,473,507	17,948,332
Central R.R. Co. of New Jersey	87,616,680	87,228,265	388,414
Chicago & North Western Trans.	487,064,700	471,305,452	15,759,246
Chicago, Milwaukee, & St. Paul	479,818,908	454,594,100	25,224,807
Chicago, Rock Island & Pacific	415,229,744	383,730,592	31,499,152
Delaware & Hudson Ry. Co.	70,151,828	63,522,972	6,628,855
Erie-Lackawanna Ry. Co.	402,912,812	399,379,340	3,533,470
Grand Trunk Western R.R. Co.	128,457,490	128,219,389	238,100
Gulf Mobile & Ohio R.R. Co.	135,887,774	131,146,463	4,741,310
Illinois Central R.R. Co.	477,482,120	477,052,768	429,351
Missouri Pacific R.R. Co.	477,885,928	455,203,800	22,682,128
Penn Central Transportation Co.	2,742,794,560	2,732,732,640	10,061,908
Seaboard Coast Line R.R. Co.	678,351,816	673,628,224	4,723,592
Southern Pacific Transportation	1,120,593,680	1,106,579,344	14,014,329
Southern Ry. Co.	458,881,412	456,686,924	2,194,486
Texas & Pacific Ry. Co.	127,276,619	122,040,630	5,235,989
Union Pacific R.R. Co.	759,129,584	758,227,048	902,528
Western Pacific R.R. Co.	105,523,420	92,065,614	13,457,806

level. It should be noted, however, that for several railroads it is the case that these losses are comparatively large; for these roads it is improbable that these losses are transient.

Nonetheless, relatively large capital misallocations can be accommodated with little economic loss. The efficiency loss of the Penn Central's $1 billion capital shortage, for example, is $10 million; the capitalized value of this inefficiency is $110 million. The reason for this relatively small efficiency loss is that the elasticity of substitution between equipment capital and structures capital is quite high.

In table 4.12 we present the estimates of the long-run returns to scale corresponding to the three capital stocks of table 4.10. Almost without exception these estimates indicate increasing returns to scale. An interesting aspect of these estimates is that under the assumption of a 4-percent opportunity cost the railroads face greater returns to scale than they do with a 9-percent opportunity cost. Thus, a program of government

Table 4.12 Long-Run Returns to Scale, by Railroad, 1969

	Assuming observed point is a long-run equilibrium	Assuming a 9-percent opportunity cost	Assuming a 4-percent opportunity cost
Atchison, Topeka & Santa Fe Ry.	0.9588	0.9577	0.9179
Boston & Maine Corp.	0.5304	0.6635	0.6120
Central R.R. Co. of New Jersey	0.5415	0.5589	0.5170
Chicago & North Western Trans.	0.8764	0.9235	0.8813
Chicago, Milwaukee, & St. Paul	0.8325	0.8949	0.8516
Chicago, Rock Island & Pacific	0.8625	0.9686	0.9186
Delaware & Hudson Ry. Co.	0.5292	0.6506	0.5976
Erie-Lackawanna Ry. Co.	0.7488	0.7714	0.7311
Grand Trunk Western R.R. Co.	0.5889	0.5756	0.5293
Gulf Mobile & Ohio R.R. Co.	0.7647	0.8281	0.7792
Illinois Central R.R. Co.	0.8616	0.8687	0.8299
Missouri Pacific R.R. Co.	0.9263	1.0020	0.9539
Penn Central Transportation Co.	0.9670	0.9558	0.9238
Seaboard Coast Line R.R. Co.	0.9481	0.9271	0.8871
Southern Pacific Transportation	0.9990	0.9710	0.9317
Southern Ry. Co.	0.9156	0.9371	0.8909
Texas & Pacific Ry. Co.	0.7110	0.7954	0.7430
Union Pacific R.R. Co.	0.9622	0.9538	0.9136
Western Pacific R.R. Co.	0.5227	0.6789	0.6248

subsidized loans for track improvement will move railroads further from a position for which unsubsidized[17] marginal cost pricing would be feasible.

The reason for this result can be seen as follows. Increasing the capital stock lowers the elasticity of variable (short-run) cost with respect to output ($\Sigma \ \partial \ln C^s / \partial \ln \psi_i$) since (heuristically) greater WS capital represents greater capacity.[18]

Since

$$\frac{\partial C^s}{\partial x} = \frac{\partial \ln C^s}{\partial \ln x} \frac{C^s}{x},$$
(4.7)

however, it is possible that increases in x lower $\partial C^s / \partial x$ in absolute value without affecting $\partial \ln C^s / \partial \ln x$ since such increases unambiguously lower C^s / x. This is in fact the case as table 4.13, which presents

Table 4.13 $\partial \ln C^s / \partial \ln x$ under Alternative Assumptions, by Railroad, 1969

	Observed point	9-percent opportunity cost	4-percent opportunity cost
Atchison, Topeka & Santa Fe Ry.	−0.3698	−0.3699	−0.3591
Boston & Maine Corp.	−0.1855	−0.2142	−0.2030
Central R.R. Co. of New Jersey	−0.3931	−0.3968	−0.3870
Chicago & North Western Trans.	−0.3215	−0.3336	−0.3227
Chicago, Milwaukee, & St. Paul	−0.3011	−0.3170	−0.3059
Chicago, Rock Island & Pacific	−0.1481	−0.1721	−0.1604
Delaware & Hudson Ry. Co.	−0.1592	−0.1847	−0.1735
Erie-Lackawanna Ry. Co.	−0.3841	−0.3900	−0.3796
Grand Truck Western R.R. Co.	−0.3185	−0.3150	−0.3044
Gulf Mobile & Ohio R.R. Co.	−0.2137	−0.2284	−0.2170
Illinois Central R.R. Co.	−0.4033	−0.4052	−0.3949
Missouri Pacific R.R. Co.	−0.1883	−0.2062	−0.1947
Penn Central Transportation Co.	−0.5461	−0.5428	−0.5333
Seaboard Coast Line R.R. Co.	−0.3780	−0.3724	−0.3620
Southern Pacific Transportation	−0.3807	−0.3736	−0.3628
Southern Ry. Co.	−0.2512	−0.2565	−0.2453
Texas & Pacific Ry. Co.	−0.1429	−0.1611	−0.1496
Union Pacific R.R. Co.	−0.3633	−0.3615	−0.3506
Western Pacific R.R. Co.	−0.1180	−0.1499	−0.1387

$\partial \ln C^s / \partial \ln x$ under the three assumptions, shows. Thus, the estimates of $\Sigma \ \partial \ln C^l / \partial \ln \psi_i$, given by the right-hand side of (4.7), decrease as the optimal WS capital stock grows, that is, as the relative price of WS capital falls.

This brings us to four questions. The first, posed previously, is whether the current rate structure reflects long-run marginal costs. If it does, then rate adjustments will not be necessary to achieve a neoclassical social welfare optimum provided the railroads can be appropriately subsidized. The second question is the size of the subsidy necessary to keep the railroads solvent assuming a 9-percent opportunity cost for WS capital, marginal cost pricing, and unchanged output and technological conditions. The third question is whether the economies of scale of table 4.12 could be exhausted by increasing freight traffic. If so, there is the possibility that a subsidy program could be avoided. Finally, the fourth question concerns the administration of a subsidy program: would

Table 4.14 Ratio of Average Revenues to Long-Run Marginal Costs for Passenger Service, by Railroad, 1969

	Observed point	9-percent opportunity cost	4-percent opportunity cost
Atchison, Topeka & Santa Fe Ry.	0.5283	0.5363	1.3528
Boston & Maine Corp.	−3.6034	0.8059	1.7434
Central R.R. Co. of New Jersey	2.6119	1.7884	6.0923
Chicago & North Western Trans.	1.4907	0.5925	1.3085
Chicago, Milwaukee, & St. Paul	1.6692	0.4392	0.9482
Chicago, Rock Island & Pacific	2.0600	0.1694	0.3189
Delaware & Hudson Ry. Co.	0.2771	0.0923	0.1358
Erie-Lackawanna Ry. Co.	1.8251	0.9448	4.9107
Grand Trunk Western R.R. Co.	0.2526	0.3000	0.6666
Gulf Mobile & Ohio R.R. Co.	0.3446	0.1936	0.2963
Illinois Central R.R. Co.	0.6179	0.5610	1.0158
Missouri Pacific R.R. Co.	0.2356	0.0543	0.1117
Penn Central Transportation Co.	2.6572	4.3857	−9.0206
Seaboard Coast Line R.R. Co.	0.4511	0.6148	1.4352
Southern Pacific Transportation	0.1319	0.2051	0.5594
Southern Ry. Co.	0.2694	0.2008	0.4144
Texas & Pacific Ry. Co.	0.0736	0.0303	0.0489
Union Pacific R.R. Co.	0.3105	0.3540	0.8785
Western Pacific R.R. Co.	0.3918	0.1203	0.1648

a government program that lowered the opportunity cost of WS capital, either through direct loans or guarantees, be feasible if accompanied by quantity constraints on the amount of the loans?

In tables 4.14 and 4.15 we present estimates of average revenue–long-run marginal cost ratio for passenger and freight service under each of the three assumptions concerning the cost-minimizing capital stock. As can be seen by comparing the appropriate columns of these tables, the effect of lowering the opportunity cost of WS capital is to increase these ratios, since a larger capital stock would lower marginal costs. At a 9-percent opportunity cost, most roads would face adverse incentives at the margin for freight service, whereas a 4-percent opportunity cost would, at the cost-minimizing capital stock, generate favorable or nearly favorable marginal incentives for most roads. Since marginal costs are of course estimated with error, it is possible that the freight rate structure in 1969 roughly reflected long-run marginal costs calculated at a 4-percent

Table 4.15 Ratio of Average Revenues to Long-Run Marginal Costs for Freight Service, by Railroad, 1969

	Observed point	9-percent opportunity cost	4-percent opportunity cost
Atchison, Topeka & Santa Fe Ry.	0.8340	0.8368	0.9658
Boston & Maine Corp	1.1748	0.9135	1.0113
Central R.R. Co. of New Jersey	1.0624	0.9942	1.1659
Chicago & North Western Trans.	0.7698	0.6631	0.7582
Chicago, Milwaukee, & St. Paul	0.8230	0.6844	0.7789
Chicago, Rock Island & Pacific	0.8988	0.7656	0.8287
Delaware & Hudson Ry. Co.	1.7941	1.4554	1.5999
Erie-Lackawanna Ry. Co.	0.8794	0.8071	0.9390
Grand Trunk Western R.R. Co.	1.0974	1.1436	1.3116
Gulf Mobile & Ohio R.R. Co.	1.2415	1.0868	1.2053
Illinois Central R.R. Co.	0.8305	0.8069	0.9420
Missouri Pacific R.R. Co.	0.9751	0.8475	0.9283
Penn Central Transportation Co.	0.5195	0.5548	0.6682
Seaboard Coast Line R.R. Co.	0.7305	0.7898	0.9129
Southern Pacific Transportation	0.8165	0.9065	1.0465
Southern Ry. Co.	1.0107	0.9597	1.0706
Texas & Pacific Ry. Co.	1.2080	1.0665	1.1543
Union Pacific R.R. Co.	0.8866	0.9129	1.0512
Western Pacific R.R. Co.	1.9085	1.5262	1.6564

opportunity cost for WS capital; but at the more realistic 9-percent opportunity cost, it would appear that rates were generally below long-run marginal costs. Thus, marginal cost pricing would probably have required an overall increase in freight rates in 1968–1970.

The size of the subsidy required to sustain long-run cost minimization and marginal cost pricing at existing output levels is calculated in table 4.16. The first column presents long-run total costs assuming a 9-percent opportunity cost for capital, while the second column presents the revenues that would be generated by marginal cost pricing. In calculating both columns, the actual output levels and technological conditions observed in 1969 were used. Since marginal cost pricing would generally have raised rates and thus lowered traffic, both columns are overstated, though, as we shall see, this source of error is probably small. The third column, the difference between costs and revenues, is the required subsidy. Since every road but the Missouri Pacific faces long-run increasing

Table 4.16 Subsidy Calculation for 9-Percent Opportunity Cost of Capital, by Railroad, 1969

	Costs ($)	Revenues ($)	Subsidy ($)
Atchison, Topeka & Santa Fe Ry.	921,168,528	882,186,944	38,981,582
Boston & Maine Corp.	116,473,507	77,279,898	39,193,609
Central R.R. Co. of New Jersey	87,228,265	48,748,391	38,479,874
Chicago & North Western Trans.	471,305,452	435,238,544	36,066,907
Chicago, Milwaukee, & St. Paul	454,594,100	406,818,048	47,776,051
Chicago, Rock Island & Pacific	383,730,592	371,688,644	12,041,948
Delaware & Hudson Ry. Co.	63,522,972	41,326,929	22,196,042
Erie-Lackawanna Ry. Co.	399,379,340	308,091,724	91,287,618
Grand Trunk Western R.R. Co.	128,219,389	73,799,945	54,419,444
Gulf Mobile & Ohio R.R. Co.	131,146,463	108,601,508	22,544,955
Illinois Central R.R. Co.	477,052,768	414,420,440	62,632,329
Missouri Pacific R.R. Co.	455,203,800	456,107,256	−903,456
Penn Central Transportation Co.	2,732,732,640	2,611,873,440	120,859,211
Seaboard Coast Line R.R. Co.	673,628,224	624,548,384	49,079,841
Southern Pacific Transportation	1,106,579,344	1,074,521,600	32,057,740
Southern Ry. Co.	456,686,924	427,964,984	28,721,943
Texas & Pacific Ry. Co.	122,040,630	97,075,089	24,965,541
Union Pacific R.R. Co.	758,227,048	723,171,344	35,055,705
Western Pacific R.R. Co.	92,065,614	62,498,912	29,566,701

returns to scale (see table 4.12, column 2), each road except the Missouri Pacific requires a subsidy if WS capital is to receive a 9-percent net rate of return and marginal cost pricing is to obtain. The sum of these subsidies in 1969 would have been about $785 million. Since these calculations assume an optimal capital stock, the $180 million efficiency loss calculated in table 4.11 would have been the economic losses borne by railroad owners under a policy of long-run marginal cost pricing and optimal subsidization in 1969.

Comparing the two figures—the $785 million economic loss (negative economic rent) and the $180 million efficiency loss—it would seem that the railroads' main long-run problem (provided they could obtain marginal cost pricing from the ICC) is one of classical long-run returns to scale at existing output levels rather than capital misallocation. As mentioned previously, however, it might be possible to exhaust the observed returns to scale by increasing traffic levels, so that traffic increases might obviate a subsidy program.

Since the long-run cost elasticities can be directly estimated from the short-run cost elasticities [by (4.6)], it is useful to consider these equations explicitly and analyze the role that output plays in determining short-run cost elasticities. The elasticity of short-run cost with respect to the fixed factor x_F, passenger output ψ_1, and freight output ψ_2 are given, respectively, by

$$
\frac{\partial \ln C}{\partial \ln x_F} = \underset{(0.117)}{-0.427} + \underset{(0.503)}{0.029 \ln x} - \underset{(0.184)}{0.087 \ln t_1} + \underset{(0.235)}{0.197 \ln t_2}
$$
$$
- \underset{(0.196)}{0.024 \ln t_3} + \underset{(0.100)}{0.028 \ln t_4} - \underset{(0.084)}{0.142 \ln \psi_1} - \underset{(0.360)}{0.035 \ln \psi_2}, \tag{4.8}
$$

$$
\frac{\partial \ln C}{\partial \ln \psi_1} = \underset{(0.0548)}{0.1129} - \underset{(0.0836)}{0.1417 \ln x} + \underset{(0.0477)}{0.0619 \ln \psi_1} + \underset{(0.0581)}{0.0573 \ln \psi_2}, \tag{4.9}
$$

$$
\frac{\partial \ln C}{\partial \ln \psi_2} = \underset{(0.0833)}{1.1289} - \underset{(0.3604)}{0.0346 \ln x} + \underset{(0.1495)}{0.1117 \ln t_1} - \underset{(0.1672)}{0.0847 \ln t_2}
$$
$$
- \underset{(0.1457)}{0.0312 \ln t_3} - \underset{(0.0820)}{0.03104 \ln t_4} + \underset{(0.0581)}{0.0573 \ln \psi_1}
$$
$$
+ \underset{(0.2260)}{0.1772 \ln \psi_2}, \tag{4.10}
$$

where:

$x = $ WS capital.

$t_1 = $ low-density route-miles.

$t_2 = $ total route-miles.

$t_3 = $ average length of haul.

$t_4 = $ traffic mix.

$\psi_1 = $ passenger output.

$\psi_2 = $ freight output.

These equations show that the main determinants of short-run returns to scale $(\partial \ln C^s / \partial \ln \psi_i)$ are the effects of ψ_1 and ψ_2. Although these effects are estimated with comparatively large standard errors, the differences in ψ_1 and ψ_2 among railroads are so large that differences between roads in $\Sigma \, \partial \ln C^s / \partial \ln \psi_i$ apparently can be discerned. Since the terms associated with $\ln \psi_1$ and $\ln \psi_2$ in (4.9) and (4.10) are positive, it is the case that there always exists some opportunity cost and traffic level such that scale economies are exhausted; but the required traffic levels

Table 4.17 Ton-Miles Required to Exhaust Returns to Scale for Capital Stock Optimal at 9-Percent Opportunity Cost, by Railroad, 1969

	Required ton-miles	Actual ton-miles	Ratio
Atchison, Topeka & Santa Fe Ry.	63,178,980	47,361,984	1.33
Boston & Maine Corp.	22,593,600	2,922,028	7.73
Central R.R. Co. of New Jersey	38,385,520	1,754,425	21.87
Chicago & North Western Trans.	31,028,090	18,624,224	1.66
Chicago, Milwaukee, & St. Paul	34,330,490	17,188,160	1.99
Chicago, Rock Island & Pacific	23,514,120	19,604,048	1.19
Delaware & Hudson Ry. Co.	27,880,920	3,514,551	7.93
Erie-Lackawanna Ry. Co.	75,924,440	15,505,454	4.89
Grand Trunk Western R.R. Co	48,183,330	2,949,481	16.33
Gulf Mobile & Ohio R.R. Co.	24,829,580	8,640,978	2.87
Illinois Central R.R. Co.	59,951,100	23,842,000	2.51
Missouri Pacific R.R. Co.	26,217,220	26,581,344	0.98
Penn Central Transportation Co.	123,858,900	88,155,744	1.40
Seaboard Coast Line R.R. Co.	51,311,400	31,131,520	1.64
Southern Pacific Transportation	80,596,840	66,205,376	1.21
Southern Ry. Co.	37,972,240	25,600,512	1.48
Texas & Pacific Ry. Co.	18,438,570	5,622,334	3.27
Union Pacific R.R. Co.	63,556,030	46,482,800	1.36
Western Pacific R.R. Co.	30,978,590	4,886,429	6.33

are typically quite high. For example, at the point of approximation, achieving the exhaustion of economies of scale by changing just freight traffic ψ_2 requires that ψ_2 increase by a factor of 2.3. For smaller firms even greater relative increases would be required, as shown in table 4.17. Moreover, it is not the case that, for every opportunity cost of WS capital and set of values for the arguments of the cost function other than ψ_2, one can construct a point such that long-run economies of scale are exhausted. Of course, since the standard errors of the coefficients of (4.8)–(4.10) are large, and since one is extrapolating far beyond the sample range, these calculations may well be meaningless. The purpose of such calculations however, is not to establish that returns to scale cannot be exhausted by increased traffic levels, but rather to establish that our estimates do not actively support the view that the exhaustion of returns to scale is "just around the corner." The former issue is probably best addressed by examining the measure of long-run returns to scale ($\Sigma \, \partial \ln C^l / \partial \ln \psi_i$) under the assumption that the point of approximation represents a long-run equilibrium. As calculated previously, $\Sigma \, \partial \ln C^l / \partial \ln \psi_i$ at that point is 0.8655 with an estimated standard error of 0.0809. In short, it appears that a decisive rejection of constant returns to scale at existing levels of output is not possible based upon the evidence produced in this study; but the evidence does *tend* to deny that hypothesis.

Since a subsidy program for the railroads appears necessary *if* long-run marginal cost pricing is to be adopted and technological conditions and output levels are to remain unchanged, it is appropriate to consider the administration of such a program. In theory, of course, one need only transfer to each road the appropriate amount of money; but the calculation of the appropriate subsidy presents obvious political and administrative difficulties. Current policy calls for loan guarantees and purchases of preference shares; as such it lowers the opportunity cost of WS capital. If firms face no quantity constraint under such a program, it is equivalent to lowering the price of one factor, namely, WS capital. As already noted, such a program would make unsubsidized marginal cost pricing even more infeasible. But the policy does contain quantity constraints; thus a natural question to consider is whether a policy of limited subsidized loans could be designed which would be administratively simple and convey the appropriate subsidy.

One way of envisioning such a policy is to compare it to nationalization. In the neoclassical theory of nationalization, the government sets the capital stock, using the market rate of interest as the social opportunity cost ("shadow price") of capital, and sets prices equal to marginal costs; the result, of course, is that revenues net of payments to variable factors do not meet the imputed fixed factor costs. However, if there are some funds left over after payments to variable factors, the government is earning some rate of return—lower than the market rate—on its investment in the fixed factor. In principle, then, it would be possible for the government to lend the entire fixed factor stock at this rate of interest to a private firm which would operate in the socially optimal manner.

Of course, the government need not lend the entire fixed factor stock for such a scheme to be feasible; the criterion is that the gap between the market rate of interest and that charged by the government times the amount lent by the government equal the total subsidy. Thus, if the total subsidy required by the railroads in 1969 was $785 million, then the minimum government investment required to achieve this subsidy would be ($785 million/0.09) = $8.72 billion. Obviously, this would be the capitalized cost of the government loan program regardless of the interest rates charged.

Table 4.18 Subsidy as a Percentage of Current Dollar Value of Way-and-Structures Capital, by Railroad, 1969

	Subsidy	Value of way-and-structures capital	Percentage
Atchison, Topeka & Santa Fe Ry.	38,981,582	2,037,850,608	1.91
Boston & Maine Corp.	39,193,609	168,371,034	23.27
Central R.R. Co. of New Jersey	38,479,874	203,227,538	18.93
Chicago & North Western Trans.	36,066,907	965,913,000	3.73
Chicago, Milwaukee, & St. Paul	47,776,051	896,297,544	5.33
Chicago, Rock Island & Pacific	12,041,948	460,751,692	2.61
Delaware & Hudson Ry. Co.	22,196,042	81,203,701	27.33
Erie-Lackawanna Ry. Co.	91,287,618	918,529,672	9.93
Grand Trunk Western R.R. Co.	54,419,444	251,855,708	21.60
Gulf Mobile & Ohio R.R. Co.	22,544,955	199,679,628	11.29
Illinois Central R.R. Co.	62,632,329	1,127,603,824	5.55
Missouri Pacific R.R. Co.	−903,456	636,955,600	−0.14
Penn Central Transportation Co.	120,859,211	7,881,023,424	1.53
Seaboard Coast Line R.R. Co.	49,079,841	1,497,839,584	3.27
Southern Pacific Transportation	32,057,740	2,466,198,560	1.29
Southern Ry. Co.	28,721,943	763,751,816	3.76
Texas & Pacific Ry. Co.	24,965,541	138,623,488	18.00
Union Pacific R.R. Co.	35,055,705	1,649,392,752	2.12
Western Pacific R.R. Co.	29,566,701	98,386,621	30.05

In table 4.18 we calculate the amount of the subsidy from table 4.16 as a percentage of the optimal stock (measured in 6/30/69 dollars). For eight roads comprising 9.8 percent of the sample's route-miles, this percentage exceeds the 9-percent opportunity cost of capital, indicating that the government could not achieve the required subsidy by lending funds for WS use only, but would also have to subsidize equipment capital.

The Railroad Revitalization and Regulatory Reform Act of 1976 provides for up to $600 million in redeemable preference share financing and $1 billion in loan guarantees for the rehabilitation and improvement of rail facilities and equipment. The former at best provides the equivalent of 30-year loans with no interest for the first 10 years and 2 percent thereafter; the latter is envisioned as lowering effective interest rates by 2 percentage points. In addition, the act provides for up to $2.1 billion in loans to Conrail, $1.75 billion in grants for a high-speed rail passenger system between Boston and Washington, and $360 million for operating subsidies for low-density service over 5 years.

With the exception of the low-density service subsidy and the passenger system grant, these programs are designed to increase the WS capital intensity of the railroads. Aside from implicit restrictions which limit funding to those "self-sustaining" railroads which are not abandoning the industry by excessive dividend payouts or diversification, there are no effective criteria in the act for distributing the $1.6 billion in preference shares and loan guarantees. Thus those roads which do qualify for the aid have an incentive, provided by the below-market interest rates, to overcapitalize. As noted above, this causes greater returns to scale at the margin, making marginal cost pricing even more infeasible. Moreover, if the opportunity cost of capital is evaluated at the nonsubsidized ("shadow price") rate, the total subsidy (which is the operating subsidy plus the foregone interest on the subsidized loan) required under marginal cost pricing to make the roads viable increases, and marginal costs will no longer represent social opportunity costs. In contrast, those roads which do not qualify, or do not choose to qualify (by refusing to meet the restrictions on dividends and diversification), receive no subsidy at all under this program, and will, if profit maximizing and not generating revenues sufficient to cover full economic costs, continue to follow a plan of "strategic" bankruptcy in the absence of merger alternatives.

If our analysis concerning returns to scale is correct, then the optimal policy must convey a subsidy to (nearly) all railroads without distorting the price of WS capital at the margin.[19] To do this through a loan program requires that an explicit calculation of the cost-minimizing capital stock be made and that the interest subsidy and loan amounts be calculated to convey the appropriate subsidy. Under an optimal program, restricting the loans to "self-sustaining" firms or those not abandoning the industry would be unnecessary since all firms would become viable and realize rates of return on shareholders' equity comparable to those available elsewhere in the economy.

Unfortunately, our analysis indicates that if output and technological conditions are to remain at their historical levels, the optimal program will require large government subsidies to maintain the rail system in its current configuration even if prices are set equal to marginal costs (and thus on the whole raised) and no traffic is thereby lost. While it must be emphasized that the estimate of the size of the subsidy is subject to considerable error, this suggests that a reconfiguration of the rail system would be desirable. In the next subsection we consider this possibility in the context of national transportation policy, and discuss some of the limitations of our analysis.

4.3.4 Long-Run Competitive Equilibrium

The discussion of the previous chapter indicated that if the railroads achieved a competitive equilibrium with their existing capital stock, they would still obtain a return to capital somewhat below the opportunity cost of capital, while the previous discussion in this chapter indicated that if the railroads achieved an optimal capital stock at existing output levels, they would also earn a return to capital that would be less than its opportunity cost. This raises the obvious question of what would happen to rail profitability if the railroads simultaneously achieved a competitive equilibrium and an optimal capital stock. Thus this section analyzes the implication of a long-run competitive equilibrium in which price equals long-run marginal cost and the capital stock is permitted to adjust to ensure that costs are minimized.

The optimal stock of capital can be obtained by equating the derivative of the total cost function with respect to WS capital with the opportunity cost of capital, that is, by solving the equation $\partial C^s / \partial x_F = -w_F$ for the amount of capital x_F. Since the arguments of $\partial C^s / \partial x_F$ contain the outputs of bulk and manufactured commodities, and since the arguments of the rail marginal cost functions contain the WS capital, the long-run competitive equilibrium can be obtained by adding (4.4) to the system of equations (3.1)–(3.8) that were used to calculate the short-run competitive equilibrium.

Table 4.19 presents the rates, output levels, costs, revenues, and profits that would obtain under a short-run competitive equilibrium under existing railroad WS capital and the values of these variables that would obtain under a long-run competitive equilibrium with the optimal capital stock. As opposed to the existing equilibrium, it is important to note that rail output would fall in a short-run competitive equilibrium. This implies that the existing capital stock is probably too large at the short-run competitive equilibrium and that short-run marginal costs are below long-run marginal costs. Table 4.19 corroborates this intuition. In the Official Region, which experienced a substantial reduction in rail output under competitive pricing, long-run marginal costs are substantially above short-run marginal costs, and a movement from short-run marginal cost pricing to long-run marginal cost pricing would raise rates by almost 40 percent on manufactured goods and by 15 percent on bulk commodities. In contrast, rail rates would only rise by approximately

Table 4.19 Short-Run and Long-Run Competitive Equilibria, Rail and Trucking Industries, Bulk and Manufactured Goods, Official and South-West Regions, 1972

| | Short-run competitive equilibrium | | | | Long-run competitive equilibrium | | | |
| | Rail | | Truck | | Rail | | Truck | |
	Official	South-West	Official	South-West	Official	South-West	Official	South-West
Manufactured output (bill. ton-mile)	30.284	148.932	49.206	42.122	18.302	139.193	54.365	43.124
Bulk output (bill. ton-mile)	76.469	237.234	22.248	16.002	63.243	226.241	24.121	16.500
Manufactured rate (¢/ton-mile)	4.590	2.979	4.505	4.610	6.385	3.143	4.444	4.613
Bulk rate (¢/ton-mile)	1.521	1.043	3.693	3.975	1.747	1.085	3.622	3.977
Total revenue ($bill.)[a]	3.634	8.194	3.045	2.578	3.354	8.117	3.290	2.645
Total costs ($bill.)[b]	2.440	6.567	3.654	2.716	2.355	6.575	3.933	2.775
Profits ($bill.)	1.194	1.627	−0.609	−0.138	0.999	1.542	−0.643	−0.130
Way-and-structures capital ($bill.)	17.997	19.000	na	na	8.962	15.136	na	na
Net return to capital (%)	3.43	5.36	na	na	7.948	6.988	na	na
Subsidy required to achieve 9% return to capital ($bill.)	1.001	0.691	na	na	0.094	0.305	na	na

a. Rail revenues include $1.080 from "other" bulk commodities and passenger traffic in the Official Region, and $1.287 from "other" bulk commodities and passenger traffic in the South-West Region.
b. Rail variable costs; truck total costs.

5 percent in the South–West Region. Thus compared with the short-run competitive equilibrium, the long-run competitive equilibrium would be characterized by less rail output and high rail rates and marginal costs, and more truck output and slightly lower truck rates and marginal costs.

It is interesting to compare the profitability of the railroads in the short-run and the long-run competitive equilibria. In the first case, railroads in each region would cover variable costs and earn a net return on their capital of 3.43 percent in the Official Region and 5.36 percent in the South–West Region. Given the size of their capital stock, this implies substantial subsidies in the Official Region of approximately $1.0 billion, and in the South–West Region of $0.7 billion, to permit the railroads sufficient revenue to maintain their capital stock adequately and to achieve a net return of 9.0 percent. The corresponding subsidies in the long-run equilibrium would be approximately $0.1 and $0.3 billion in the Official and South–West Regions, respectively, indicating that nearly normal returns to capital could be obtained. If accompanied by other infrastructure changes, such as abandonment of low-density lines, it is possible that the railroads could be self-supporting in a long-run competitive equilibrium.

In assessing the feasibility of achieving a long-run competitive equilibrium, however, it is important to stress that it reflects a major departure from the existing equilibrium. This is particularly true in the Official Region, where a long-run competitive equilibrium would be characterized by a 50-percent reduction in WS capital, rate increases on manufactured goods in excess of 100 percent, and reductions in traffic in manufactured goods in excess of 75 percent. Similar changes would occur in the South–West Region, although of considerably smaller magnitudes. A long-run competitive equilibrium would be characterized, therefore, by even greater income changes than the short-run competitive equilibrium.

Nevertheless, this analysis does indicate that there may be a combination of rates and WS capital that could permit the railroads to be self-sufficient and earn returns on capital that are competitive with other sectors in the economy. However, as opposed to the existing situation, this rail system would be characterized by a heavy reliance on bulk traffic, high rates on manufactured goods, limited manufactured traffic, and a greatly reduced network and scope of service. Thus while this rail system could be economically viable, it would also be one that performed relatively few of the quasi-public functions that the current rail system provides.

4.4 Implications for National Transportation Policy

The analysis of railroad costs given in this chapter has some clear implications for railroad policy with respect to mergers and abandonments. In particular, the findings of this chapter indicate that mergers of similar railroads that do not substantially affect operations (by changing average length of haul, for instance) or do not eliminate low-density line are not likely to be successful. The reason for this, and similar results, is that while a 1-percent increase in traffic at constant network size, average length of haul, and low-density branchline mileage increases long-run costs by less than 1 percent, the elasticity of long-run cost with respect to a uniform percentage increase in traffic, network size, and low-density line is more than 1. Since the current freight rate structure does not distinguish branchline traffic or traffic switching roads [see Harris (1977a) on the former], the traffic of the combined roads will generate the same revenues but actually cost more.

This indicates that at least around the point of approximation,[20] which corresponds to a rather large hypothetical railroad, there are managerial diseconomies of railroad size. Thus mergers of large roads which do not increase average length of haul are likely to be unsuccessful, while those increasing average length of haul (end-to-end mergers) balance a real operational economy against the managerial diseconomy and therefore have better prospects.

A second policy that is likely to be unsuccessful is the rehabilitation of low-density branchline track. As we have seen, the total effect of capital misallocations is small, and low-density branchline service is at least as labor intensive as other service; thus savings on branchline track rehabilitation are likely to be small. Moreover, it should be recognized that providing service along these lines is very expensive; thus, a move in the direction of marginal cost pricing would be to raise rates on shipments originating or terminating on such lines. This would further reduce traffic on these lines, so that the total savings would be even less than otherwise anticipated.

An important limitation of our analysis is that it cannot quantify the effects of a massive abandonment of low-density branchlines. This is a limitation imposed both by the functional form we have used (which is not well behaved as its arguments approach zero) and by the fact that such an abandonment would cause fundamental changes in the underlying technology. This latter limitation also applies to any large change in the technological conditions faced by railroads.

Nevertheless, the marginal effects of such changes can be evaluated, so that a sort of piecemeal welfare analysis can be performed. In doing so, two issues must be distinguished. The first is whether the proposed changes are welfare increasing, that is, whether the changes will reduce costs by more than the eliminated services are worth. (Evaluating the latter is particularly difficult since we do not have marginal cost pricing.) The second is whether the proposed changes make unsubsidized marginal cost pricing more feasible. As a practical matter, one prefers schemes that will allow unsubisidized marginal cost pricing because of the administrative and political difficulties of calculating and conveying the appropriate subsidy. In principle, of course, once the technological conditions are fixed, marginal cost pricing and, if necessary, appropriate subsidies, are always preferred to other pricing schemes.

At the margin, low-density branchline abandonment is almost certainly desirable, given its high cost [see Harris (1977a) for a simulation of the effects of branchline abandonments]. Our estimates of $\partial \ln C^s/\partial \ln \psi_1$, $\partial \ln C^s/\partial \ln \psi_2$, and $\partial \ln C^s/\partial \ln x$ are such that it appears that the infeasibility of marginal cost pricing would not be affected by such abandonment, but these estimates are imprecise. One cause for optimism is that our estimates do tend to indicate that such abandonment would lower the marginal costs of other shipments, so that traffic levels under marginal cost pricing might not fall.

An analogous situation obtains with respect to short-haul traffic in manufactured goods: roads specializing in such traffic tend to have higher costs. Without a detailed analysis of the rate structure and a cost function more disaggregated by commodity type, it is not possible to determine whether a reallocation of this traffic to motor carriers would be desirable. But certainly such a policy should be considered, and the tools for such an analysis are now available.

Finally, perhaps the most pressing policy issue facing the railroads is whether they can be economically viable and self-sustaining without government subsidy. In this connection, the analysis of this and the previous chapter are generally encouraging. Specifically, the previous chapter indicated that if a competitive equilibrium were achieved with the existing stock of WS capital, the railroads in the Official and South-West Regions would earn respective returns of 3.43 and 5.36 percent. If, however, a long-run competitive equilibrium were achieved, these railroads would earn respective returns of 7.95 and 6.99 percent. Thus this analysis indicates that competitive pricing in conjunction with optimal adjustments in the capital stock and some truck abandonment could possibly permit the railroads to earn a normal return on capital.

These findings should give considerable encouragement to rail policy planners. While we find some evidence of long-run economies of scale at existing levels of output, it appears that they are substantially attenuated at a long-run competitive equilibrium. In particular, if the long-run competitive equilibrium were accompanied by some low-density line abandonment, the railroads could probably be self-sufficient. Therefore, there appears to be no inherent tendency toward increasing returns to scale or natural monopoly.

Nevertheless, it is important to stress that although a long-run competitive equilibrium may reflect a viable economic solution, it also represents a dramatic shift in government policy regarding the structure of rail rates and rail service. This is particularly true in the Official Region, where its establishment would cause considerable dislocation to shippers of manufactured goods since rail rates on these goods are projected to rise by more than 100 percent and rail carriage of these goods is projected to fall by approximately 75 percent. Thus in the Official Territory at least, it appears that the primary beneficiaries of the current policies are the shippers of manufactured goods. Indeed, the subsidy required to enable the railroads in the Official Region to be self-supporting is quite close to the income transfer that was estimated to arise from current pricing policies. In a very real sense, then, the subsidy that is required to permit the continuation of the present policies is not a rail subsidy but is in fact a shipper subsidy.

This analysis indicates, therefore, that there does appear to be a rail system that could be self-supporting. But, particularly in the Official Region, this railroad would be quite different from the current rail system and would perform very different services at very different rates than those presently performed. Consequently the real policy choice is whether society wants financially viable railroads that perform services that meet the standards of private market profitability, or whether it wants railroads to perform public service activities that require subsidy. In view of the declining nature of the Northeast economy, it may well be that subsidies are the appropriate policy. But in this case, it is imperative to make clear that the railroads are merely the vehicle through which shipper subsidies are made.

If the railroads are currently earning low returns on capital (or even making losses on their variable cost), it is not primarily because they are poorly managed or inefficient, but because current regulatory policies require them to carry large volumes of traffic at rates that are noncompensatory and to maintain large infrastructures that are inherently uneconomic. With smaller infrastructure and compensatory rates the railroads could be self-sufficient. Thus the rail problem is not really a rail problem per se but rather a public policy problem of the rate and service levels that are deemed to be socially acceptable to certain shipper groups. If these rate and service levels differ from profitable rate and service levels, a subsidy may be justified. But in making this subsidy, it should be clear that it is to shippers rather than to railroads. To place the discussion, as is currently done, in terms of rail subsidies rather than shipper subsidies only serves to confuse the issue since it transforms what should be a shipper problem into a rail problem. Thus at the very least, it is important that the debate be posed in its proper context: does social policy requires the railroads to perform noncompensatory uneconomic service?; if so, to what extent is society willing to pay a shipper subsidy through the railroads for the maintenance of this service?

Notes

1. Harris (1977b) has attempted to incorporate the route network into his analysis and has found that the nature of the route utilization has a significant impact on costs.

2. See, for example, Keeler (1974), Caves et al. (1980a), and appendix B.

3. For example, Keeler (1974) argues that the bulk of rail track is superfluous and that savings of approximately $3 billion could be obtained by suitable abandonment.

4. Harris (1977b) has found that light-density lines generate substantial traffic volumes.

5. Although WS capital is a fixed factor instead of a technological variable, we refer to it as a technological variable for notational simplicity.

6. These figures were based on a restricted model in which the coefficients' interaction terms between the technological variables are restricted to equal zero. These restrictions cannot be rejected using the likelihood ratio test [$\chi^2 = 1.68$; $\chi^2(5) = 1.92$ at the 0.75 level].

7. These figures are also based on the regression which restricts the coefficients on the interaction terms between the technological variables to be zero.

8. Moreover, the functional form employed allows $\partial \ln C / \partial \ln t_1$ to vary only with factor prices, capital, and the level of freight output, so that estimates of $\partial C / \partial t_1$ for firms with small amounts of low-density mileage—such as the Western Pacific and the Delaware and Hudson—may be spuriously high since C/t_1 will be large.

9. As an alternative, we could assume that capital is evenly distributed over mainline track and low-density track and reduce WS capital by 7.3 percent in the South–West Region and by 6.4 percent in the Official Region, reflecting the distribution of low-density track. Since this doubtless underestimates the capital reduction associated with an abandonment of ordinary track, it was felt that the other approach was preferable. Thus a 10-percent reduction in ordinary track in conjunction with no changes in WS capital and a 10-percent change in WS capital set the limits for the cost changes associated with such a change.

10. In determining the rate of return to investments we subtract 3.2 percentage points from

the gross return to reflect depreciation and property taxes. Thus an opportunity cost of capital of 9.0 percent corresponds to a gross return on capital of 12.2 percent.

11. Given the confidence intervals on the individual railroads given in table 4.4, it should be clear that the figures of $3 and $4 million are not significantly different from zero.

12. These figures are somewhat higher than the average cost savings of $66,313 that were estimated at the mean in the previous section, and reflect the impact on traffic levels and factor utilization as output diverges from the mean.

13. For the stylized firm in the Official Region, low-density route-miles account for 35.8 percent of the total, while for the South–West Region this figure is 27.0 percent.

14. The differentials between these figures and those obtained directly from increases in WS capital reflect the differences in the allocation of capital between general track and low-density track.

15. Note that these changes in marginal costs are not comparable to the changes in marginal costs estimated in table 4.5 since the points of evaluation are somewhat different.

16. Although this result may appear counterintuitive, it arises because output rises proportionately more than costs fall.

17. That is, marginal cost pricing would require subsidies in addition to those of the hypothetical loan program.

18. Actually, in our estimates nearly all of this effect on elasticity is related to passenger service.

19. The latter is important not only because it preserves the equality of marginal and social opportunity costs, but also because lowering this price makes marginal cost pricing even more infeasible.

20. At small network sizes, increases in network size actually decrease costs somewhat; this indicates that smaller roads might benefit from "uniform" size increases of the type discussed. This seems to imply that an "optimal" railroad size for given traffic, characterized by haul, mix, etc., exists; but our estimates are too imprecise to calculate such a size with any degree of confidence.

Chapter 5

Deregulation and Competition among Common Carriers of General Commdities

5.1 Introduction and Overview

The regulated trucking market can be segmented into two distinct groups: common carriers of general commodities and common carriers of specialized commodities. General commodity carriers tend to specialize in relatively small shipments and hence are characterized by less-than-truckload (LTL) carriage and terminal consolidation. As LTL carriers of general commodities, their traffic encompasses the spectrum of manufactured and related goods that are suitable for truck transport, and their customers tend to be relatively small shippers who do not generate a sufficient volume to support rail or full-truckload operations. In contrast, the carriers of specialized commodities utilize full-truckload (TL) operations and perform few, if any, consolidation functions. While their traffic also includes the spectrum of manufactured goods, these carriers tend to compete directly with the railroads and hence concentrate on large-load, long-haul traffic.

Since common carriers of general commodities tend to serve small shippers in rural areas who have few other sources of transportation, considerable concern has arisen whether the interests and needs of these shippers would be adequately served in an environment in which trucking were deregulated. Particular concern has focused upon the possible existence of economies of scale among these carriers and the possible existence of cross subsidies between shipments utilizing high-density corridors and shipments using low-density corridors. If economies of scale exist, in the advent of deregulation these shippers might find themselves captives of monopolistic trucking firms who would then attempt to raise rates to their monopoly levels. If a cross subsidy exists between light-density and high-density traffic, in the advent of deregulation shippers in light-density corridors might find themselves subject to substantial rate increases as carriers attempted to raise their profit margins to "normal" levels on low-density traffic. Thus there is a fundamental concern that deregulation might lead to substantial rate increases to shippers in rural areas and small cities and towns.

Economists generally believe that the general commodity trucking industry would be competitively organized in the absence of regulation.

Since this industry is characterized by low capital requirements, they feel that there is nothing inherent in the structure of technology that would indicate the existence of barriers to entry or economies of scale. Thus, in the absence of regulation, one would expect the general commodity trucking industry to be characterized by a large number of small firms, each operating at the minimum point of its average cost curve. In this case, the costs and service levels available to firms serving light-density regions would be the same as those available to high-density regions. Consequently, small shippers in small, rural communities should expect to face the same rate structure and receive the same levels of service as large shippers in large, urban areas. Thus, most economists believe that there is nothing inherent in the structure of the industry to indicate that the general public interest is served by regulation.

Advocates of regulation take a diametrically opposed view. According to them, the trucking industry is not only characterized by economies of scale but also economies of density. Thus, average costs not only fall with the size of the firm, but also with the volume of traffic over the network. Since small rural communities do not have sufficient traffic volumes to support a large number of efficiently sized firms, advocates of regulation feel that in the absence of regulation these communities could expect to experience a reduction in service and higher rates as they faced either efficient monopolistic carriers or small, inefficient carriers.

The recent merger movement in the general commodity trucking industry has lent considerable support to the regulationists' view. In recent years, the industry has been marked by a large number of mergers and acquisitions, in that large firms have either acquired or merged with smaller firms to extend their operating rights. Thus, the industry has become more concentrated, and large firms have become significantly larger. Since trucking firms essentially face a regulated price, this indicates that they perceive the existence of rather marked economies of scale; for a given regulated rate structure, a larger scale of operations should yield lower costs and thus higher profits. But if larger firms are in fact more efficient than smaller firms, small rural communities could suffer substantial reductions in service and increases in rates in the advent of deregulation.

It may be possible to reconcile these conflicting views by distinguishing between technological and regulatory economies of scale. Technological economies of scale are inherent in the structure of technology, while regulatory economies of scale are caused by the structure of regulation.

Because regulated trucking firms are typically limited in the commodities they can carry or the routes they can cover, by acquiring firms with different operating rights regulated trucking firms can obtain longer hauls, higher load factors, fewer empty backhauls, and thus lower operating costs. Consequently, larger firms may be more profitable not because their costs are inherently lower, but because they can obtain higher utilization of equipment through diversified operating rights. Since many of the recent mergers have been characterized by the extension of operating rights and authorities, this indicates that if economies of scale do in fact exist, they may be of a regulatory rather than a technological nature. This implies, of course that economies of scale would not exist if any carrier were free to carry any commodity to any place along any route. Thus, in a deregulated environment, the presently observed cost differentials among firms of different sizes and different kinds of operating authorities would not exist.

The question of the existence of regulatory as opposed to technological economies of scale has been analyzed by Friedlaender (1978b), Spady (1979), and Spady and Friedlaender (1978), who find evidence that the apparent economies of scale in the general commodity trucking industry arise primarily from operating characteristics rather than from size per se. Thus, once differences in length of haul, size of shipment, etc., are taken into account, one finds little, if any, evidence of economies of scale. In the absence of regulation, therefore, it is likely that shippers would generally face carriers with essentially constant or even increasing costs.

However, even if carriers in a given market may not have any monopoly power, it is important to note that since operating characteristics have a significant impact upon costs, differences in operating characteristics associated with certain types of traffic can lead to substantial cost differentials. In this connection, we find clear evidence that the costs associated with traffic in light-density rural areas, which is characterized by short hauls, small shipment sizes, and small loads, are significantly higher than those associated with high-density traffic between large urban areas, which is characterized by long hauls, large shipment sizes, and large loads. It is likely, therefore, that shippers in small cities and towns and rural areas face fundamentally higher trucking costs than shippers in large urban areas.

Nevertheless, these cost differentials would only imply that rates would increase to small shippers in rural areas in the absence of regulation if this traffic were currently subsidized. Thus before a judgement can be made concerning the adverse effect of deregulation upon these shippers, a full analysis must be made of the relationships between prices, marginal costs, and the elasticities of demand for this traffic. In this respect, this chapter will argue that there is little evidence of systematic subsidies to light-density traffic.

In analyzing the behavior of the markets for common carriers of general commodities, it is important to recognize that substantial differences exist in the nature of trucking firms. In particular, common carriers of general commodities present substantial differences in firm size, age of capital stock, nature of terminal operations, route density, and so forth, not only between geographic regions but also between the relatively localized regional carriers and the geographically dispersed interregional and trans-continental carriers. For this reason it makes little sense to regard general commodity carriers as homogeneous entities within homogeneous markets. Indeed, one of the most important lessons of this analysis is that just as wide discrepancies exist in costs among railroads and specialized commodity carriers, similar discrepancies exist among general commodity carriers. It follows that policy prescriptions that might seem appropriate for one segment of the industry might be highly inappropriate for another; therefore without a full understanding of the differences in technology among carriers of general commodities, it is quite likely that policy changes that might improve performance in one sector could reduce it in others.

This chapter presents an initial attempt to confront some of these issues by focusing on the costs, technology, and pricing relationships of common carriers of general freight, which account for approximately one-half of the revenues and ton-miles of the regulated trucking industry.

Ideally, we would have liked to segment this market as fully as possible on a regional basis and thus analyze geographic differences in trucking technology on a relatively disaggregate scale. Because of limitations in the number of observations, we were forced to settle on a somewhat more aggregate breakdown for our econometric analysis: regional carriers in the Official Territory, which comprises the New England, Middle Atlantic, and Central Regions; all other regional carriers, which comprise carriers in the Southern, South–Western, and Western Regions, and which we refer to as carriers in the South–West Region for notational simplicity; and interregional and transcontinental carriers. Although we recognize that this level of aggregation may introduce some bias, we believe that this bias is minimal.

Since appendix C presents the discussion of the structure and nature of technology for common carriers of general commodities, this chapter will focus upon the policy implications of this analysis. Section 5.2 will consider the evidence concerning the existence of economies of scale and argue that workable competition is a likely outcome in a deregulated environment. Section 5.3 directly addresses the question of the extent and nature of the differences in the cost structure of the three types of carriers and argues that the costs and technologies are sufficiently different that it is unlikely that one type of carrier would encroach on the operations of the others in the absence of regulation. Section 5.4 considers the relationships between prices and marginal costs that presently exist for each type of carrier and argues that current regulatory practices appear to compensate carriers of light-density traffic adequately, indicating that there would be little upward pressures on rates on this traffic in the absence of regulation.

5.2 Economies of Scale in Common Carriers of General Commodities

The general specification used to describe trucking costs and technology postulates that trucking costs depend upon output levels y, factor prices w, and operating characteristics t, which can be expressed in general terms as

$$C = C(y, w, t), \tag{5.1}$$

where w and t represent vectors of factor prices and operating characteristics, respectively, and y represents aggregate ton-miles. We give this operational content by assuming that this general cost function can be described by a translog approximation (the specific functional form and the estimated coefficients are discussed in detail in appendix C).

For the purposes of this chapter, however, it is important to note that the econometric analysis discussed in appendix C indicates that production is characterized by significant nonhomotheticities between the operating characteristics (the t vector) and output y, and between the t vector and factor prices. Thus not only are the elasticities of substitution affected by the levels of the operating characteristics, but more important for policy, the elasticities of cost are also affected by the levels of the operating characteristics.[1] Consequently, in analyzing the nature of returns to scale, considerable care should be used to incorporate the effect of the operating characteristics where appropriate.

The nature of returns to scale can be characterized by the elasticity of cost with respect to output, given by $\partial \ln C / \partial \ln y$. If this is less than one, the industry is characterized by increasing returns to scale, and if this is greater than one, the industry is characterized by decreasing returns to scale. A cost elasticity of one implies constant returns to scale.

The general behavior of returns to scale in each of our three samples can be seen by considering the elasticity of cost facing a hypothetical firm that faces the mean factor prices, utilizes the mean output characteristics, and produces at the mean output level of each sample. These cost elasticities are given as follows for each sample, with their standard errors in parentheses:

Official Region, 1.0864 (0.0376).
South–West Region, 1.0759 (0.0273).
Interregionals, 0.8969 (0.0501).

Thus the "typical" regional carrier appears to face decreasing returns to scale, while the "typical" interregional carrier appears to face increasing returns to scale. In evaluating these results, however, it is important to note that although the "typical" regional carrier closely resembles the individual firms in the regional samples, no firm in the interregional sample closely resembles the hypothetical firm of the sample mean. Indeed, 33 of the 47 interregional carriers actually face decreasing returns to scale, and only 1 has an estimated cost elasticity falling more than two standard errors below one. Moreover, as will become apparent below, the estimated cost function for the interregional carriers is anomalous in a number of other respects. Thus while we can infer that the regional carriers are subject to decreasing returns to scale, we cannot infer that the "typical" interregional carrier is subject to increasing returns to scale.

Because of nonhomotheticities in production, however, it is not particularly useful to characterize returns to scale by the "typical" firm in each region. Since output characteristics affect the elasticities of cost, it is useful to consider the elasticity of cost with respect to output for a firm facing mean factor prices.[2] Within the translog cost function used in this analysis, this expression is given as follows:

$$\frac{\partial \ln C}{\partial \ln y} = \gamma_y + \sum_j E_{jy}(\ln t_j - \ln \bar{t}_j) + F_{yy}(\ln y - \ln \bar{y}), \tag{5.2}$$

where γ_y represents the coefficient on the linear output term, E_{jy} the coefficients on the interaction terms between output and the operating characteristics, and F_{yy} the coefficient on the squared output term (see appendix C). Thus the E_{jy} coefficients measure the effect of operating characteristics upon the cost elasticities, with positive E_{jy} coefficients indicating that the elasticities of cost fall with operating characteristics below their mean values and rise with operating characteristics above their mean values, and conversely for negative values of the E_{jy} coefficients. Similarly, a positive F_{yy} coefficient indicates that the firm faces a U-shaped average cost curve, while a negative F_{yy} coefficient indicates that a hypothetical firm faces an inverted (and asymmetric) U-shaped average cost curve. Finally, the γ_y term measures the economies of scale facing a "typical" firm operating with mean output level, operating characteristics, and factor prices.

The data related to firm operating characteristics that are generally available for general commodity carriers are given as follows: total tons; tons in shipments of less-than-truckload (LTL) size; total vehicle-miles, number of shipments;[3] insurance costs; and number of terminals. From these variables, six firm averages of service characteristics can be constructed: AVSIZE ≡ average shipment size (total tons/number of shipments); ALH ≡ average length of haul (ton-miles/total tons); LTL ≡ percentage of freight in LTL lots (LTL tons/total tons); AVLOAD ≡ average load per vehicle (ton-miles/total vehicle-miles); INSUR ≡ average insurance cost per ton/mile (insurance costs/ton-miles); and TERMINAL ≡ ton-miles/terminal.

Given the nature of the common carrier industry, it is realistic to regard the first four of these operating characteristic variables as beyond the firm's determination and hence as exogenous. Since common carriers must serve the general public, these four variables will be determined by the orders received by the firm and the firm's operating rights. The firm cannot charge prices to discourage undesirable traffic,[4] and the ICC ostensibly exerts pressure concerning the quality of service as measured by time in transit. (Unfortunately, no direct measure of this service dimension is available.) While firms may engage in sales efforts to encourage desirable traffic, their common carrier obligation to accept all customers at established rates also makes them vulnerable to undesirable traffic for their own fleet. Consequently, we will regard these four variables as exogenous.[5]

It is also probably reasonable to view insurance costs per ton-mile as exogenous. Even though firms can choose the desired levels of their insurance premiums, their common carrier obligations typically prevent them from exerting a substantial influence upon the composition of their output. Since, however, insurance premiums are likely to be closely tied to the value of the commodity and its characteristics with respect to fragility and perishability, it is likely that the firm has relatively little control over its insurance payments per ton-mile. Therefore it is probably reasonable to treat this variable as being beyond the control of the firm and hence as being an exogenous variable in the cost function.

The rationale for including ton-miles per terminal as an exogenous operating characteristic is less clear-cut. On the one hand, it is clear that costs are affected by route network configurations and by traffic density, which are partially captured by this variable. On the other hand, since we estimate a long-run cost function, the number of terminals is presumably under the control of the firm and hence is not an exogenous variable. Nevertheless, on balance it seems useful to include ton-miles per terminal since it is important to incorporate some measure of network density into the analysis. It should be pointed out, however, that this variable only proved useful in the estimated cost function of the inter-regional carriers, and hence only enters into the cost function for these carriers.[6]

Table 5.1 presents the estimates of (5.2) for each of the three types of carriers. The coefficients on the linear and squared output terms (γ_y and F_{yy}) indicate that a regional carrier operating with mean factor prices and operating characteristics will operate along the rising portion of a U-shaped average cost curve. In contrast, an interregional carrier operat-

Table 5.1 Estimated Cost Elasticities at Mean Factor Prices, by Type of Carrier, 1972

Parameter	Region		
	Official	South–West	Interregionals
γ_y	1.0864	1.0759	0.8969
	$(0.0376)^a$	(0.0273)	(0.0501)
$E_{1y}(\ln \text{ALH})$	0.0365	−0.0467	−0.0932
	(0.0504)	(0.0606)	(0.0600)
$E_{2y}(\ln \text{AVLOAD})$	0.0128	0.1604	0.2602
	(0.0562)	(0.0705)	(0.0957)
$E_{3y}(\ln \text{LTL})$	0.1434	0.0681	−0.2664
	(0.0679)	(0.0722)	(0.0819)
$E_{4y}(\ln \text{AVSIZE})$	0.0014	0.0086	−0.3223
	(0.0447)	(0.0454)	(0.0862)
$E_{5y}(\ln \text{INSUR})$	0.0035	0.0388	−0.0413
	(0.0271)	(0.0283)	(0.0581)
$E_{6y}(\ln \text{TERMINAL})$	–	–	0.0990
			(0.0338)
$F_{yy}(\ln y)$	0.0248	0.0533	−0.0880
	(0.0347)	(0.0256)	(0.0329)

a. Standard errors are in parentheses.

ing at mean factor prices and output levels will operate along the declining portion of an inverted U-shaped average cost curve.

Since, however, firms do not typically operate at mean levels of the operating characteristics, it is important to analyze the impact of operating characteristics upon economies of scale. Nevertheless, table 5.1 shows that the coefficients on the E_{jy} terms for the regional carriers are generally small and insignificant, indicating that the estimate of returns to scale at the mean for these carriers is not a poor approximation. However, the sign and magnitude of the LTL coefficient for carriers in the Official Region and of the AVLOAD coefficient for the carriers in the South–West Region indicate that as these variables increase beyond their mean value, the observed diseconomies of scale increase. In general, the E_{jy} coefficients tend to increase the likelihood that any given large regional carriers will be operating under conditions of decreasing returns to scale.[7]

In contrast, the evidence concerning returns to scale among the Inter-regionals is ambiguous. While a hypothetical firm with sample mean characteristics operates on the falling portion of an inverse U-shaped average cost curve, actual firms (as mentioned above) typically have cost elasticities exceeding one. In table 5.2, the estimated cost elasticities for the 21 largest interregional firms and 4 small firms are presented along with their estimated standard errors. Of the 16 firms falling above the sample mean, fully half have cost elasticities exceeding one, as do 3 of the 5 largest firms.

Part of the explanation for this phenomenon lies in the generally large and significant values of the E_{jy} coefficients for the Interregionals. As table 5.3 shows, the six operating characteristics and ton-miles are generally weakly correlated within the interregional sample; the strongest relation is between LTL and AVSIZE, with $r = -0.6096$. Thus, the Interregionals display a wide variety of combinations of firm size and operating characteristics; these combinations are generally such that applying (5.2) (given in table 5.1 at mean factor prices) results in an estimate of declining returns to scale (which are significantly different from constant returns) for most interregional carriers.

Since one of the main concerns about deregulating the trucking industry is that the large interregional carriers will drive the smaller firms out of business, it is important to understand the relationship between average cost levels, service characteristics, and firm size both within and between carrier types as defined by our three samples. What is the nature of returns to scale within each group? Are differences in average cost levels due to differences in service characteristics, or could the large interregional

Table 5.2 Elasticity of Cost with Respect to Output for Interregional Carriers, by Firm, at 1972 Output Levels

Trucking firm	Ton-miles[a]	$\partial \ln C / \partial \ln y$	Standard error
Roadway Express Inc.	4,287,290	0.871	0.067
Consolidated Frtways.—Del.	4,042,558	1.046	0.051
Yellow Freight Sysm. Inc.	3,607,552	0.936	0.058
Time—DC Inc.	2,338,241	1.044	0.054
Pacific Intermtn. Exp. Co.	2,228,369	1.066	0.056
McLean Trkg. Co.	2,206,066	0.948	0.064
Transcon. Lines	2,152,124	1.100	0.063
Ryder Truck Lines Inc.	1,584,476	0.954	0.060
Lee Way Motor Frt. Inc.	1,290,082	0.984	0.054
IML Freight Inc.	1,265,653	1.050	0.055
Interstate Mtr. Frt. Sys.	1,183,377	0.896	0.057
Carolina Frt. Carriers	1,049,303	1.024	0.051
Arkansas-Best Frt. Sys.	1,029,541	0.955	0.063
Gateway Trptn. Co. Inc.	1,015,200	1.009	0.056
Transamerican Frt. Lines	990,136	1.041	0.069
Mason & Dixon Lns. Inc.	939,218	0.991	0.047
Eastern Express Inc.	846,973	1.031	0.043
Werner Continental Inc.	805,003	1.069	0.063
Garrett Frt. Lns. Inc.	753,982	1.105	0.058
Johnson Mtr. Lns. Inc.	741,143	0.995	0.060
Western Gillette Inc.	682,963	1.121	0.077
RC Motor Lines Inc.	280,934	0.935	0.061
Overland Trptn Co.	67,938	1.024	0.064
Billings Trf. Corp. Inc.	67,325	1.062	0.062
Henry CS Trf. Inc.	18,577	1.058	0.075

a. Unit = 1,000.

Table 5.3 Correlation Matrix of Firm Characteristics for the Interregionals

	ALH	AVLOAD	LTL	AVSIZE	INSUR	TERMINAL	TM	TCOST	REV
ALH	1.0	0.3348	0.1982	−0.1211	−0.1933	0.2494	0.5458	0.4523	0.4506
AVLOAD		1.0	−0.3083	0.1240	−0.2657	0.2818	0.1544	0.0771	0.0760
LTL			1.0	−0.6096	0.3200	−0.2873	0.1507	0.2171	0.2279
AVSIZE				1.0	−0.2733	0.0423	−0.1511	−0.1780	−0.1781
INSUR					1.0	−0.1705	0.0847	0.1355	0.1334
TERMINAL						1.0	0.2695	0.2169	0.2071
TM							1.0	0.9836	0.9833
TCOST								1.0	0.9995
REV									1.0

carriers produce output with the service characteristics of the other two samples at lower cost?

5.3 Cost Differences among the Common Carriers

The differences among the three samples of motor carriers in operating characteristics, ton-miles, and other variables can be seen in table 5.4, which gives the means and standard deviations of these variables. In general, in moving from the Official to the South–West to the Inter-regionals, one moves from short-haul, small-load operations conducted by small firms to long-haul large-load operations conducted by large firms.

One naturally expects that average costs will generally be highest for the Official carriers and lowest for the Interregionals. In table 5.5 we tabulate average cost for each carrier type over a wide range of output, using weighted (by ton-miles) mean operating characteristics and factor prices. The marginal and average cost curves corresponding to table 5.5 are plotted in figures 5.1–5.3.[8]

Two aspects of table 5.5 and figures 5.1–5.3 are noteworthy. First, at "typical" levels of output, average costs in the South–West Region are roughly 50 percent higher than those of the Interregionals, while the Official Region has costs about twice as high as the Interregionals. Second, the Interregionals average and marginal costs, while rather peculiarly shaped at high and low output levels, are relatively constant between 250 million and 2 billion ton-miles. The peculiarities at the extremes are due to the estimate of F_{yy} being less than zero. While F_{yy} is statistically significant, it is worth noting that its value is not stable across alternative specifications.[9] Given this evidence and the firm-by-firm calculation of $\partial \ln C / \partial \ln y$ in the previous section, it must be admitted that scale economies among the Interregionals are not well understood. In particular, while it seems that some combinations of operating characteristics lead to scale economies, these combinations are not often observed; moreover, even these combinations yield average cost curves which are relatively flat for a wide range of output, with substantial economies accruing at sizes currently reached by only a handful of carriers.

Since operating characteristics differ so much among the three types of carriers, it is important to understand the extent to which differences in operating characteristics and factor prices, as opposed to differences of technology as embodied in the cost function, are responsible for the differences in average and marginal costs among carrier types. Of particular

Table 5.4 Means and Standard Deviations for Costs, Revenues, Operating Characteristics, and Ton-Miles, by Type of Carrier, 1972

Variable	Abbreviation	Unit	Official Mean	Official Standard deviation	South–West Mean	South–West Standard deviation	Interregionals Mean	Interregionals Standard deviation
Average length of haul	ALH	miles	120.014	65.0765	185.566	94.044	673.957	284.170
Average load per vehicle	AVLOAD	tons	7.5316	3.3825	10.0812	3.1381	14.6831	2.6325
Proportion of freight in LTL lots	LTL	LTL ton/ total tons	0.4829	0.1988	0.5109	0.1733	0.3657	0.1234
Average shipment size	AVSIZE	tons/shipment	1.2783	1.4102	0.8837	0.7028	1.3378	1.9265
Insurance	INSUR	insurance cost/ ton-miles	0.0035	0.0038	0.0025	0.0018	0.0009	0.0004
Ton-miles per terminal	TERMINAL	ton-miles/ no. of terminals	na	na	na	na	18,209.8	15,923.9
Ton-miles	TM	millions	20.955	30.708	57.241	86.751	931.628	1,010.780
Total cost	TCOST	$millions	4.198	4.584	8.090	10.169	68.449	72.673
Revenues	REV	$millions	4.418	4.873	8.787	11.397	72.928	79.363

Table 5.5 Average Costs (Weighted Mean) of Trucking Firms, by Type of Carrier, 1972

Output	Average costs (¢/y-miles)		
y-millions	Official	South–West	Interregionals
5	13.0	12.0	2.9
10	13.5	11.6	3.8
20	14.2	11.4	4.9
30	14.7	11.5	5.5
40	15.1	11.6	5.9
50	15.5	11.7	6.3
100	16.7	12.3	7.2
150	17.6	12.8	7.7
200	18.3	13.2	8.0
250	18.9	13.6	8.2
300	–	14.0	8.3
400	–	14.6	8.5
500	–	15.2	8.5
750	–	17.4	8.6
1,000	–	–	8.6
1,500	–	–	8.4
2,000	–	–	8.2
3,000	–	–	7.9
3,500	–	–	7.7
4,000	–	–	7.6
Range of output (mill. ton-miles)	1.0–180.2	1.4–635.1	18.6–4,287.3
Mean output (mill. ton-miles)	20.955	57.241	931.6
Stand dev. of output (mill. ton-miles)	30.708	86.751	1,010.8

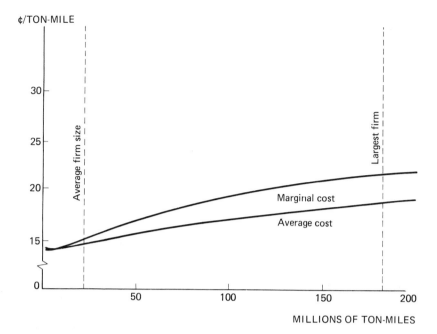

Figure 5.1   Average and marginal cost curve of "typical" firm in Official Region.

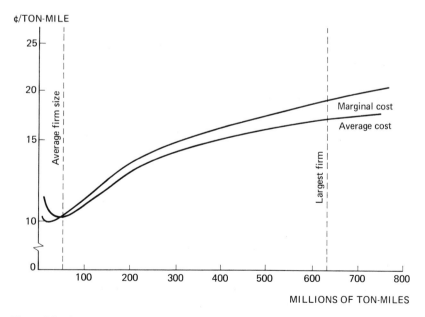

Figure 5.2   Average and marginal cost curve of "typical" firm in South–West Region.

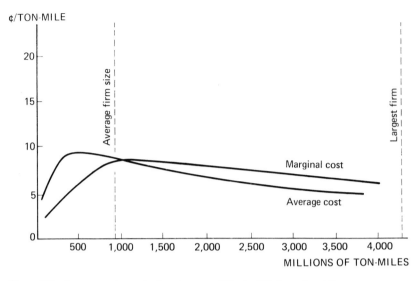

Figure 5.3   Average and marginal cost curve of "typical" Interregional firm.

interest is whether one group of carriers, such as the South–West or Inter-regionals, could, under the operating characteristics and factor prices of another group (e.g., the Official), produce at average costs substantially below those currently experienced by the second group. One way of answering this question is to compare the behavior of $C_j(y, w_i, t_i)$ and $C_i(y, w_i, t_i)$ over a wide range of y, where C_i and C_j denote, respectively, the cost function of the ith and jth group of carriers and w_i and t_i the factor prices and operating characteristics, respectively, of a typical firm in the ith group (in practice, weighted mean values).

Figure 5.4 plots average cost curves using the factor prices and operating characteristics of the wrighted mean firm of the Official Region; the cost functions used are those of the Official and South–West carriers. Until output levels of about 150 million ton-miles are reached, the average cost given by the Official cost function is lower than that of the South–West cost function. Moreover, at higher levels of output the advantage of the South–West is not very great, particularly considering the fact that the relevant prediction intervals are growing since these output levels are well beyond the mean level of both samples. Finally, since there are disecono-mies of scale for both types of carriers, it would seem that the lower output ranges are most relevant. Thus, it appears that the Official carriers would be virtually immune to encroachment by the South–West carriers under deregulation.

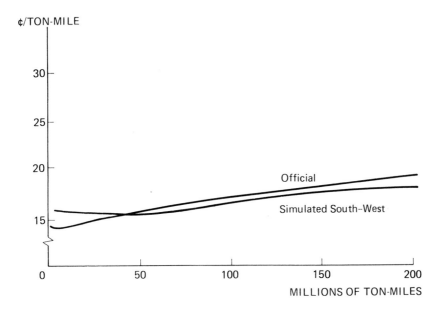

Figure 5.4 Comparison of official and South–West average cost curves for firms facing factor prices and operating characteristics of the Official carriers.

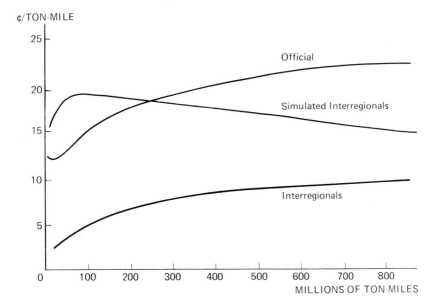

Figure 5.5 Comparison of Official and Interregional average cost curves for firms facing factor prices and operating characteristics of the Official carriers.

In figure 5.5, we perform a similar exercise comparing the Official and the Interregionals. In addition, we plot the Interregionals' own average cost curve (i.e., using the factor prices and service characteristics of the weighted mean Interregional firm, as in figure 5.3). From this it is apparent that most of the difference in average costs between the Official and Interregional carriers is due to differences in service characteristics and factor prices rather than cost functions.[10]

Up to about the size of the largest Official firm (180 million ton-miles), the average costs of the Official carriers are lower than those of the Inter-regionals. Beyond this point, the Interregionals have an everincreasing advantage, growing to about 10¢/ton-mile at 1 billion ton-miles. Of course, this is not the relevant comparison, since the Official firms face declining returns to scale. Two hundred 5-million ton-mile Official firms could produce 1 billion ton-miles at about 0.1¢ less per ton-mile than one Interregional firm, if we take the estimated cost functions literally. Since the scale of operations of the two types of firms are so different, it is difficult to make meaningful comparisons because the prediction intervals are very large due to the necessary extrapolation beyond the sample point. Nevertheless, at conditions anywhere near those faced by the current Official firms, encroachment by the Interregionals is very unlikely. The only reason such encroachment cannot be entirely ruled out is because no firm facing conditions similar to those of the Official carriers is operating on the (ton-mile) scale of the Interregionals. Since no such firm exists, it is virtually impossible to determine (at least using current statistical methods) whether such a firm could compete with the current Official firms. However, the evidence, such as it is, suggests that it could not.

In figure 5.6 we compare the South–West and Interregional carriers. Many of the features of the Official–Interregional comparison hold for figure 5.6 also. At output levels of up to about 200 million ton-miles, the South–West carriers have average costs below those of the Interregionals, with the Interregionals gaining an ever greater advantage thereafter. The minimum average cost that our hypothetical South–West firm could attain would be about 11.4¢/ton-mile at an output of 20 million ton-miles; an Interregional firm would attain the same average costs at about 900 million ton-miles.[11] Since South–West carriers operate under conditions more similar to the Interregionals than do the Official carriers, the possibility of some encroachment by the Interregionals on the South–West carriers' traffic is greater than the corresponding possibilities of either of the two cases above. Nonetheless, the prospect that such encroachment would lead to monopoly problems in the advent of deregulation is slight.

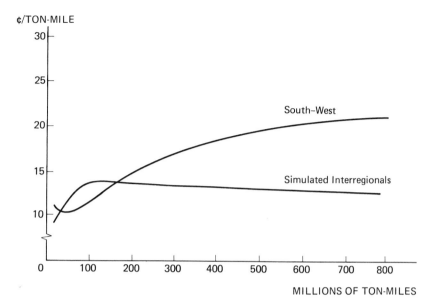

¢/TON-MILE

MILLIONS OF TON-MILES

Figure 5.6   Comparison of South–West and Interregional average cost curves for firms facing factor prices and operating characteristics of the South–West carriers (weighted mean).

One reason for this is that if one put the Interregionals' factor prices and operating characteristics into the South–West cost function, a relatively flat average cost function over the output range of 20–150 million ton-miles is obtained at average costs of 7.3–7.5¢/ton-mile; the similar "flat" region for the Interregionals has costs of 8.2–8.6¢/ton-mile. Thus, instead of one-way encroachment, one might expect a two-way realignment of traffic between the two types of carriers, that is, each type of carrier would gain some traffic (from the other) for which it currently does not have operating rights.

In conclusion, we find that fears of predatory encroachment under deregulation are generally unfounded. There is some ambiguity in the results concerning returns to scale among the very largest Interregionals, but these ambiguities appear largely to result from econometric artifacts; this remains an area in which additional research is possible and potentially fruitful. Nevertheless, the mass of evidence indicates that each carrier type has "adapted" to its environment, in that each class generally attains lowest average costs for the type of traffic it most often handles. In the event of deregulation, existing inefficient firms will face their greatest competition not from "superlarge" firms but from firms which will essentially replicate the current modes of operation by following a policy of simultaneous route consolidation *and* route "fill-ins." Thus, short-haul small-shipment traffic will remain in the hands of small firms specializing in such traffic.

5.4 Marginal Costs and Pricing Structure of Carriers of General Commodities

Given a cost function such as (5.1) and its translog approximation, it is possible to differentiate it with respect to output y to obtain the marginal costs of producing at any given level of output. Since marginal cost pricing is generally viewed as an efficiency norm, a question of obvious interest is whether the prices allowed by the ICC are close to marginal costs; in addition, it would be convenient to be able to characterize any *systematic* deviations of the commission's policy from marginal cost pricing in a simple fashion. In the motor carrier industry, for example, it could be that price is always above marginal cost, but that this gap is greater for longer-haul traffic. It may even be that for some types of traffic price is below marginal cost, while for other types of traffic price is above marginal cost; in this case, it *might* be appropriate to conclude that the latter "subsidizes" the former.

To fix ideas, suppose that price equals marginal cost for every output, and that we can approximate costs by the following translog cost function:[12]

$$\ln C = \alpha_0 + \sum_i \alpha_i \ln w_i + \sum_j \beta_j \ln t_j + \gamma_y \ln y$$

$$+ \frac{1}{2} \sum_i \sum_l A_{il} \ln w_l + \sum_i \sum_j B_{ij} \ln w_i \ln t_j$$

$$+ \sum_i C_{iy} \ln w_i \ln y + \frac{1}{2} \sum_j \sum_m D_{jm} \ln t_j \ln t_m$$

$$+ \sum_j E_{jy} \ln t_j \ln y + \frac{1}{2} F_{yy} (\ln y)^2 + \varepsilon_C, \tag{5.3}$$

where the w's represent factor prices, the t's technological or operating characteristics, y aggregate output, and ε_C a disturbance term. Thus by logarithmically differentiating this equation with respect to output y, if price equals marginal cost, we readily obtain

$$\frac{\partial \ln C}{\partial \ln y} = \frac{\partial C}{\partial y}\frac{y}{C} = \frac{py}{C}$$

$$= \gamma_y + \sum_i C_{iy} \ln w_i + \sum_j E_{jy} \ln t_j + F_{yy} \ln y, \tag{5.4}$$

so that the revenue–cost relationship is given by an equation analogous to the factor share equations. If there was prior knowledge to the effect that price did equal marginal cost, (5.4) could be added to the system of equations to be estimated after adding to it an appropriate disturbance.

It is important to note that this equation does not require the assumption of free competition; this estimation procedure would be appropriate for a market in which the regulatory agency explicitly divided demand among firms and set the price to be charged by each firm equal to its marginal cost. Of course, to do this, the regulatory agency would need some way of knowing or controlling demand, or of policing possible disequilibria.

Since it is unlikely, however, that the regulatory authorities enforce marginal cost pricing, an alternative and more plausible assumption is that the regulatory agency adopts a pricing policy, which in the general case sets for each firm a price for each output depending on the factor prices, technological conditions, and output levels it faces, and forces the firm to accept all demand forthcoming at the regulated prices. Suppose that this price schedule is set so that the revenue–cost equation satisfies

$$\frac{p(y, w, t)y}{C(y, w, t)} = \tilde{\gamma}_y + \sum_i \tilde{C}_{iy} \ln w_i + \sum_j \tilde{E}_{jy} \ln t_j + \tilde{F}_{yy} \ln y, \tag{5.5}$$

where the tildes indicate that the values of the coefficients are not derived from the cost function as in (5.4), but are values implicitly set by the regulatory agency. This equation can be rewritten as

$$p(y, w, t) = \frac{C}{y}\left[\tilde{\gamma}_y + \sum_i \tilde{C}_{iy} \ln w_i + \sum_j \tilde{E}_{jy} \ln t_j + \tilde{F}_{yy} \ln y\right], \tag{5.6}$$

which, after (5.3) has been appropriately substituted, gives an explicit formula for the pricing policy which corresponds to (5.5). Since (5.6) applies to the one-output case, it can be interpreted as setting price equal to a multiple of average cost (C/y), with the multiple depending on factor prices, technological conditions, and the level of output. If marginal cost pricing prevailed, the tilded coefficients in (5.6) would equal the nontilded coefficients in (5.3). Thus differences between the coefficients of these two estimated equations indicate systematic deviations from a policy of marginal cost pricing.

If one is willing to accept (5.6) as a model of the regulatory agency schedule, then a revenue–cost equation corresponding to (5.5) should be added to the system of cost and factor share equations to be estimated. The hypothesis that the regulatory agency pricing policy is to set price equal to marginal cost can then be tested by estimating a system with (5.4) substituted for (5.5), that is, by constraining the coefficients of (5.5) to equal their nontilded analogs in (5.3), and performing a likelihood ratio test.

On the other hand, if the regulatory agency does not have a pricing policy that can be expressed by (5.4) or (5.5), then adding a revenue–cost equation to the cost–factor share system adds a misspecified equation. Since the equations are estimated simultaneously, this specification error will "spread" to the cost–factor share system. Thus, we should always estimate the cost–factor share system separately before adding, to the "best" particular specification of (5.3), the equations corresponding to (5.4) or (5.5).

We thus add the revenue–cost equation (5.5) to the cost and factor share equations for each type of carrier and compare the tilded coefficients to their nontilded analogs in (5.3). For each type of carrier, we are able to reject decisively the hypothesis that the coefficients of (5.5) equal their nontilded analogs. This indicates that a marginal cost pricing policy is not followed by the ICC and that cost or production studies that assume marginal cost pricing make a serious specification error.[13]

Although we reject the proposition that price equals marginal cost, in analyzing the relationship between price and marginal cost it still may be appropriate to use the revenue–cost equation that is jointly estimated with the cost and factor share equations, but without the cross-equation restrictions on the coefficients between the revenue–cost equation and the cost and factor share equations. This procedure adjusts for the interrelationships that may exist among the disturbances of the relevant equations, but does not impose any assumptions concerning the relationship between price and marginal cost. Indeed, (5.5) postulates that prices are proportional to average costs, with the factor of proportionality depending on factor prices and operating characteristics.

The coefficients of the revenue–cost equations can be interpreted as measuring the changes in the factor of proportionality between prices and average costs, while the analogous coefficients of the cost function can be interpreted as measuring the changes in the factor of proportionality between marginal costs and average costs. Hence differences between the two types of variables measure the differences between prices and marginal costs that arise from changes in factor prices or operating characteristics. Thus if $\tilde{E}_{jy}$ represents the marginal effect upon prices of changing the jth operating characteristics and E_{jy} represents the marginal effect upon marginal costs of changing the same operating characteristic, $\tilde{E}_{jy} - E_{jy} > 0$ would imply that as the operating characteristic grew relative to the mean, we would observe an increasingly large price–marginal cost ratio. Thus, a positive difference between these two variables indicates a deviation in marginal cost pricing policies that favors firms having large values of the relevant variables. Similarly, $\tilde{E}_{jy} - E_{jy} = 0$ indicates that any deviation of price from marginal costs does not arise from systematic pricing responses of that variable. Finally, $\tilde{E}_{jy} - E_{jy} < 0$ implies that the price structure discriminates against firms with large values of the jth operating characteristic and implicity favors firms with low values of that variable.

Table 5.6 presents the differences in the coefficients in the revenue–cost equation and the analogous coefficients in the cost function for each type of carrier. In the revenue function, the constant term $\tilde{\gamma}_y$ measures the profitability of the "typical" firm facing mean factor prices, operating characteristics, and output levels, while in the cost function γ_y measures the elasticity of cost with respect to output or the long-run profitability that would accrue to the firm if price equalled marginal cost. Hence $\tilde{\gamma}_y - \gamma_y$ measures the extent to which the actual profitability of the "typical" firm deviates from the profitability that would exist under long-run marginal cost pricing. A negative value indicates that actual profitability is less than long-run equilibrium profitability, and a positive value indicates the converse. Table 5.6 indicates that these values are negative for the Official and South–West samples at the point of expansion, implying that the "typical" firm earns returns that are marginally less than those implied by marginal cost pricing. However, the standard error associated with this estimate for the South–West Region is sufficiently large that we cannot reject the hypothesis that actual profitability is greater than that which would occur under long-run marginal cost pricing. It is interesting to note, however, that $\tilde{\gamma}_y - \gamma_y$ is marginally significantly different from zero for the carriers in the Official Region, indicating that regulatory constraints probably prevent these carriers from earning as great a return as they would if marginal cost pricing were followed. For the Interregional carriers, the confidence band for $\tilde{\gamma}_y - \gamma_y$ is extremely wide, indicating a wide range in profitability among these carriers, with some tendency for firms to receive greater profits than they would under marginal cost pricing.

Table 5.6 Differences between Estimated Coefficients in Revenue Share Equation and Cost Equation, by Type of Carrier, 1972

Coefficient	Variable[a]	Official		South–West		Interregionals	
		Value	Standard error	Value	Standard error	Value	Standard error
$\tilde{\gamma}_y - \gamma_y$	Constant	−0.0533	0.0380	−0.0009	0.0285	0.0225	0.0528
$\tilde{C}_{1y} - C_{1y}$	w_1 (labor)	−0.1009	0.0337	−0.1153	0.0313	−0.1602	0.0488
$\tilde{C}_{2y} - C_{2y}$	w_2 (fuel)	0.1409	0.0393	0.2018	0.0334	0.2375	0.0541
$\tilde{C}_{3y} - C_{3y}$	w_3 (capital)	−0.0569	0.0105	−0.0491	0.0107	−0.0621	0.0077
$\tilde{C}_{4y} - C_{4y}$	w_4 (pur. trans.)	0.0169	0.0291	−0.0375	0.0281	0.0151	0.0208
$\tilde{E}_{1y} - E_{1y}$	t_1 (ALH)	−0.0294	0.0509	0.0522	0.0598	−0.0180	0.0541
$\tilde{E}_{2y} - E_{2y}$	t_2 (AVLOAD)	0.0012	0.0567	−0.1278	0.0696	0.0129	0.0903
$\tilde{E}_{3y} - E_{3y}$	t_3 (LTL)	−0.1706	0.0701	−0.0212	0.0719	0.0387	0.0708
$\tilde{E}_{4y} - E_{4y}$	t_4 (AVSIZE)	−0.0151	0.0449	0.0310	0.0457	0.1180	0.0771
$\tilde{E}_{5y} - E_{5y}$	t_5 (INSUR)	0.0071	0.0274	−0.0486	0.0285	0.1074	0.0491
$\tilde{E}_{6y} - E_{6y}$	t_6 (TERMINAL)	—	—	—	—	−0.0692	0.0306
$\tilde{F}_{yy} - F_{yy}$	y (output)	−0.0238	0.0344	−0.0581	0.0252	0.0149	0.0271

a. ln omitted for convenience.

The $\tilde{C}_{jy} - C_{jy}$ coefficients measure the differential response between price and marginal costs with respect to factor prices. They are generally statistically significant, indicating that the response of rates to changes in these variables differs from that of marginal costs. It is interesting to note that this differential is consistently large for fuel $\tilde{C}_{2y} - C_{2y}$, indicating that fuel price increases result in greater price increases than cost increases. This may reflect the commission's willingness to permit rate pass-ons resulting from fuel price increases. In any event, these findings suggest that trucking firms would not suffer from increases in fuel prices under the current regulatory structure. In contrast, the price–marginal cost differentials on labor costs $\tilde{C}_{1y} - C_{1y}$ and capital costs $\tilde{C}_{3y} - C_{3y}$ are negative and clearly indicate that firms with relatively high labor and capital costs are not fully compensated in the rate structure. This is particularly true with respect to labor costs, and perhaps explains the increasing utilization of purchased transportation and the growth of owner-operators. Finally, the price–marginal cost differentials with respect to purchased transportation $\tilde{C}_{4y} - C_{4y}$ are positive for Interregional carriers and those in the Official Region, but negative for those in the South–West Region. However, these differentials are not significant.

The $\tilde{E}_{jy} - E_{jy}$ coefficients present the price–marginal cost differentials arising from operating characteristics and do not indicate that any systematic pricing relationships exist across all types of carriers. Conventional wisdom holds that a cross subsidy exists between traffic in high-density corridors between large urban centers and traffic on low-density corridors between rural areas. Similarly, cross subsidies are believed to exist between long-haul, large-load shipments (the "cream" of the traffic) and short-haul, small-load shipments.

Cross subsidies are usually discussed in terms of absolute profitability, and it is often argued that trucking firms make actual losses on short-haul, small-load, light-density traffic, but earn sufficient profits on their long-haul, large-load, high-density traffic to compensate them for these losses. If a firm produces multiple outputs, however, average costs become undefined and it thus makes little sense to talk about the profitability of certain types of traffic. Since, however, marginal costs are well defined in a multiple-output technology, it is certainly reasonable to consider the price–marginal cost relationships among certain types of traffic. Thus if a cross subsidy existed, we would expect to find the price–marginal cost ratios of long-haul, large-load, high-density traffic significantly higher than those associated with short-haul, small-load, low-density traffic. In terms of the differentials between the coefficients of the revenue–cost equation and the cost function, if a cross subsidy existed we would consequently expect to find that $\tilde{E}_{jy} - E_{jy}$ was positive for average length of haul, average load, and average shipment size, and negative for LTL. In fact, we do not find a consistent pattern of this type and actually observe some behavior that is directly contrary to that implied by the subsidy hypothesis.

With respect to carriers in the Official Region, the only variable that is significantly different from zero is LTL, which has a negative value, indicating that firms with a large proportion of LTL traffic are less profitable than those with small values. This finding is consistent with the growth of specialized commodity carriers, and clearly indicates that the rate structure does not provide adequate compensation for the costs incurred with LTL operations. Thus to the extent that LTL operations are associated with light-density rural traffic, there appears to be an implicit subsidy of this traffic granted by the rate structure, at least in the Official Region.

A somewhat different response pattern emerges in the South–West Region, which indicates that the rate structure discriminates in favor of firms whose traffic is characterized by small loads and low insurance costs. These findings are in direct opposition to the subsidy hypothesis, and indicate that the price–marginal cost ratios are more favorable for small-load, low-value (or less fragile) shipments than for large-load, high-value (or fragile) shipments.

Three operating characteristics seem to have a significant impact upon price–marginal cost relationships for the Interregional carriers: firms with large shipment sizes, high insurance costs, and low ton-miles/terminal are apparently favored by the rate structure. This is at best a very marginal confirmation of the subsidy hypothesis.

On balance, the relationships between prices and marginal costs associated with the various operating characteristics appear to give little support to the subsidy hypothesis. While certain types of shipments appear to be favored by the rate structure for certain types of carriers, no consistent pattern emerges that implies that traffic associated with light-density rural traffic is subsidized by the rate structure. Indeed, there is some evidence that this traffic is actually favored by the rate structure and is relatively more profitable than traffic associated with high-density corridors. However, the findings of this section are sufficiently inconsistent that no single pattern of subsidy emerges. We are thus led to the conclusion that although operating and shipment characteristics affect the price–marginal cost ratios, they do not do so in a consistent or systematic fashion that would imply a pattern of cross subsidization from high-density, urban traffic to low-density rural traffic.

Finally, the difference between $\tilde{F}_{yy}$ and F_{yy} is negative for the Official and South–West carriers, but significant only for the latter. This implies that the price–marginal cost ratios tend to fall with firm size, and thus that the rate structure does not favor large firms nor encourage their expansion. For the Interregionals, firm size has virtually no effect upon price–marginal cost ratios. Thus whatever incentives firms may have to expand are probably due to an ability to attract shipments with attractive profitability characteristics (e.g., AVSIZE for the Interregionals), rather than to increased output levels per se.

In conclusion, then, this analysis indicates that we cannot characterize any of these carriers by marginal cost pricing and that prices deviate from marginal costs in ways related to factor prices, operating characteristics, and output levels. Nevertheless, these deviations between prices and marginal costs do not appear to be systematically related to output levels or operating characteristics in such a fashion as to indicate that the commission's pricing policies systematically favor any particular types of shipments, or favor large firms. Thus we find very little support for the cross-subsidy hypothesis. Consequently, fears that rates would rise dramatically on small shipments, short-haul traffic, or low-density traffic in the absence of regulation do not receive empirical support from this analysis.

Notes

1. Since significant nonhomotheticities were also found to exist between factor prices and output, the elasticities of cost are also influenced by factor prices. However, although the interaction effects between output and factor prices were generally found to be statistically significant, they were also numerically small and hence have a relatively small impact upon the estimated cost elasticities.

2. Although production is nonhomothetic and factor prices typically affect the elasticities of cost, the coefficients associated with these effects are typically small, although statistically significant. Hence it is reasonable to ignore these effects in characterizing the behavior of cost elasticities. Appendix C presents a full analysis of the nature and extent of these nonhomotheticities.

3. A shipment is a single movement of freight; it is classified as an LTL shipment if the total weight of the goods to be moved is less than 5 tons. The 5-ton definition of a TL shipment used by the ICC is highly arbitrary since 5 tons of most goods handled by a common carrier will not fill a truck. Of course, several shipments may go in the same truck, if shipments are small; on the other hand, one shipment may be split among several vehicles. In this way it is possible that a firm that handles a high proportion of large shipments has an average shipment size greater than its average load, though the reverse is almost always the case.

4. We will examine pricing policies extensively in section 5.4.

5. It should be pointed out, however, that many analysts in the trucking industry believe that firms are able to discourage undesirable traffic by performing poor service, etc. Unfortunately, there are no data to corroborate these assertions.

6. The terminal variable is apparently subject to greater measurement errors in the two samples of regional carriers since it also includes "terminal authorities" as well as "terminals." Moreover, the terminal variable is unavailable for a substantial number of regional carriers.

7. The distribution of observed elasticities of costs with respect to output is as follows: in the Official Territory, 22.7 percent of firms in the sample less than 1.0, 9.7 percent less than 0.95; in the South–West Region, 36 percent of the firms in the sample less than 1.0, 19.3 percent less than 0.95.

8. The marginal and average costs can be calculated from

$$AC = \frac{\exp(\ln(C/w_4))w_4}{y},$$

$$MC = AC\frac{\partial \ln(C/w_4)}{\partial \ln y}.$$

9. For example, when in section 5.4 we estimate this cost model jointly with a "revenue share" equation whose coefficients are *not* constrained to be derived from the cost function, we find γ_y is about one and F_{yy} is virtually zero. While this is possibly indicative of specification error in the "revenue share" equation (which is spread to the cost function through the simultaneous estimation of the variance–covariance matrix of disturbances), alternative specification of the Interregionals' cost function yielded a variety of results for γ_y and F_{yy}. In constrast, the results for the regional carriers were remarkably stable in this respect.

10. The same conclusion is reached when the Interregionals' characteristics and factor prices are put in the Official cost function. If the Official firms had Interregionals prices and characteristics, their average costs would be much lower. For example, at 50 million ton-miles, average cost would drop from 15.5 to 9.7¢.

11. We disregard the average cost levels that Interregionals could obtain by shrinking since we are interested in the predatory prospects of large Interregionals under deregulation.

12. See Spady (1979) for a discussion of the relationships between prices and marginal costs in the multiple-output case.

13. As noted above, adding (5.5) to the cost–factor share system substantially affects the results for the Interregionals. For the other two samples, there are also shifts, but these appear to be considerably less serious.

Chapter 6

Regulatory Analysis and Regulatory Reform: A Summing-Up

A basic motivation of this book is the belief that rational decisions concerning regulatory reform can only be made if policymakers have sufficient information concerning the efficiency and distributional consequences of changes in existing regulatory practices. Thus a major focus of this book has been the development of a consistent analytical framework that could be applied to evaluate issues of regulatory reform and its subsequent application to regulatory problems in the rail and trucking industry. Consequently, although this book certainly leaves considerably more questions unanswered than it attempts to answer, we nevertheless hope that we have provided an analytical framework that can be used in subsequent research and policy analysis.

From a methodological viewpoint, a basic premise of this book has been that the neoclassical theory of the firm, the industry, and competitive behavior can be used to provide a consistent framework to evaluate the behavior of the transportation sectors. We have thus developed neoclassical cost and demand functions from the underlying production functions that incorporate operating characteristics as well as conventional variables such as factor prices, outputs, and rates. In terms of the specification of transportation cost functions, the inclusion of these operating characteristics proves to be particularly important in terms of understanding the nature of scale economies, factor substitutions, and the underlying technology of these industries. From the point of view of policy analysis, the inclusion of these operating characteristics is extremely important since these are the primary variables upon which transportation policy operates.

In addition to stressing the theory of production that lies behind the cost and demand functions, this analysis has stressed the need for a general equilibrium analysis of transportation markets. Thus, changes that take place in any one transport market will engender changes in related markets, which will, in turn, engender further changes in the initial markets. Since these general equilibrium effects may be rather large, it is important to utilize an analysis that encompasses all of the interrelationships among the relevant markets. By developing a consistent set of cost and demand functions across modes and commodities and by simulating their joint equilibrium, this research provides such a general equilibrium analysis.

Finally, since transportation policy is not only concerned with aspects of economic efficiency but also with distributional questions concerning the beneficiaries of current transportation policies, any analysis of transportation policy must include measures of income changes as well as measures of efficiency gains and losses. To this end, this research has developed a regional income model that links regional income levels to freight rates and thus provides a means of assessing the aggregate income effects associated with changes in transportation policies.

Consequently, in stressing the theoretical foundations of the transport cost and demand functions, the general equilibrium nature of transportation markets, and the distributional consequences of changes in regulatory policy, we hope that we have strengthened the analytical foundations of regulatory policy analysis. However, in the absence of cost and demand data on water transportation, exempt carriage, and private trucking, we cannot hope to provide a complete picture of the consequences of regulatory reform. Thus although this analysis provides a somewhat broader analytical scope than its predecessors, it is important to note that it still leaves many areas of concern uncovered.

Nevertheless, the methodological framework developed in this book has proved to be useful in analyzing three major transportation policies: the maintenance of the value-of-service rate structure; the adoption of programs to upgrade the railroad infrastructure; and deregulation of the trucking common carriers of general commodities.

6.1 Value-of-Service Pricing

The value-of-service rate structure was analyzed within a framework that considered two modes (rail and truckload truck—carriers of specialized commodities), two commodities (bulk and manufactured goods), and two regions (the Official Territory and the rest of the country, which we denote by the South–West Region). Rates, marginal costs, and traffic allocation that existed in 1972 were compared to the levels of these variables that would have existed if a competitive equilibrium had existed at that time.

In terms of policy, perhaps the most surprising result of this analysis was a refutation of the existence of the value-of-service rate structure. In particular, not only did the empirical evidence suggest that the price–marginal cost ratios on bulk commodities were actually higher than those on manufactured goods, but also that the price–marginal cost ratios on manufactured goods were actually less than unity within the railroad industry. Consequently, this analysis suggests that to the extent that a subsidy may exist in the rate structure, it goes from bulk commodities to manufactured goods rather than from manufactured goods to bulk commodities, as is held by the conventional wisdom.

In terms of the efficiency losses associated with the existing rate structure, this analysis showed that in virtually all markets substantial deviations from marginal cost pricing were found to exist, with the greatest discrepancies appearing in the rail market for manufactured goods in the Official Territory and the rail market for bulk commodities in the South–West Region. Although price was generally found to be above marginal costs under the existing value-of-service rate structure, rail rates appeared to be substantially below marginal costs for manufactured goods in the Official Territory and somewhat below marginal cost for manufactured goods in the South–West Region. Thus, within both regions, abandonment of value-of-service pricing and the establishment of a competitive rate structure would lead to rate increases on rail shipments of manufactured goods, rate reductions on truck shipments of both bulk and manufactured commodities, and a marked shift in the modal split in favor of rail for bulk commodities and in favor of truck for manufactured goods.

Since railroads in the Official Territory appear to carry considerable traffic at rates below marginal cost, a switch to marginal cost pricing would increase their profitability considerably, enabling them to earn a return to capital of 3.44 percent. While this is still less than the rates of return earned in most industries, it is a considerable improvement over the situation implied by existing pricing policies under which the Eastern railroads failed to cover variable costs. Although marginal cost pricing would reduce the profitability of railroads in the South–West Region, they would still earn a return to capital of approximately 5.36 percent.

Since the rate changes occasioned by marginal cost pricing would be rather large, the associated income changes would also be rather large. A switch from the regulated rate structure to competitive pricing policies would lead to direct income losses to rail shippers of manufactured goods, to trucking firms in the Official Territory, and to rail and trucking firms in the South–West Region. Thus with the important exception of rail shippers of manufactured goods, the income transfers resulting from the adoption of a competitive pricing policy would be from the carriers to the shippers. The fact that rail rates rise substantially on manufactured commodities in the Official Territory is important, however, since it leads to further income losses to manufacturing workers in the Official Territory. Thus in the Official Territory, the direct and indirect income losses resulting from a competitive pricing policy appear to exceed its efficiency and income gains. Nevertheless, the income gains accruing to the South–West Region from such a policy are sufficiently large to ensure that the aggregate benefits of a competitive pricing policy are considerably greater than the aggregate costs. However, the costs to specific shipper groups and carrier types are sufficiently large to suggest that efforts to ensure that these losers receive adequate compensation should be an item of high priority if a rationalization of the present rate structure in favor of competitive pricing is undertaken.

6.2 Railroad Costs and Infrastructure Investments

Since the railway roadbed has deteriorated considerably in recent years, this research also considers the implications of policies aimed at improving the railroads' infrastructure. We find that considerable cost savings could be obtained from abandoning light-density track; in 1972, a 10-percent reduction in light-density track would have saved the railroads approximately $440 million.

Although it is widely believed that the railroads suffer from excess capacity, it is important to distinguish between track, which represents common carrier obligations to haul traffic, and way-and-structures (WS) capital, which represents the capital embodied in the roadway. While virtually all railroads have some excess track, a large number of railroads appear to have insufficient capital. These railroads have apparently let their maintenance expenditures on way-and-structures decline to such an extent that increases in capital are actually needed to move them to a point of long-run equilibrium. For the majority of railroads, therefore, a policy that would provide them with resources to increase investments in way-and-structures capital by 10 percent, while permitting them to abandon the more costly segments of their low-density track, would lead to substantial cost savings of $708 million at 1972 output levels.

Finally, it is important to note that although this study finds evidence of long-run increasing returns to scale at existing output levels or at output levels consistent with a *short-run* competitive equilibrium, it finds newly constant returns to scale at output and infrastructure levels that are consistent with a *long-run* competitive equilibrium. This indicates the possibility that there are combinations of output levels and capital stock that would permit the railroads to earn a normal return on capital and hence be financially self-sufficient. In a long-run competitive equilibrium with the current route structure, we estimate that the railroads in the Official Region could earn a return on way-and-structures capital of 7.95 percent, while those in the South–West Region could earn a return of 6.99 percent; with a more favorable route structure these returns could certainly be increased. Thus it appears that the railroads could achieve rates of return that are comparable to those in other sectors in the economy with appropriate adjustments in rates and infrastructure.

6.3 Deregulation of Trucking Carriers of General Commodities

The less-than-truckload (LTL) trucking market has long been a source of concern to policymakers, with carriers and shippers generally making dire predictions about the likely consequences of deregulation, and economists generally arguing that competition could better serve the public interest than regulation. This research performed an extensive analysis of the costs and revenue structures of interregional carriers and small regional carriers in the Official and South–West Regions. Evidence of increasing costs and decreasing returns to scale is found for the regional trucking firms, indicating that these carriers should be competitively organized in the absence of regulation. While the interregional carriers give some evidence of increasing returns to scale, the bulk of these carriers appear to have exhausted their scale economies. Thus there seems little likelihood that the large interregional carriers would attempt to expand their operations significantly in the absence of regulation.

It is interesting to note that these three types of carriers exhibit widely different cost levels, with carriers in the Official Region having the highest costs and the Interregionals having the lowest. Nevertheless, our analysis suggests that these cost differentials arise primarily from differences in operating characteristics. Thus were the Interregionals to attempt to encroach on the traffic of the other carriers, it is likely that their costs would rise as their operations would take on the characteristics of the regional carriers. Consequently, the cost structure of carriers of general commodities gives little reason to believe that workable competition is not a reasonable possibility in a deregulated environment.

In addition to finding no evidence that deregulation of common carriers of general commodities would lead to the domination of the industry by a few firms, this research finds no evidence that rates are held down on traffic generated by small cities and towns or by rural and agricultural areas. In particular, an analysis of the differentials that exist between prices and marginal costs for these carriers found no evidence that the price–marginal cost ratios were systematically related to operating or shipment characteristics in such a way that the price–marginal cost ratios were held down for short-haul, small-load, small-size, LTL traffic. Indeed, there was some evidence that the rate structure may actually reward carriers for transporting traffic of this nature. If, however, the rate structure adequately compensates carriers for short-haul, small-load traffic, so that the rate differentials fully reflect cost differentials, there is little reason to believe that rates on this type of traffic would rise in a deregulated environment. Hence shippers in light-density areas appear to have little reason to fear that deregulation would be accompanied by rate increases; this traffic already appears to be earning an adequate return.

With a few important caveats, the findings of this book indicate that the public interest would be served by deregulation. This is particularly true in the case of regional carriers of general commodities, for which competition would appear to allocate resources efficiently and equitably and cause relatively few disruptions in the existing equilibrium. In contrast, although a movement toward a competitive equilibrium in the rail and truckload trucking markets would clearly generate aggregate efficiency and distributional benefits considerably in excess of the costs, it is likely that substantial income transfers would result from such a change. This implies that some means of providing adequate compensation must be developed for those who would face substantial income losses in the event of such a change.

Therefore, this book closes with a challenge to policymakers and legislators to develop the institutional mechanisms that would provide transitional protection to the losers from increased competition in the transport markets, while permitting society to benefit from the clear efficiencies that competition would provide. Thus the issue should not be *whether* the transportation industries should be deregulated or not, but *how* they can be deregulated to ensure an orderly transition from the present equilibrium to one that would represent a more rational allocation of the nation's scarce resources.

Appendix A

General Specifications of Costs and Technology

A.1. Introduction

Neoclassical economic theory makes very few assumptions about the technology of firms, in that the restrictions on the functional representation of a technology are derived from behavioral assumptions about the firm, such as cost minimization, profit maximization, or merely production efficiency (i.e., output maximization from given inputs). Consequently, in the empirical estimation of a technology, it is desirable to use all available prior knowledge about both the technology itself and the firm's economic environment, without implicitly imposing restrictions that are not true. Of course, every empirical investigator strives to incorporate a priori knowledge in his estimation procedure, and there is a well-developed theory of how correctly implemented restrictions improve the efficiency of one's estimates and how false restrictions usually (but not always) spell disaster. Moreover, there are formal decision-theoretic models which in special circumstances can significantly aid the incorporation of a priori knowledge into estimation procedures, and, more important for this study, there is the conventional Neyman–Pearson theory of statistical inference once a general model has been specified. But in no case do the data "tell their own story" unaided.

With respect to the transportation industries, the lack of a homogeneous output and the need to incorporate shipment characteristics directly into the analysis pose several problems. In particular, measuring the quantity and type of services produced by transportation firms is extremely difficult, as is explicitly modeling the technology that produces them. In the freight transportation industries, the generic measure of output is the ton-mile; but this is an obviously inadequate measure when the commodities hauled are diverse, and when average lengths of haul, average shipment sizes and average loads, and amount and type of area served vary widely from firm to firm. Similarly, there is the more technical question of how a difference in, say, average length of haul or route structure should be modeled; can firms whose services differ in these respect be viewed as producing for a given quantity of ton-miles different amounts of quality-adjusted output using otherwise identical technologies, or should they be viewed as having different but related technologies?

A.2 General Cost Function Specifications

The general neoclassical joint cost function can be written

$$C = C(y, w), \tag{A.1}$$

where y is a vector of output quantities and w a vector of factor prices. It is "dual" to the production frontier $F(y, x) = 0$, where x is a vector of factor quantities (to which w corresponds), as $C(y, w)$ gives the solution to

$$\min_{x} \sum_{i} w_i x_i \quad \text{subject to } F(y, x) = 0. \tag{A.2}$$

An explanation of the conditions under which $C(y, w)$ exists and its relation to $F(y, x)$ can be found in Lau (1976). For our purposes it is sufficient to note that $C(y, w)$ gives the firm's minimum cost of producing y at factor prices w, assuming it faces no binding constraints in the choice of x. It is nondecreasing in its argument and concave in w for all y.

McFadden (1978) has suggested a simple but powerful extension of (A.1) which can be written as

$$C = C(y, w, t), \tag{A.3}$$

which solves

$$\min_{x} \sum_{i} w_i x_i \quad \text{subject to } F(y, x, t) = 0, \tag{A.4}$$

where t is a vector summarizing what we shall call "technological conditions." An example of a technological condition would be the route structure of a motor carrier or railroad; a variable which would help summarize this condition might be the number of route-miles which generate very little traffic but which must be served nonetheless.

A further extension of (A.1) is to adjust the generic outputs y for quality differences in a simple way. Let q be a vector of qualities, with q^i being the qualities associated with the ith generic output y^i. Furthermore, suppose each quality is associated with only one output, and denote the vector $[y^i, q^i]$ by z^i and $([y^1, q^1], \ldots, [y^m, q^m])$ by z. Then writing

$$C(y, q, w, t) = C(\psi^1(y^1, q^1), \ldots, \psi^m(y^m, q^m), w, t) \tag{A.5a}$$

or

$$C(z, w, t) = C(\psi^1(z^1), \ldots, \psi^m(z^m), w, t) \tag{A.5b}$$

is equivalent to assuming

$$\frac{\partial}{\partial w}\left[\frac{C_{z_j^i}}{C_{z_k^i}}\right] = \frac{\partial}{\partial t}\left[\frac{C_{z_j^i}}{C_{z_k^i}}\right] = \frac{\partial}{\partial z^l}\left[\frac{C_{z_j^i}}{C_{z_k^i}}\right] = 0, \qquad i = 1, \ldots, m, \tag{A.6}$$

where $C_{z_j^i}$ is the partial derivative of C with respect to the jth component of z^i and $i \neq l$. Equation (A.6) expresses the Leontief (1947) conditions corresponding to (A.5a) or (A.5b). The notation of (A.5b) makes conspicuous the formal equivalence of (A.5a) to the conventional aggregation of several outputs (the elements of z^i) to one output (ψ^i) through an aggregator function $[\psi^i(\cdot)]$. The interpretation of (A.6) in conventional aggregation theory is that the marginal rates of transformation (marginal cost ratios) between components of an aggregate are independent of factor prices, technological conditions, and outputs not in the aggregate. Thus the mix of outputs within an aggregate does not affect the optimal factor intensities, and technological conditions do not affect the (component) output combinations feasible at a given level of the aggregate.

The interpretation of the components of z^i as a generic output and its corresponding qualities yields and model equivalent to one considered by Fisher and Shell (1972, pp. 26–37, 105–107) in the context of price indices. The very simplest case of this model, which we will use in both of the studies that follow, is the pure repackaging case given by

$$\psi^i(y^i, q^i) = y^i\phi^i(q^i). \tag{A.7}$$

The analogy of repackaging as applied, for example, to trucking, is that trucking services are packaged in ton-miles, and the service content of the package is a function of the characteristics of the ton-miles—the size of the shipment, the length of haul, etc.

The specification of (A.5a) already imposes the conditions that (for a given level of effective output) quality changes do not affect optimal factor intensities and technological conditions do not affect feasible generic output–quality combinations. Without these restrictions, which can be relaxed by including qualities in the technological conditions vector, it is impossible to preserve the simple notion of quality change embodied in the condition that the relative marginal costs of two different (y^i, q^i) combinations be independent of w, t, and $[y^l, q^l]$, $l \neq i$.[1] Using (A.7), in which we impose the requirement that $\psi^i(y^i, q^i)$ be homogeneous of degree 1 in y, is in contrast a matter of convenience; in the contexts in which (A.7) is to be employed there is a natural generic output such that it is convenient to think of a doubling of generic output at constant qualities as a doubling of effective output.[2]

It is convenient to take $\phi(q)$ as a simple Cobb–Douglas function of qualities. While this has the disadvantage of imposing a very specific curvature on quality–quality isoquants whose reasonableness must be evaluated on a case-by-case basis, it has the usual advantage of a simple interpretation and an economy of parameters. More important, in the translog specification adopted below the Cobb–Douglas specification of $\phi(q)$ is nested in the translog specification in which the elements of q are included in t. Thus it is possible to conveniently test the restriction of the general model to a quality-adjustment model in which $\phi(q)$ is Cobb–Douglas.

Finally, if the firm is unable to choose the levels of some factors but chooses the quantities of the variable factors to minimize the expenditures on those factors, the appropriate short-run or restricted cost function is

$$C = C(\psi, x_F, w_V, t), \tag{A.8}$$

which solves

$$\min_{x_V} \sum_i w_i x_{V_i} \quad \text{subject to } F(\psi, x_F, x_V, t) = 0, \tag{A.9}$$

where the subscripts F and V refer to fixed and variable factors, respectively. It is often useful to regard x_F as part of the t vector; this viewpoint is explicitly adopted, for example, in McFadden (1978).

A.3 The Translog Cost Function

In the studies that follow, the specific functional form used for (A.5) or (A.8) will be

$$
\begin{aligned}
\ln C = {} & \alpha_0 + \sum_i \alpha_i \ln w_i + \sum_j \beta_j \ln t_j + \sum_k \gamma_k \ln \psi_k \\
& + \tfrac{1}{2} \sum_i \sum_l A_{il} \ln w_i \ln w_l + \sum_i \sum_j B_{ij} \ln w_i \ln t_j \\
& + \sum_i \sum_k C_{ik} \ln w_i \ln \psi_k + \tfrac{1}{2} \sum_j \sum_m D_{jm} \ln t_j \ln t_m \\
& + \sum_j \sum_k E_{jk} \ln t_j \ln \psi_k + \tfrac{1}{2} \sum_k \sum_h F_{kh} \ln \psi_k \ln \psi_h + \varepsilon_C,
\end{aligned} \tag{A.10}
$$

where ε_C is a disturbance. This is the transcendental logarithmic functional form, which has been widely used in cost and production studies since its first systematic interpretation as a flexible[3] functional form by Christensen et al. (1973). By including fixed factor quantities in the t vector, (A.10) becomes a translog short-run cost function corresponding to (A.8); when all factors are variable (A.10) is the long-run translog cost function corresponding to (A.5).

One interpretation of the translog functional form is that it represents a second-order Taylor series approximation to an unknown underlying function. To view (A.10) explicitly as such a Taylor series approximation, replace $\ln w_i$ by $\ln w_i - \ln w_i^0$, $\ln t_j$ by $\ln t_j - \ln t_j^0$, and $\ln \psi_k$ by $\ln \psi_k - \ln \psi_k^0$; then the point (w_i^0, t_j^0, ψ_k^0) is the point of approximation or expansion. In the studies that follow, the point of approximation is the sample arithmetic mean of the (w, t, y, q) vector. Since, for example, $\ln w_i - \ln \bar{w}_i$ equals $\ln(w_i/\bar{w}_i)$, this corresponds to normalizing each variable[4] to have a mean of one, and using the normalized variables in (A.10). Since (A.10) as written can be viewed as a Taylor series approximation around the point $(1, 1, \ldots, 1)$, and $\ln 1 = 0$, a number of important economic calculations are simplified at the point of approximation, which corresponds to a hypothetical firm whose values of factor prices, technological conditions, generic outputs, and qualities are those of the sample arithmetic means.

In the approximation interpretation of the translog function, the properties (i.e., the value of the function and its first and second derivatives) of the underlying function are inherited by the approximating function only at a single point—in this case, the sample arithmetic mean of the (w, t, y, q) vector. For some properties, this equality at a point guarantees that the approximating translog function will have the property globally. This is the case with homogeneity, for example, so that the translog approximation to a homogeneous function is homogeneous. Concavity, on the other hand, cannot hold globally for any translog function (unless it reduces to a Cobb–Douglas function)—no restrictions on the coefficients of a translog function will guarantee global negative semidefiniteness of its Hessian. Since concavity in w is an important property that any well-defined cost function must have, it is difficult to argue that a translog cost function is an exact representation of a cost function throughout the conceivable range of its arguments.

This indicates that an approximation interpretation of the translog function is nearly inevitable, and brings up the problem how to interpret violations of essential conditions at points other than the point of approximation.[5] In some sense, of course, a "good" approximation will not violate essential conditions within the sample, but the more important question is whether satisfaction of the essential conditions throughout the sample range (or possibly excepting fringe points) is indicative of a satisfactory approximation. Here, the only evidence appears to be a simulation study by Wales (1977), which indicates that translog estimates of important elasticities are quite good for cases in which monotonicity and concavity hold for all points in a sample, and generally very good if the violations occur only for a small number of points. Conversely (and not unexpectedly), Wales finds that translog estimates which violate these conditions for a large number of sample points do not indicate that a maximization or minimization process is not at work, but that the translog function is a poor approximation to its functional representation.

If firms are indeed cost minimizers, so that (A.10) is valid, then Shephard's lemma holds:

$$\frac{\partial C(\psi, w, t)}{\partial w_i} = x_i, \tag{A.11}$$

or

$$\frac{\partial \ln C(\psi, w, t)}{\partial \ln w_i} = \frac{\partial C(\psi, w, t)}{\partial w_i} \cdot \frac{w_i}{C} = \frac{w_i x_i}{C}. \tag{A.12}$$

Thus, corresponding to (A.10) are the cost share equations

$$\frac{w_i x_i}{C} = \alpha_i + \sum_l A_{il} \ln w_l + \sum_j B_{ij} \ln t_j + \sum_k C_{ik} \ln \psi_k + \varepsilon_i, \tag{A.13}$$

where ε_i is a disturbance.

Since

$$\sum_i \left(\frac{w_i x_i}{C} \right) = 1,$$

it follows that $\Sigma_i \varepsilon_i = 0$, so that the variance–covariance matrix of $(\varepsilon_C, \varepsilon_i)$ is singular. Moreover, there is reason to believe that the disturbances among both the share equations and the cost equation are contemporaneously correlated. We specify that the disturbances are multivariately normally distributed, and estimate the cost and factor share equations jointly using the FIML estimation and inference procedures outlined in Berndt et al. (1974). This is achieved by dropping one factor share equation from the system to be estimated; the FIML estimators are invariant to the share equation dropped.[6]

We also impose the coefficient restrictions upon (A.10) which ensure that the cost function be homogeneous of degree 1 in factor prices, and the symmetry conditions $A_{il} = A_{li}$, $D_{jm} = D_{mj}$, and $F_{kh} = F_{hk}$, for all h, i, j, k, l, and m. Equation (A.10) is homogeneous of degree 1 in w if and only if

$$\sum_i \alpha_i = 1, \tag{A.14a}$$

$$\sum_i A_{il} = 0, \qquad l = 1, \ldots, I, \tag{A.14b}$$

$$\sum_i B_{ij} = 0, \qquad j = 1, \ldots, J, \tag{A.14c}$$

$$\sum_i C_{ik} = 0, \qquad k = 1, \ldots, K, \tag{A.14d}$$

where I, J, and K are the number of (variable) factors, technological conditions, and outputs, respectively. Both factor price homogeneity and symmetry are implied by cost minimization, and these properties hold globally for a translog function if they hold at one point.[7] Thus, even under the approximation interpretation of the translog cost function, in which the estimated cost function has the (up to second-order) properties of the true underlying function only at a point, these restrictions are implied by cost-minimizing behavior.

To estimate the cost–factor share system, it is necessary to substitute for each appearance of ψ_k in (A.10) and (A.13):

$$\psi_k = y_k \phi^k(q^k), \tag{A.15}$$

or

$$\ln \psi_k = \ln y_k + \ln \phi^k(q^k). \tag{A.16}$$

Using a Cobb–Douglas form for $\phi^k(q^k)$ yields

$$\ln \psi_k = \ln y_k + \sum_i \delta_i^k \ln q_i^k. \tag{A.17}$$

Substituting (A.17) into (A.10) and (A.13) and imposing the symmetry and factor price homogeneity restrictions gives the final estimating form.

As mentioned earlier, using a Cobb–Douglas form for $\phi^k(q^k)$ allows the specification of $C(\psi(y, q), w, t)$ (the hedonic model) to be nested inside of $C(y, w, t, q)$, in which q can be interpreted as being appended to the t vector. This can be seen by writing both models explicitly in the form of (A.10) and substituting (A.17) for $\ln \psi_k$. The hedonic model is thus the more general model with a complicated series of nonlinear restrictions on the coefficients.[8] It is not necessary to directly consider these restrictions in testing the restriction to the hedonic model since it is computationally simpler to estimate both models in their natural forms and perform the likelihood ratio test.

Notes

1. By an argument analogous to Fisher and Shell (1972, theorem 5.1, pp. 31–32).

2. A more general $\psi^i(y^i, q^i)$ could be estimated by including q^i in the t vector and imposing appropriate separability constraints.

3. The translog functional form is called "flexible" since it is capable of providing a second-order approximation to an arbitrary function. Two concepts of approximation, both satisfied by the translog function, have been distinguished by Lau (1974b). In the first concept, a function $H(Z)$ provides a second-order differential approximation to $G(Z)$ at Z_0 provided $H(Z_0) = G(Z_0)$ and

$$\left. \frac{\partial H}{\partial Z} \right|_{Z=Z_0} = \left. \frac{\partial G}{\partial Z} \right|_{Z=Z_0},$$

$$\left[\frac{\partial^2 H}{\partial Z_i \partial Z_j} \right]_{Z=Z_0} = \left[\frac{\partial^2 G}{\partial Z_i \partial Z_j} \right]_{Z=Z_0}.$$

In the second concept, $H(Z)$ provides a second-order numerical approximation to $G(Z)$ at Z_0 if $H(Z_0) = G(Z_0)$ and

$$|H(Z) - G(Z)| \leq \frac{K\|Z - Z_0\|^3}{\|Z_0\|^3}$$

for all Z in a given neighborhood of Z_0, where k is a constant depending on Z_0 and the chosen neighborhood, and $\|Z\|$ denotes a norm of Z.

Any function $H(Z)$ that can be interpreted as a second-order Taylor series approximation to $G(Z)$ around Z_0 is both a numerical and a differential second-order approximation; a translog function can be so interpreted. A very wide and interesting class of functions with this interpretation, which includes the translog, Diewert (1971) (generalized Leontief), and quadratic functions as special cases, has been examined by Denny (1974).

4. For ψ_k we have $\ln \psi_k = (\ln y_k - \ln \bar{y}_k) + \Sigma_i \delta_i^k (\ln q_i - \ln \bar{q}_i)$, so that ψ_k^0 is not $\bar{\psi}_k$ but $\bar{y}_k \phi(\bar{q}) = \bar{y}_k$.

5. If a condition is violated at the point of approximation, then it can be imposed at that point by suitable coefficient restrictions; these restrictions allow the hypothesis to be tested at that point (Lau, 1974b). In practice, however, these restrictions are complicated and difficult to implement; fortunately, in both the studies that follow, all essential conditions are satisfied at the point of approximation and throughout most, if not all, of the range of the sample.

6. A survey of specifications and estimation procedures with a singular covariance matrix can be found in Berndt and Savin (1975); see also Barten (1969).

7. In the case of homogeneity, this can be seen as follows. Since the underlying function is homogeneous, both it and its approximating function satisfy Euler's equation at the point of approximation. But for the translog function, satisfaction of Euler's equation

at that point is equivalent to (A.14). Direct calculation shows that (A.14) implies global homogeneity.

8. There is a comparatively wide literature on using the translog functional form to test for the existence of consistent aggregates of factors. If the translog function were an exact representation of the technology, the Leontief conditions would hold globally. Two sets of restrictions for which this is true were developed and applied by Berndt and Christensen (1973a, 1974). In independent simultaneous papers, Blackorby et al. (1977) and Denny and Fuss (1977) pointed out that the translog function that approximates a separable function need only satisfy the Leontief conditions at the point of approximation. It turns out that this implies much weaker restrictions than those employed by Berndt and Christensen.

Denny and Fuss prove a proposition (1977, p. 405) concerning the undesirable effects of the stronger restrictions: it is equivalent to forcing the function to "be either a Cobb–Douglas function of translog subaggregates or a translog function of Cobb–Douglas subaggregates." The extension of this result to the current case is this: the general model $C(y, w, t, q)$ restricted to globally satify the Leontief conditions (A.6) is either a translog function of Cobb–Douglas $\phi(q)$'s or a Cobb–Douglas function of translog $\phi(q)$'s, in the case where $\psi(y, q)$ is homothetic in y. [For more general $\psi(y, q)$, the $\psi(\cdot)$ functions themselves would play the role of the $\phi(q)$'s.] We will assume that the case of the Cobb–Douglas function of translog $\phi(q)$'s is without interest since it specifies a simple technology of complicated aggregates. We will also not formally test the general model for local separability since the implied nonlinear restrictions seem in practice to be far from true and their imposition, while reducing slightly the number of independent parameters, does not yield a simpler model from either the computational or interpretive viewpoint.

Appendix B

Cost Functions for US Railroads, 1968–1970

B.1 Introduction: Previous Cost and Production Studies of US Railroads

The estimation of cost and production functions for the railroad industry has, by econometric standards, a long history. Nonetheless, previous studies have generally been inadequate in two respects. First, they have failed to distinguish the effect of way-and-structures capital on costs from that of track or route-miles. While more way-and-structures capital should lower expenditures on other factors, ceteris paribus, an increase in route-miles represents an increase in common carriage obligation so that one might expect expenditures on other factors to increase. Second, previous studies have ignored the effect of such variables as traffic mix by commodity type, average length of haul, and low-density route-mileage on costs. Our intention in this appendix is to demonstrate the methodological and practical advantages of a more careful specification of railroad technology. Towards this end, we will review several recent studies that employ methods similar to those outlined in appendix A.

Brown et al. (1979) and Hasenkamp (1976a, b) have recently estimated models using Klein's (1947, 1953) cross-sectional data on US railroads for the years 1928 and 1936. Hasenkamp's models are production frontiers of the form

$$h(y) = g(x),$$

where y is a vector of outputs, specifically passenger-miles and freight ton-miles, and x a vector of inputs, specifically labor measured as man-hours, fuel measured as tons of coal equivalent, and capital services measured as car-miles or train-hours. The functions h and g were Cobb–Douglas, CES, or the generalized quadratic function suggested by Diewert (1974). Hasenkamp found in all formulations increasing returns to scale, and that the production possibility frontier (or, in the cost function case, isocost contour) was not concave. The former result was also obtained in Klein's original study, and the latter was imposed through the use of a Cobb–Douglas form for both h and g.

Among the obvious shortcomings of both Hasenkamp's and Klein's studies is the separability of outputs from inputs, so that, for example, optimal factor intensities are independent of output mix. Brown et al. (1975) remedied this by estimating a translog cost function (and factor share system) with Klein's data. They again find increasing returns to scale and a convex isocost contour, but also are able to reject both separability and homogeneity of arbitrary degree in output.

In a time-series cross-section study, Caves et al. (1980a) estimate a generalized translog short-run cost function in which way-and-structures capital is taken as a fixed factor, and labor, fuel, and materials and equipment are the variable factors. This represents an advance in that investment in way-and-structures is fixed in the short run; unfortunately, however, the marginal product of this factor is negative (i.e., increasing way-and-structures capital increases *variable* costs). In contrast with earlier results, they find long-run constant returns to scale.[1]

These results are in many respects similar to those of Keeler (1974), who studied a cross section of railroads over the years 1968–1970. Keeler specified passenger and freight output to be separate Cobb–Douglas functions of the way-and-structures, equipment, fuel, and labor resources devoted to each output. Unlike Caves et al., who used a value of investment figure for way-and-structures capital, Keeler used track-miles. After assuming factor prices were constant across his sample, Keeler estimated a total cost function of the form

$$TC = rT + C(\psi, T), \tag{B.5}$$

where TC is the cost of both variable and fixed factors, T is miles of track, and $C(\psi, T)$ a short-run cost function whose functional form is dual to the specification of nonjoint, Cobb–Douglas production functions; r is a parameter to be estimated representing the true (unobservable) cost of a track-mile. Keeler estimated r to be about \$19,000, whereas $\partial C / \partial T$ can be calculated from his estimates to be about \$6,700. That is, the way-and-structures resources represented by 1 track-mile cost a railroad \$19,000, but reduced other costs by only \$6,700; for the latter figure to equal the former, over 200,000 track-miles, or about 65 percent of the US total in 1969, would have to be abandoned.

Keeler's results resemble Caves et al. in that both seem to imply large excess trackage or overcapitalization in way-and-structures along with a technology of long-run constant returns to scale. If this characterization were accurate, the policy prescription that would likely follow would be massive track abandonment combined with some form of deregulation, as Keeler cautiously advocates. In Keeler's study, there is an explicit identity of capital with track-miles, while in Caves et al. track mileage is not considered in any explicit manner; but both studies give the somewhat counterintuitive result that railroads are harmed (in that their current or "out-of-pocket" costs increase) by an additional unit of way-and-structures capital.

The usual explanation for this is that an additional unit of way-and-structures capital "represents" additional trackage which is "in excess" at the margin. But while it may be true that track-miles and reproduction value are positively correlated, there is no a priori reason to identify or conflate the two: two railroads with an identical number of track-miles may have very different reproduction values if, for example, the condition of their track is different. For a given railroad, an improvement in the condition or quality (heavier rail track) of its track surely lowers variable costs, for the operations possible on lower-quality track are possible on higher-quality track.

What is almost certainly being captured by the fixed factor formulations that do not distinguish trackage from way-and-structures capital is that, ceteris paribus, the cost of producing a given combination of freight and passenger traffic increases with network size as measured by route-miles. Increasing route-miles without changing measured traffic characteristics (such as ton-miles and average length of haul) might be expected to increase equipment requirements, for example. Conversely, one might expect that reducing route-miles while holding ton-miles constant would have no deleterious effects save congestion, which could probably be alleviated by building second mainlines and expanding classification yards and terminals. In addition, the distribution of route-miles by traffic density should have an effect on cost and factor intensities; it is widely believed, for example, that branchlines generating a small amount of traffic are particularly burdensome. Thus, using a conventional specification analysis argument, if capital is positively correlated with higher-cost route structures, ceteris paribus, an underestimation of the marginal product of capital would be expected; if this correlation were strong enough, an estimate of a negative marginal product of capital could result.

This suggests that route-miles and low-density route-miles be made technological arguments of the cost function in the manner outlined in appendix A. In addition, since average length of haul indicates the relative importance of linehaul and loading operations, we would expect it to be an important technological factor in railroad cost functions. A longer average length of haul will result in lower cost per ton-mile and a shift in factor intensities. Since average length of haul is correlated with network size, excluding it from the cost function would probably result in spurious estimates of increasing returns to scale.

Another technological factor affecting rail operations not accounted for in most previous studies is freight traffic mix. Railroads handle a wide range of commodities, from comparatively fragile manufactured commodities to mine and forest products. One would expect that the carriage of the latter is less costly than the former, since the latter requires less costly equipment and has smaller handling costs. Since US railroads vary widely in their freight traffic mix, it is likely that including some measure of traffic mix as a technological condition will improve our results considerably, even though there is no strong prior expectation as to the biases which would result from excluding this variable.

In summary, previous studies have failed to provide a satisfactory understanding of the role of way-and-structures capital in railroad operations. While way-and-structures capital is certainly a factor of production, it has not generally been appropriately distinguished from the rail route-mileage with which it is associated. In terms of the technological model presented in previous chapters, total and low-density route-mileage are measures of the service obligations of a railroad: to each level of these obligations (and other technological conditions) there corresponds a neoclassical technology. In such a model, one can characterize the changes in operations (factor intensities) and costs occasioned by changes in service obligations while still preserving the ordinary concept of a factor of production.

In the next section of this appendix we give an explicit specification of our model, while the following section presents and interprets estimates of this model for a cross section of US railroads for the years 1968–1970.

B.2 Specification of a Cost Function for US Railroads

We will assume that way-and-structures capital is fixed in the short run so that firms minimize expenditures on the remaining factors given the exogenously determined fixed factor quantity, technological conditions, and outputs. It is appropriate to regard way-and-structures capital as fixed not only because its quantity is difficult to vary over short periods, but also because railroads are generally believed to have allowed this factor to decay rapidly in many instances. Since it is unlikely that the optimal adjustment of this factor can be obtained through such depreciation, it would be inappropriate to treat this factor as variable.

The technological conditions the firm faces are exogenous since route structure and branchline mileage are explicitly controlled by the ICC, and average length of haul and traffic mix are determined by the route structure and shipper demands along these routes. Since railroads are obligated by their status as common carriers to satisfy all shipper demands at fixed prices, the technological conditions and output, both influenced by demand, are exogenous.

Thus, the following equation applied in the current context is appropriate:

$$C = C(\psi_P, \psi_F, x, w, t),   \text{(B.6)}$$

where ψ_P is passenger service output, ψ_F freight service output, x the quantity of way-and-structures capital, w a vector of prices of variable factors, and t a vector of technological conditions.

In the remainder of this section we consider the following topics in detail: (1) the arguments of the cost function and their definitions; (2) the sample over which (B.6) is to be estimated; (3) the functional form employed; and (4) the specification of an autoregressive structure for the disturbances of the cost and factor share equations.

B.2.1 The Arguments of the Cost Functions and Their Definitions

Passenger service output is passenger-miles y_P adjusted for two qualities, passenger average travel length (PATL) and passenger-miles per passenger route-mile (PDENS), using

$$\psi_P = y_P \phi(\text{PATL, PDENS}),   \text{(B.7)}$$

where ϕ is a translog function.[2] One expects that increases in passenger density will decrease the cost of producing a given amount of passenger-miles not only because of economies of utilization of equipment and centralization of ancillary services (ticket offices, terminals, etc.), but also because passenger service requires that track be kept in better condition. The effect of passenger average travel length on passenger service, however, may be ambiguous. Handling fewer passengers per passenger-mile lowers the cost associated with ticketing and boarding passengers; but increases in passenger average travel length are also associated with a shift in the type of passenger service provided from commuter to interstate. If the latter is more expensive than the former, we would expect $\partial \psi_P / \partial \text{PATL} < 0$ for larger values of PATL.

For freight service output revenue ton-miles is used. Since average length of haul and traffic mix are liable to have a direct effect on factor shares, they have been included as technological conditions, which is a less restrictive condition than including them in a hedonic function altering ton-miles. While it would be desirable to disaggregate ton-miles by commodity type, there are data and specification limitations which prohibit this; these limitations are discussed under traffic mix, below.

The measure of way-and-structures capital employed is the reproduction cost of land, way, and structures estimated by R. A. Nelson (1974) for the American Association of Railroads (AAR). In this study, Nelson adopted the basic methodology employed by the ICC in constructing its 1963 *Elements of Value* and used railroad reports to the ICC and the AAR to estimate reproduction cost as of December 31, 1971. ICC data on changes in railroad investment, the GNP deflator for investment in railroad structures, and a depreciation rate of 2 percent were used to extrapolate middle-of-year reproduction costs of way-and-structures measured in 12/31/71 dollars to the data used in this sample. Details of the construction of this and other variables are included in the technical supplement to this appendix (section B.5).

The variable factors employed in the specification are equipment, general and maintenance labor, traffic and transportation labor (other than train), on-train labor, and fuel and materials. For the three classifications of labor, Divisia price indexes were calculated from the railroads' A-200 wage reports to the ICC; these provide wage and man-hour data for 128 categories of labor; those categories are aggregated into seven broad classifications by the ICC. Adjusting the expenditures in the seven classifications for fringe benefits and labor taxes as reported by the railroads in the ICC *Transport Statistics I*, Divisia price indexes using the data on the seven classifications were calculated for our three classifications. Since labor payments reported in the A-200 statistics include those for investment activities (e.g., laying new track), the discrepancy between total A-200 wages and the *Transport Statistics* item "employee compensation chargeable to operating expenses" was subtracted from the expenditures on general and maintenance labor, after appropriate adjustment for fringe benefits and taxes. This is equivalent to assuming that investment expenditure on labor is proportionately distributed among the four subcategories of general and maintenance labor. Unfortunately, the ICC collects no data on distribution of these expenditures, but since these expenditures typically account for only 2–4 percent of the total labor bill and can be accurately attributed to one of our three classifications, the main effect of this procedure will be slightly erroneous share weights in the calculation of the Divisia index.

While good firm-specific data are thus available for labor prices, we use the AAR's time-series index of fuel and materials prices for our fuel and materials expenditure category. This category includes all nonlabor expenditures included in *Transport Statistics*' operating costs, net of equipment, and way-and-structures depreciation. It consists primarily of expenditures for fuel, maintenance materials, insurance, damage to property and cargo losses, injuries to persons, and office supplies.

An implicit rental price of equipment capital w_e was constructed using

$$w_e = (r + d) p_k, \tag{B.8}$$

where r is an interest rate, d a depreciation rate of 5 percent, and p_k the GNP deflator for the price of rail equipment. Interest rates for each railroad were calculated from *Moody's Transportation Annual* by using the appropriate index of yields for each road's lowest- (i.e., worst-) rated equipment trust certificate. Our intention here was to obtain an approximation to the marginal market rate at which funds could be borrowed if secured by equipment; these rates are of course substantially below those of general obligations.

An estimate of each firm's owned equipment capital stock was calculated from the AAR's estimate of reproduction cost at the end of 1971, as presented in R. A. Nelson (1974). The method used was similar to that employed for way-and-structures, with a 5-percent depreciation rate assumed. Each firm's quantity of equipment capital was multiplied by its capital rental price to provide the opportunity and depreciation costs of owned capital in current dollars, and to this figure each firm's net equipment rentals as reported in *Transport Statistics* was added to derive net total expenditures on equipment.

Each railroad's variable costs are the sum of its expenditures on the five variable factors, as explained above. In terms of the ICC's accounting system, variable cost is operating cost net of way-and-structures and equipment depreciation, plus fringe benefits and labor taxes on employee compensation chargeable to operating expenses, plus net equipment rentals, plus imputed opportunity and depreciation costs on equipment capital.

Of the four technological conditions variables used in our model, two are taken from *Transport Statistics*. Freight route-miles is average mileage operated in freight transportation service [not total track-mileage, as used in Keeler (1974)] while average length of haul is revenue ton-miles/ revenue tons.

The other two variables used as technological conditions are derived from data made available by the Federal Railroad Administration (FRA). In 1976 the FRA conducted a survey of rail route utilization for the years 1970–1975 as part of a study mandated by the Railroad Revitalization and Regulatory Reform Act. On the basis of this survey, the FRA classified 51,555 route-miles as B (lowest-density) branchlines, accounting for 25.6 percent of the nation's total and 27.1 percent of those not classified as "other." The main criterion of classification is annual freight density; those lines carrying less than one million gross ton-miles annually are classified as B branchlines. By contrast, roughly 25 percent of the nation's route-miles fall in each of the other three classifications: 1–5 million gross ton-miles carried annually; 5–20 million; over 20 million.

From the FRA classification, B branchline-miles for the sample year 1968–1970 were simply extrapolated by assuming that the ratio of B branchlines to total route-miles was the same as reported for each railroad by the FRA. This procedure is probably accurate since the 1968–1970 route-miles by road show only a small deviation from the FRA figures; on a national basis, rail route-miles were reduced from 207,500 in 1968–1970 to 201,500 in 1975, with tons per route-mile staying virtually constant.

An additional FRA data source was the *Carload Waybill Statistics*, a 1-percent sample of waybills. From this sample and the ICC's *Quarterly Commodity Statistics*, an estimate of ton-miles in each of seven commodity categories was obtained. To do this, average length of haul by commodity was estimated from the waybill sample (see technical supplement, section B.5); these were multiplied by tons as given in the *Quarterly Commodity Statistics*. The inherent limitations of the data make this disaggregation highly suspect; moreover, as table B.1 shows, railroads vary widely in the types of commodities they carry. This makes expansion of the output vector in the translog functional form especially difficult as a practical matter, since not only will many of the additional coefficients required by the increase in outputs occur only in the cost equation (a point discussed below) but also because "extreme" values will be common. In the approximation interpretation of the translog, this may be a difficulty since the approximation error grows with the distance from the point of approximation. Moreover, since the translog satisfies global monotonicity conditions only when reduced to the very restrictive Cobb–Douglas, a large deviation from Cobb–Douglas curvature at the point of approximation, which would imply large second-order terms, would

Table B.1 Percentage Distribution of Ton-Miles by Commodity Groups, 1970

	Agricultural products	Coal	Manufactured products	Chemical, mineral, petroleum, & other bulk commodities
Atchison, Topeka & Santa Fe Ry.	18.0	2.2	48.9	31.0
Baltimore & Ohio R.R. Co.	2.5	35.5	35.4	26.6
Bangor & Aroostook R.R. Co.	5.9	0.3	24.7	69.1
Bessemer & Lake Erie R.R. Co.	0.0	49.6	6.7	43.7
Boston & Maine Corp.	4.7	7.9	57.4	29.9
Burlington Northern Inc.	24.7	10.1	35.8	29.4
Central R.R. Co. of New Jersey	1.0	13.9	31.5	53.6
Chesapeake & Ohio Ry. Co.	1.0	70.9	14.2	14.0
Chicago & Eastern Illinois R.R.	3.5	20.8	42.3	33.4
Chicago & North Western Trans.	16.4	16.8	35.6	31.1
Chicago, Milwaukee, & St. Paul	14.3	9.4	55.7	20.6
Chicago, Rock Island & Pacific	25.7	1.0	50.3	23.0
Clinchfield R.R. Co.	0.9	76.8	11.5	10.8
Delaware & Hudson Ry. Co.	5.7	4.6	37.1	52.6
Denver & Rio Grande Western R.R.	6.1	43.5	35.7	14.6
Duluth, Missabe & Iron Range R.R.	0.0	2.6	2.4	95.0
Erie-Lackawanna Ry. Co.	5.1	8.2	72.8	13.9
Florida East Coast Ry. Co.	0.8	0.0	46.6	52.6
Fort Worth & Denver Ry. Co.	41.1	0.2	31.4	27.2
Grand Trunk Western R.R. Co.	5.6	8.7	67.5	18.2
Gulf Mobile & Ohio R.R. Co.	8.0	22.2	38.8	31.1
Illinois Central R.R. Co.	8.3	12.1	46.7	33.0
Illinois Terminal R.R. Co.	5.1	30.6	45.4	19.0
Kansas City Southern Ry. Co.	17.2	2.8	33.8	46.3
Lehigh Valley R.R. Co.	1.7	9.2	55.9	33.2
Louisville & Nashville R.R. Co.	5.3	43.2	26.0	25.5
Maine Central R.R. Co.	5.7	0.8	45.8	47.7
Missouri Pacific R.R. Co.	13.4	1.6	34.6	50.3
Missouri-Kansas-Texas R.R. Co.	13.1	3.0	42.4	41.5
Norfolk & Western Ry. Co.	4.7	55.3	23.9	16.1
Norfolk Southern Ry. Co.	9.1	8.7	20.8	61.4
Penn Central Transportation Co.	3.6	26.8	46.7	22.9
Pittsburgh & Lake Erie R.R. Co.	0.0	51.8	9.9	38.2

Table B.1 (continued)

	Agricul- tural products	Coal	Manufac- tured products	Chemical, mineral, petroleum, & other bulk com- modities
Reading Co.	2.1	41.5	21.4	35.1
Seaboard Coast Line R.R. Co.	4.7	10.2	38.4	46.7
Soo Line R.R. Co.	22.9	1.9	28.3	46.9
Southern Pacific Transportation	9.3	0.2	44.8	45.7
Southern Ry. Co.	10.5	14.7	39.5	35.3
St. Louis Southwestern Ry. Co.	3.4	0.0	69.1	27.4
St. Louis-San Francisco Ry. Co.	7.7	7.4	46.2	38.6
Texas & Pacific Ry. Co.	9.2	0.9	45.0	44.9
Union Pacific R.R. Co.	17.1	5.8	44.6	32.6
Western Maryland Ry. Co.	0.7	80.0	7.0	12.3
Western Pacific R.R. Co.	2.2	0.9	84.4	12.6

result in violation of the regularity conditions for a large number of points in the sample.

Thus, given the limitations of the data and the possible force of the above reservations, it may not be desirable or practical to disaggregate output by commodity type. On the other hand, one would expect traffic mix by commodity type to have some effect on costs and factor intensities, so that even given relatively poor data it may be prudent to include some measure of traffic mix as an element of the technological conditions vector. For this reason the ratio of ton-miles of manufactured commodities to other ton-miles is included as a technological condition.[3]

Unfortunately, the number of railroads for which the above variables are available is comparatively limited. Railroads that do not provide any passenger service cannot be used since the translog specification cannot handle values of zero for its arguments; more important, it is difficult to conceive of a convenient specification capable of characterizing the technologies of both passenger and nonpassenger roads.

This directs our attention to railroads producing passenger services. Since the inception of Amtrak, however, interstate passenger service has been progressively transferred from the railroads to Amtrak, with the railroads providing some services to Amtrak under contract. Operations of the latter type are not included in *Transport Statistics*, a basic data source. Moreover, the operations which remain covered by *Transport Statistics* are likely to have undergone a structural shift due to Amtrak's operation.

These considerations suggest that one must concentrate on either the pre- or post-Amtrak era, with attention devoted in the latter case to examining the relation between Amtrak and the railroads. We have chosen to concentrate on the pre-Amtrak era.

B.2.2 The Sample

Data were available[4] for 26 railroad systems providing passenger service within the years 1968–1970. Of these systems, one (the Burlington Northern) was formed in 1970; comparable data were not available for its constituent systems. A second system, the Texas and Pacific, apparently abandoned its passenger service (or at least a very large portion thereof) early in 1970.

This leaves 75 observations. In preliminary estimation, however, 6 railroads were consistent outliers[5] for which important regularity conditions (such as positive marginal costs and a positive marginal product of way-and-structures capital) were violated. Upon investigation it was found that these 6 roads had the six highest relative coal traffic levels; these are listed by percentage of ton-miles in table B.2. Of the 6 roads, the Baltimore and Ohio had the smallest coal percentage (35.5 percent), while of the 20 other roads, the Penn Central had the highest coal percentage (26.8 percent). The Penn Central had a relatively high percentage of traffic in manufactured commodities (46.7 percent versus the Baltimore and Ohio's 35.4 percent), while the Baltimore and Ohio is controlled by

Table B.2 Percentage Distribution of Ton-Miles by Commodity Type for Six Coal Roads and the Penn Central

	Agricultural products	Coal	Manufactures	Chemical, mineral, & other
Baltimore & Ohio	2.52	35.49	35.43	26.56
Chesapeake & Ohio	1.03	70.85	14.17	13.95
Denver & Rio Grande	6.15	43.55	35.70	14.60
Louisville & Nashville	5.31	43.15	26.00	25.54
Norfolk & Western	4.71	55.27	23.92	16.09
Reading	2.08	51.56	21.37	35.09
Penn Central	3.59	26.84	46.71	22.85

the Chesapeake and Ohio, which is the most coal-oriented of the major railroads. Moreover, when the Baltimore and Ohio is included in the sample, it displays properties similar to the other 5 coal railroads, whereas the Penn Central does not.

Excluding the 6 coal railroads leaves a sample of 20 railroad systems and 57 observations. These 20 systems, however, account for over 70 percent of the US total of most measures of railroad size and activity, including capital stock, operating cost, revenues, passenger-miles, and route-miles. For ton-miles the figure falls to 68 percent, since the coal railroads account for a disproportionate number of ton-miles relative to other activities, which is consistent with our finding (below) that their technology differs significantly from other roads.

Our specification has 5 variable factors, 1 fixed factor, 4 technological conditions, and 2 outputs; the translog functional form with 12 variables has 91 coefficients. In addition, there are 5 coefficients in the hedonic function to be applied to passenger-miles, and 15 elements of the covariance matrix of disturbances if contemporaneous correlation between the disturbances of the cost and factor share equations is assumed. There are 57 observations available for each of the five simultaneously estimated equations.

B.2.3 Functional Form
Of the 91 coefficients of the cost function, 13 can be eliminated by imposing homogeneity of degree one of the cost function factor prices. Together with the 5 hedonic coefficients, this leaves 83 coefficients to be estimated if the full translog functional form is to be employed. From one point of view, there are 285 observations [57 observations × (4 independent factor share equations + 1 cost equation)], but this is misleading since not every coefficient appears in every equation. In particular, terms in ψ (outputs), t (technological conditions) and x (the fixed factor), appear only in the cost equation, excepting their interaction terms with the w's (factor prices), which each appear in one factor share equation. Counting these coefficients and the constant term, the full translog specification of the cost function contains 40 coefficients which appear in no factor share equation. Moreover, 4 of the variables generating these terms— the 4 technological conditions—show little within-firm variation (i.e., over time).

Fortunately, it is possible to eliminate a significant number of these terms by imposing some mild separability constraints and limiting the way the t's enter the functional form. In particular, consider

$$\ln C(\psi_P, \psi_F, x, w, t) = \ln g(\psi_F, x, w, t) + \ln h(\psi_P, \psi_F, x, w), \qquad \text{(B.9)}$$

where h is a translog function of its arguments, and can therefore be interpreted as corresponding to a conventional short-run translog cost function whose arguments are outputs, fixed factors, and variable factor prices. This specification, regardless of the functional form of $g(\cdot)$, imposes separability of the technological conditions from passenger output; this eliminates four coefficients from the general translog functional form, namely, the four $\psi_P - t$ interaction terms. This is not too restrictive since the technological conditions refer only to freight service variables, and heuristically, passenger service, particularly at the margin, is a small portion of railroad activity.

We shall employ the following functional form for $g(\cdot)$:

$$\ln g(\psi_F, x, w, t) = \sum_j \beta_j \ln t_j + \sum_i \sum_j B_{ij} \ln w_i \ln t_j$$
$$+ \sum_j D_j \ln x \ln t_j + \sum_j E_{jF} \ln t_j \ln \psi_F, \qquad \text{(B.10)}$$

where the coefficients follow the notation established in appendix A, provided x, the fixed factor, is interpreted as corresponding to the "zeroth" component of the t vector.[6] This convention is adopted both to conform to that of the previous analysis (and thereby obviate a new series of letters) and to emphasize the functionally similar roles played by technological conditions and fixed factors. It is important to note, however, that in both $h(\cdot)$ (since it is translog) and (B.10), the fixed factor has a full set of nonzero interaction terms, and in this respect is analogous to the variable factor prices. Otherwise, one would be arbitrarily imposing separability conditions upon the fixed factor that were not imposed upon the variable factors.

There are two other aspects of (B.10) that should be noted. The first is that we have adopted the convention of writing (B.10) without a constant term, thereby subsuming it in the intercept of $\ln h(\cdot)$. The second is that (B.10) differs from the full translog specification by setting the coefficient on t–t interaction and quadratic terms to zero; thus $D_{jm} = 0$, for all j, $m \neq 0$. Thus, one way of interpreting (B.10) is that for given ψ_F, x, and w, the function $g(\cdot)$ is Cobb–Douglas in t. This is somewhat restrictive in its implications, but has the advantage of reducing the number of coefficients to be estimated by 10; moreover, the eliminated coefficients appear exclusively in the cost equation. The final function nevertheless contains 69 coefficients which must be estimated, 26 of which appear only in the cost equation.

B.2.4 Autoregressive Structure of the Disturbances

Finally, since our sample consists of time-series cross-sectional data, it is not unreasonable to expect autocorrelated disturbances due to the persistence of unmeasured road characteristics over time. Berndt and Savin (1975) have shown that the singularity of the contemporaneous disturbance covariance matrix of the full factor share and cost equation system imposes restrictions on the autoregressive process. If the model estimated does not satisfy these restrictions, then maximum likelihood estimation will not be invariant to the deleted factor share equation. A consequence of this, of course, is that likelihood ratio test statistics will also be affected by the factor share equation deleted.

The autoregressive structure we will estimate satisfies the restrictions outlined by Berndt and Savin, and corresponds to their Model 7 (1975, p. 949). Departing from our usual notation, our nonlinear[7] multivariate regression model can be expressed for each railroad as

$$y_t = f(X_t, \beta) + u_t, \qquad t = 1, 2, 3 \text{ (at best)}, \tag{B.11}$$

where y_t is an $n \times 1$ vector of dependent variables, X_t a $k \times 1$ vector of independent variables, β an $m \times 1$ coefficient vector, u_t an $n \times 1$ vector of random disturbances, and the subscript t denotes a given time period. A simple specification of a process generating u_t that satisfies Berndt and Savin's restrictions is

$$u_t = \rho u_{t-1} + \varepsilon_t, \tag{B.12}$$

where ε_t is an $n \times 1$ vector of independently identically distributed normal random vectors with mean zero and covariance matrix Σ, and ρ is a scalar. That is, each equation's disturbance is equal to ρ times its previous disturbance plus an innovation, and the innovations are multivariately normally distributed independently over time but contemporaneously correlated; ρ is the same for every equation.[8] To estimate (B.11) and (B.12) we assume that β and ρ are the same for every railroad. Using (B.11) and (B.12), we can obtain

$$y_t - \rho y_{t-1} = f(X_t, \beta) - \rho f(X_{t-1}, \beta) + \varepsilon_t. \tag{B.13}$$

Given an estimate of ρ, the usual maximum likelihood methods could be applied to (B.13) using those observations for which y_{t-1} and X_{t-1} existed.

There are two difficulties with this suggestion, to which we propose solutions analogous to those employed in the simple single-equation framework. To obtain a consistent estimate of ρ, estimate (B.11) by maximum likelihood methods employing all observations under the assumption $\rho = 0$,[9] and estimate ρ by

$$\frac{\sum u_t u_{t-1}}{\sum u_t^2}, \tag{B.14}$$

taking care, of course, to handle "gaps" correctly. Using the estimated ρ, (B.13) can be applied when data for the previous year are available; the consistency of the estimate of ρ would guarantee that estimating the coefficients of the cost–factor share system by maximum likelihood methods taking ρ as fixed would yield estimates with the same desirable properties of full maximum likelihood estimates,[10] namely, consistency and asymptotic efficiency. However, since 20 observations are "first" observations for which the previous year's data are not available, this leaves only 37 observations. Since there are 26 coefficients that appear in the cost equation but are not in any factor share equation, the loss of the 20 first-year observations is important. If, however, the stochastic process represented by (B.12) has been operating for many periods, the contemporaneous covariance matrix of u_t (which is, recall, a vector) approaches $\left[\dfrac{1}{1-\rho^2}\right] \Sigma_\varepsilon$, where Σ_ε is the contemporaneous covariance matrix of ε [see Theil (1971, pp. 251–253) for the single-equation case]. In this case, one can transform the 20 first observations by

$$\sqrt{1-\rho^2}\, y_t = \sqrt{1-\rho^2} f(X_t, \beta) + \sqrt{1-\rho^2}\, u_t \tag{B.15}$$

and use $\sqrt{1-\rho^2}\, u_t$ in place of ε_t in calculating the likelihood function.

An important consideration, therefore, is whether (B.12) can be viewed as having operated undisturbed for a long period prior to the first observation. (If $|\rho|$ is small, the period need not be too long.) Since u_t represents the effect of unmeasured road characteristics, ε_t the evolution of new unmeasured road characteristics, and ρ the extent to which the innovations represented by ε_t persist, a disturbance of the relation represented by (B.12) could consist, for example, of either an extraordinary value [in the sense of being drawn from a distribution different from $N(0, \Sigma_\varepsilon)$] of ε_t or a change in the operation of a road such that past road characteristics did not persist to the extent specified by ρ.

Among the obvious causes of such disturbances would be a railroad merger. In a merger, the first period disturbance u_1 can be veiwed as being composed of three parts:

$$u_1 = \rho u^* + \varepsilon_1 + m_1, \tag{B.16}$$

where u^* represents disturbances from the constituent roads' past histories which persist in the new road, ε_1 the usual innovations, and m_1 disturbances due to the merger.[11] If $m_1 = 0$ and

$$u^* = \theta u_1^0 + (1 - \theta)u_2^0, \qquad 0 < \theta < 1, \tag{B.17}$$

where u_i^0 is the disturbance of the ith road in the year preceding merger,

$$\Sigma_{u_1} = \frac{\rho^2}{1 - \rho^2}[\theta^2 + (1 - \theta)^2]\Sigma_\varepsilon + 2\rho^2\theta(1 - \theta)\Sigma_{u_1^0 u_2^0} + \Sigma_\varepsilon$$

$$= \frac{1}{1 - \rho^2}\Sigma_\varepsilon + 2\rho^2\theta(\theta - 1)\left[\frac{\Sigma_\varepsilon}{(1 - \rho^2)} - \Sigma_{u_1^0 u_2^0}\right], \tag{B.18}$$

where $\Sigma_{u_1^0 u_2^0}$ is the covariance matrix of disturbances between firms if we assume $\Sigma_{u_1^0} = [1/(1 - \rho^2)]\Sigma_\varepsilon$. Equation (B.18) has the interpretation that when the merger has no direct effect on the first period disturbance, and the persisting historical effects are a weighted average of the consitutent roads' disturbances of the preceding year, then the application of (B.15) is valid if (1) $\rho = 0$, (2) $\theta = 0$ or $\theta = 1$, or (3) $\Sigma_{u_1^0 u_2^0} = [1/(1 - \rho^2)]\Sigma_\varepsilon$. That is, the inefficiencies induced by applying (B.15) are small if (1) autocorrelation is small, (2) one constituent firm's historical experience is much more important than the other's (e.g., one firm is relatively large), or (3) the disturbances experienced by the two firms are similar. If the two firms' past disturbances have been independent, then (B.15) should be replaced by

$$\sqrt{\frac{1 - \rho^2}{1 + 2\rho^2\theta(\theta - 1)}}\, y_t = \sqrt{\frac{1 - \rho^2}{1 + 2\rho^2\theta(\theta - 1)}}\, f(X_t, \beta)$$

$$+ \sqrt{\frac{1 - \rho^2}{1 + 2\rho^2\theta(\theta - 1)}}\, u_t. \tag{B.19}$$

Since $2\rho^2\theta(\theta - 1) < 0$, this means that observations of the first year of operation of a merged railroad should be weighed more *heavily* than other first-year observations since the independence of the past disturbances of the constituent roads lowers the autoregressive effect.

Empirically, our values of ρ are such that the inefficiency of using (B.15) when (B.19) is applicable are small. But the applicability of (B.19) depends on $m_1 = 0$, that is, that the merger itself have no extraordinary effect on u_1. Thus, whether the first observation following a merger should be disregarded depends on the character of the merger.

There are two roads that experienced major mergers in our sample. The Penn Central was formed from the Pennsylvania and New York Central railroads on February 1, 1968, and the Burlington Northern was formed from the Northern Pacific, Great Northern, and Chicago, Burlington, and Quincy railroads on March 2, 1970. In the case of the Penn Central, the two roads from which it was formed had nearly identical average lengths of haul, route-miles, and passenger average travel length; in addition, the cities served by the two were nearly identical. There is no noticeable difference in the Penn Central's major operating statistics between the post- and premerger periods.

The Burlington Northern, in contrast, combined two largely similar roads—the Northern Pacific and the Great Northern—which both had mainlines running from Minneapolis to Portland and Seattle, with a rather dissimilar road—the Chicago, Burlington, and Quincy—which connected Minneapolis to Chicago, and provided lines to Kansas City, St. Louis, Omaha, Denver, Galveston, Peoria, and Paducah, Kentucky. In 1969, the average length of haul on the Burlington Northern's constituent roads was 387 miles; in the first year of operation of the merged road, 1970, this rose to 419; in 1971 it rose further to 463; and in 1972, to 476. During this period, no other railroad achieved a comparable increase in average length of haul. The merger was opposed by competing roads, as it was widely believed at the time that its route structure would offer it important advantages over its smaller competitors;[12] the Supreme Court approved the merger after a long series of appeals. On the passenger side, the Great Northern and Northern Pacific provided interstate passenger service, with passenger average travel lengths exceeding 400 miles; the Chicago, Burlington, and Quincy primarily provided commuter passenger service, with an average travel length below 50 miles. Thus, there is some reason to believe that it would be desirable to exclude the 1970 observation for the Burlington Northern from the sample.

B.3 Cost Function Estimates for US Railroads, 1968–1970

We estimated our model for three samples: the first included all 57 observations; the second excluded the 1970 observation for the Burlington Northern; and the third excluded both the Burlington Northern observation and the first, 1968, Penn Central observation. As described in the preceding section, the model was estimated for each sample assuming

$\rho = 0$ and then transformed according to (B.13) and (B.15) using the value of ρ calculated from (B.14).

In terms of their overall implications, all six sets of estimated coefficients are very similar; the ρ transformation slightly raises the estimated standard errors of most of the coefficients. The estimated values of ρ for the three samples are 0.5725, 0.4389, and 0.4271, respectively. While the ρ transformation does not affect the general results in any case, it has the greatest effect in the first sample, which includes the suspect Burlington Northern observation. The major effect of the transformation is to produce counterintuitive results concerning passenger density for observations with high densities. In addition, both estimates using the Burlington Northern observation have some minor irregularities in the behavior of the marginal product of (way-and-structures) capital. For firms with a low marginal product of capital (i.e., $-\partial C/\partial x$ is near zero), the regularity condition $\partial^2 C/\partial x^2 > 0$ is violated; when this condition is imposed [albeit inefficiently, by restricting the coefficient on $(\ln x_1)^2$ to be small in absolute value, i.e., not *too* negative] it cannot be rejected at the 0.25 level, but forces $-\partial C/\partial x < 0$ for some observations. In view of these considerations and those adduced in the previous section concerning the Burlington Northern merger, and the fact that excluding the first Penn Central observation had almost no effect on the estimates, we will concentrate on the second sample, which excludes the Burlington Northern but includes all three Penn Central observations. [See Spady (1979) for the coefficient estimates of the first sample and of the second sample under the assumption $\rho = 0$.]

In addition to estimating the railroad cost function in its general form, we estimated it with the restriction that the coefficients on the interaction terms between the technological factors t_i and the fixed factor x were zero. This was done to increase the precision of the remaining coefficients and to ensure that extreme values of the fixed factor or of the technological conditions did not bias the estimated responses of costs to changes in any of these variables. Thus in the ensuing tables, the heading marked "Normal model" refers to the estimates made with the full set of interactions, while the heading marked "Restricted model" refers to the one in which the coefficients on the x–t interactions are set equal to zero. Note that while most of the discussion in the text concerning specific railroad behavior is based on the normal model, the simulated marginal cost function and the general equilibrium analysis were based on the restricted model.

The results for the second sample with $\rho = 0.4389$ are presented in

Table B.3 Coefficients on Linear Terms and Economic Coefficients Not Appearing in Any Factor Share Equation

Coefficient	Variable	Normal model		Restricted model	
		Value	Standard error	Value	Standard error
α_0	Constant	15.15460	0.03271	15.16580	0.02904
α_1	w_1 (equipment)	0.25338	0.00641	0.25435	0.00629
α_2	w_2 (general labor)	0.30383	0.00766	0.30245	0.00693
α_3	w_3 (yard & switching labor)	0.05618	0.00193	0.05578	0.00578
α_4	w_4 (on-train labor)	0.18798	0.00309	0.18823	0.00298
α_5	w_5 (fuel & materials)	0.19864	0.00839	0.19919	0.00763
β_0	x (WS capital)	−0.42678	0.11738	−0.45746	0.10134
β_1	t_1 (low-density route-miles)	0.29108	0.06655	0.33130	0.05765
β_2	t_2 (route-miles)	0.08641	0.09038	0.07438	0.06695
β_3	t_3 (average length of haul)	−0.55757	0.07081	−0.54699	0.05854
β_4	t_4 (traffic mix)	0.33977	0.05320	0.33044	0.04842
γ_1	ψ_1 (passenger service)	0.11289	0.05475	0.14212	0.04819
γ_2	ψ_2 (revenue ton-miles)	1.12192	0.08328	1.09562	0.07046
D_{00}	$\frac{1}{2}(x)^2$	0.02875	0.50316	–	–
D_{01}	xt_1	−0.08756	0.18392	–	–
D_{02}	xt_2	0.19670	0.23459	–	–
D_{03}	xt_3	−0.02408	0.19584	–	–
D_{04}	xt_4	0.02759	0.09997	–	–
E_{01}	$x\psi_1$	−0.14172	0.08363	−0.12179	0.05304
E_{02}	$x\psi_2$	−0.03461	0.36043	0.02364	0.08531
E_{12}	$t_1\psi_2$	0.11171	0.14954	0.07295	0.03649
E_{22}	$t_2\psi_2$	−0.08474	0.16725	−0.04502	0.07647
E_{32}	$t_3\psi_2$	−0.03121	0.14572	−0.03928	0.05894
E_{42}	$t_4\psi_2$	−0.03104	0.08196	−0.01791	0.02891
F_{11}	$\frac{1}{2}(\psi_1)^2$	0.06191	0.04766	0.07701	0.03857
F_{12}	$\psi_1\psi_2$	0.05731	0.05812	0.03496	0.04743
F_{22}	$\frac{1}{2}(\psi_2)^2$	0.17725	0.22595	0.08227	0.12545

Cost equation

R^2		0.99701		0.99708	
RMSE		0.05474		0.05420	
Mean absolute residual		0.04279		0.04193	
Mean residual		1.773×10^{-3}		1.677×10^{-3}	
LLF		863.35		862.797	

Table B.4 Factor Share Equation for Equipment Capital

Coefficient	Variable	Normal model Value	Standard error	Restricted model Value	Standard error
α_1	Constant	0.25338	0.00641	0.25435	0.00630
A_{11}	w_1 (equipment)	0.00799	0.03384	0.01493	0.03325
A_{12}	w_2 (general labor)	0.11337	0.04562	0.10290	0.04491
A_{13}	w_3 (yard & switching labor)	0.00817	0.01137	0.00547	0.01124
A_{14}	w_4 (on-train labor)	−0.00396	0.01648	−0.00825	0.01611
A_{15}	w_5 (fuel & materials)	−0.12552	0.03552	−0.11506	0.03937
B_{10}	x (WS capital)	−0.16156	0.01699	−0.16293	0.00968
B_{11}	t_1 (low-density route-miles)	0.00536	0.00937	0.00579	0.00938
B_{12}	t_2 (route-miles)	0.10100	0.01648	0.10031	0.01655
B_{13}	t_3 (average length of haul)	−0.17593	0.01683	−0.17403	0.01691
B_{14}	t_4 (traffic mix)	0.09713	0.00978	0.09712	0.00989
C_{11}	ψ_1 (passenger service)	−0.01140	0.00744	−0.01020	0.00754
C_{12}	ψ_2 (ton-miles)	0.10113	0.01446	0.10112	0.10223
R^2		0.8047		0.80221	
RMSE		0.02137		0.02150	
Mean absolute residual		0.01758		0.01773	
Mean residual		-8.664×10^{-4}		-8.641×10^{-4}	

tables B.3–B.9. As a table of 69 coefficients would be cumbersome, we present the coefficients on the cost function's "linear" log terms and those cross terms which appear only in the cost equation in table B.3; the factor share equations are presented in tables B.4–B.8 and table B.9 contains the coefficients of the hedonic function that is applied to passenger-miles.[13] We have standardized the variables so that terms in $\ln z$ are actually $\ln(z/\bar{z}) = \ln z - \ln \bar{z}$, where $\bar{z}$ is the sample mean of z. The sample means of the variables are given in table B.10.

B.4 Properties of the Estimated Cost Function at the Sample Mean

Although the characteristics of the estimated rail costs differ substantially by railroad (cf. chapter 4), it is useful to consider the behavior of the cost function at the point of approximation. In this discussion we will focus on the normal model and discuss the implications of the estimated

Table B.5 Factor Share Equation for General, Maintenance, and Administrative Labor

Coefficient	Variable	Normal model		Restricted model	
		Value	Standard error	Value	Standard error
α_2	Constant	0.30383	0.00766	0.30245	0.00693
A_{21}	w_1 (equipment)	0.11337	0.04562	0.10290	0.04491
A_{22}	w_2 (general labor)	−0.06170	0.10222	−0.04988	0.10222
A_{23}	w_3 (yard & switching labor)	−0.05214	0.02643	−0.04614	0.02623
A_{24}	w_4 (on-train labor)	−0.09409	0.03574	−0.08037	0.03462
A_{25}	w_5 (fuel & materials)	0.09442	0.06422	0.07348	0.06306
B_{20}	x (WS capital)	0.03680	0.01766	0.04105	0.01685
B_{21}	t_1 (low-density route-miles)	0.00582	0.00884	0.00449	0.00886
B_{22}	t_2 (route-miles)	−0.07285	0.01475	−0.07155	0.01477
B_{23}	t_3 (average length of haul)	0.15528	0.01562	0.15281	0.01570
B_{24}	t_4 (traffic mix)	−0.06547	0.00881	−0.06884	0.00878
C_{21}	ψ_1 (passenger service)	0.04909	0.00754	0.04829	0.00730
C_{22}	ψ_2 (ton-miles)	−0.06488	0.01448	−0.06764	0.01495
R^2		0.7902		0.78454	
RMSE		0.01621		0.01643	
Mean absolute residual		0.01250		0.012585	
Mean residual		-1.345×10^{-4}		-1.3567×10^{-4}	

cost function for a hypothetical railroad that faced mean values of factor prices, technological conditions, the fixed factor, and output.

Table B.3 indicates that for a hypothetical firm facing the sample mean values of the variables, the elasticity of cost with respect to passenger service is estimated to be about 0.113, while the elasticity of cost with respect to ton-miles is about 1.122. The effect of the technological conditions on costs is as expected: increases in low-density route-mileage and the ratio of ton-miles of manufactured commodities to ton-miles of nonmanufactured commodities increase costs, while an increase in average length of haul decreases costs; an increase in total route-mileage raises costs by a small amount, but this effect is not statistically significant. An increase in way-and-structures capital decreases variable costs; this is a result consistent with neoclassical production theory which has not been obtained previously.

In table B.11 we evaluate the magnitude of these effects at the sample

Table B.6 Factor Share Equation for Yard and Switching Labor

Coefficient	Variable	Normal model Value	Normal model Standard error	Restricted model Value	Restricted model Standard error
α_3	Constant	0.05618	0.00193	0.05578	0.00178
A_{31}	w_1 (equipment)	0.00817	0.01137	0.00547	0.01134
A_{32}	w_2 (general labor)	−0.05214	0.02643	−0.04613	0.03633
A_{33}	w_3 (yard & switching labor)	−0.06351	0.02289	−0.06602	0.02279
A_{34}	w_4 (on-train labor)	0.04443	0.01268	0.04704	0.01263
A_{35}	w_5 (fuel & materials)	0.06304	0.01818	0.05963	0.01817
B_{30}	x (WS capital)	0.00772	0.00474	0.00891	0.00466
B_{31}	t_1 (low-density route-miles)	0.00851	0.00244	0.00818	0.00747
B_{32}	t_2 (route-miles)	−0.01678	0.00393	−0.01654	0.00392
B_{33}	t_3 (average length of haul)	0.00608	0.00447	0.00567	0.00453
B_{34}	t_4 (traffic mix)	−0.00789	0.00240	−0.00822	0.00242
C_{31}	ψ_1 (passenger service)	0.01119	0.00201	0.01088	0.00199
C_{32}	ψ_2 (ton-miles)	−0.01380	0.00372	−0.01441	0.00370
R^2		0.82624		0.81549	
RMSE		0.00493		0.005076	
Mean absolute residual		0.00413		0.004268	
Mean residual		6.077×10^{-5}		6.7384×10^{-5}	

mean by using

$$\frac{\partial C}{\partial z} = \frac{\partial \ln C}{\partial \ln z} \frac{\hat{C}}{z}, \tag{B.22}$$

where $\hat{C}$ is the fitted value of C in dollars.[14] The marginal cost of a low-density route-mile is estimated to be \$63,292, while a route-mile has a marginal cost of \$5,170; since low-density route-miles are included in route-miles, the total cost of adding a low-density route-mile is \$68,462. The marginal cost of passenger service (i.e., a passenger-mile at the mean levels of PATL and PDENS) is 10¢, while the marginal cost of a ton-mile is 1.88¢. A dollar of way-and-structures capital lowers variable cost by 13 percent, or, equivalently, a dollar of capital in 12/31/71 prices lowers variable costs 11¢.

On the input side, the estimated cost function is concave at the sample mean and at every observation. The estimated short-run Allen–Uzawa elasticities of substitution and elasticities of factor demand at the point

Table B.7 Factor Share Equation for On-Train Labor

Coefficient	Variable	Normal model		Restricted model	
		Value	Standard error	Value	Standard error
α_4	Constant	0.18798	0.00309	0.18823	0.00298
A_{41}	w_1 (equipment)	−0.00396	0.01648	−0.00825	0.01611
A_{42}	w_2 (general labor)	−0.09409	0.03574	−0.08037	0.03462
A_{43}	w_3 (yard & switching labor)	0.04443	0.01268	0.04704	0.01263
A_{44}	w_4 (on-train labor)	−0.00617	0.02062	−0.01011	0.01965
A_{45}	w_5 (fuel & materials)	0.05972	0.02463	0.05168	0.02444
B_{40}	x (WS capital)	0.04376	0.00823	0.04294	0.00807
B_{41}	t_1 (low-density route-miles)	0.02266	0.00460	0.02323	0.00454
B_{42}	t_2 (route-miles)	−0.06529	0.00775	−0.06512	0.00771
B_{43}	t_3 (average length of haul)	0.02332	0.00862	0.02429	0.00850
B_{44}	t_4 (traffic mix)	−0.01507	0.00451	−0.01530	0.00454
C_{41}	ψ_1 (passenger service)	0.00634	0.00355	0.00689	0.00353
C_{42}	ψ_2 (ton-miles)	−0.00913	0.00670	−0.00947	0.00676
R^2		0.83451		0.83563	
RMSE		0.00942		0.00938	
Mean absolute residual		0.00738		0.00733	
Mean residual		4.904×10^{-4}		5.025×10^{-4}	

of approximation, together with their estimated standard errors, are contained in table B.12.

Table B.12 indicates that three pairs of factors are complements, while all other factor pairs are substitutes. While the two types of traffic and transportation labor are substitutes, they are both complements to general labor, which consists of administrative and maintenance labor. The complementarity of general and on-train labor is slight, however, and the hypothesis of independence (AES = 0) cannot be rejected. Equipment and fuel and materials are also complements, which is the expected short-run effect.

Since the elasticities of substitution describe the effect of factor prices on factor intensities, we now turn to analyze the effects of the technological conditions and output upon factor intensities. However, because we have fully discussed the impact of the infrastructure-related technological conditions upon factor intensities in chapter 4, in this appendix we will focus upon the impact of the other technological conditions upon costs.

Table B.8 Factor Share Equation for Fuel and Materials

Coefficient	Variable	Normal model		Restricted model	
		Value	Standard error	Value	Standard error
α_5	Constant	0.19862	0.00839	0.19919	0.00762
A_{51}	w_1 (equipment)	−0.12552	0.03552	−0.11506	0.03437
A_{52}	w_2 (general labor)	0.09442	0.06422	0.07348	0.06306
A_{53}	w_3 (yard & switching labor)	0.06304	0.01818	0.05964	0.01817
A_{54}	w_4 (on-train labor)	0.05972	0.02463	0.05168	0.07494
A_{55}	w_5 (fuel & materials)	−0.09166	0.05804	−0.06974	0.05663
B_{50}	x (WS capital)	0.07328	0.01903	0.07003	0.01798
B_{51}	t_1 (low-density route-miles)	−0.04235	0.00949	−0.04169	0.00938
B_{52}	t_2 (route-miles)	0.05393	0.01638	0.05350	0.01616
B_{53}	t_3 (average length of haul)	−0.00877	0.01671	−0.00873	0.01659
B_{54}	t_4 (traffic mix)	−0.00868	0.00993	−0.00677	0.00973
C_{51}	ψ_1 (passenger service)	−0.05522	0.00843	−0.05586	0.00819
C_{52}	ψ_2 (ton-miles)	−0.01331	0.01623	−0.00960	0.01563
R^2		0.7266		0.73499	
RMSE		0.02035		0.02004	
Mean absolute residual		0.01660		0.01643	
Mean residual		4.497×10^{-4}		4.2989×10^{-4}	

Table B.9 Hedonic Function for Passenger Service

Term	Normal model		Restricted model	
	Value	Standard error	Value	Standard error
PATL	−0.25190	0.08972	−0.29334	0.07536
PDENS	−0.16464	0.18235	−0.21485	0.15875
$\frac{1}{2}(\text{PATL})^2$	−0.52989	0.10189	−0.55471	0.09025
PATL · PDENS	0.00945	0.08016	0.01773	0.07387
$\frac{1}{2}(\text{PDENS})^2$	0.18603	0.11354	0.15646	0.10425

Table B.10 Sample Means and Standard Deviations of the Cost Function's Arguments

Variable	Mean	Standard deviation
x = way and structures capital (billions of 12/31/71 dollars)	1.570	1.798
t_1 = miles of low-density route-mileage	1,860.1	1,726.8
t_2 = route-miles	6,760.4	5,220.9
t_3 = average length of haul	326.90	149.90
t_4 = ratio of manufactured to nonmanufactured ton-miles	1.223	1.004
y_P = passenger-miles (millions)	454.41	731.59
y_F = ton-miles (billions)	24.086	22.691
PATL = passenger average travel length	209.28	237.77
PDENS = passenger-miles per passenger route-mile (thousands)	257.57	220.53
w_1 = rental price of equipment ($[r + d]p_k$)	0.1099	0.0123
w_2 = general labor (index)	0.8829	0.0608
w_3 = yard & switching labor (index)	0.9131	0.0594
w_4 = on-train labor (dollars/man-hour)	6.5249	0.8359
w_5 = fuel & materials (index)	106.002	2.8476

Table B.11 Marginal Cost Effects of Capital, Route-Mileage, and Output at Sample Mean

Variable z	$\partial C/\partial z$ at sample mean (dollars)
x = way-and-structures capital	-0.1099[a]
t_1 = low-density route miles	63,291.8
t_2 = route-miles	5,169.18
ψ_1 = passenger service	0.1005
ψ_2 = freight service (thousands of ton-miles)	18.8401

a. To convert this to a rate of return, 12/31/71 asset prices must be converted to [(19 × 1968) + (19 × 1969) + (18 × 1970)/56] asset prices. This yields an estimated rate of return of 13.08%, before depreciation.

Table B.12 Short-Run Factor Demand Elasticities and Allen Partial Elasticities of Substitution at Point of Approximation

	Equipment	General labor	Yard & switching labor	On-train labor	Fuel & materials
Equipment	–	2.4718 (0.5889)	1.5734 (0.7954)	0.9164 (0.3460)	−1.4948 (0.6846)
General labor		–	−2.0538 (1.5453)	−0.6461 (0.6227)	2.5669 (1.0640)
Yard & switching labor			–	5.2105 (1.2412)	6.6503 (1.7123)
On-train labor				–	2.6011 (0.6580)
Own price elasticity	−0.7149 (0.1354)	−0.8989 (0.3360)	−2.0749 (0.4177)	−0.8449 (0.1084)	−1.2629 (0.2961)

The elasticity of demand for factor i with respect to technological condition j is given by

$$\beta_j + \frac{B_{ij}}{\alpha_i} \tag{B.23}$$

at the point of approximation. For output j the corresponding expression is

$$\gamma_j + \frac{C_{ij}}{\alpha_i}. \tag{B.24}$$

Table B.13 presents the estimates of (B.23) and (B.24) for the fixed factor, technological conditions, and outputs: the first column gives the elasticity of cost with respect to the appropriate argument, which can be viewed as being the weighted sum of the factor demand elasticities of the remaining five columns; the weights are the factor shares at the point of approximation, which are given by α_i.

Viewing table B.13 from another perspective, the difference between the elasticity of cost with respect to a technological condition and a corresponding factor demand elasticity is a measure of the effect of including the technological condition in the factor demand equation. The statistical significance of this effect can be evaluated from the t statistic of the appropriate B_{ij} (or C_{ij}) coefficient. In general, these effects are very significant by the usual statistical standards; this indicates that a functional specification that does not allow for these effects is inadequate.

Table B.13 Elasticities of Factor Demand with Respect to Way-and-Structures Capital, Technological Conditions, and Output at the Point of Approximation

	Elasticity of cost	Equipment	General labor	Yard & switching labor (traffic & transportation)	On-train labor	Fuel & materials
x = way-and-structures capital	−0.42678	−1.065 (0.142)	−0.306 (0.131)	−0.289 (0.137)	−0.194 (0.118)	−0.058 (0.304)
t_1 = low-density route-miles	0.29108	0.311 (0.083)	0.310 (0.071)	0.442 (0.072)	0.412 (0.065)	0.078 (0.119)
t_2 = route miles	0.08641	0.485 (0.127)	−0.153 (0.100)	−0.212 (0.100)	−0.261 (0.083)	0.358 (0.105)
t_3 = average length of haul	−0.55757	−1.252 (0.117)	−0.046 (0.085)	−0.449 (0.092)	−0.434 (0.066)	−0.602 (0.107)
t_4 = traffic mix	0.33977	0.723 (0.073)	0.124 (0.061)	0.199 (0.064)	0.260 (0.050)	0.296 (0.100)
ψ_1 = passenger service	0.11289	0.068 (0.068)	0.274 (0.061)	0.312 (0.064)	0.147 (0.054)	−0.166 (0.075)
ψ_2 = ton-miles	1.12192	1.521 (0.113)	0.908 (0.101)	0.876 (0.105)	1.074 (0.080)	1.055 (0.100)

Table B.13 indicates that the elasticity of cost with respect to average length of haul is −0.56, so that a 1-mile increase in the average length of haul at the point of approximation reduces costs by \$690,000, or about 2.86¢ per 1,000 ton-miles. Since table B.13 also shows that the elasticity of cost with respect to freight output is 1.12, a 1-percent increase in ton-miles accompanied by a 1-percent increase in average length of haul would increase costs by 0.56 percent [= 1.12 + (−0.56)]. While it would be tempting to conclude from this that roughly half the short-run *marginal* costs associated with an increase in freight traffic are associated with linehaul operations, this may be overstating the case because the distribution of shipments by length of haul probably changes with changes in the average length of haul.

This may be the explanation of the estimate of −1.252 for the elasticity of equipment demand with respect to average length of haul found in table B.13. If a 1-percent increase in average length of haul could be thought of as every shipment traveling 1 percent further, it would seem that the ceteris paribus effect on equipment demand could not exceed 1 percent. If, however, short-haul shipments are particularly equipment intensive, then a shift in the distribution of shipments away from very short hauls may yield a greater-than-1-percent savings in equipment.

The other effects of average length of haul on factor intensities are in accord with prior expectations, with the estimate of -0.046 for the elasticity of general labor demand being particularly satisfying since the only savings one could expect in this factor would be associated with efficiencies in waybill processing. (That is, there will be fewer waybills per ton-mile.) Similarly, the cost savings of 0.45 percent on yard and switching labor and the cost savings of 0.60 percent on fuel and materials that would be associated with a 1-percent increase in average length of haul accord well with intuition since an increase in average length of haul implies a movement in the traffic distribution away from yard and switching activities, which are labor- and fuel-intensive.

The effects of a shift in the composition of traffic toward manufactured goods also accord well with prior expectations. Since these shipments have smaller loads per freight car and generally require more careful handling, the value of the equipment used to service such shipments is greater, ceteris paribus. The estimates of table B.13 indicate that about 54 percent of the increased costs engendered by such traffic shifts are due to increased equipment requirements.

The results concerning the effect of passenger service on factor intensities are somewhat puzzling. While it might be expected that passenger service is labor intensive, particularly with respect to nontrain traffic and transportation labor, which includes station personnel, there seems to be no satisfactory explanation of its estimated effect on fuel and materials. The estimated elasticity of -0.166 implies that an increase in passenger service causes an absolute decline in the use of fuel and materials, ceteris paribus. One conceivable explanation is that passenger service provides a positive external economy to freight service in those components of the fuel and materials factor which are neither fuel nor materials per se—namely, injuries to persons, lost freight and property damage—and which may be decreased by the increased safety standards and better track conditions required by passenger service. This would be consistent with the observed intensity of passenger service in general and maintenance and nontrain traffic and transportation labor.

It is these last two factors whose cost shares fall when freight service increases, while a 1-percent increase in such service causes a slightly greater than 1-percent increase for on-train labor and fuel and materials. The cost share of equipment rises with increased freight service; this is probably due to the disproportionate increase in train length (relative to the number of trains) associated, ceteris paribus, with increased traffic levels.

The foregoing analysis of the effects of way-and-structures capital, technological conditions, and output upon factor intensities indicates that these variables are important arguments of the factor share equations; their inclusion is not only required from a formal statistical point of view, but also informative in that a comparatively detailed description of the operation of the technology is made available.

B.5 Technical Supplement: Data Sources

Many of the underlying data for this study were provided by the ICC on magnetic tape. Where possible, these data have been checked for consistency and accuracy against published sources, notably *Transport Statistics of the United States*, Part I, various years. We provide in this technical supplement only those details of data construction not described in subsection B.2.1 above.

Capital stock   Estimates of the reproduction cost of each railroad's capital stock as of 12/31/71 can be found in R. A. Nelson (1974). Nelson's values for way-and-structures and land were combined to form a way-and-structures category; his categories of locomotives, freight cars, and other equipment were combined into an equipment category. The ICC's *Transport Statistics* provides end-of-year values for the undepreciated value of investment in way-and-structures and equipment for each railroad. By first differencing these values, the current dollar investment in each category was found for each year. When corporate reorganizations affected the ICC's accounts for value of investment, corresponding estimates of yearly investment, as provided by *Moody's Transportation Annual* from unpublished ICC data, were used instead. (For those railroads for which such a substitution was not necessary, the two sources give nearly identical figures.) The value of the yearly investments in each category in 12/31/71 prices was obtained by deflating by the times-series indexes of railroad equipment and railroad structures prices which are calculated by the Commerce Department as part of the implicit price deflator of the investment component of GNP. Once a depreciation rate is assumed, one can extrapolate backward from Nelson's 12/31/71 estimates using the yearly investment figures to construct a value for the capital stock at the end of each year. The depreciation rates assumed were 1.9 percent for the way-and-structures category (an average of 2 and 0 percent for the nonland and land components, respectively, with the weights taken as the national average of the percentage in each category), and 5 percent for equipment; these are commonly accepted estimates [see Harris (1977a)]. End-of-year capital stock values thus obtained were averaged to obtain average values for the calendar year.

Labor   For each labor category, labor expenditures were defined as wage and salary disbursements, plus employees' health and welfare benefits, plus an apportionment of employers' contributions to unemployment compensation and retirement programs. Wage and salary data are from the A-200 wage statistics, unpublished, as provided on tape by the ICC, which also includes figures for hours *actually* worked. (In the case of on-train labor, union rules allow full-day pay for less than eight hours of actual work—a typical worker in this category may be *paid* for 2,800 hours a year, but work about 2,000.) Wage rates for each subcategory were defined as labor expenditures divided by man-hours actually worked.

For general labor, a Divisia price index from the following subcategories was constructued:

1. Executive, office, and staff.
2. Professional, clerical, and general.
3. Maintenance of way and structures.
4. Maintenance of equipment.

As explained in section 2.1, employee compensation not chargeable to operating expenses was assumed to have been spent on this category. A Divisia price index for the yard and switching labor category, (more properly, transportation labor other than train and engine), was constructed from data for:

5. Transportation other than train and engine, yard and switching.
6. Yard and switching labor.

The final category, on-train labor, corresponds to the ICC's classification of transportation: train and engine.

Ton-miles by commodity type were estimated by multiplying an estimate of average length of haul by commodity by tons as given in the ICC's *Quarterly Commodity Statistics*. Estimates of average length of haul by commodity were constructed from the ICC–FRA *Carload Waybill Statistics*, various years, which is a 1-percent random sample of all shipments' waybills. Unfortunately, when a shipment is interlined (moves across two or more railroads), it is not possible to tell from the waybill how many miles it traveled on each road. Rather than make an arbitrary allocation of distance to each road for interlined shipments, we restricted our attention to shipments originating and terminating on the same road.

From these an average length of *intraline* haul was calculated for each of seven commodity groups. Since overall average length of haul is known, one can calculate average length of haul by commodity if one is willing to assume that the ratio of interline to intraline length of haul does not vary across commodities (but does vary across roads). Clearly, this is a big assumption, but we make it *faute de mieux*. Using the resulting estimate of ton-miles, the ratio of manufactured ton-miles to nonmanufactured ton-miles was calculated; the STCC codes and commodities that are included in our definition of "manufactured" are given in table B.14. An alternative measure of traffic mix, which makes no use of the *Carload Waybill Statistics* whatever, is the ratio of tons of manufactured commodities to nonmanufactured tons. The results obtained with this measure, however, are uniformly inferior.

Table B.14 STCC Codes for Commodities Classified as Manufactured

Code	Commodity
19	Ordnance and accessories
20	Food and kindred products
21	Tobacco products
22	Basic textiles
23	Apparel and other finished textile products
25	Furniture and fixtures
26	Pulp, paper, and allied products
27	Printed matter
30	Rubber and miscellaneous plastic products
31	Leather and leather products
33	Primary metal products
34	Fabricated metal products
35	Machinery, except electrical
36	Electrical machinery, equipment, and supplies
37	Transportation equipment
38	Instruments, photo & optical goods, watches and clocks
39	Miscellaneous products of manufacturing
44	Freight forwarder traffic
45	Shipping associations or similar traffic
46	Miscellaneous mixed shipments
47	Small packaged freight shipments

Notes

1. Caves et al. (1980a) estimate a short-run cost function of the form

$$C^s = C^s(y_P, y_F, \text{PATL}, \text{ALH}, x, \tilde{w}), \tag{B.1}$$

which corresponds to the long-run cost function

$$C^l = C^l(y_P, y_F, \text{PATL}, \text{ALH}, w_k, \tilde{w}), \tag{B.2}$$

where $\tilde{w}$ represents a vector of variable factor prices, x represents WS capital, w_k represents the price of WS capital, and the other variables have their previous meanings.

Returns to scale are defined by

$$R = \left(\sum_i \frac{\partial \ln C^l}{\partial \ln z_i} \right)^{-1}. \tag{B.3}$$

This is estimated from [see (4.6)]

$$R = \left(1 - \frac{\partial \ln C^s}{\partial \ln x} \right) \Big/ \sum_i \frac{\partial \ln C^s}{\partial \ln z_i}, \tag{B.4}$$

where the z's are either $y_P, y_F, \text{PATL}, \text{ALH}$, or simply y_P and y_F. In the former case, returns to scale are measured assuming that increases in output arise from increases in ALH and PATL; in the latter case, ALH and PATL are assumed constant. Using the latter measure, which corresponds to the measure used in this and most other studies, the R ranges between 1.01 and 1.03 for a railroad with sample mean characteristics.

2. We depart from a Cobb–Douglas specification of $\phi(\cdot)$ since we wish to allow for the possibility that it is not monotonic in its arguments.

3. The ratio of manufactured ton-miles to total ton-miles is an obvious alternative measure of traffic mix, but performs less well empirically.

4. Actually, data were collected for 44 class I linehaul railroads for the years 1968–1972. For the other railroads in the United States, the *Carload Waybill Statistics* sample was clearly inadequate; for the years preceding 1968 mergers made much of the B branchline and capital data useless, and other data were difficult to obtain, particularly in machine-readable form. The years 1971 and 1972 were not used due to Amtrak operations.

5. It is possible to include the observations for 4 of these roads—the Denver and Rio Grande, the Louisville and Nashville, the Norfolk and Western, and the Reading—with the observations for the other 20 roads and obtain results which generally satisfy the regularity conditions but which have somewhat different implications from those obtained using the 20 noncoal roads alone. Using the estimates presented in section B.3, for which the sample consisted of 19 noncoal roads, a prediction interval test permits rejection of the hypothesis that coal and noncoal roads have the same technology at the 0.005 level (see below).

6. The relevant equation is reproduced here for convenience:

$$\ln C = \alpha_0 + \sum_i \alpha_i \ln w_i + \sum_j \beta_j \ln t_j + \sum_k \gamma_k \ln \psi_k$$
$$+ \frac{1}{2} \sum_i \sum_l A_{il} \ln w_i \ln w + \sum_i \sum_j B_{ij} \ln w_i \ln t_j$$
$$+ \sum_i \sum_k C_{ik} \ln w_i \ln \psi_k + \frac{1}{2} \sum_j \sum_m D_{jm} \ln t_j \ln t_m$$
$$+ \sum_j \sum_k E_{jk} \ln t_j \ln \psi_k + \frac{1}{2} \sum_k \sum_h F_{kh} \ln \psi_k \ln \psi_h + \varepsilon_C.$$

7. As pointed out in appendix A, our model can be viewed as linear with nonlinear restrictions on the parameters, but it is more convenient here to treat it as a general nonlinear model.

8. While it is not necessary in this context for ρ to be the same for every equation, it is necessary for ρ to be the same for every factor share equation. Empirically, it turns out that ρ for the cost share equation is about the same as ρ for the factor share equations.

9. These estimates are invariant to the equation deleted, since they are the maximum likelihood estimates if ρ is truly zero.

10. It is a matter of considerable computational convenience to take ρ as fixed: the slightly nonlinear nature of our problem introduced by the hedonic specification makes an iterative algorithm necessary even when ρ is fixed. One could recalculate ρ at the end of these procedures and reiterate until ρ converged, a considerable computational burden, or one could rewrite the program to view ρ as an argument of the likelihood function, a considerable programming task. Since the asymptotic properties of these two procedures and the one we adopt are identical, and there is no basis for distinguishing between them on the basis of their finite sample properties, the additional expense does not seem justified.

11. If $u_2 = \rho u_1 + \varepsilon_2$ [i.e., (B.12) holds in the second period], the application of (B.13) is appropriate since it requires the operation of (B.12) for only one period.

12. To some extent that appears prima facie to be the case: two of its Midwest competitors have since declared bankruptcy, and two more are said to be near bankruptcy (*Business Week*, 1978). These systems, which are included in our sample, are Chicago, Milwaukee, St. Paul, and Pacific; Chicago, Rock Island and Pacific; Chicago and North Western; Illinois Central Gulf (formed in 1972 from the Illinois Central and the Gulf, Mobile, and Ohio).

13. As mentioned above, this model was used to test the hypothesis that the regression model which we estimated for the noncoal roads also applies to the coal railroads: the Denver and Rio Grande, the Louisville and Nashville, the Norfolk and Western, and the Reading. Since these railroads do not provide sufficient observations to estimate a model for them alone, we face a situation analogous to that of applying the Chow test for the equality of the full set of regression coefficients when the degrees of freedom of one sample are inadequate. If we regard ρ and the contemporaneous variance–covariance matrix of residuals Σ (after differencing by ρ) as given and equal to their estimates from the noncoal samples, then

$$[\varepsilon'(\Sigma^{-1} \otimes I)\varepsilon/T_2]/[\varepsilon^{*'}(\Sigma^{-1} \otimes I)\varepsilon^*/T_1 - K], \tag{B.20}$$

where ε is a $T_2 \times 1$ vector of residuals calculated from (B.13) and (B.15) for the coal roads and ε^* the $T_1 \times 1$ vector of residuals calculated for the 56 observations of the noncoal roads, is distributed $F(T_2, T_1 - k)$. Here $T_2 = 4$ roads $\times$ 3 years $\times$ 5 equations $= 60$, and $T_1 = 56$ "observations" $\times$. 5 equations $= 280$; $k = 60$, the number of estimated coefficients. Calculating (B.20) we obtain a test statistic value of 4.94, while the 0.01 value of $F(60,211)$ is between 1.47 and 1.66.

Since Σ and ρ are not in fact given but only consistently estimated, the above test is only asymptotically valid. An alternative test statistic in the same notation is

$$\varepsilon'(\Sigma^{-1} \otimes I)\varepsilon, \tag{B.21}$$

which is asymptotically χ^2 with T_2 degrees of freedom. Its value is 393.25; the 0.005 level of $\chi^2(60)$ is 91.95. Thus both tests, while only approximate, allow rejection of the null hypothesis at the 0.01 level.

14. Factor prices are measured relative to the price of fuel and materials, which has a sample mean of 106.002. Thus $\hat{C} = [\exp(15.1546)]106.002 = \$404,457,800$, $\partial \ln C/\partial \ln t_1 = 0.29108$, and $t_1 = 1860.129$. Applying (B.22) yields $\$63,291.08$ for $\partial C/\partial t_1$.

Cost Functions for Regulated Motor Carriers

C.1 Introduction: Industry Structure and Previous Studies

The ICC classifies motor carriers of property engaged in interstate operations into four groups: common; contract; private; and exempt. Common carriers, the subject of this study, serve the general public and carry a wide range of (usually manufactured) commodities. Contract carriers either specialize in the carriage of a small number of specific commodities, such as household goods, or have long-term contracts with a small number of shippers, usually less than ten. Private carriers are firms which carry their own products in the furtherance of their primary business. Exempt carriers carry commodities that are exempt from regulation, usually agricultural products.

There are three categories of ICC-regulated carriers:[1] common carriers of general freight; special commodities carriers; and contract carriers. The last category is a relatively small segment of the trucking industry. General freight carriers and special commodity carriers each comprise about 20 percent of the market for intercity freight trucking (Roberts, 1977). Both sets of carriers are "common carriers" in that they must provide the service of transporting certain commodities at fixed rates along fixed routes to all customers. The fixed route and commodity rates, while not determined by the ICC, must meet its approval.[2]

Although the two sectors of the trucking industry analyzed in this study both transport general freight, most of the firms in the category of carriers of other specialized commodities transport specified commodities rather than general freight. Each operating authority possessed by a specialized freight carrier entitles it to transport a specified product. If that specified product requires peculiar transportation facilities (e.g., automobiles, refrigerated products, petroleum), the firm transporting the product is placed by the ICC in a particular subcategory of specialized commodities carriers. The term "other special commodities" as used by *Trinc's Blue Book of the Trucking Industry* includes eight ICC commodity groups—heavy machinery, dump trucking, armored truck service, films and associated commodities, forest products, mine ores not including coal, retail store delivery, and explosives or dangerous articles—as well as an all-inclusive group: ICC subgroup number 17, "specific commodities not subgrouped." This last subgroup, in which the vast majority of carriers of other specialized commodities is found, consists primarily of large firms with several operating authorities for different commodities to different areas. Many of these firms are heavily reliant on owner-operators whose vehicles are readily adaptable to transporting different types of freight. Most of those firms transporting specialized commodities that do not require peculiar facilities (i.e., different from facilities required by common carriers of general freight) are placed in the subcategory of this study—specialized carriers of other commodities. In this sense, both sectors carry freight that requires roughly the same facilities and vehicles to transport.

The difference in technologies between the two sectors results primarily from differences in operating authorities. While operating authorities for specialized carriers are more restrictive in specifying commodities for transport than are common general freight operating authorities, specialized carrier authorities are less restrictive in routing entitlements. Carriers of specialized commodities have authorities to carry products from one region to another region. Thus, if a specialized product is manufactured, processed, or distributed at one plant, an operating authority for a specialized carrier might enable the carrier to distribute the product to all major consumers in a given region. This type of operating authority does not require the capital-intensive consolidated terminal distribution systems that are necessitated by operating authorities for carriers of general freight, because operating authorities of special commodity carriers allow for direct delivery to large consumers. At the same time, without consolidated terminal distribution systems, small shipments of less-than-truckload freight become quite costly. In contrast, carriers of general freight have operating authorities that allow service to a mapping of specific points, but not to entire regions. Pointwise authorities encourage consolidated pickup and distribution centers at each point of operating authority. Consolidation terminals permit carriers of general freight to achieve economies in the linehaul journey for less-than-truck-load freight inasmuch as more than one shipment can be made per haul. The expense of terminal usage, both in overhead and delay of delivery, make general freight carriers more expensive than specialized freight carriers for large truckload shipments. For large shipments, particularly for medium or long distances, rail carriers and trucking carriers of specialized commodities compete for the same market.[3]

Consolidated distribution terminals require the specialization of labor assignments from the scheduled transportation of freight between certain terminals to the distribution and processing of freight at the terminal. This specialization of labor has perhaps in part fostered the growth of unionized labor for carriers of general freight. Carriers of other specialized commodities, without the need for specialized labor of distribution terminals or scheduled service on fixed-point routes, can rely more on nonunion labor and particularly on rented owner-operators.

During the past decade, carriers of specialized commodities, particularly other specialized commodities, have grown rapidly (see table C.1). Ton-mileage for other specialized commodities grew by over 100 percent whereas ton-mileage for general freight carriers rose by only 40 percent. Note that carriers of specialized commodities raised their market share of regulated trucking from about 17 to 33 percent. During that time, the number of firms carrying other specialized commodities, as in other sectors of the regulated trucking industry, decreased.

A question of interest to observers of the trucking industry is whether this increase in the relative importance of carriers of other specialized commodities is a result of technological changes or regulatory policy. More specifically, what are the causes of the increased utilization of specialized carriers of other commodities, and what are the causes of the decrease in the number of firms?

Part of the growth in the carriers of specialized commodities might be explained by regulatory procedures over the past decade. Roberts[4] suggests that the preponderance of new route authorities applied for, and granted to, carriers of specialized commodities occurs because those carriers have greater ease than common carriers of general freight in demonstrating the "convenience and necessity" of such authorities. While

Table C.1 Freight in Billions of Ton-Miles (by Number of Firms)

Year	General freight	Specialized	Other specialized
1966	71.9 (1,536)	50.4 (2,079)	22.6 (1,110)
1967	72.1 (1,213)	49.9 (1,956)	22.2 (1,187)
1972	92.5 (1,176)	93.7 (2,188)	41.6 (1,201)
1973	102.2 (1,136)	98.9 (2,092)	45.4 (1,152)
1974	102.0 (971)	96.7 (1,573)	47.5 (982)
1976	98.0 (978)	101.9 (1,553)	48.4 (959)

Source: *Trinc's Blue Book of the Trucking Industry (1967–1977)*.

no carrier for a particular specialized commodity may service a given area currently covered by a commodity-specific operating authority, it may enter into areas that are only serviced by common carriers of general freight. The effect of this regulatory procedure may be severalfold in the encouragement of returns to scale in specialized carrier operation:

1. Because many carriers of other specialized commodities have little overhead and rely heavily on owner operators, the initial expense for a regional operating authority will create a general decreasing average cost curve since the cost of the operating authority does not increase with utilization.

2. The specialization of each commodity in an operating authority may enable specialized carriers to expand services without fear of new market entry in a given region for a given specialized commodity.[5]

3. The granting of regional operating authorities to specialized commodities carriers may lead to differences between the two sectors in trucking technologies suggested above.

4. Delays and the expense of application procedures for new operating authorities encourage mergers and discourage entry into both sectors of the regulated trucking industry. Although mergers may induce some returns to scale in the general freight sector from a more efficient network of routes, there are constraints on size from terminal usage and distributions. In contrast, mergers in the specialized commodities sector might induce economies of scale by more efficient utilization of capital and regular service.

Several econometric studies of the cost structure of general freight carriers have previously been made. These studies have usually consisted of cross-sectional regressions of costs on output, with a number of variations in functional form and some differences in the measurement of output. While some early studies using vehicle-miles as an output measure found constant returns to scale, more recent studies using ton-miles as an output measure and including service characteristics as independent variables have tended to find increasing returns to scale.[6] In most cases the degree of returns to scale is small; many models assume homogeneity and estimate the degree to be about 0.95.[7]

However, most of these studies use a Cobb–Douglas cost function or other functional forms that impose severe restrictions on the nature of the underlying trucking technology. Since, however, it is likely that non-homotheticities exist among output, factor inputs, and the operating characteristics of the firm, it is desirable to estimate a neoclassical cost function for regulated motor carriers that takes these possible nonhomotheticities into account.[8] In the next section, we outline the cost function specification for regulated motor carriers. Section C.3 presents the findings with respect to specialized commodity carriers, while section C.4 presents the findings with respect to carriers of general commodities.

C.2 Specification of Cost Functions for Regulated Motor Common Carriers

Since the trucking industry is characterized by relatively small capital requirements, we estimate a long-run cost function, which assumes that firms are able to make optimal adjustments in capacity. In addition, we utilize a technological specification in which the shipment characteristics enter directly into the cost function.[9] Hence, the general form of the estimated trucking cost function is given by the following expression:

$$C = C(y, w, t),$$ (C.1)

where C represents long-run total costs, y total ton-miles, w a vector of factor prices, and t a vector of shipment characteristics.

We use a translog approximation to (C.1), which then takes the following general form:

$$\ln C(y, w, t) = \alpha_0 + \sum_i \alpha_i (\ln w_i - \ln \bar{w}_i) + \sum_j \beta_j (\ln t_j - \ln \bar{t}_j)$$
$$+ \gamma(\ln y - \ln \bar{y}) + \tfrac{1}{2}\sum_i \sum_l A_{il}(\ln w_i - \ln \bar{w}_i)(\ln w_l - \ln \bar{w}_l)$$
$$+ \sum_i \sum_j B_{ij}(\ln w_i - \ln \bar{w}_i)(\ln t_j - \ln \bar{t}_j)$$
$$+ \sum_i C_i(\ln w_i - \ln \bar{w}_i)(\ln y - \ln \bar{y})$$
$$+ \tfrac{1}{2}\sum_j \sum_m D_{jm}(\ln t_j - \ln \bar{t}_j)(\ln t_m - \ln \bar{t}_m)$$
$$+ \sum_j E_j(\ln t_j - \ln \bar{t}_j)(\ln y - \ln \bar{y}) + \tfrac{1}{2}F(\ln y - \ln \bar{y})^2,$$ (C.2)

where each variable has been normalized by the sample mean (represented by a bar over the variable).

Since we assume cost minimization, the following restrictions on the parameters in (C.2) should be imposed to ensure that the cost function is homogeneous of degree 1 in factor prices:

$$\sum_i \alpha_i = 1, \quad \sum_i A_{il} = 0 \qquad \text{for all } l,$$
$$\sum_i B_{ij} = 0 \qquad\qquad \text{for all } j.$$ (C.2a)

In addition, the following symmetry conditions should be satisfied:

$$A_{il} = A_{li}$$
$$D_{jm} = D_{mj} \qquad \text{for all } i, j, l, \text{ and } m. \tag{C.2b}$$

If firms are indeed costminimizing, from Shephard's lemma the factor demand equations can be derived:

$$\frac{\partial C(y, w, t)}{\partial w_i} = x_i \qquad \text{for all } i. \tag{C.3}$$

For translog cost functions, it is mathematically more attractive to derive the following factor share equations instead of a factor demand equation:

$$\frac{\partial \ln C(\psi, w, t)}{\partial \ln w_i} = \frac{\partial C(\psi, w, t)}{\partial w_i} \frac{w_i}{C} = \frac{x_i w_i}{C} = S_i$$
$$= \alpha_i + \sum_l A_{il}(\ln w_l - \ln \bar{w}_l) + \sum_j B_{ij}(\ln t_j - \ln \bar{t}_j)$$
$$+ C_i(\ln \psi - \ln \bar{\psi}) + \varepsilon_i, \tag{C.4}$$

where ε_i is a disturbance term.

Since the cost shares sum to one for each observation, it follows that $\Sigma \varepsilon_i = 0$, so that the variance–covariance matrix of these disturbances is singular. A survey of appropriate estimation methods for this case is contained in Berndt and Savin (1975); Barten (1969) seems to have been the first to have noticed that if ε_c and ε_i are multivariately normal, then maximum likelihood methods can be applied to the system with one factor share equation removed. The resulting estimates are invariant to the equation deleted, and consistent, asymptotically normal, and asymptotically efficient.

C.3 Estimated Costs of Specialized Commodity Carriers

To estimate the cost function given in (C.2), we need to specify the costs, factor prices, and technological variables included in the cost function. Since we estimate a long-run cost function, to each firm's operating cost was added a 12-percent opportunity cost for capital, with capital measured as "carrier operating property—net." The firm's total costs were then divided into the following four categories of factor payments: labor costs; fuel costs (expenditures plus taxes); purchased transportation; and "other." "Other expenditures" consist mostly of the imputed opportunity cost of capital, depreciation, and maintenance of capital items (tires, etc.), and were assumed to be payments for capital services. Each firm's "carrier operating property—net" was taken as a measure of the quantity of capital (and thus of capital services), so that "other expenditures" divided by "carrier operating property–net" gave a firm-specific price of capital. A firm-specific price of labor was obtained by dividing labor expenditures by the average number of employees. Since direct quantity measures of purchased transportation and fuel were not available, regional prices for these inputs were estimated by a method whose assumptions and results are given in the technical supplement.

With respect to the operating characteristics, the following variables were available for carriers of specialized commodities:

t_1 = AVLOAD = average load per vehicle (ton-miles/total vehicle-miles).

t_2 = AVHAUL = average length of haul (ton-miles/total tons).

t_3 = INSUR = insurance (insurance expenditures/total ton-miles).

The variables AVLOAD and AVHAUL attempt to reflect the operating characteristics of the firm. Presumably those firms with full capacity utilization and long hauls will have larger values of AVLOAD and AVHAUL and concomitant reduction in their costs. The insurance variable attempts to reflect differences in the composition of output. Carriers of specialized commodities have distinguishable differences in the value of the composition of their freight. Thus even though most carriers in this group have a large number of operating authorities for different commodities, there still is a significant level of specialization that provides for a composition of output distinguishable from that of another specialized commodities carrier.

One would expect that the estimated coefficient for an insurance quality variable would reflect added expense for outputs with higher insurance value per composition.[10] Shipments may require higher insurance because of their intrinsic value or because of special handling characteristics such as fragility, perishability, and number of handling operations. In contrast, large average lengths of haul and average loads per vehicle suggest reduced handling expenses and better equipment utilization, thus leading to lower average costs. One would consequently expect that linear coefficients for these latter variables would be negative.

Since it is likely that regional differences exist among carriers of specialized commodities, we estimated cost functions for carriers in the

Official Region and in the rest of the country, which we designate as the South–West Region. Thus our sample consisted of 201 firms in the Official Region and of 161 firms in the South–West Region.[11]

All firms were included in the sample for which there were adequate data and that met the following criteria:

1. Each firm purchased insurance for freight loss or damage.
2. Each firm had a price of labor of $5,500 or more. Special commodities carriers rely heavily on nonunionized labor and on independent owner-operators, and wages for the nonunionized labor are probably lower than those for the unionized general freight carriers. Further, the number of employees reported by a firm may include owner-operators whose commission may not be reflected in labor expenses. Thus it was felt that although $5,500 reflects a low annual salary, it probably reflects a realistic minimum. Note that the mode of the price of labor in the specialized commodities sample is $8,500.
3. There were no obvious errors in the data; for example, one firm reported an average load of 78 tons.

Table C.2 presents the coefficient estimates of the jointly estimated cost and factor share equations for specialized commodity carriers in the Official and South–West Regions. In general, the coefficients are statistically significant and the R^2's of the cost and factor share equations indicate a reasonable goodness of fit.[12]

Before turning to the implications of these results for specific costs and technology, it is useful to discuss their implications for modeling trucking technology. First, since the linear coefficients on the operating characteristics t_i are all significant, and the quadratic coefficients on these variables are generally significant, this indicates that these variables affect costs and technology and should enter directly into the cost function. Second, since the coefficients on the interaction terms among factor prices and operating coefficients $w_i t_j$ are generally significant, this indicates that technology is not separable in operating characteristics. Thus not only do operating characteristics affect costs, but they also affect factor shares and factor utilizations. This implies that the technological specification $C = C(y, w, t)$ is preferable to the hedonic specification $C = C(y\phi(t), w)$.[13] Finally, since the coefficients on the interaction terms among factor prices and output $w_i y$ are generally significant, this indicates that production is nonhomothetic and nonseparable; factor shares and intensities do vary with levels of output. These results imply that we cannot make global generalizations about the nature of technology and returns to scale since measures of cost elasticities will not

Table C.2 Estimated Coefficients in Cost Function and Associated Factor Share Equations for Carriers of Specialized Commodities, by Region

Coefficient	Official		South–West	
	Value	Standard error	Value	Standard error
k	8.8839	0.0288	9.5417	0.0806
w_1 (labor)	0.3485	0.0139	0.2675	0.0175
w_2 (fuel)	0.0423	0.0041	0.0498	0.0648
w_3 (capital)	0.2925	0.0121	0.3003	0.0164
w_4 (pur. trans.)	0.3167	0.0228	0.3841	0.0291
t_1 (AVLOAD)	−0.8441	0.0167	−0.5346	0.1204
t_2 (AVHAUL)	−0.1767	0.0163	−0.1769	0.0694
t_3 (INSUR)	0.0319	0.0167	0.2679	0.0722
psi (ψ)	0.7873	0.0280	0.9362	0.0563
$w_1 w_1$	0.1223	0.0271	0.0781	0.0339
$w_1 w_2$	−0.0099	0.0071	0.0136	0.0114
$w_1 w_3$	−0.0136	0.0122	−0.0035	0.0148
$w_1 w_4$	−0.0990	0.0339	−0.0882	0.0404
$w_2 w_2$	−0.0178	0.0083	−0.0122	0.0172
$w_2 w_3$	−0.0258	0.0039	−0.0192	0.0058
$w_2 w_4$	0.0535	0.0137	0.0178	0.0249
$w_3 w_3$	−0.0343	0.0113	−0.0386	0.0152
$w_3 w_4$	0.0737	0.0207	0.0613	0.0251
$w_4 w_4$	−0.0282	0.0533	0.0090	0.0660
$w_1 t_1$	−0.0059	0.0138	−0.0311	0.0168
$w_1 t_2$	−0.0046	0.0095	−0.0244	0.0110
$w_1 t_3$	0.0055	0.0079	−0.0103	0.0086
$w_2 t_1$	−0.0054	0.0042	−0.0046	0.0062
$w_2 t_2$	0.0096	0.0028	0.0073	0.0041
$w_2 t_3$	−0.0086	0.0024	−0.0067	0.0032
$w_3 t_1$	0.0184	0.0119	−0.0199	0.0157
$w_3 t_2$	0.0079	0.0078	−0.0123	0.1027
$w_3 t_3$	−0.0016	0.0065	0.0036	0.0081
$w_4 t_1$	−0.0071	0.0231	0.0158	0.0278
$w_4 t_2$	−0.0129	0.0153	0.0293	0.0182
$w_4 t_3$	0.0046	0.0128	0.0134	0.0143
w_1 psi	−0.0238	0.0083	−0.0316	0.0086
w_2 psi	−0.0081	0.0024	−0.0091	0.0032
w_3 psi	−0.0396	0.0066	−0.0336	0.0079
w_4 psi	0.0715	0.0132	0.0743	0.0141
$t_1 t_1$	0.3563	0.0152	−0.1427	0.1142

Table C.2 (continued)

Coefficient	Official		South–West	
	Value	Standard error	Value	Standard error
$t_1 t_2$	−0.1116	0.0111	−0.0423	0.0534
$t_1 t_3$	−0.0530	0.0102	0.0562	0.0464
$t_2 t_2$	0.0646	0.0130	0.1330	0.0617
$t_2 t_3$	−0.0203	0.0086	−0.0559	0.0268
$t_3 t_3$	0.0088	0.0098	0.0793	0.0326
t_1 psi	−0.2007	0.0167	−0.0457	0.0527
t_2 psi	−0.0135	0.0105	−0.0144	0.0313
t_3 psi	−0.0635	0.0134	0.0155	0.0346
psi psi	0.0273	0.0238	0.0874	0.0346

	Official		South–West	
	R^2	RMSE	R^2	RMSE
Cost equation	0.8877	0.3192	0.9108	0.3354
Labor equation	0.1531	0.1166	0.0746	0.0407
Fuel equation	0.2123	0.0344	0.2835	0.1800
Capital equation	0.1913	0.0924	0.2597	0.1098
Purch. trans. equation	0.1958	0.1863	0.1044	0.0843
Log of likelihood function	752.683		489.460	

only vary with the level of output but also with the level of factor prices and the level of the operating characteristics.

Nevertheless, to obtain some feel for the nature of trucking technology and interregional differences in this technology, it is useful to discuss briefly the estimates of cost elasticities and elasticities of factor substitution and demand evaluated at the mean levels of the variables. Since the equations were estimated by using variables that were measured as deviations from the mean, the calculation of these elasticities is considerably simplified by the standardization of the variables so that their (standardized) value is one at the sample mean since $\ln 1 = 0$.

Table C.3 presents the elasticities of cost with respect to output and operating characteristics and their associated standard errors for carriers in the Official and South–West Regions, where all variables are evaluated at the mean. This indicates that a hypothetical carrier in the Official Region facing mean factor prices and operating characteristics and producing at mean output levels would exhibit strongly increasing returns to scale ($\partial \ln C / \partial \ln y = 0.7873$ with a standard error of 0.0280), while a

Table C.3 Elasticity of Costs with Respect to Output and Operating Characteristics at the Point of Approximation, Carriers of Specialized Commodities

Elasticity of cost with respect to	Official		South–West	
	Value	Standard error	Value	Standard error
Output ($\partial \ln C / \partial \ln \psi$)	0.7873	0.0280	0.9362	0.0563
Average load ($\partial \ln C / \partial \ln t_1$)	−0.8841	0.0167	−0.5346	0.1204
Average length of haul ($\partial \ln C / \partial \ln t_2$)	−0.1767	0.0163	−0.1769	0.0694
Insurance ($\partial \ln C / \partial \ln t_3$)	0.0319	0.0167	0.2679	0.0722

similar hypothetical carrier in the South–West Region would exhibit mildly increasing returns to scale ($\partial \ln C / \partial \ln y = 0.9362$ with a standard error of 0.0563). Similarly, such a carrier would exhibit relatively high economies of capacity utilization with respect to average load and relatively modest economies of utilization with respect to average haul ($\partial \ln C / \partial \ln$ AVLOAD equals −0.8841 with a standard error of 0.0167 in the Official Region and −0.5346 with a standard error of 0.1204 in the South–West Region). Finally, such a carrier would exhibit significant diseconomies associated with the handling of high-value goods in the South–West Region, but be relatively insensitive to this operating characteristic in the Official Region ($\partial \ln C / \partial \ln$ INSUR equals 0.2679 with a standard error of 0.0722 in the South–West Region and 0.0319 with a standard error of 0.0167 in the Official Region). Thus these findings indicate that costs are quite sensitive to output levels and operating characteristics, with carriers in the Official Region being substantially more responsive to economies associated with increases in output and increases in average load than those in the South–West Region.

Since, however, we have indicated that substantial nonhomotheticities exist with respect to output levels and operating characteristics, it is useful to consider how these cost elasticities vary as the levels of output and the operating characteristics change. Table C.4 therefore presents expressions for these elasticities evaluated at mean factor prices, but at variable output levels and values of the operating characteristics. With respect to economies of scale, it is interesting to note that average load has a strong effect upon the cost elasticity in the Official Region, but a negligible one in the South–West Region. Thus not only do firms in the Official Region exhibit marked economies of scale, but those with large loads exhibit even greater economies of scale. This implies that there is a clear relationship between firm size, average load, and costs, with large

Table C.4 Elasticities of Cost with Respect to Output and Operating Characteristics at Mean Factor Prices, Carriers of Specialized Commodities, by Region

	$\partial \ln C/\partial \ln y$		$\partial \ln C/\partial \ln$ AVLOAD		$\partial \ln C/\partial \ln$ ALH		$\partial \ln C/\partial \ln$ INSUR	
	Value	Standard error	Value	Standard error	Value	Standard error	Value	Standard error
Official								
Constant	−0.7873	0.0280	−0.8441	0.0167	−0.1767	0.0163	0.0319	0.0167
AVLOAD	−0.2007	0.0167	0.3563	0.0152	−0.1116	0.0111	−0.0530	0.0102
ALH	−0.0135	0.0105	−0.1116	0.0111	0.0646	0.0130	−0.0203	0.0086
INSUR	−0.0635	0.0134	−0.0530	0.0102	−0.0205	0.0086	0.0088	0.0098
y	0.0273	0.0238	−0.2007	0.0167	−0.0135	0.0105	−0.0635	0.0134
South–West								
Constant	0.9362	0.0563	−0.5346	0.1204	−0.1760	0.0694	0.2679	0.0722
AVLOAD	−0.0457	0.0527	−0.1427	0.1142	−0.0423	0.0534	0.0562	0.0464
ALH	−0.0144	0.0313	−0.0423	0.0534	0.1330	0.0617	−0.0559	0.0268
INSUR	0.0155	0.0346	0.0562	0.0464	−0.0554	0.0268	0.0793	0.0326
y	0.0874	0.0345	−0.0144	0.0313	−0.0144	0.0313	0.0155	0.0346

firms utilizing large loads having substantially lower costs than small firms with small loads. While admittedly inferential, this tends to support the hypothesis that the observed economies of scale are of a regulatory rather than a technological nature.

The findings concerning the elasticities of cost with respect to operating characteristics are interesting and support the hypothesis of different regional technologies. In particular, while costs become less sensitive to average load as the size of the load increases in the Official Region, they become more sensitive to size of load as load increases in the South–West Region. Thus while carriers facing mean shipment loads in the South–West Region have costs that are considerably more sensitive to load than those in the Official Region, this differential is even greater for carriers facing shipment loads that are twice the mean. However, elasticity of costs with respect to average length of haul becomes greater in absolute value in the Official Region as load increases and smaller in absolute value in the South–West Region as average load increases. Thus, on balance there appear to be greater economies of equipment utilization associated with high average loads in the Official Region than in the South–West Region. Finally, the elasticity of cost with respect to insurance appears to be relatively insensitive to the values of output or of the operating characteristics.

Having discussed the elasticity of costs, we now consider the elasticities of substitution among factors and the elasticities of demand for each factor.[14] Table C.5 presents the elasticities of factor substitution and the own price elasticity of each factor at the point of approximation. The own price elasticity of demand for fuel is quite high in both regions, but relatively low for all of the other factors, with remarkable regional similarities. Since carriers of specialized commodities tend to substitute owner-operators for their own equipment, we would expect to see a high elasticity of substitution between purchased transportation and capital on the one hand and between purchased transportation and fuel on the other. Table C.5 indicates that this is indeed the case, with the elasticities being somewhat higher in the Official Region than in the South–West Region. Similarly, insofar as equipment and fuel are related, we would expect to see a complementary relationship between these two factors, which again appears to be the case.

Thus carriers of specialized commodities appear to fit the neoclassical model of production remarkably well, with the elasticities of substitution behaving as expected, as do the elasticities of cost with respect to operating

Table C.5 Own Factor Demand Elasticities and Allen–Uzawa Cross Elasticities, Carriers of Other Specialized Commodities

	Labor	Fuel	Capital	Purchased transportation
Official				
Labor	–	0.3264 (0.4911)	0.8668 (0.1216)	0.1026 (0.3111)
Fuel		–	−1.0875 (0.4316)	4.9973 (1.2362)
Capital	·		–	1.7960 (0.2532)
Own price elasticity	−0.2998 (0.0778)	−1.3782 (0.2030)	−0.8249 (0.0453)	−0.7725 (0.1752)
South–West				
Labor	–	2.0266 (0.8812)	0.9559 (0.1862)	0.1366 (0.4100)
Fuel		–	−0.2811 (0.4493)	1.9294 (1.3126)
Capital			–	1.5313 (0.2296)
Own price elasticity	−0.4405 (0.1276)	−1.1952 (0.3476)	−0.8282 (0.0578)	−0.5923 (0.1749)

characteristics. What is surprising, however, is the marked economies of scale exhibited by these carriers in the Official Region. While it is likely that these are due to regulatory effects under which large firms obtain extensive operating rights and thus enjoy better equipment utilization, it is certainly true that these effects are not fully captured by the operating characteristics included in the analysis. Thus whether these carriers are subject to technological economies of scale or regulatory economies of scale must remain a question to be resolved by further research.

C.4 Estimated Costs of Common Carriers of General Commodities

Chapter 5 analyzed the behavior of the common carriers of general commodities, which tend to specialize in LTL carriage, and found significant differences in the cost structures and technologies of the three different types of carriers: regional carriers in the Official Region; regional carriers in the rest of the country, which we denote by the South–West Region; and interregional or transcontinental carriers (Interregionals). In this section, we present the estimated cost function for these carriers and discuss the structure of their technology, which forms the basis of the policy discussion in chapter 5.

As was true in the case of the special commodity carriers, we employ a general technological specification that includes operating characteristics as well as the usual arguments of the cost function. There are six output-related variables that we treat as operating characteristics: average length of haul; average load per vehicle; percentage of freight in LTL; average shipment size; insurance cost; and terminal density. Large average lengths of haul, large average loads per vehicle, and large average sizes of shipments all suggest reduced handling expenses at terminals and, therefore, lower average costs. One would expect that linear coefficients for these variables would all be negative. Large percentages of LTL shipments suggest many shipments per truck and consequently larger handling expenses at terminals. One would therefore expect a positive linear coefficient for percentage LTL. Since insurance costs reflect differences in fragility and costs of special handling, the inclusion of insurance as a quality variable should serve to capture further differences in the composition of outputs. Since high-value and fragile goods should require more special handling and also have high insurance costs, one would expect the insurance variable to have a positive effect upon costs. Terminal density is specified as terminals per ton-mile, and enters the cost function as the reciprocal for mathematic convenience.[15] Since terminal consolidations are expensive, because of the way that terminal density has been specified, one would expect its linear coefficient to have a negative sign. Although the cost functions for all three types of carriers were estimated using the terminal variable, it only added to the explanatory power of the estimated equation in the case of the interregional carriers.[16] Hence the estimated cost functions for the Official and South–West regional carriers do not include the terminal variable.

As indicated before, it is quite reasonable to suspect that there are differences in the structure of the technology of common carriers of general freight with respect to geographic regions that cannot be accounted for solely by differences in factor prices or the quality variables that attempt to measure the nature of trucking operations. We thus divided the regulated common carriers of general commodities into the following three groups: regional carriers in the Official Territory; regional carriers in the rest of the country; and interregional and transcontinental carriers. The distinction between the regional and the interregional carriers primarily arises due to differences in the scale of operation. While regional carriers typically may have an output of 50 million ton-miles annually, transcontinental carriers often have outputs of 1 billion ton-miles. Thus while the regional carriers generally act as small consolidators in a relatively localized market, the interregional carriers are truly national firms consolidating and shipping goods throughout the country. Hence there are good reasons to believe that the small regional carriers and the large interregional carriers may have significantly different technologies.

The distinction between regional carriers is considerably more arbitrary. To make the regional trucking analysis consistent with conventional regional rail analysis, we originally planned to use a regional breakdown that followed the ICC's regional railroad aggregation. Because of a paucity of data, however, we were forced to aggregate the trucking regions into two general categories: The Official Territory, which comprises the New England, Middle Atlantic, and Central trucking regions as defined by the ICC; and the rest of the country, which we denote by the South–West Region.

All of the data except terminal information were taken from *Trinc's Blue Book of the Trucking Industry* (1973) which summarizes the individual firm reports to the ICC. Terminal information was from *National Highway and Airway Carriers and Routes* (1973). In constructing the samples used in this analysis, however, we found that not all of the firms listed in *Trinc's* could be included. About half, for example, were not required by the ICC to report all the information necessary to calculate the operating characteristics. In addition, during the sample period, the ICC did not require consolidated reports from wholly owned subsidiaries. Thus, it was necessary to limit our samples to firms that met the following five conditions:

1. They purchased some of all four factors, but no more than 10 percent of their costs were for purchased transportation. (The first restriction affects firms reporting either no fuel or no purchased transportation costs; a firm reporting no purchased transportation is probably not in a long-run cost-minimizing position. Firms that rent most of their vehicles do so from subsidiaries set up for tax and regulatory purposes. Due to an ICC ruling allowing the deduction of such expenses as current costs, a firm that establishes such a subsidiary can artificially lower its operating ratio, which was a primary regulatory target in the early 1970s. Subsequent ICC rulings required that the operations of such subsidiaries be reported.)
2. They reported an average annual salary of $8,000 or more per employee. (Some firms implicitly reported salaries as low as $2,000, presumably because they counted owner-operators whose trucks they rented as employees, even though they did not directly pay them any wages.)

3. They had a calculated price of capital of less than 10. [Due to reasons related to (1) above, a few carriers report almost no operating property, as it is (presumably) owned by subsidiaries. Note that carrier operating property is the value of the property that the firm owns, *not* its equity in that property.]

4. They handled some LTL shipments. Since a translog function is not defined for zero value of the variables, firms that had no LTL shipments were omitted.[17]

5. They had no other "obvious" error in the data. (For instance, one firm reported an average load of 92 tons.)

Samples of size 154, 161, and 47 for the Official carriers, the other South–West carriers and the Interregional carriers, respectively, were finally prepared for estimation.

Definitions of variables   Total costs for each firm are calculated as ICC operating costs plus a 12-percent opportunity cost for capital, with the item "carrier operating property—net" (of depreciation) taken as a measure of the quantity of capital. These costs were then divided into four parts: labor costs; fuel expenditures and fuel taxes; purchased transportation;[18] and other expenditures. This last category consists mostly of the imputed opportunity cost of capital and depreciation and maintenance of capital items; thus, these expenditures were assumed to be payments for capital services.

Firm-specific factor prices for labor and capital were obtained by defining the former as labor costs per employee and the latter as capital service payments per unit of capital. Firm-specific prices for fuel and purchased transportation cannot be calculated, however, since only indirect quantity measures (e.g., rented vehicle-miles—but vehicle characteristics vary greatly) are available. Consequently, we have estimated regional prices for these factors by a method whose assumptions and results are contained in the technical supplement. The specific variable definitions are given as follows:

C = the total expenditures of the firm, to be the sum of labor costs, fuel expenditures and fuel taxes, purchased transportation, and "other expenditures."

w_1 = factor price of labor, defined as labor costs divided by number of employees.

w_2 = factor price of fuel, defined as fuel expenditures and fuel taxes per adjusted vehicle-mile.

w_3 = factor price of capital, defined as "other expenditures" plus a 12-percent opportunity cost of capital divided by "carrier property—net." Since "other expenditures" include depreciation and maintenance of capital items, this category largely reflects expenditures on capital services. Dividing this by carrier property net yields a price of capital services, to which is added a 12-percent opportunity cost of capital.

w_4 = factor price of purchased transportation, defined as expenditures on purchased transportation per adjusted rented vehicle-mile. The assumptions and formulas to derive factor price of fuel and factor price of purchased transportation are given in the technical supplement.

S_1 = factor share of labor, defined as labor costs divided by total expenditures.

S_2 = factor share of fuel, defined as fuel expenditures and fuel taxes divided by total expenditures.

S_3 = factor share of capital, defined as "other expenditures" plus the opportunity cost of capital divided by total expenditures.

S_4 = factor share of purchased transportation, defined as expenditures on purchased transportation divided by total expenditures.

y = TM = the physical output, defined as the total ton-miles carried by the firm.

R = revenue/cost ratio for a firm, defined as total revenues divided by total costs.

q_1 = ALH = average length of haul, defined as total ton-miles divided by total tons.

q_2 = AVLOAD = average load per vehicle, defined as total ton-miles divided by total vehicle-miles.

q_3 = LTL = percentage of freight in less-than-truckload lots, defined as total LTL tons divided by total tons.

q_4 = AVSIZE = average shipment size, defined as tons per shipment.

q_5 = INSUR = unit insurance cost, defined as insurance costs per ton-mile.

q_6 = TERMINAL = terminal density, defined as ton-miles per terminal (used only in the Interregionals cost function).

We have estimated the cost equation (C.2) and its associated factor share equations (C.4) using FIML methods, subject to the restrictions given in (C.2a) and (C.2b). This requires deleting one factor share equation, since the disturbances of the factor share equations sum to zero and thus have a singular covariance matrix; FIML is invariant to the equation dropped [see Barten (1969) or Berndt and Savin (1975)]. In this context, imposition of (C.2a) is easily achieved by choosing the price of the factor whose equation is deleted as numeraire; the coefficients on the terms containing this factor's price can then be calculated from (C.2a).

In addition, to make our results easier to interpret, we have standardized each variable to have a mean value of 1.0; that is, we have divided the raw measure of each variable in each sample by its sample arithmetic mean. In the approximation interpretation of the translog function, this standardization is equivalent to taking the sample mean of (y, w, t) as the point of approximation. This facilitates computation of elasticities of the factor demand, substitution, and so forth for a hypothetical firm with sample mean characteristics since $\ln 1.0 = 0$.

When all coefficients in (C.2) and (C.4) are estimated, this standardization does not affect the results. For the Official and South–West carrier samples, there are 56 coefficients to be simultaneously estimated after (C.2a) are imposed by normalization; since there are 154 and 161 firms, respectively, in the samples, this poses no problem.

For the interregional carriers, however, there is an additional component of the t vector which increases the number of coefficients to be estimated to 66; there are only 47 firms in this sample. This situation is not so bad as it first appears, however, since 30 of the coefficients appear in at least one factor share equation, leaving 36 coefficients that may enter into the cost function. However, since this leaves only 11 degrees of freedom for an estimation method whose desirable properties are only asymptotic, we decided to impose as a priori restrictions on (C.2) and (C.4) the additional coefficient restriction

$$D_{jm} = 0, \qquad j, m = 1, \ldots, 6, \tag{C.7}$$

that is, that the coefficients on terms of the form $\ln t_j \ln t_m$ be constrained to zero. This eliminates 21 coefficients which appear only in the cost equation, leaving effectively 32 degrees of freedom for the remaining 15 coefficients. One way of viewing (C.2) with (C.7) imposed is

$$\ln C(y, w, t) = \ln g(t, y, w) + \ln h(y, w), \tag{C.8}$$

where $h(y, w)$ is a neoclassical cost function and $g(t, y, w)$ is Cobb–Douglas for given y and w and homogeneous of degree 0 in w. While estimating (C.2) with eq. (C.7) imposed no longer provides a second-order approximation to an arbitrary $C(y, w, t)$, it is equivalent to specifying (C.8) with a translog functional form for $h(y, w)$. Thus, (C.8) retains the advantage of modeling the effect of t on costs and factor shares, while sacrificing some of the flexibility of the general translog form.

Table C.6 presents the estimated cost functions for the regional carriers in the Official and South–West Regions, while table C.7 presents the cost function for the Interregional carriers. In general, the coefficients are significant and the R^2's indicate an acceptable goodness of fit.

Table C.6 Coefficient Estimates for Cost Functions of the Official and South–West Regional Carriers

Coefficient[a]	Variable[b]	Official Value	Official Standard error	South–West Value	South–West Standard error
α_0	Constant	8.6919	0.0595	9.7507	0.0391
α_1	w_1 (labor)	0.5902	0.0057	0.5929	0.0056
α_2	w_2 (fuel)	0.0401	0.0014	0.0454	0.0011
α_3	w_3 (capital)	0.3358	0.0057	0.3259	0.0054
α_4	w_4 (purchased transportation)	0.0339	0.0038	0.0358	0.0033
β_1	t_1 (ALH)	−0.5112	0.0862	−0.6220	0.0706
β_2	t_2 (AVLOAD)	−0.4897	0.0959	−0.2338	0.0893
β_3	t_3 (LTL)	0.3327	0.1431	0.0140	0.1403
β_4	t_4 (AVSIZE)	−0.2483	0.0931	−0.2656	0.0725
β_5	t_5 (INSUR)	0.0074	0.0550	0.0244	0.0501
γ_y	y (output)	1.0864	0.0376	1.0759	0.0273
A_{11}	$\frac{1}{2}(w_1)^2$	0.0322	0.0158	0.0659	0.0143
A_{12}	$w_1 w_2$	−0.0277	0.0050	−0.0273	0.0042
A_{13}	$w_1 w_3$	−0.0137	0.0079	−0.0189	0.0070
A_{14}	$w_1 w_4$	0.0092	0.0130	−0.0197	0.0113
A_{22}	$\frac{1}{2}(w_2)^2$	0.0346	0.0060	0.0388	0.0046
A_{23}	$w_2 w_3$	−0.0114	0.0015	−0.0097	0.0014
A_{24}	$w_2 w_4$	0.0045	0.0042	−0.0018	0.0037
A_{33}	$\frac{1}{2}(w_3)^2$	0.0212	0.0079	0.0259	0.0070
A_{34}	$w_3 w_4$	0.0039	0.0053	0.0027	0.0042
A_{44}	$\frac{1}{2}(w_4)^2$	−0.0177	0.0133	0.0189	0.0110
B_{11}	$w_1 t_1$	−0.0427	0.0089	−0.0447	0.0097
B_{12}	$w_1 t_2$	0.0086	0.0096	0.0003	0.0114
B_{13}	$w_1 t_3$	0.0357	0.0101	0.0216	0.0136
B_{14}	$w_1 t_4$	−0.0237	0.0067	−0.0184	0.0097
B_{15}	$w_1 t_5$	−0.0022	0.0048	−0.0083	0.0063
B_{21}	$w_2 t_1$	0.0154	0.0021	0.0122	0.0019
B_{22}	$w_2 t_2$	−0.0064	0.0023	−0.0071	0.0022
B_{23}	$w_2 t_3$	−0.0063	0.0025	0.0019	0.0027
B_{24}	$w_2 t_4$	0.0051	0.0016	0.0097	0.0019
B_{25}	$w_2 t_5$	−0.0004	0.0012	0.00005	0.0012
B_{31}	$w_3 t_1$	0.0169	0.0089	0.0249	0.0094
B_{32}	$w_3 t_2$	−0.0015	0.0096	0.0187	0.0111
B_{33}	$w_3 t_3$	−0.0217	0.0101	−0.0075	0.0132

Table C.6 (continued)

Coefficient[a]	Variable[b]	Official Value	Official Standard error	South–West Value	South–West Standard error
B_{34}	$w_3 t_4$	0.0144	0.0067	0.0061	0.0094
B_{35}	$w_3 t_5$	0.0036	0.0048	0.0090	0.0061
B_{41}	$w_4 t_1$	0.0104	0.0060	0.0076	0.0057
B_{42}	$w_4 t_2$	−0.0006	0.0064	−0.0120	0.0068
B_{43}	$w_4 t_3$	−0.0076	0.0067	−0.0161	0.0081
B_{44}	$w_4 t_4$	0.0043	0.0045	0.0026	0.0057
B_{45}	$w_4 t_5$	−0.0011	0.0032	−0.0008	0.0037
C_{1y}	$w_1 y$	0.0157	0.0038	0.0145	0.0038
C_{2y}	$w_2 y$	−0.0035	0.0009	−0.0018	0.0008
C_{3y}	$w_3 y$	−0.0118	0.0038	−0.0161	0.0037
C_{4y}	$w_4 y$	−0.0003	0.0025	0.0034	0.0023
D_{11}	$\frac{1}{2}(t_1)^2$	0.3716	0.1636	0.0419	0.1892
D_{12}	$t_1 t_2$	−0.5550	0.1455	−0.4445	0.1311
D_{13}	$t_1 t_3$	−0.1485	0.1276	0.0675	0.1485
D_{14}	$t_1 t_4$	0.2405	0.0822	0.1301	0.1176
D_{15}	$t_1 t_5$	−0.0361	0.0569	−0.1210	0.0802
D_{22}	$\frac{1}{2}(t_2)^2$	0.7874	0.1878	−0.0699	0.2030
D_{23}	$t_2 t_3$	−0.0900	0.1582	0.0426	0.1769
D_{24}	$t_2 t_4$	−0.4934	0.1124	0.0056	0.1419
D_{25}	$t_2 t_5$	−0.0150	0.0658	−0.1945	0.1033
D_{33}	$\frac{1}{2}(t_3)^2$	0.5234	0.1875	−0.5860	0.3100
D_{34}	$t_3 t_4$	0.0160	0.0822	−0.1377	0.1640
D_{35}	$t_3 t_5$	−0.1398	0.1120	0.0781	0.0786
D_{44}	$\frac{1}{2}(t_4)^2$	0.0562	0.0505	0.2748	0.0983
D_{45}	$t_4 t_5$	−0.2054	0.0708	0.1234	0.0583
D_{55}	$\frac{1}{2}(t_5)^2$	0.0226	0.0248	−0.0164	0.0580
E_{1y}	$t_1 y$	0.0365	0.0504	−0.0467	0.0606
E_{2y}	$t_2 y$	0.0128	0.0562	0.1604	0.0705
E_{3y}	$t_3 y$	0.1434	0.0699	0.0681	0.0722
E_{4y}	$t_4 y$	0.0014	0.0447	0.0086	0.0454
E_{5y}	$t_5 y$	0.0035	0.0271	0.0388	0.0283
F_{yy}	$\frac{1}{2}(y)^2$	0.0248	0.0347	0.0533	0.0256

Table C.6 (continued)

	R^2	RMSE
Official (log of likelihood function = 1208.497)		
Cost equation	0.9533	0.2074
Labor equation	0.3974	0.0392
Fuel equation	0.3312	0.0095
Capital equation	0.1766	0.0393
Purchased transportation equation	0.1013	0.0261
South–West (log of likelihood function = 1251.433)		
Cost equation	0.9743	0.1823
Labor equation	0.2693	0.0442
Fuel equation	0.4391	0.0086
Capital equation	0.2211	0.0431
Purchased transporation equation	0.1619	0.0262

a. As defined in (C.2).
b. We have omitted ln for convenience.

Table C.7 Coefficient Estimates for Cost Functions of the Interregional Carriers

Coefficient[a]	Variable[b]	Value	Standard error
α_0	Constant	11.7986	0.0698
α_1	w_1 (labor)	0.5795	0.0114
α_2	w_2 (fuel)	0.0625	0.0036
α_3	w_3 (capital)	0.3002	0.0101
α_4	w_4 (purchased transportation)	0.0577	0.0161
β_1	t_1 (ALH)	−0.3804	0.1055
β_2	t_2 (AVLOAD)	−0.5799	0.2300
β_3	t_3 (LTL)	−0.1434	0.1506
β_4	t_4 (AVSIZE)	−0.4480	0.1648
β_5	t_5 (INSUR)	−0.0758	0.0808
β_6	t_6 (TERMINAL)	−0.0311	0.0766
γ_1	y (output)	0.8969	0.0501
A_{11}	$\frac{1}{2}(w_1)^2$	0.0645	0.0201
A_{12}	$w_1 w_2$	−0.0017	0.0094
A_{13}	$w_1 w_3$	−0.0103	0.0075
A_{14}	$w_1 w_4$	−0.0376	0.0174
A_{22}	$\frac{1}{2}(w_2)^2$	0.0336	0.0103
A_{23}	$w_2 w_3$	−0.0128	0.0013
A_{24}	$w_2 w_4$	−0.0043	0.0033
A_{33}	$\frac{1}{2}(w_3)^2$	−0.0154	0.0063

Table C.7 (continued)

Coefficient[a]	Variable[b]	Value	Standard error
A_{34}	$w_3 w_4$	0.0385	0.0079
A_{44}	$\frac{1}{2}(w_4)^2$	0.0033	0.0195
B_{11}	$w_1 t_1$	-0.0506	0.0163
B_{12}	$w_1 t_2$	0.0658	0.0348
B_{13}	$w_1 t_3$	0.1371	0.0217
B_{14}	$w_1 t_4$	0.0225	0.0257
B_{15}	$w_1 t_5$	-0.0245	0.0133
B_{16}	$w_1 t_6$	-0.0272	0.0112
B_{21}	$w_2 t_1$	0.0103	0.0053
B_{22}	$w_2 t_2$	-0.0010	0.0109
B_{23}	$w_2 t_3$	0.0376	0.0069
B_{24}	$w_2 t_4$	0.0330	0.0080
B_{25}	$w_2 t_5$	-0.0047	0.0042
B_{26}	$w_2 t_6$	-0.0053	0.0036
B_{31}	$w_3 t_1$	0.0105	0.0147
B_{32}	$w_3 t_2$	0.0212	0.0310
B_{33}	$w_3 t_3$	0.0171	0.0194
B_{34}	$w_3 t_4$	0.0024	0.0223
B_{35}	$w_3 t_5$	-0.0025	0.0119
B_{36}	$w_3 t_6$	-0.0252	0.0100
B_{41}	$w_4 t_1$	0.0298	0.0232
B_{42}	$w_4 t_2$	-0.0861	0.0492
B_{43}	$w_4 t_3$	-0.1918	0.0307
B_{44}	$w_4 t_4$	-0.0579	0.0359
B_{45}	$w_4 t_5$	0.0317	0.0189
B_{46}	$w_4 t_6$	0.0576	0.0159
C_{1y}	$w_1 y$	0.0220	0.0061
C_{2y}	$w_2 y$	0.0019	0.0019
C_{3y}	$w_3 y$	0.0021	0.0053
C_{4y}	$w_4 y$	-0.0260	0.0085
E_{1y}	$t_1 y$	-0.0932	0.0600
E_{2y}	$t_2 y$	0.2602	0.0957
E_{3y}	$t_3 y$	-0.2664	0.0819
E_{4y}	$t_4 y$	-0.3222	0.0862
E_{5y}	$t_5 y$	-0.0413	0.0581
E_{6y}	$t_6 y$	0.0990	0.0338
F_{yy}	$\frac{1}{2}(y)^2$	-0.0880	0.0329

Table C.7 (continued)

	R^2	RMSE
Cost equation[c]	0.9811	0.1818
Labor equation[c]	0.8537	0.0315
Fuel equation[c]	0.4598	0.0102
Capital equation[c]	0.1790	0.0286
Purchased transportation equation[c]	0.8035	0.0451

a. As defined in Eq. (2).
b. We have omitted ln for convenience.
c. Log of likelihood function = 407.964.

As was true in the case of carriers of specialized commodities, we see that the coefficients of the operating characteristics are generally significant, as are the coefficients of the interaction terms between operating characteristics and factor prices and the coefficients of the interaction terms between factor prices and output. Taken together, these findings indicate that production is *not* characterized by separability between inputs and outputs, nor by separability between operating characteristics and outputs or factor prices. Thus global generalizations about technology are difficult to make for these carriers.

Table C.8 presents estimated Allen–Uzawa partial elasticities of substitution and elasticities of demand at the sample mean for each of the three samples. Neoclassical production theory requires that $C(y, w, t)$ be concave in w for all y and t. In the approximation interpretation of the translog function, the properties of the underlying function are generally only preserved at the point of approximation, which in our case is the sample mean. The estimated cost functions are concave at the point of approximation for all three samples. Moreover, concavity holds for nearly all points in the samples, with some exceptions occurring in the Official and South–West samples. Upon examination we found that these cases consisted entirely of observations for which the estimated elasticity of fuel demand was greater than -0.05. Since, heuristically, the violation of the concavity condition occurs when elasticities of substitution are large (in absolute value) compared to elasticities of demand, it seems appropriate to view these violations as benign given the plausibility of the estimate of the fuel demand elasticity and the comparatively large estimates of the standard errors of the relevant elasticities of substitution.

The estimated elasticities of table C.8 in general accord with prior expectations. Capital and purchased transportation are substitutes in all three samples. Purchased transportation is also a substitute for labor and

Table C.8 Factor Demand Elasticities and Allen–Uzawa Partial Elasticities of Substitution, by Type of Carrier

	Labor	Fuel	Capital	Purchased transportation
Official				
Labor	–	−0.1715	0.9309	1.4606
		(0.2166)	(0.0396)	(0.6481)
Fuel		–	0.1510	4.3218
			(0.1137)	(3.1307)
Capital			–	1.3452
				(0.4686)
Own price	−0.3552	−0.0960	−0.6011	−1.4871
elasticity	(0.0271)	(0.1527)	(0.0244)	(0.3958)
South–West				
Labor	–	−0.0137	0.9023	0.0718
		(0.1584)	(0.0363)	(0.5282)
Fuel		–	0.3430	−0.1367
			(0.0947)	(2.2702)
Capital			–	1.2317
				(0.3589)
Own price	−0.2960	−0.0987	−0.5946	−0.4378
elasticity	(0.0247)	(0.1006)	(0.0221)	(0.3031)
Interregionals				
Labor	–	0.5419	0.9405	−0.1226
		(0.2621)	(0.0433)	(0.5753)
Fuel		–	0.3188	−0.1770
			(0.0917)	(0.9586)
Capital			–	3.2215
				(0.8716)
Own price	−0.3091	−0.3995	−0.7510	−0.8849
elasticity	(0.0366)	(0.1671)	(0.0262)	(0.3383)

fuel in the Official sample (although the estimated standard errors are relatively large), but not in the other samples; these differences may arise from the fact that rented vehicles may or may not include fuel and/or driver. Labor and capital have an elasticity of substitution of just under one in all three samples, while the elasticity of fuel–labor substitution is roughly zero for the Official and South–West carriers. The apparent substitutability of fuel for labor among the Interregionals is a paradox unless large vehicles are fuelinefficient and firms substitute heavily loaded large vehicles for small vehicles as driver wages increase. The comparatively high elasticity of demand for fuel among the Interregionals probably derives from the long-haul nature of their operations. The elasticities of demand for labor and capital are roughly the same in all three samples, while the variations in the demand elasticity of purchased transportation may derive from differences in its composition as outlined above or from defects in the procedure used to estimate its price.

C.5 The Effect of Operating Characteristics on Factor Intensities

The factor share equations implied by (C.4) at mean factor prices are given in table C.9. The necessity of modeling the impact of operating characteristics directly by the model $C = C(y, w, t)$ rather than as quality differences, as in $C = C(\psi(y, t), w)$ is heuristically indicated by the large number of significant coefficients in table C.10 which correspond to B_{ij}'s in (C.2).

A convenient way to summarize the results of table C.9 is to classify operating characteristics by their effect on labor's share of total costs, since when an operating characteristic increases labor's share it generally decreases all the others, and vice versa. An increase in average length of haul, for example, decreases labor's cost share and increases the cost shares of all other factors in all three samples. Note, however, that an increase in cost share caused by an increase in ALH does not mean that the absolute level of that factor rises: the elasticity of demand for factor i with respect to operating characteristic j is given by

$$\beta_j + \frac{B_{ij}}{\alpha_i}. \tag{C.9}$$

The estimated values (and standard errors) of (C.9) are presented in table C.10. Thus, in the Official sample, a 1-percent increase in ALH at the sample mean lowers costs by 0.51 percent; labor utilization falls by 0.58 percent, fuel by 0.13 percent, capital by 0.46 percent, and purchased transportation by 0.20 percent. As one would expect, the savings achieved by producing the same number of ton-miles with slightly greater average length of haul are mostly in labor and capital; the percentage reduction in fuel requirements is substantially less.

Similarly, increases in LTL are particularly labor intensive, as are declines in average shipment size except among the Interregionals. While AVSIZE has a positive sign in the Interregional labor share equation, the Interregional elasticity of labor demand with respect to AVSIZE is still -0.4091 since the elasticity of cost with respect to AVSIZE among the Interregionals is of a rather large magnitude: -0.4480. The corresponding Interregional elasticities of demand with respect to AVSIZE for the other

Table C.9 Factor Share Equations at Mean Factor Prices and Output, by Type of Carrier

Equation	Labor	Fuel	Capital	Purchased transportation
Official				
Constant	0.5902	0.0401	0.3358	0.0339
	(0.0057)	(0.0014)	(0.0057)	(0.0038)
ALH	−0.0427	0.0154	0.0169	0.0104
	(0.0089)	(0.0021)	(0.0089)	(0.0060)
AVLOAD	0.0086	−0.0064	−0.0015	−0.0006
	(0.0096)	(0.0023)	(0.0096)	(0.0064)
LTL	0.0357	−0.0063	−0.0217	−0.0076
	(0.0101)	(0.0025)	(0.0101)	(0.0067)
AVSIZE	−0.0237	0.0051	0.0144	0.0043
	(0.0067)	(0.0016)	(0.0067)	(0.0045)
INSUR	−0.0022	−0.0004	0.0036	−0.0011
	(0.0048)	(0.0012)	(0.0048)	(0.0032)
South–West				
Constant	0.5929	0.0454	0.3259	0.0358
	(0.0056)	(0.0011)	(0.0054)	(0.0033)
ALH	−0.0447	0.0122	0.0249	0.0076
	(0.0097)	(0.0019)	(0.0094)	(0.0057)
AVLOAD	0.0003	−0.0071	0.0187	−0.0120
	(0.0114)	(0.0022)	(0.0111)	(0.0068)
LTL	0.0216	0.0019	−0.0075	−0.0161
	(0.0136)	(0.0027)	(0.0132)	(0.0081)
AVSIZE	−0.0184	0.0097	0.0061	0.0026
	(0.0097)	(0.0019)	(0.0094)	(0.0057)
INSUR	−0.0083	0.00005	0.0090	−0.0008
	(0.0063)	(0.0012)	(0.0061)	(0.0037)
Interregionals				
Constant	0.5795	0.0625	0.3002	0.0577
	(0.0114)	(0.0036)	(0.0101)	(0.0161)
ALH	−0.0506	0.0103	0.0105	0.0298
	(0.0163)	(0.0051)	(0.0147)	(0.0232)
AVLOAD	0.0658	−0.0010	0.0212	−0.0861
	(0.0348)	(0.0109)	(0.0310)	(0.0492)
LTL	0.1371	0.0376	0.0171	−0.1918
	(0.0217)	(0.0069)	(0.0194)	(0.0307)
AVSIZE	0.0225	0.0330	0.0024	−0.0579
	(0.0257)	(0.0080)	(0.0223)	(0.0359)
INSUR	−0.0245	−0.0047	−0.0025	0.0317
	(0.0133)	(0.0042)	(0.0119)	(0.0189)
TERMINAL	−0.0272	−0.0053	−0.0252	0.0576
	(0.0112)	(0.0036)	(0.0100)	(0.0159)

Table C.10 Elasticities of Cost and Factor Demand with Respect to Operating Characteristics, by Region[a]

	Cost	Labor	Fuel	Capital	Purchased transportation
Official					
ALH	−0.5112	−0.5837	−0.1273	−0.4609	−0.2034
	(0.0862)	(0.0871)	(0.0844)	(0.0927)	(0.4014)
AVLOAD	−0.4897	−0.4752	−0.6504	−0.4943	−0 5075
	(0.0959)	(0.0968)	(0.0919)	(0.1032)	(0.1994)
LTL	0.3327	0.3932	0.1745	0.2680	0.1075
	(0.1431)	(0.1439)	(0.1408)	(0.1483)	(0.2383)
AVSIZE	−0.2483	−0.2886	−0.1215	−0.2056	−0.1218
	(0.0931)	(0.0937)	(0.0909)	(0.0965)	(0.2267)
INSUR	0.0074	0.0037	0.0015	0.0182	−0.0252
	(0.0550)	(0.0554)	(0.0534)	(0.0582)	(0.1407)
Ton-miles	1.0864	1.1130	0.9980	1.0512	1.0771
	(0.0376)	(0.0378)	(0.0365)	(0.0406)	(0.1016)
South–West					
ALH	−0.6220	−0.6973	−0.3540	−0.5457	−0.4092
	(0.0706)	(0.0745)	(0.0721)	(0.0756)	(0.3124)
AVLOAD	−0.2338	−0.2333	−0.3891	−0.1764	−0.5680
	(0.0893)	(0.0941)	(0.0907)	(0.0940)	(0.1882)
LTL	0.0140	0.0505	0.0569	−0.0089	−0.4352
	(0.1403)	(0.1442)	(0.1413)	(0.1456)	(0.2382)
AVSIZE	−0.2656	−0.2967	−0.0511	−0.2468	−0.1934
	(0.0725)	(0.0764)	(0.0729)	(0.0777)	(0.2341)
INSUR	0.0244	0.0104	0.0256	0.0522	0.0015
	(0.0501)	(0.0524)	(0.0513)	(0.0532)	(0.1654)
Ton-miles	1.0759	1.1004	1.0367	1.0264	1.1705
	(0.0273)	(0.0288)	(0.0278)	(0.0296)	(0.1117)
Interregionals					
ALH	−0.3804	−0.4678	−0.2163	−0.3453	−0.1363
	(0.1055)	(0.4650)	(0.0629)	(0.0975)	(0.3587)
AVLOAD	−0.5799	−0.4664	−0.5959	−0.5090	−2.0709
	(0.2300)	(0.3301)	(0.1270)	(0.1946)	(0.5086)
LTL	−0.1434	0.0931	0.4584	−0.0864	−3.4654
	(0.1506)	(0.1442)	(0.1121)	(0.1460)	(1.2482)
AVSIZE	−0.4480	−0.4091	0.0789	−0.4399	−1.4506
	(0.1648)	(0.1550)	(0.1114)	(0.1563)	(0.6950)
INSUR	−0.0758	−0.1181	−0.1511	−0.0840	0.4724
	(0.0808)	(0.0803)	(0.0581)	(0.0822)	(0.7656)
TERMINAL	−0.0311	−0.0781	−0.1155	−0.1149	0.9672
	(0.0766)	(0.0774)	(0.0559)	(0.0743)	(0.4650)
Ton-miles	0.8969	0.9349	0.9269	0.9041	0.4465
	(0.0501)	(0.0490)	(0.0409)	(0.0483)	(0.3301)

a. At sample mean; standard error in parentheses.

factors are as follows: fuel, 0.0789; capital, -0.4399; and purchased transportation, -1.4506.

The elasticities of factor usage with respect to average load are all negative, indicating that usage of all factors for all types of carriers declines as average load increases. Moreover, the savings in factor utilization appear to be relatively greater for fuel and purchased transportation, indicating that as carriers obtain relatively greater equipment utilization, they are able to obtain increased fuel economies and require less utilization of purchased transportation. The effect of increases in average size of shipment upon factor usage is similar to that of increases in average load, but of a generally smaller magnitude. Thus the economies associated with increases in average shipment size appear to be somewhat less than increases in average load.

Increases in the percentage of LTL shipments generally lead to increases in labor and fuel usage, although the effect is not always statistically significant. Moreover, for the South–West and Interregionals carriers, increase in the percentage of LTL shipments also leads to significant reduction in the use of purchased transportation; this is to be expected, since purchased transportation primarily consists of owner-operators, who specialize in truckload carriage.

Increases in insurance costs are generally statistically insignificant except for the interregional carriers, where increases in insurance costs per ton-mile lead to reduced fuel utilization. Finally, increases in ton-miles per terminal for the interregional carriers lead to equiproportionate reductions in fuel and capital usage and increases in the usage of purchased transportation. Thus, ceteris paribus, a firm whose route structure permits the maintenance of fewer terminals uses purchased transportation to a greater extent. This is what one would expect if high ton-miles–terminal ratios were indicative of simple high-density point-to-point operations. Such operations resemble those of contract carriers and carriers of special commodities, which typically employ substantial numbers of owner-operators and whose purchased transportation shares often exceed 30 percent.

This analysis clearly indicates that the service characteristics of the common carriers of general commodities have significant influences on effective output and on cost structure for all types of carriers. Moreover, their effects on cost and factor utilization are characterized by fundamental differences among the carriers, as reflected in the behavior of the shipment size, length of haul, percentage of LTL traffic, and load variables. Although it is admittedly difficult to determine whether these differences are due to regulation, the evidence provided by this study suggests that differences in the nature of the trucking operations between the small regional carriers and the large interregional carriers are fundamental and are due to technology rather than to regulation per se.

Regional carriers in the Official Region and the South–West Region also show significant differences in technology. These differences are further tested statistically by the likelihood ratio test.[19] We pooled samples of the two regions and reestimated the technology model against the pooled sample. The log of likelihood is 2396.569 for the pooled sample. The sum of log of the likelihood of the two unpooled samples is 2459.930. The test statistic is 126.722, which is greater than the value of χ^2 at the 0.005 significance level with 65 degrees of freedom. Therefore, the hypothesis that there is a common trucking technology across the two groups of regional carriers in our sample is clearly rejected at the 99.5-percent confidence level.

In conclusion then, neoclassical production theory appears to describe the carriers of general commodities extremely well, with production being characterized by distinct nonhomotheticities in output and in operating characteristics. Consequently, considerable caution must be used in making global generalizations about trucking technology, for measures of factor substitutability, returns to scale and so forth will typically vary by firm. In this respect, common carriers of general commodities are quite similar to carriers of specialized commodities since both their technologies clearly indicate complex interactions among output levels, operating characteristics, and factor utilization.

C.6 Technical Supplement: The Estimation of Regional Factor Prices for Regulated Common Carriers

The basic problem in establishing prices for both fuel and purchased transportation is that while each firm's total expenditures on these goods are observed, the quantities purchased are not. Thus it is necessary to utilize an indirect measure of the price of these factors. This technical supplement consequently outlines the methodology used and the estimates obtained for the prices of fuel and purchased transportation on the part of specialized commodity carriers and the general commodity carriers.

C.6.1 Specialized Commodity Carriers

Fuel The factors that would appear to have the most direct effect on fuel mileage on the part of specialized commodity carriers are vehicle size, the percentage of miles driven on interstate highways, and the number of stops (and therefore, presumably, side trips to more congested areas) made. Reasonable proxies for these variables are average load and average length of haul. Thus, there is an identity

$$\frac{\text{fuel \$}}{\text{veh-mile}_{i,r}} = \frac{\text{fuel \$}}{\text{fuel gallon}} \frac{\text{fuel gallon}}{\text{veh-mile}_{i,r}}$$

$$= P_r \phi(\text{ALH}_i, \text{AVLOAD}_i) + \varepsilon_i, \tag{C.10}$$

where P_r is the price of fuel in region r, i subscripts denote firm-specific variables, and the ε_i's are normal and independently identically distributed (i.i.d.). The function $\phi(\text{ALH}_i, \text{AVLOAD}_i)$ of gallons per mile is approximated by a translog function, and its parameters and the P_r's are estimated by applying FIML to

$$\frac{\text{fuel \$}}{\text{veh-mile}_i} = P_r \exp(\ln \phi(\text{ALH}_i, \text{AVLOAD}_i)) + \varepsilon_i. \tag{C.11}$$

Results of the fuel price estimation are presented in table C.11. The nonprice coefficients are all significant and have the expected sign.

Purchased Transportation   Of the 362 firms, 49 reported unusable data on purchased transportation. For the remaining 313 firms purchased transportation includes vehicle-miles rented with and without driver. Unfortunately, for these vehicle-miles separate figures for average load, average length of haul, LTL percentage, and average shipment size are not available; it is necessary to assume that the firm's average values for these variables are reasonable representations of the characteristics of the rented vehicle-miles.

Because the estimating procedure for an additive error specification similar to (C.11) did not converge, OLS was applied to the following multiplicative error specification:

$$\ln \frac{\text{purchased trans. \$}}{\text{rented veh-mile}_i} = \ln P_r + \ln \phi(\text{ALH}_i, \text{AVLOAD}_i, \text{RWD}_i) + \varepsilon_i, \tag{C.12}$$

where $\phi(\cdot)$ is a translog function similar to (C.11) and RWD represents the proportion of purchased transportation that was rented with driver. A full translog specification was used. The results are reported in table C.12, with $e^{\ln P_r}$ reported as the estimated regional purchased trans-

Table C.11 Estimation of Regional Fuel Prices (362 Observations)

Coefficient	Estimated coefficient	Standard error
A1 (NY and NE)	0.053133	0.0059597
A3 (NJ)	0.031397	0.0048272
A4 (PA)	0.019607	0.0035367
A5 (MD, VA, WV)	0.024307	0.0053329
A6 (OH)	0.025678	0.0044231
A7 (MI, IN, IL)	0.016480	0.0031568
A8 (South)	0.037839	0.0043765
A9 (Southwest)	0.064922	0.0063898
AA (Plains)	0.031669	0.0052700
AC (Rockies and Pacific)	0.039625	0.0048178
lnLOAD	0.241694	0.0719511
lnHAUL	−0.231660	0.0630407
$\frac{1}{2}$(lnLOAD)^2	0.424576	0.0659365
$\frac{1}{2}$(lnHAUL)^2	0.390460	0.0616291
lnLOAD · lnHAUL	−0.394282	0.0399173

Log of the likelihood function = 654.631
R^2 = 0.4635
SSR = 0.569510

portation prices.[20] The nonprice coefficients are in logarithmic terms.

In general, the nonprice coefficients are of the predicted sign and significant. The price terms, however, are not as reasonable as in the fuel case. With large standard errors, the restriction of (C.12) to a single price for purchased transportation might not be rejected. However, in the absence of good reasons to treat the regions identically, the estimated purchased transportation prices have been used in the cost functions.

Both estimations were made on a nationwide sample. Six subregions were represented by separate P_r's in the Official Territory: (1) New England and New York; (2) New Jersey; (3) Pennsylvania; (4) Maryland, Virginia, and West Virginia; (5) Ohio; and (6) Michigan, Indiana, and Illinois.

C.6.2 General Commodity Carriers

Fuel   Using a fuel cost per vehicle-mile for each firm as fuel price is not an appropriate measure since it implies that every vehicle gets the same mileage per gallon, while, in fact, mileage per gallon is highly variable among vehicles. The factors that would appear to affect most directly

Table C.12 Estimation of Regional Purchased Transportation Prices (313 Observations)[a]

Variable	Estimated coefficient (natural terms)	Values (logarithmic terms)	Standard error
A1 (NY and NE)	0.488	−0.717	0.169
A3 (NJ)	0.466	−0.766	0.185
A4 (PA)	0.371	−0.993	0.123
A5 (MD, VA, WV)	0.299	−1.201	0.174
A6 (OH)	0.399	−0.921	0.153
A7 (MI, IND, ILL)	0.292	−1.230	0.152
A8 (South)	0.300	−1.203	0.148
A9 (Southwest)	0.406	−0.902	0.172
AA (Plains)	0.324	−1.118	0.142
AC (Rockies & Pacific)	0.369	−0.997	0.150
lnLOAD		0.131	0.079
lnHAUL		−0.199	0.054
ln% RWD		1.382	0.297
$\frac{1}{2}$(lnLOAD)^2		0.145	0.100
$\frac{1}{2}$(lnHAUL)^2		0.022	0.072
$\frac{1}{2}$(ln% RWD)^2		4.178	2.184
lnLOAD · lnHAUL		−0.106	0.063
lnLOAD · ln% RWD		−0.084	0.176
lnHAUL · ln% RWD		0.034	0.154

Log of the liklihood function = 306.749
$R^2 = 0.2396$
SSR = 130.110
a. Observations omitted: rented rail or water; rent = 0; dependent variable < −3.5; dependent variable > 2.5.

fuel mileage of general commodity carriers are vehicle size, the percentage of miles driven on interstate highways, fuel taxes (different by region), and the number of stops (and, therefore, presumably side trips to more congested areas) made. Reasonable proxies for these variables are average load, average length of haul, percentage LTL traffic and ton-miles per terminal. Thus, as an identity we have

$$\frac{\text{fuel \$}}{\text{veh-mile}_{i,r}} = \frac{\text{fuel \$}}{\text{fuel gallon}} \frac{\text{fuel gallon}}{\text{veh-mile}_{i,r}}$$

$$= P_r \phi(\text{ALH}_i, \text{AVLOAD}_i, \text{LTL}_i, \text{TERMINAL}_i), \qquad (\text{C.13})$$

where P_r is the price of fuel in region r and i subscripts denote firm-specific variables. While a number of stochastic specifications of (C.13) suggest themselves, some of which are very complicated, the simplest is

$$\frac{\text{fuel \$}}{\text{veh-mile}_{i,r}} = P_r \phi(\text{ALH}_i, \text{AVLOAD}_i, \text{LTL}_i, \text{TERMINAL}_i)$$

$$+ \varepsilon_i, \qquad (\text{C.14})$$

where the ε_i's are normal and i.i.d.[21] The function $(\text{ALH}_i, \text{AVLOAD}_i, \text{LTL}_i, \text{TERMINAL}_i)$ of gallons per mile is approximated by a translog function, and its parameters and the P_r's are estimated by applying FIML to[22]

$$\frac{\text{fuel \$}}{\text{veh-mile}_{i,r}} = P_r \exp(\ln \phi(\text{ALH}_i, \text{AVLOAD}_i, \text{LTL}_i, \text{TERMINAL}_i)),$$

$$+ \varepsilon_i, \qquad (\text{C.15})$$

where

$$\ln \phi = \alpha_1 (\ln \text{ALH}_i - \ln \overline{\text{ALH}}) + \alpha_2 (\ln \text{AVLOAD}_i - \ln \overline{\text{AVLOAD}})$$
$$+ \alpha_3 (\ln \text{LTL}_i - \ln \overline{\text{LTL}}) + \alpha_4 (\ln \text{TERMINAL}_i$$
$$- \ln \overline{\text{TERMINAL}}) + \frac{1}{2} \beta_{11} (\ln \text{ALH}_i - \ln \overline{\text{ALH}})^2 + \cdots. \qquad (\text{C.16})$$

The above equations were estimated for each type of carrier. In order to capture more geographical differences in fuel prices within the several commodity carriers, each type among these carriers was further classified into subgroupings: New England; North Mid-Atlantic; Middle Atlantic; Central States East; Central States West for the Official Region; Central States, Eastern, South, Midwest and Pacific Region for the South–West Region; Eastern–Central, East–South, Transcontinental, and South–

Central, East–Midwest, and East–Southwest for the Interregionals. The estimating results are given in table C.13–C.15.

The coefficients of the linear terms give the elasticities of gallons per mile with respect to each service characteristic. These elasticities have the expected sign and are significantly different from zero, except for the sign of TERMINAL for the Interregionals. The positive (negative) squared terms indicate fuel requirements are increasingly (decreasingly) sensitive as each service characteristic increases. The overall picture given by these results is that firms specializing in small-load, short-haul, LTL traffic require more fuel per vehicle-mile.

Purchased Transportation   The stochastic specifications for regional purchased transportation prices are

$$\ln \frac{\text{purchased trans. \$}}{\text{rented veh-mile}_i} = \ln P_r + \ln \phi(\text{ALH}_i, \text{AVLOAD}_i, \text{RWD}_i, \text{LTL}_i, \text{AVSIZE}_i, \text{TERMINAL}_i) + \varepsilon_i, \quad \text{(C.17)}$$

Table C.13 Maximum Likelihood Estimates of Regional Fuel Prices for the Official Region (158 Observations)[a]

Coefficient	Value	Standard error
Price, New England[b]	0.07064	0.00500
Price, North Mid–Atlantic[b]	0.07600	0.00301
Price, Middle Atlantic[b]	0.06864	0.00280
Price, Central States East[b]	0.07094	0.00340
Price, Central States West[b]	0.07337	0.00333
ALH[c]	−0.33531	0.05595
AVLOAD[c]	0.55277	0.05861
LTL[c]	0.25204	0.05444
$(\text{ALH})^{2}$[c]	0.45625	0.16180
$(\text{AVLOAD})^{2}$[c]	0.32373	0.16522
$(\text{LTL})^{2}$[c]	0.12273	0.05475
AVLOAD · ALH[c]	−0.43988	0.14533
LTL · AVLOAD[c]	0.47324	0.09504
LTL · ALH[c]	−0.41311	0.08249

Log of likelihood function = 435.514
R^2 = 0.6189
SSR = 0.037324
a. Dependent variable is fuel expenditures per vehicle-mile.
b. Natural terms.
c. Logarithmic terms.

Table C.14 Maximum Likelihood Estimates of Regional Fuel Prices for the South–West Region (155 Observations)[a]

Coefficient	Value	Standard error
Price, Central States[b]	0.07101	0.0030
Price, Eastern States[b]	0.07576	0.0035
Price, Southern States[b]	0.07498	0.0024
Price, Midwest States[b]	0.07495	0.0024
Price, Pacific region[b]	0.07880	0.0028
ALH[c]	−0.2756	0.0412
AVLOAD[c]	0.4895	0.0590
LTL[c]	0.2896	0.1569
$(ALH)^{2c}$	−0.1009	0.0624
ALH · LTL[c]	0.2330	0.2322
$(LTL)^{2c}$	−4.9335	1.8112

Log of likelihood function = 460.380
$R^2 = 0.4336$
SSR = 0.0239
a. Dependent variable is fuel expenditures per vehicle-mile.
b. Natural terms.
c. Logrithmic terms.

where $\phi(\cdot)$ is a translog function similar to (C.16). RWD refers to the percentage of miles rented with driver. Purchased transportation includes vehicle-miles rented with and without driver. Unfortunately, for these vehicle-miles separate figures for average load, average length of haul, LTL percentage, average shipment size, and ton-miles per terminal are not available; it is necessary to assume that the firm's average values for these variables are reasonable representations of the characteristics of the rented vehicle-miles.

Equation (C.17) is estimated by OLS for each type of carrier. The estimating results are shown in tables C.16–C.18, with $e^{\ln P_r}$ reported as the estimated regional purchased transportation prices;[23] their standard errors are calculated from the usual first-order Taylor expansion formula. The nonprice coefficients are of logarithmic terms, as implied by (C.17), and the numerous insignificant cross terms are not reported. In general, some of the nonprice coefficients are of the expected sign and significant; some of the coefficients have counterintuitive signs or are statistically insignificant.[24]

With these large standard errors, the restriction of (C.17) to a single

Table C.15 Maximum Likelihood Estimates of Regional Fuel Prices for the Interregionals (42 Observations)[a]

Coefficient	Value	Standard error
Price, Eastern–Central[b]	0.06024	0.0031
Price, East–South[b]	0.06082	0.0025
Price, Transcontinental[b]	0.06345	0.0040
Price, South–Central, East–Midwest, East–Southwest[b]	0.06326	0.0028
ALH[c]	−0.2060	0.0901
AVLOAD[c]	0.1547	0.1417
LTL[c]	0.9241	0.3486
TERMINAL[c]	0.0210	0.0381
$(ALH)^{2c}$	0.1384	0.1612
$ALH \cdot LTL^c$	1.8447	0.9496
$(LTL)^{2c}$	−21.2851	5.5715
$(TERMINAL)^{2c}$	0.1477	0.05425

Log of likelihood function = 153.825
$R^2 = 0.7312$
SSR = 0.00155
a. Dependent variable is fuel expenditures per vehicle-mile.
b. Natural terms.
c. Logarithmic terms.

Table C.16 Maximum Likelihood Estimates of Regional Purchased Transportation Prices for the Official Region (89 Observations)[a]

Coefficient	Value	Standard error
Price, New England[b]	0.87412	0.32681
Price, North Mid–Atlantic[b]	0.70126	0.18651
Price, Middle Atlantic[b]	0.64462	0.22709
Price, Central States East[b]	0.63978	0.21541
Price, Central States West[b]	0.88892	0.25918
ALH[c]	−0.50282	0.31926
AVLOAD[c]	0.72775	0.37182
LTL[c]	0.38025	0.34245
$(1 + \%RWD)^c$	1.65275	0.41913
AVSIZE	0.05649	0.28422

Log of likelihood function = −128.594
$R^2 = 0.2399$
SSR = 93.7397
a. Dependent variable is log(purchased transportation expenditures/rented vehicle-mile).
b. Natural terms.
c. Logarithmic terms.

Table C.17 Maximum Likelihood Estimates of Regional Purchased Transportation Prices for the South–West Region (152 Observations)[a]

Coefficient	Value	Standard error
Price, Central States[b]	0.63857	0.3606
Price, Eastern[b]	0.46316	0.3721
Price, South[b]	0.45022	0.3359
Price, Midwest[b]	0.66102	0.3427
Price, Pacific[b]	0.47661	0.3369
ALH[c]	−0.5211	0.2042
AVLOAD[c]	0.4224	0.2841
LTL[c]	0.9037	1.0195
AVSIZE[c]	−0.0304	0.2007
$(1 + \%RWD)$[c]	−0.1825	1.0213
$(ALH)^2$[c]	−0.3753	0.3464
AVLOAD · AVSIZE[c]	0.4833	0.3792
LTL · AVSIZE[c]	1.1063	1.2990
LTL · $(1 + \%RWD)$[c]	1.0736	2.7447
$(1 + \%RWD)^2$[c]	11.7035	6.3953

Log of likelihood function $= -193.467$
$R^2 = 0.2964$
SSR $= 113.479$
a. Dependent variable is log (purchased transportation expenditures/rented vehicle-mile).
b. Natural terms.
c. Logarithmic terms.

price for purchased transportation might not be rejected at the usual levels. However, in the absence of good reasons to treat the regions identically, the estimated purchased transportation prices have been used in the cost functions.

It is also important to note that the variables used to reflect the price of purchased transportation are not precisely defined. Thus, firm expenditures of purchased transportation include a broad range of rentals, many of which do not have corresponding ton-miles. In particular, firms with very long hauls often do not have operating rights on some segments of their routes. Transportation along these route segments must be rented, but this is not reflected in the rented miles of these firms. Therefore, firms that often use routes without operating rights have high purchased transportation costs that are not reflected in the rental miles. This problem is particularly acute with respect to the Interregional carriers.

Table C.18 Maximum Likelihood Estimates of Regional Purchased Transportation Prices for the Interregionals (42 Observations)[a]

Coefficient	Value	Standard error
Price, Eastern–Central[b]	1.4954	0.4002
Price, East–South[b]	2.2340	0.3315
Price, Transcontinental[b]	1.5056	0.4533
Price, South–Central, East–Midwest[b]		
East–Southwest[b]	2.7379	0.3284
ALH[c]	0.8920	0.5798
AVLOAD[c]	−1.1294	1.0410
LTL[c]	14.6727	4.5023
AVSIZE[c]	2.0433	0.6621
$(1 + \%RWD)^c$	2.2000	0.5482
TERMINAL[c]	0.2007	0.2619

Log of likelihood function = −48.1994
$R^2 = 0.5574$
SSR = 24.4103
a. Dependent variable is log(purchased transportation expenditures/rented vehicle-miles).
b. Natural terms.
c. Logarithmic terms.

Notes

1. The larger part of the trucking industry is not regulated by the ICC. Such carriers include those engaged exclusively in intrastate and local freight as well as certain interstate carriers—exempt are agricultural haulers, private carriers, and owner-operators. These unregulated carriers are of some interest to this study because much of the transportation provided by carriers of other special commodities is rented from owner-operators.

2. See Wyckoff and Maister (1977) and Chow (1978) for further discussion of the trucking industry.

3. See Roberts (1977, pp. 11–13).

4. See Roberts (1977, p. 18).

5. This suggested effect does not imply monopoly pricing, merely expansion of services without great risk of loss of market power from entry. Roberts (1977, p. 20) suggests that the pricing mechanism for carriers of specialized commodites is competitive. A carrier may also object to the application of another firm for an operating authority for a commodity in a region already serviced.

6. The earlier studies are M. J. Roberts (1956) and R. A. Nelson (1956). Emery (1965), Warner (1965), and Lawrence (1976) find returns to scale; Oramas (1975) does not. Chow (1978) finds no evidence of economies of scale for carriers of specialized commodities, but some evidence of economies of scale for carriers of general commodities.

7. In some cases where ostensible evidence of returns to scale has been found, it has been recognized by the investigators that these were not returns to firm size, but to economies of "density" or "utilization." Meyer et al. (1959, p. 88), for example, concluded that "observ-

able economies of scale are probably a function of the intensity to which a given geographical route pattern is utilized and not of the total volume of the firm. These economies of scale in traffic density are equally available to the absolute large and small firm."

8. Related studies are given by Spady and Friedlaender (1978). Spady (1979), Furchtgott (1978), and Chiang (1979).

9. For a discussion of estimated trucking costs that use a hedonic formulation or that omit the technological factors entirely, see, Spady and Friedlaender (1978), Spady (1979), Furchtgott (1978), and Chiang (1979).

10. There is some ambiguity about the interpretation of this variable since increases in insurance costs will also affect total costs. By standardizing this variable upon ton-miles, however, this effect is probably diminished. Moreover, in terms of total costs, insurance is a minor expense and one whose fluctuations probably do not directly affect total expense but do indirectly reflect higher expenses as a proxy for a more expensive or risky commodity to transport.

11. All of the data used to estimate the trucking cost functions came from *Trinc's Blue Book of the Trucking Industry (1973)*, which reports on the behavior of these firms in 1972.

12. When estimating cost functions and their associated factor share equations, the R^2's associated with the latter are almost always substantially lower than those of the former. This indicates that there is more unexplained interfirm variation in factor shares than in costs.

13. For a discussion of the results using hedonic and nonhedonic specifications see Furchtgott (1978).

14. Within a translog framework, the Allen–Uzawa elasticity of substitution $AUES_{ij}$ between factors i and j is given by

$$AUES_{ij} = 1 + \frac{A_{ij}}{\hat{M}_i \hat{M}_j}, \tag{C.5}$$

where A_{ij} represents the estimated coefficient on the interaction term between factor i and factor j, and $\hat{M}_i$ and $\hat{M}_j$ the fitted factor shares. Since $\hat{M}_i$ and $\hat{M}_j$ equal the coefficient of the linear w_i term and the linear w_j term, respectively, at the point of approximation, the calculation of the $AUES_{ij}$ is quite simple when evaluated at the mean. Within a translog framework, the own price elasticity of factor demand is also given by

$$e_i = \hat{M}_i + \frac{A_{ii}}{\hat{M}_i} - 1. \tag{C.6}$$

15. Although a better measure of the network effects would have been given by terminals per route-mile, data on route-miles are not available.

16. The terminal variable is considerably less reliable for firms in the Official and South–West samples.

17. In order to include observations that had no LTL carriage, we also estimated the cost function using $1 + \%LTL$ as a variable instead of $\%LTL$. The choice of the LTL variable made little difference in the estimated equation. Since it was felt that the variable $\%LTL$ was somewhat easier to interpret than the variable $1 + \%LTL$, the former variable was used in the analysis. For an analysis using $1 + \% LTL$ see Spady and Friedlaender (1978).

18. "Purchased transportation" consists of payments for rented vehicles; the vehicles may include a driver, in which case they usually include fuel.

19. Since a cost function with terminal as one of the quality variables is not available for the

regional carriers at the moment, the likelihood ratio test to test the differences between regional carriers and interregional carriers is not implemented.

20. Under the assumption that the disturbances in (C.12) are normal i.i.d., the estimated prices reported in Table C.12 are maximum likelihood estimates.

21. For the results given below, there is little evidence of regional heteroskedasticity; beyond this, the specification of the disturbance has not been further analyzed.

22. TERMINAL was used only for the Interregionals.

23. Under the assumption that the disturbances in (C.17) are normal i.i.d., the estimated prices reported in Table C.17 are maximum likelihood estimates.

24. A firm in the sample should purchase no rail or water transportation. Presence of such expenses might bias the purchased transportation share of expenses in a way that could not be easily explained among estimates of trucking costs. But almost all Interregional firms do purchase rail or water transportation. We are unable to omit all of these firms from the sample to obtain the price of purchased transportation. Actually, comparing the vehicle-miles for rail and water to the total vehicle-miles, we find that including these firms would be better than omitting them all.

Freight Rates and Regional Income

In this appendix we discuss the models used to analyze and quantify the relationships among freight rates, regional output, regional income, and regional employment. Section D.1 presents the relationship between freight rates and regional output, while section D.2 presents the relationship between regional output and regional employment. Section D.3 then links these relationships to regional income and presents estimates of the elasticities of regional income and employment with respect to freight rates.

D.1 Freight Rates and Regional Output

D.1.1 Scope of the Analysis

Although freight rate cases usually involve very specific commodities in very specific regions, data limitations make it virtually impossible to build models that would enable the policymaker to estimate the precise impacts of such changes upon regional incomes. By utilizing considerably more aggregative models, however, it is possible to obtain fairly precise quantitative measures of the impact of changes in the rates of fairly broad commodity types upon income in fairly broad geographical regions. As such, these models should yield useful insights into the income effects associated with specific rate changes.

Our choice of commodity aggregation was in large part determined by data limitations. Although there are excellent data on rail flows and rates, outside of the manufacturing industries data are extremely scarce for rates and regional flows of other commodities. Thus we were forced to confine our analysis to a set of manufactured commodities for which sufficient regional data existed.

With respect to modes, we were equally circumscribed by data limitations, and our analysis is limited to rail and trucking rates.

While data limitations largely prescribe the permissible level of commodity and modal aggregation, considerably more choice is available with respect to regional aggregation. The ICC usually presents rail data on the basis of five major regions, while it presents trucking data on the basis of nine major regions. In addition, the Census of Transportation not only presents data on a state level, but also on a level as disaggresate as the production area, which usually consists of one or two SMAs. Finally, the Census Bureau and the Commerce Department's Bureau of Economic Analysis typically present data at the state level as well as that of the census region.

Because this analysis focuses on the relationship of rail and trucking rates to regional incomes, we chose to perform our regional analysis on a level that was compatible with the rail data. Thus we utilized the following regional aggregation:

Official Territory.

Southern Region.

South–Western Region.

Mountain–Pacific Region.

Western Trunk Line.

D.1.2 The Methodological Approach

The Model   Most regional modeling has been done at the state or the city level and has made use of the assumption that causality is unidirectional and runs from national to subnational variables.[1] Thus national variables regarding income, employment, etc., ultimately drive these regional models, which essentially make the small-country assumption in the context of a world of international trade. While, strictly speaking, it is of course inaccurate to assume the exogeneity of national variables even if one is modeling the economy of a state, such as Massachusetts or Mississippi, since national variables are definitionally either the sum or weighted averages of state variables and are therefore affected to some extent by changes within the economy of a state, the small size of the state or local economies should lead to relatively little bias due to simultaneity. Moreover, the paucity of income and output data at the state level, and even more so at the city or county level, has made it infeasible to construct a model which avoids placing primary stress on national aggregates.

Since we are dealing with large regional aggregates, such a small-country assumption is clearly unwarranted.[2] For example, the Official Territory contained 46 percent of national income in 1975. Thus, while it may be reasonable to ignore problems of simultaneity in modeling state or local economies, it would clearly be unacceptable to assume that the portion of the country producing such a large fraction of GNP could have no effect on the size of GNP.

Consequently, we have attempted to model the regional economies in a way that takes regional linkages directly into account. We have therefore chosen to construct a model that makes use of the available data insofar as possible without relying on the assumption of unidirectional causality. Indeed, the economic activity in each region is explicitly linked to that of other regions in this model, and the national economy is implicitly treated as the sum of its component regions. While such an approach is clearly theoretically superior to utilizing the small-country assumption, data limitations have forced us to make many compromises and simplifying assumptions that somewhat vitiate the strength of the analysis.[3] Nevertheless, we feel that in spite of its limitations, the interregional approach is clearly superior to the unidirectional approach. In this section we thus describe the central equations of the model that describe the interregional linkages and show how these fit into a more general regional model that can be used to estimate regional employment and income.

Since the regional models that we are developing encompass the entire country, it is important to specify the linkages among these regions, rather than simply specify how one region reacts to changes in other regions or the nation as a whole. In our analysis this linkage is established by means of equations that attempt to explain the flow of goods between regions as a function of market prices, freight rates, and income.

To a certain extent this analysis is analogous to an international trade problem of separate countries (in this case, large regions of a single country) trading with one another, but attempts to apply basic theorems such as the Heckscher–Ohlin theorem encounter theoretical difficulties when the setting is a five-region, many-commodity, many-factor framework. The Heckscher–Ohlin theorem predicts that a country or region will export that commodity in which it has a comparative advantage, but it is impossible to judge in which of the many commodities one of our five regions might be said to have a comparative advantage. In addition, the empirical fact that most regions both export and import most of the many commodities throws into doubt any conceivable classification.

The basic assumption we make is that, ceteris paribus, a region A will import more from another region B if the price of the good produced in B falls for consumers in A. This can occur if costs of production fall in region B or if the cost of transporting the commodity from region B to A decreases. Similarly, if incomes rise in region A, and if the good is a normal good, more should be imported into A, not only from B, but from all other regions.

Although an analysis based on strict profit or utility maximization would indicate that each region should only purchase commodities from the least-cost region, inclusive of transportation costs, we recognize that any given region will typically import a commodity from a number of regions while at the same time exporting it to these same regions. Perhaps the most reasonable explanation for this is that our commodity groupings are extremely aggregate and hence contain considerable variation in the components of the aggregate. Thus, the composition of any two-digit industry may be very different among regions. Consequently, although theoretical considerations would lead us to believe that we would not observe simultaneous imports and exports of any given commodity between any two regions, differences in the two-digit aggregates could make this phenomenon possible and indeed probable. Similarly, fixed contracts or poor information could also lead to a region importing a commodity at a price which is higher than it need pay, and increases in relative prices could also be expected to lead to an increase in consumption of the lower-priced commodity under these conditions.

Unfortunately, adequate data are not available to permit the estimation of a full set of equations that have as the dependent variable the flow of a good from each region to every other region. Thus, let Y_K^{OD} be the flow of good K from region O to region D, where O indexes the region of origin and D indexes the region of destination of the flow, $O = 1, \ldots, 5$, and $D = 1, \ldots, 5$. Then we hypothesize that Y_K^{OD} is a function of its own price, prices of substitute commodities, and the level of income in the importing region:

$$Y_K^{OD} = Y(I^D, P_K^{OD}, \tilde{P}_K^{OD}, \tilde{P}_{SK}^{OD}),\qquad\qquad (D.1)$$

where

P_K^{OD} is the price of Y_K^{OD}.

$\tilde{P}_K^{OD}$ is a vector of prices of good K in region D if it were imported from another region. For example, $\tilde{P}_K^{12} = (\tilde{P}_K^{22}, \tilde{P}_K^{32}, \tilde{P}_K^{42}, \tilde{P}_K^{52})$.

$\tilde{P}_{SK}^{OD}$ is a vector of prices of substitute commodities. For example, if Y_K is coal, $\tilde{P}_{SK}^{OD}$ might be a vector of prices of competing fuels such as oil and gas.

I^D is the income in the region of destination.

Equation (D.1) is really the reduced form of two structural equations that describe two distinct but simultaneous decisions. The first is the decision how much of good K, say machinery, to consume in region D, and the second is the decision where in the country to purchase that total amount of machinery. The first decision depends on the aggregate price level of the commodity, the price of other goods that substitute for it in consumption, and regional income. The second decision depends on the price of the commodity and transportation costs. Thus (D.1) expresses both of these decisions in a reduced form, single equation.

In terms of estimation, we found that a linear approximation to (D.1) performed the best according to the usual statistical criteria. Moreover, we introduced a number of dummy variables to permit interregional variations in the response of commodity flows to income and price differentials. Thus the general estimating equation took the following form:[4]

$$Y_K^{OD} = \alpha_0 + \alpha_1 P_K^{OD} + \alpha_2 \tilde{P}^{OD} + \alpha_3 I^D + \sum_m \alpha_m D_m, \qquad (D.2)$$

where:

Y_K^{OD} = production of commodity K in region O and shipped to region D.

P_K^{OD} = delivered price of commodity K in region D produced in region O (production costs plus transportation).

$\tilde{P}^{OD}$ = the delivered price of commodity K in region D if it is purchased from any region other than O.

I^D = income in region D.

D_m = a regional dummy variable representing areas of production or consumption.

The Data   The basic data on interstate shipments of manufactured commodities are collected by the US Bureau of the Census in the *Commodity Transportation Survey*, which was conducted in 1963, 1967, and 1972. Because of irreconcilable data differences between 1963 and the subsequent two census years, we have limited our analysis to cross-section, time-series estimation of regional flows for the years 1967 and 1972, and the five regions discussed above: the Official Territory; the Southern Region; the Western Trunk Line; the Southwestern Region; and the Mountain–Pacific Region.[5]

In keeping with our aggregate analysis, we originally combined the twenty two-digit manufacturing industries into two aggregate industries of durable and nondurable manufactured goods. However, when the flow analysis described above was applied to the data, the equations had almost no explanatory power. This was apparently due to aggregation bias. Since a number of diverse commodities were combined to form the aggregate commodities of durables and nondurables, the different production prices that exist in different regions are more likely to reflect the different composition of production among regions than actual differences in the price of a given commodity. While this same aggregation problem is likely to exist at the two-digit level of aggregation, the empirical results indicate that the problem is not as great.[6]

Unfortunately, we have only been able to estimate flow equations for those industries for which a sufficient number of observations exist. The nine industries for which the analysis was performed are those for which there was a substantial amount of the commodity flowing between all regions. Since data were available for 1967 and 1972, there were fifty observations for each of the nine industries.[7]

To obtain an estimate of the cost of production of manufactured commodities in the originating region (PRODCOST) we have divided the total value of shipments of manufactured commodities, as reported in the Census of Manufacturers, by the total tonnage of shipments, which was obtained from the tapes of the census of Transportation. The analysis outlined above predicts that the flow of commodities between regions will depend upon the total price of the good in the consuming region, which consists of the production cost (PRODCOST) plus the cost of transporting the good to the destination region. Since data limitations made it impossible to calculate a transportation price index for every two-digit transport commodity classification (TCC) code commodity group,[8] we have therefore made the assumption that the cost of transporting all durable or nondurable goods between any two points is the same. We have thus calculated an index of transportation costs for all durable (TRANSDUR) and all nondurable (TRANSND) goods. The appropriate index was then added to the producer cost of the good to give the total price of the commodity as perceived by the consumer in the region of destination: $P(OD)$, where O is the region of origin and D the region of destination.

Because data from two different years are used in the analysis, we have deflated $P(OD)$ by the wholesale price index for durable or non-durable commodities, and multiplied the resulting figure by 100. Therefore, the price term used in our equations is given as follows:

(i) For durable goods having standard industrial classifications SIC24, 28, 32, 33, 34, 35)

$$P(OD) = \frac{\text{PRODCOST}(O) + \text{TRANSDUR}(OD)}{\text{WPI(DUR)}} \times 100.$$

(ii) For nondurable goods (SIC20, 25, 26)

$$P(OD) = \frac{\text{PRODCOST}(O) + \text{TRANSND}(O, D)}{\text{WPI(ND)}} \times 100.$$

Here WPI(DUR) and WPI(ND), respectively, refer to the wholesale price index for durable and nondurable goods.

For some of the commodities, the transportation price index was found to have a negative and significant coefficient if included both on its own in the equation and also as a component of the price term. This finding appears somewhat implausible since it implies that consumers respond to a change in the price of a good resulting from a change in the cost of production differently than they respond to a price increase resulting from a change in freight rates.

However, a more reasonable explanation may exist since shipping goods involves costs other than the actual transportation costs. Insurance and packing costs are two examples of costs that are likely to be directly and positively related to the distance over which a good is shipped. Since there is a high correlation between the calculated transportation indexes and the distance between any two regions, or between major commercial centers within any two regions, it is very likely that these freight indexes are acting as proxies for distance and that this variable is significant due to the inventory and related costs of shipping goods over longer distances. If this is true, a negative bias is likely to have been imparted to the estimated freight rate coefficients because of problems associated with errors in variables. This problem arises because the transportation rates do not perfectly measure the inventory and related costs of shipping goods.

Another possible explanation for the significance of the transportation cost index in the manufacturing flow equations arises from lack of perfect information. Since consumers are poorly informed about prices and commodities in alternative markets, they are more likely to make purchases at markets close to home simply because of the transaction costs involved in becoming more fully informed about commodities and prices in distant markets. Since these transaction costs are also likely to be positively correlated with distance and the transportation cost indexes, these indexes may in part be serving as proxies for these transaction costs.

Because of the ambiguous interpretation of the freight rate used as an independent variable, it is not clear whether the elasticity of output with respect to freight rates should include the effect of the freight rate when used as an independent argument in the estimating·equation. On balance, however, since there is little reason to believe that a change in rail or trucking rates will affect the variables for which it may be acting as a proxy (either inventory costs or informational costs), when estimating the response of output to changes in freight rates it seems reasonable to consider only the value of the price term, which includes production costs plus freight rates, and to omit the effect of the freight rate acting independently.

The income term used in the equation is per capita regional disposable income deflated by the national consumer price index (CPI). Although it would have been preferable to have used regional price deflators, these do not exist.[9]

The Results   In addition to the variables described above, we included a number of regional dummy variables. Because the model presented in (D.1) is highly restrictive and forces the price and income coefficients to be constant across regions, we introduced regional dummy variables on both the intercept and the price and income terms, allowing their coefficients to vary across the destination regions and origin regions. In addition, for most commodities the intraregional flows were too large to be explained by the price and income variables alone. We therefore added a dummy variable with a value of 1 if the flow was intraregional. While we recognize that this variable acts as a proxy for the large number of variables that may account for the size of intraregional flows and as such has no direct explanatory power, its inclusion improved the performance of most equations substantially.

We thus used the following dummy variables in our analysis:[10]

DUMXX $= 1$ if flow in intraregional; 0 otherwise.

DUM$(OO) = 1$ if flow originates in region O; 0 otherwise.

DUM$(DD) = 1$ if D is the destination region; 0 otherwise.

DUM$(EE) = 1$ if flow is within the Mountain–Pacific Region; 0 otherwise.

DUMPRD = DUM(*OO*)*PRD, where PRD represents the delivered price to region D.

DUMI(D) = DUM(*OO*)*YDISPD, where YDISPD represents the real per capita disposable income of region D.

Note that in terms of region of destination, we standardize on the Official Territory and hence do not explicitly include a regional dummy variable for it. Moreover, in terms of the region of origin, we only include dummy variables for the Official Territory and the Mountain–Pacific Region. While the use of dummy variables obviously creates more flexibility than that provided by (D.1) alone, the form of the equation is still moderately restrictive in that it permits price and income elasticities to vary by the region of destination, but not by the region of origin.

Many different equations were estimated for each commodity, and only the "best" equation is reported in table D.1.[11] Regressions were run in both linear and logarithmic form, and the linear form always proved superior. In some equations, the constant term was insignificant and dropping it from the equation had a negligible impact on the size of the other coefficients, but usually increased their significance.

Table D.1 shows that the price and income terms were generally highly significant and that the R^2's were generally high, indicating that the basic model gives a reasonable explanation of interregional commodity flows. It is interesting to note, however, that the dummy price variables were not statistically significant, indicating that there is little regional variation in the response of commodity flows to delivered prices.[12] This result should not be particularly surprising, however, in view of the "footloose" nature of manufacturing activity, and it is consistent with the fact that manufacturing activity is relatively evenly dispersed throughout the country, at least at this high level of regional and commodity aggregation.

In contrast, the income dummy variable was significant in a number of industries (food, lumber and wood products, chemicals and plastics, and stone, clay and glass) and a number of regions. Table D.2 presents the regional income coefficient for those industries in which statistically significant regional variation was found,[13] and indicates that while there is some regional income variation, it is relatively slight.

Table D.3 presents the elasticities calculated at the mean of the variables for the price and income variables and for the transportation cost component of the price term.[14] This shows that while the elasticities of regional output with respect to income are generally high, the elasticities

Table D.1 Regression Results for Interregional Commodity Flow Equations, Selected Manufacturing Industries

	Industry								
Variable	Food & kindred (SIC20)	Lumber & wood (SIC24)	Furniture & fixtures (SIC25)	Pulp, paper & allied (SIC26)	Chemicals & allied (SIC28)	Clay, concrete, glass & stone (SIC32)	Primary metal (SIC33)	Fabricated metal (SIC34)	Machinery (SIC35)
Constant	–	-49.29 (88.15)	–	–	–	–	-228.78 (110.20)	-26.2 (15.9)	–
Price	-0.3289 (0.061)	-0.35 (0.0008)	-0.0002 (0.000054)	-0.1367 (0.039)	-0.1549 (0.0324)	-0.2173 (0.188)	–	-0.00578 (0.00319)	-0.00176 (0.0004)
DUMI(2)	0.092 (0.012)	0.0187 (0.009)	–	–	0.0292 (0.01)	–	–	–	–
DUMI(3)	0.0224 (0.0115)	0.019 (0.008)	–	–	0.0332 (0.0097)	–	–	–	–
DUMI(4)	0.0388 (0.0104)	0.018 (0.006)	–	–	–	-0.0196 (0.0057)	–	–	–
DUMI(5)	–	–	–	–	–	–	–	–	–
DUMXX	350.0 (27.5)	–	1.800 (0.614)	96.29 (11.07)	247.6 (24.74)	202.78 (18.56)	103.0 (36.0)	26.9 (5.24)	11.56 (2.5)
DUM(O5)	–	–	–	–	-102.35 (25.02)	–	–	–	–
DUM(D1)	43.42 (27.7)	–	5.377 (0.578)	51.69 (11.57)	–	108.78 (18.77)	329.6 (33.3)	72.39 (5.37)	41.87 (2.47)
DUMEE	–	310.5 (28.2)	–	–	–	–	–	–	–
TRANSDUR	–	–	-0.0329 (0.016)	–	–	-1.79 (0.521)	-4.132 (0.97)	-0.632 (0.141)	-0.136 (0.067)
TRANSND	–	–	–	-0.994 (0.299)	–	–	–	–	–
R^2	0.82	0.795	0.776	0.815	0.768	0.87	0.75	0.886	0.920
SE	77.83	36.9	1.47	26.27	70.0	44.15	87.05	12.56	6.000

Table D.2 Income Coefficients, Selected Manufacturing Industries

Region	Food & kindred (SIC20)	Lumber & wood (SIC24)	Chemicals & allied (SIC28)	Clay, concrete, glass, & stone (SIC32)
1 (Official)	0.093	0.307	0.047	0.040
	(0.015)	(0.028)	(0.008)	(0.016)
2 (Southern)	0.122	0.326	0.077	0.040
	(0.019)	(0.022)	(0.013)	(0.016)
3 (South–Western)	0.117	0.326	0.081	0.040
	(0.019)	(0.026)	(0.013)	(0.016)
4 (Western Trunk Line)	0.132	0.320	0.047	0.021
	(0.019)	(0.023)	(0.008)	(0.018)
5 (Mountain–Pacific)	0.093	0.307	0.047	0.040
	(0.015)	(0.028)	(0.008)	(0.016)

Table D.3 Price Elasticities of Commodity Flows with Respect to Delivered Price, Real Disposable Income, and Freight Rates, Calculated at the Mean

| Industry group | Elasticity with respect to | | |
	Price	Income	Freight rates
Food & kindred (SIC20)	−1.50	1.66	−0.051
Lumber & wood (SIC24)	−0.72	1.96	−0.022
Furniture & fixtures (SIC25)	−0.34	1.13	−0.002
Pulp, paper, and allied (SIC26)	−0.26	1.88	−0.065
Chemicals and allied (SIC28)	−0.75	1.21	−0.038
Clay, concrete, glass & stone (SIC32)	−0.74	1.60	−0.075
Primary metal (SIC33)	−	3.61	−
Fabricated metal (SIC34)	−0.44	2.32	−0.006
Machinery (SIC35)	−0.49	1.04	−0.003

of regional output with respect to delivered price are relatively low, ranging from a high of -1.50 for food to a low of -0.34 for furniture and fixtures. From this we can infer that changes in production costs inclusive of transportation rates have a relatively unimportant impact on regional production. Moreover, since freight rates form a relatively minor component of the delivered goods price, the elasticity of regional production with respect to transportation costs is extremely low, ranging from a high of -0.075 for stone, clay, and glass to a low of -0.002 for furniture and fixtures. Thus a 10-percent change in aggregate rate and trucking rates would only lead to a 0.75-percent reduction in the stone, clay, and glass industries and a 0.02-percent reduction in the output of furniture and fixtures.

Of course, these elasticities represent the mean response over regions, and for policy purposes we are really interested in the regional variation in the income and price elasticities. These are calculated for each region and each commodity for 1972, and are presented in table D.4 for each manufacturing industry for which we were able to obtain a significant price coefficient. This table indicates that the elasticity of regional manufacturing flows with respect to freight rates is generally quite low for all regions and all commodities.[15]

D.2 Regional Output and Regional Employment

D.2.1 The Employment Model

Once we have estimated the flow equations, they fit conceptually into a larger model in the following way:

$$Y_K^O = \sum_{D=1}^{5} Y_K^{OD}. \tag{D.3}$$

The sum of the inter- and intraregional flows of good Y_K from a region O equals the total output of that good in that region. In order to determine employment in region O in industry K, total output is related, through specification of a production function, to the quantity of labor demanded (and by assumption of perfectly elastic labor supply, to the quantity supplied).

On a conceptual level, the simplest regional production function is of a fixed coefficient type that requires fixed proportions of inputs to give any level of output. This is the basic assumption of models that derive employment multipliers or use input–output analysis.[16] In addition to limitations posed by large data requirements, these models also suffer

Table D.4 Elasticities of Commodity Flow with Respect to Aggregate Freight Rates, by Region of Origin and Destination and Commodity Type, 1972

OD pair[a]	Food & kindred (SIC20)	Lumber & wood (SIC24)	Furniture & fixtures (SIC25)	Paper & allied (SIC26)	Chemical & allied (SIC28)	Stone, clay, & glass (SIC32)	Fabricated metals (SIC34)	Machinery, except electrical (SIC35)
O, O	−0.0114	−0.3071	−0.0002	−0.0109	−0.0060	−0.0058	−0.0005	−0.0003
O, S	−0.0391	−1.6417	−0.0008	−0.0665	−0.0270	−0.0507	−0.0025	−0.0009
O, W	−0.0478	−0.7241	−0.0005	−0.0449	−0.0212	−0.0737	−0.0011	−0.0007
O, SW	−0.1499	−2.8584	−0.0150	−0.2158	−0.0756	−0.3575	−0.0047	−0.0017
O, MP	−0.5929	−3.5976	−0.0037	−0.9047	−0.2816	−1.2539	−0.0118	−0.0043
S, O	−0.2171	−0.2623	−0.0012	−0.0292	−0.0711	−0.6038	−0.0190	−0.0056
S, S	−0.0153	−0.0122	−0.0002	−0.0072	−0.0039	−0.0044	−0.0095	−0.0011
S, W	−0.6116	−0.2507	−0.0013	−0.0496	−0.0737	−0.8323	−0.0188	−0.0064
S, SW	−0.3494	−0.0386	−0.0007	−0.0444	−0.0588	−0.0871	−0.0082	−0.0026
S, MP	−2.0596	−4.7486	−0.0027	−1.1250	−0.7063	−5.5454	−0.1393	−0.0328
W, O	−0.0601	−1.0562	−0.0023	−0.1230	−0.3747	−0.0736	−0.0150	−0.0017
W, S	−0.1132	−1.1756	−0.0025	−0.4077	−0.9636	−0.1609	−0.0245	−0.0023
W, W	−0.0053	−0.1182	−0.0011	−0.0159	−0.0697	−0.0397	−0.0022	−0.0004
W, SW	−0.0369	−4.3044	−0.0025	−0.1463	−0.2534	−0.2182	−0.0180	−0.0024
W, MP	−0.1614	na	−0.0043	−0.6362	−2.4520	−1.7764	−0.0803	−0.0093
SW, O	−0.5099	−2.1556	−0.0093	−0.1510	−0.0543	−2.7737	−0.0326	−0.0535
SW, S	−0.0887	−0.4697	−0.0030	−0.0730	−0.0143	−0.4353	−0.0189	−0.0183
SW, SW	−0.0084	−0.0263	−0.0061	−0.0093	−0.0019	−0.0049	−0.0011	−0.0014
SW, MP	−0.3926	na	−0.0058	−0.2982	−0.0142	−0.2491	−0.0234	−0.0158
MP, O	−0.3229	−0.2986	−0.0368	−0.4474	−3.1512	na	−0.1854	−0.0408
MP, S	−0.6467	−0.2961	−0.0748	−0.6890	−6.4740	−7.1660	−0.1358	−0.0535
MP, W	−0.1481	−0.0674	−0.0316	−0.1446	−0.6446	−7.3159	−0.1785	−0.0149
MP, SW	−0.1641	−0.1356	−0.0036	−0.3378	−0.9012	−0.4598	−0.0373	−0.0126
MP, MP	−0.0129	−0.0124	−0.0004	−0.0111	−0.0126	−0.8998	−0.0040	−0.0043

a. O = Official; S = Southern; W = Western Trunk Line; SW = South-Western; MP = Mountain-Pacific.

from the assumption of a constant technology, which is hardly realistic in a changing economy. Although work is being done to develop models with coefficients that can change over time,[17] these have not been entirely satisfactory and the alternative assumption that substitution between factors is impossible in the short run does not seem realistic.[18] A more practical problem with these models is that the application of the simple linear model is unlikely to give meaningful results when actual production is more complex.

Other regional studies, which assume that substitution between factors may occur, have related factor prices, output, and factor levels through a production function, usually of Cobb–Douglas form. These studies frequently assume Hicks neutral technological change and constant returns to scale (CRS).[19] A major criticism of this work is that there is no a priori reason to expect the elasticity of substitution between factors to be one. Although this particular criticism may be obviated by the use of the constant elasticity of substitution (CES) production function, the CES function imposes a constant elasticity over all relative factor levels and over time, and thus is only moderately less restrictive than the Cobb–Douglas production function.[20] More basically, both the CES and Cobb–Douglas forms of the production function pose problems of aggregation since neither is able to model joint production in a satisfactory fashion. Consequently, if estimation were done at an aggregate level of output, these functions would impose constant elasticities of substitution, even though the aggregate elasticity of substitution should change as the composition of different microoutputs change. Moreover, neither production function is particularly flexible in permitting differences in the elasticities of substitution between pairs of inputs when more than two exist.[21]

Other regional models have imposed restrictions on technology by postulating that regional and national technologies are the same. Among these are models that specify regional employment as a share of national employment.[22] Regional technologies could be expected to differ from national technology and among themselves for three reasons. First, since each region has a different mix of factors that are not mobile in the short run, there is likely to be some regional specialization in production. Second, microlevel technology will differ among regions if the resources to develop new technologies are not accessible to some regions. Third, even if technology were the same everywhere in each industry, the differing composition of output would give the national and regional technologies different properties.

Consequently, although the regional literature has unquestionably made important contributions to the understanding of the determinants of regional employment, it has used excessively restrictive assumptions concerning the nature of technology, which have tended to vitiate the usefulness of the analysis. Thus it is desirable to derive a labor demand equation based on a technology that does not impose CRS, CES, or even a specific form of the production function.[23] Moreover, to allow for the effects of technological change and for aggregation in inputs and outputs, the technology should be variable over time and among regions.

This analysis therefore uses a labor demand equation based on a flexible technology that can vary over time, and in particular, estimates a labor share equation based on a translog cost function. As such it is considerably more general than most labor demand equations used previously. Indeed, one of the findings of this research is that labor demand equations used in previous regional analyses have generally been misspecified because they have been based on two erroneous assumptions: first, the hypothesis of CRS or CES is generally rejected in this analysis; second, the hypothesis of identical regional technologies is generally rejected.[24]

We thus assume that we can represent regional technology by the following cost function:

$$C = C(y, w_L, w_K, w_E, t), \tag{D.4}$$

where y is an output measure, w_L, w_K, w_E are the factor prices of labor, capital, and energy, respectively, and t is time.[25] The associated translog function is given by[26]

$$\ln C = \alpha_0 + \sum_i \alpha_i \ln w_i + \alpha_y \ln y + \alpha_t \ln t$$
$$+ \frac{1}{2} \sum_i \sum_j B_{ij} \ln w_i \ln w_j + \frac{1}{2} B_{tt}(\ln t)^2 + B_{yt} \ln y \ln t$$
$$+ \frac{1}{2} B_{yy}(\ln y)^2 + \sum_i B_{iy} \ln w_i \ln y + \sum_i B_{it} \ln w_i \ln t \qquad i = L, K, E. \tag{D.5}$$

The derived factor share equation for labor is

$$S_L = \frac{\partial \ln C}{\partial \ln w_L} = \alpha_L + B_{LL} \ln w_L + B_{LK} \ln w_K$$
$$+ B_{LE} \ln w_E + B_{Lt} \ln t + B_{Ly} \ln y. \tag{D.6}$$

Since cost minimization implies that the cost function is homogeneous of degree 1 in factor prices, we impose the following restrictions on the coefficients of this equation:

$$\sum_i B_{Li} = 0, \qquad i = L, K, E. \tag{D.6a}$$

Econometric estimation of a translog approximation to a cost function normally involves estimating the entire system of equations (minus one factor share equation because of the constraint that the shares sum to one). Because of data restrictions, however, in this analysis we estimate the factor share equation for labor alone.[27]

D.2.2 Empirical Results

The factor share equation for labor was estimated for each of the five geographic regions.[28] From the estimated coefficients we can determine the elasticity of labor demand with respect to output.

Although the primary data are described in Friedlaender et al. (1977), a few points are worth noting. First, total costs were measured as value added plus energy costs. Thus, economic profits are assumed to be zero, and the data are thus probably constructed to indicate that production is subject to constant returns to scale. Second, since data are unavailable for physical output, which is the variable that should technically enter the equation, we have been forced to use value added as a proxy for physical output, and will hence refer to the output variable as VA rather than y.

The use of value added instead of physical output introduces two major specification problems. First, value added is net of some raw materials and supplies that probably would appropriately be treated as factors of production. Second, value added is measured in current dollar terms. Algebraically, we can write VA as

$$VA = \underbrace{(py + p^I y^I)}_{\text{value of shipments}} - \underbrace{(p^m M + p^I y^I)}_{\text{cost of materials}}, \tag{D.7}$$

where py is the dollar value of final production in manufacturing, $p^I y^I$ is the dollar value of intermediate manufacturing production, and $p^m M$ is the dollar value of raw materials. The problem is not solved, as some have speculated,[29] by assuming that materials are proportional to real output (y in this case), because the prices are likely to vary if the data are cross sectional, and they are certain to vary in time series. Assuming proportionality, the VA term can be written

$$\ln VA = \ln(p - \alpha p^m) + \ln y, \qquad \alpha = M/y, \tag{D.8}$$

or

$$\ln y = \ln VA - \ln(p - \alpha p^m). \tag{D.8a}$$

The net effect on the estimates may be to bias the coefficient of $\ln t$ toward a negative value since t and $p - p^m$ could be fairly highly correlated, and to bias the estimated coefficient of the output term toward zero. Since it was not obvious that constant proportionality between y and M obtained over time, no correction was made to VA. Nevertheless, if we are willing to assume that some proportionality may exist between y and M, then (D.8a) clearly indicates that the elasticity of value added with respect to output equals one, which clearly simplifies our efforts to relate the production analysis to the employment analysis.

Because data on energy and capital prices were unavailable on a two-digit basis, the labor share equation was estimated for the manufacturing sector as a whole. Thus the manufacturing factor share equation for aggregate labor was estimated for each of the five regions over the years 1956–1972.[30] Although all equations were originally run using OLS, in a number of cases the Durbin–Watson statistic indicated a

Table D.5 Labor Share Equations for Manufacturing Activity by Region

Coefficient[a]	Region				
	Official	Southern	Western Trunk Line	South–Western	Mountain–Pacific
α_2	0.521 (0.0005)	0.446 (0.0014)	0.478 (0.0011)	0.396 (0.0014)	0.526 (0.0107)
β_{LL}	0.137 (0.014)	0.161 (0.023)	0.127 (0.034)	0.184 (0.018)	0.149 (0.054)
β_{LK}	−0.119 (0.009)	−0.139 (0.017)	−0.871 (0.022)	−0.162 (0.019)	−0.146 (0.054)
β_{LE}[b]	−0.0185 (−)	−0.0219 (−)	−0.0140 (−)	−0.0022 (−)	−0.0030 (−)
β_{LY}	0.0041 (0.0112)	0.0564 (0.0241)	0.0454 (0.0230)	0.0563 (0.0340)	0.0619 (0.0456)
β_{Lt}	18.2 (2.10)	−27.0 (4.89)	−22.5 (5.10)	−29.4 (6.15)	−33.6 (14.2)
ρ	−0.537 (0.211)	−	0.409 (0.228)	−	0.770 (0.160)
R^2	0.989	0.945	0.956	0.964	0.907

a. Standard errors in parentheses.
b. Coefficient value implied by restriction; hence standard error not calculated.

strong likelihood of autocorrelation in the residuals. Hence the equations were reestimated using the Cochrane–Orcutt interactive procedure. The final equations are given in Table D.5. All the variables are highly significant and the R^2's are uniformly high. The Cochrane–Orcutt procedure was used to estimate the equations in the Official Territory, the Western Trunk Line, and the Mountain–Pacific Region, while the equations for the Southern and South–Western Regions were estimated using OLS.

In terms of transportation policy analysis, our main concern is with the impact of a change of freight rates upon regional incomes and employment. If we assume that wages are exogenously given, then changes in income will arise only from changes in employment. Thus by relating changes in employment to changes in output, and changes in output to changes in freight rates, we can determine the change in regional income and employment in the manufacturing industries arising from changes in transportation policy.

It is a straightforward algebraic exercise to show that within the translog framework the elasticity of demand for a factor x_i with respect to output is given by the following expression:

$$E_{x_i y} = \hat{B}_{iy}/\hat{S}_i + E_{cy}, \tag{D.9}$$

where $E_{x_i y}$ represents the elasticity of demand of x_i with respect to output, $\hat{B}_{iy}$ the relevant estimated coefficient from the factor share equation, $\hat{S}_i$ the estimated factor share, and E_{cy} the elasticity of cost with respect to output, that is, $(\partial C/\partial y)(y/C)$.

The expression $\hat{B}_{iy}/\hat{S}_i$ can be obtained directly from the estimated labor equation. However, without estimating a full cost equation, we cannot know the elasticity of costs with respect to output. Nevertheless, most estimates of technology indicate that aggregate production functions

Table D.6 Estimated Elasticity of Manufacturing Employment with Respect to Output, by Region, 1972

Region	Elasticity
Official	1.008
Southern	1.129
Western Trunk Line	1.100
South–Western	1.143
Mountain–Pacific	1.130

often appear to be subject to constant returns to scale. Hence as a first approximation, the assumption that $E_{cy} = 1$ would not be unreasonable. Moreover, by permitting E_{cy} to range over a reasonable spectrum of values representing different degrees of economies and diseconomies of scale, it should be possible to obtain limits to the value of $E_{x_i y}$.[31]

Table D.6 gives the elasticities of manufacturing employment with respect to output in each of the five regions used in our analysis. Thus a 10-percent reduction in output would lead to a 10.08-percent reduction in employment in the Official Territory and an 11.43-percent reduction in output in the South–Western Region. Hence the response of manufacturing employment to output, which does not appear to be significantly different from one in any region, shows little regional variation.

D.3 The Impact of Changing Freight Rates on Manufacturing Income

Having analyzed the relationship between regional output in the manufacturing industries and freight rates and employment, let us consider how much change in manufacturing income could be expected to arise from a change in freight rates.

To relate the change in total manufacturing output in any given region, we must first determine the change in the output of any given industry arising from a change in freight rates and then relate that to the change in total manufacturing activity.

Since the total production in any region of origin is identically equal to the shipments it makes to all other regions, including itself, the percentage change in regional output resulting from a change in regional freight rates can be given by the following expression:

$$\hat{Y}_i^O = \sum_D \mu_i^{OD} E_i^{OD} \hat{f}_i^{OD}, \qquad (D.10)$$

where:

$\hat{Y}_i^{OD} \equiv dY_i^O/Y_i^O$, the percentage change in output of industry i in region of origin O.

$\mu_i^{OD} \equiv Y_i^{OD}/Y_i^O$, the percentage of total output in region O that is shipped to region D for industry i.

$E_i^{OD} \equiv (\partial Y_i^{OD}/\partial f_i^{OD})(f_i^{OD}/Y_i^{OD})$, the elasticity of shipments between regions O and D with respect to freight rates for industry i.

$\hat{f}_i^{OD} \equiv \partial f_i^{OD}/f_i^{OD}$, the percentage change in freight rates between regions O and D for industry i.

Note that if we assume that freight rates change by the same proportion in all regions, $\hat{Y}_i^O$ can be derived directly from the weighted elasticity of output of each industry in each region, with the weights being determined by the flow shares.

Since total manufacturing activity in the region of origin O is equal to the sum of all output, it is readily apparent that [32]

$$\hat{Y}_M^O = \sum_i \sigma_i^O \, \hat{Y}_i^O \tag{D.11}$$

where:

$\hat{Y}_M^O \equiv dY_M^O / Y_M^O$, the percentage change in total manufacturing output in the region of origin O.

$\sigma_i^O \equiv Y_i^O / Y_M^O$, the share of total manufacturing output accounted for by industry i.

$Y_i^O = $ the percentage change in output of industry i in the region of origin.

Similarly, if freight rates change proportionately for all commodities, then $\hat{Y}_M^O$ can be obtained from the weighted elasticity of all output in each region, with the weights being determined by the commodity shares.

As indicated above, if we assume that material inputs are proportional to total shipments, the elasticity of value added with respect to total output or shipments equals one. While obviously an approximation, it does not appear to be unreasonable, and we hence assume that the elasticity of value added with respect to freight rates equals the elasticity of total ouput with respect to freight rates.

Regional income in the manufacturing industries in region of origin O is given by

$$I_M^O = w_M^O \, L_M^O, \tag{D.12}$$

where I_M^O refers to income, w_M^O to the average manufacturing wage, and L_M^O to employment.

Thus the percentage change in regional income in the manufacturing industries is given by

$$\hat{I}_M^O = \hat{w}_M^O + \hat{L}_M^O, \tag{D.13}$$

where the hats denote percentage change. Since, however, we assume that wages are given exogenously, we can assume that $\hat{w}_M^O = 0$.

We have previously derived an expression for the elasticity of total manufacturing employment with respect to changes in value added, which we will now denote by the symbol λ_M^O. Hence we can readily deduce that

$$\hat{L}_M^O = \lambda_M^O \, \widehat{VA_M^O}. \tag{D.14}$$

Thus, given a postulated change in manufacturing freight rates, we can obtain the change in regional output, the change in value added, the change in employment, and hence the change in manufacturing income occasioned by that change in freight rates.

Let us assume that all freight rates increase by 10 percent and estimate the changes in income that would be generated by this change in freight rates. Table D.7 gives the weighted elasticities of output for each industry in each region, and the weighted elasticity of total output in each region, which correspond, respectively, to the expressions given in (D.10) and (D.11). This table indicates that the elasticity of output with respect to freight rates is generally higher for low-value goods (lumber and wood, stone, clay, and glass) than for high-value goods (machinery), and that the elasticity of total output with respect to freight rates in generally quite small, ranging from a low of -0.039 in the Official Territory to a high of -0.441 in the Mountain–Pacific Region.

Since we assume that our sample of eight industries is representative of the entire manufacturing sector and that materials purchased are

Table D.7 Weighted Elasticities of Output with Respect to Freight Rates, by Region of Origin, 1972

Industry	Region of origin				
	Official	Southern	Western Trunk Line	South–Western	Mountain– Pacific
Food & kindred	−0.0422	−0.0989	−0.0525	−0.1300	−0.2181
Lumber & wood	−1.1462	−0.1331	−1.7981	−0.4862	−0.1063
Furniture & fixtures	−0.0018	−0.0011	−0.0023	−0.0060	−0.0332
Paper & allied	−0.0446	−0.0324	−0.1434	−0.0867	−0.1075
Chemicals & allied	−0.0228	−0.0422	−0.5705	−0.0457	−0.1501
Stone, clay & glass	−0.0245	−0.3853	−0.1491	−0.1516	−1.9027
Fabricated metals	−0.0019	−0.0210	−0.0172	−0.0192	−0.0552
Machinery, except electrical	−0.0008	−0.0063	−0.0029	−0.0299	−0.0232
Weighted elasticity of total output	−0.0390	−0.1087	−0.0827	−0.0990	−0.4410

Table D.8 Estimated Change in Regional Manufacturing Employment and Income Arising from a 10-Percent Increase in Freight Rates, by Region of Origin

	Region of Origin				
	Official	Southern	Western Trunk Line	South–Western	Mountain–Pacific
Percentage change in employment	−0.3931	−1.2272	−0.9097	−0.1029	−4.9833
Actual change in employment (1,000)	20.8	48.9	10.9	1.3	118.1
Actual change in income ($mill.)	393.0	366.3	99.1	10.6	1,148.7

proportional to total shipments, the elasticities of value added with respect to freight rates also equal the weighted elasticity of total output with respect to freight rates. Thus by utilizing (D.14) and the value of λ_M^O given in table D.6, we can readily obtain the change in regional employment and income occasioned by a 10-percent across-the-board increase in freight rates. These figures are given in table D.8, which indicates that although the percentage changes in total manufacturing employment are relatively low, the actual changes in employment and income are not trivial. In particular, given the 1972 levels of income and employment, the total reduction in manufacturing income that would occur equals $2.017 billion. Although the Official Territory has the largest manufacturing base, the Mountain–Pacific Region suffers the largest absolute losses in employment and income because of its high elasticity of employment with respect to freight rates.

In conclusion then, this analysis demonstrates that changes in freight rates can have a significant impact upon regional production and employment in the manufacturing industries. In view of the relatively small component of freight rates in the delivered goods price of manufactured commodities, this result is somewhat surprising. However, when one recognizes the essentially "foot loose" nature of these commodities, this finding appears to be more reasonable. In particular, if producers really are cost minimizers, then changes in freight rates should affect relative production costs and hence locational decisions. This analysis indicates that although these locational effects are not large in terms of elasticities, they are significant in terms of actual magnitudes of income and employment.

Notes

1. For examples of this approach see Friedlaender et al. (1975) for Massachusetts, Adams et al. (1975) for Mississippi, and Glickman (1971) for Philadelphia.

2. However, Crow (1973) has built a model of the Northeast Corridor, which comprises the ten states in the Northeast plus the District of Columbia and is thus of a comparable level of regional aggregation to our analysis, by assuming that the linkages are only unidirectional, going from the national economy to the regional economy.

3. For example, our original intentions were to include a category for other bulk commodities and an "aggregate" local industry in such a way that would enable us to model gross regional product as the sum of production in the separate industries. However, an intensive data search indicated that this was not feasible. In addition to a lack of data on bulk commodity flows, no reasonable output measure for bulk commodities existed (other than coal) that did not necessitate complex conversions (such as would be entailed in aggregating natural gas, measured in cubic feet; gasoline, measured in barrels; and copper, measured in short tons). We were also unable to model all of the durable and nondurable industries. The equations explaining flows of commodities between different regions of the country have been estimated for the eight of the twenty two-digit SIC code manufacturing industries for which adequate data are available. However, the employment equations have been estimated for total manufacturing.

4. In a few cases we introduced freight rates as explicit arguments. While the theoretical justification for this is somewhat counterintuitive since it implies that consumers are influenced by freight rates per se, in a number of cases the freight rates were found to enter as significant explanatory variables.

5. Although state-to-state flows are reported in publicly available CTS computer tapes at the five-digit level, we used data tapes that had been prepared by the Transportation Systems Center in Cambridge, Massachusetts, which had aggregated state-to-state flows on the two-digit level. In either case, however, the Census of Transportation excludes establishments of less than twenty employees and those plants shipping 90 percent or more of their volume less than 25 miles. While our measures of shipments ideally should have included data from both of these sources, data limitations have made this impossible.

6. For example, aggregation at the durable level would require the combination of fabricated metal products (SIC34) and lumber products (SIC24), while aggregation at the two-digit level would require the combination of metal cans (SIC341) and plumbing and heating apparatus (SIC343). While both levels of aggregation obviously pose difficulties with regional differences in the composition of output, the problems posed at the two-digit level appear to be considerably less than those posed at the durable or nondurable level.

7. Since there are approximately twenty two-digit SIC manufacturing codes, our manufacturing analysis is obviously not fully complete. Nevertheless, we should be able to extrapolate from these nine industries to make reasonable inferences about the nature of the behavior of the entire manufacturing sector.

8. For a full discussion of the derivation of the interregional freight rates see Friedlaender et al. (1977).

9. While the Bureau of Labor Statistics does estimate CPIs for a wide range of SMAs, the level of regional aggregation used in this analysis was sufficiently great that it seemed preferable to use the national CPI rather than attempt a regional aggregation of the various CPIs calculated within each region.

10. Of course, it is not possible to include a full range of slope and intercept dummy variables since this would eliminate all of the relevant degrees of freedom. We have therefore experi-

mented with a wide range of alternative combinations of the dummy variables and present those that were statistically the most significant.

11. This was determined by a combination of factors, which included the R^2, the standard error of the regression, and the sign and significance of the relevant variables.

12. Of course, since the equations were run in linear form, the calculated price elasticities will vary among regions.

13. For the most part, the regional coefficients are not significantly different from each other at the 10-percent level of significance.

14. The elasticity of the flow with respect to the transportation cost variable on it that enters separately in the equation has not been calculated since its interpretation, as discussed above, is so unclear.

15. The origin–destination pairs that exhibit high elasticities generally have very low flows. Thus their estimated elasticities are biased upward.

16. See Isard (1960) for a development of these models. Polenske (1974) has made extensive use of these types of regional models.

17. Miernyk (1965) gives an introduction to this literature. See, in addition, Hudson and Jorgenson (1974) and Friedlaender and Hammer (1976) for approaches to this problem.

18. Glickman's Philadelphia model (1971) has exactly this property.

19. Among these are Bell (1967), Engle (1976), Friedlaender et al. (1975), and Roberts et al. (1972).

20. Among the CES regional estimates are Glickman (1971) and Ratajczak (1972). Bell (1967) found that the CES added no information.

21. For a full discussion of this point see McFadden (1963) and Uzawa (1962).

22. Friedlaender et al. (1975) and Roberts (1972) give a detailed description of this approach.

23. The CES or Cobb–Douglas production function implies separability in production between inputs and outputs. When there is more than one microoutput, separability implies that there is no way to relate the microoutputs to inputs in separate production functions. See Spady and Friedlaender (1976) and Hall (1973).

24. See Rodrigues (1977) for a full discussion of these points. In this work we will present the preferred specifications in our empirical analysis and will not consider the problems posed by specification error related to the specific form of the production function or its regional aggregation.

25. Note that in introducing time in this fashion we are treating it as a technological variable that can interact with output and factor prices. Hence this formulation does not assume neutral technical changes.

26. Note that each variable should be interpreted as a deviation from the sample median. Thus $\ln w_i = \ln w_i - \ln \tilde{w}_i$, where $\tilde{w}_i$ represents the sample median. See Spady and Friedlaender (1976) for a discussion of the importance of the choice of the point of approximation. In this analysis, which was based on a time series, the sample median seemed more appropriate than the sample mean since it represented the midpoint of the sample over time.

27. The usual stochastic specification is given by writing

$$\ln(C) = \text{(translog terms)} + \text{(higher-order terms)}$$

and assuming that errors enter through the effects of the higher-order terms. Here the higher-order terms are assumed to equal zero and the error term enters through error in measurements of the labor share. See Burgess (1975) for more on the specification of the translog error term.

28. The data used in this analysis are given in appendix B of Friedlaender et al. (1977). Each variable was measured as a deviation from the sample median.

29. See Lucas (1975).

30. Rodrigues (1977) estimated regional employment equations on a nine-region basis as well as the five-region basis used in this analysis and found that the chosen level of regional aggregation for the employment equations was not entirely appropriate. Because, however, our regional flow analysis is based on five-region aggregates, some form of regional aggregation would be necessary to relate the nine-region employment equations to the five-region commodity flow equations. Hence, for the purpose of this analysis, it was decided to use the five-region level of aggregation for the employment equations.

31. In general, E_{cy} would appear to lie within the range 0.9–1.1. Thus the estimated value of $E_{x,y}$ should not be particularly sensitive to the assumed value of the elasticity of costs with respect to output. For a discussion of aggregate production functions see Johansen (1972).

32. Of course, we only have data on elasticities for eight of the two-digit manufacturing industries. If we are willing to assume, however, that these eight industries are representative of the entire manufacturing sector, then we can assume that the percentage change in the entire manufacturing sector will be equal to the aggregate percentage change in the nine industries that we have analyzed.

Simulating the Rail–Truck Competitive Equilibrium
Laurence P. Michaels

E.1 The Competitive Model

This appendix will attempt to describe the model of competition between rail and trucking and address the various issues in the determination of the competitive equilibrium. The level of detail will be sufficient so that with different cost and demand functions, a similar model could be constructed for a different year and/or region. A basic familiarity with hedonic translog functions will be assumed. The following description is somewhat generalized and applies equally well to either region.

In general, there are three steps involved in the construction of the competitive model. They are:

1. The development of industry demand curves from the estimated derived demand relations (section E.2).
2. The development of industry supply curves from the estimated cost relations (section E.3–E.5).
3. Solving the system of equations to obtain the competitive equilibrium (section E.7).

The model considers two modes—rail and truck—for two types of traffic—manufactured and bulk goods. The supply relation for each mode is simultaneous because cost depends on the output of both types of traffic. The demand relation is also simultaneous because the amount of a mode's services demanded depends both on the rate and trip characteristics of that mode as well as on the rate and trip characteristics of the competing mode. The basic structure of the model used in this analysis is

$$\text{MC}_{tm} = S_{tm}(\psi_{tm}, \psi_{tb}, w_t, t_{tm}), \tag{E.1}$$

$$\text{MC}_{tb} = S_{tb}(\psi_{tb}, \psi_{tm}, w_t, t_{tb}), \tag{E.2}$$

$$\text{MC}_{rm} = S_{rm}(\psi_{rm}, \psi_{rb}, \psi_{ro}, w_r, t_r, pq_r), \tag{E.3}$$

$$\text{MC}_{rb} = S_{rb}(\psi_{rb}, \psi_{rm}, \psi_{ro}, w_r, t_r, pq_r), \tag{E.4}$$

$$\psi_{tm} = D_{tm}(P_{tm}, P_{rm}, q_{tm}, q_{rm}, X_m), \tag{E.5}$$

$$\psi_{tb} = D_{tb}(P_{tb}, P_{rb}, q_{tb}, q_{rb}, X_b), \tag{E.6}$$

$$\psi_{rm} = D_{rm}(P_{rm}, P_{tm}, q_{rm}, q_{tm}, X_m), \tag{E.7}$$

$$\psi_{rb} = D_{rb}(P_{rb}, P_{tb}, q_{rb}, q_{tb}, X_b), \tag{E.8}$$

where:

$$MC = \text{marginal cost.}$$
$$\psi = \text{output.}$$
$$w = \text{factor prices.}$$
$$t = \text{technology variables.}$$
$$pq = \text{passenger trip qualities.}$$
$$q = \text{freight trip qualities.}$$
$$X = \text{other nontransportation variables.}$$
$$S, D = \text{supply and demand, respectively.}$$
$$t, r \text{ subscripts} = \text{truck and rail, respectively.}$$
$$m, b, o \text{ subscripts} = \text{manufactures, bulk and "other" outputs,}$$
$$\text{respectively.}$$

Obviously, this system is not solvable per se. There are a myriad of variables, but only eight equations. Basic economic theory states that under competition, firms equate their marginal cost with the market price. This would allow us to replace the marginal cost expressions on the left-hand side of (E.1)–(E.4) with the market prices. Simplifying assumptions (described later) will be made about factor prices, technology variables, passenger trip qualities, freight trip qualities, and the other nontransportation variables. This leaves a system of eight simultaneous nonlinear equations in eight unknowns. This should be solvable, although the method of solution may not be simple. A solution would provide equilibrium values for the eight variables:

ψ_{tm}, trucking manufactures output.

ψ_{tb}, trucking bulk output.

ψ_{rm}, rail manufactures output.

ψ_{rb}, rail bulk output.

P_{tm}, the rate for trucking manufactures.

P_{tb}, the rate for trucking bulk.

P_{rm}, the rate for rail manufactures.

P_{rb}, the rate for rail bulk.

The competitive model will also provide information on the various modes' costs of providing service and the profitability of those industries.

This basic framework can be used to study a number of different situations. Those of primary concern in this analysis are the status quo for 1972 (section E.6), the competitive equilibrium, and some comparative static experiments (section E.7). The comparative static experiments will address the issue of how the competitive equilibrium will shift under conditions of different factor prices, trip characteristics, or with a different number of firms in the market. How these various situations will be modeled will be described in later sections.

The cost relation for rail was estimated for the short run, when the amount of way-and-structures capital was viewed as fixed. This was necessary because observed firms may not be in long-run equilibrium. It is, however, theoretically possible to derive long-run marginal costs from the short-run cost relation by choosing at each level of output the quantity of the fixed factor that minimizes cost. These long-run marginal costs could then be used to obtain a long-run competitive equilibrium. The derivation of a long-run supply curve and its associated competitive equilibrium will be discussed in section E.8.

A model of this size and complexity raises many issues concerning realism, simplicity, theory, and feasibility. Often these objectives conflict. A number of modeling decisions were required to insure reasonable performance. The apparent arbitrariness of some decisions should not be permitted to obscure their basic rationale. When modeling different circumstances, some of these decisions may have to be varied.

Since the estimated cost and derived demand functions were nonlinear and functionally complex, it was necessary to resort to a computer and simulation to derive the industry supply and demand relations. Because of the simultaneity and nonlinearity of these relations, solution techniques suitable for a computer were necessary to find a solution to the system of equations. The method employed will be described in section E.7 and a copy of the computer program will be supplied upon request.

E.2 The Generation of Industry Demand Relations

This section attempts to derive industry demand curves for truck and rail for both commodity types from the estimated demand relation. The demand relation was in the form of a mode share equation:

$$S_T = \alpha_T + A_{TT} \ln(P_T/P_R) + \sum_{i=1}^{5} B_{Ti} \ln q_i + C_{Ty} \ln y$$

$$+ \sum_{i=2}^{3} D_i \text{RDUM}_i + \sum_{i=2}^{4} E_i \text{CDUM}_i, \tag{E.9}$$

where:

S_T = the trucking share of the transportation input, defined as truck revenue divided by truck plus rail revenues.

P_T/P_R = the ratio of revenue per ton-mile for truck to revenue per ton-mile for rail.

q_1 = truck average load.

q_2 = truck average length of haul.

q_3 = value of the commodity.

q_4 = rail average load.

q_5 = rail average length of haul.

y = wage and salary payments (used as a proxy for the output of the nontransportation firms).

RDUM_2 = dummy variable for the Southern Region.

RDUM_3 = dummy variable for the Western Region.

CDUM_2 = dummy variable for nondurable manufactures.

CDUM_3 = dummy variable for petroleum and petroleum products.

CDUM_4 = dummy variable for "other" bulk commodities.

The estimated coefficients for this equation may be found in chapter 2.

Naturally, since there are only two variable inputs—truck and rail—the rail share may be computed:

$$S_R = 1 - S_T. \tag{E.10}$$

It should be noted that all of the independent logged variables have been "normalized" by their mean values. That is, the ratio P_T/P_R, each q, and y have all been divided by their respective sample means. For example, each q_i in (E.9) is really

$$q_i = \frac{q_i'}{\hat{q}_i}, \tag{E.11}$$

where:

q_i = the normalized trip quality.

q_i' = the observed trip quality.

$\hat{q}_i$ = the sample mean of the observed trip qualities.

This process insures that the translog approximation is best near the mean value of the independent variables; the approximation performs less well as one moves away from the mean. Also, because the natural logarithm is only defined over positive numbers, the translog approximation is only valid when the variables' values are greater than zero.

The "base case" of this estimated equation was for durable manufactured goods in the Official Region. Manufactured goods, as defined for the supply functions, consisted of both durable and nondurable manufactures. Bulk goods consisted of both petroleum and petroleum products and "other" bulk commodities. Separate studies were done for the Official Region and for the combined Southern and Western Regions. How the regional and commodity dummy variables were handled will be described later.

The task at hand is the derivation of industry demand curves by mode, commodity group, and study area from this estimated mode share equation.

The expenditures on a particular transportation mode by the nontransportation producers of a particular commodity group in an area is

$$E_i = S_i E_t, \tag{E.12}$$

where:

E_i = the expenditures on mode i.

S_i = the share spent of mode i.

E_t = total expenditures on transportation for a commodity group.

The ton-miles produced by mode i for that commodity group can be found by dividing expenditures on mode i by the rate for that mode, or

$$\psi_i = \frac{S_i E_t}{P_i}, \tag{E.13}$$

where:

ψ_i = the output by transportation mode i in ton-miles.

P_i = the rate for mode i.

An expression for the share of mode i can be obtained from (E.9) and is a function of rates, shipment attributes, etc. Ideally, we would like to obtain a similar expression for total transportation expenditures E_t and substitute it into (E.13). Unfortunately, however, data are lacking to make such an analysis, and consequently we are forced to assume that total transportation expenditures are constant. This is equivalent to assuming that the elasticity of demand for aggregate transport services with respect to an aggregate freight rate is equal to one. If E_t is treated as a constant, (E.13) establishes a direct relationship between the price of mode i and the ton-miles of mode i demanded. Thus,

$$\psi_i = \hat{E}_t S_i(P_T, P_R, q, y, \text{RDUM}, \text{CDUM})/P_i, \qquad i = T_j R. \qquad \text{(E.14)}$$

Note that the relationship is simultaneous in the sense that one must specify the price and trip characteristics of both modes in order to determine the demanded output of either mode.

Now all that is needed is to supply the share equation with the required variables, and (E.14) can be used to generate a demand curve. Any rail and truck rates may be chosen. It is usual to fix the rate for one mode and vary the other rate to obtain a demand schedule.

The trip qualities can be calculated from the data set over which demand was estimated. The truck-related variables (such as truck average length of haul and truck average load) should be the weighted average for the region or regions for the study year. The weighting used should be truck ton-miles. Similarly, rail-related variables should be averages weighted by rail ton-miles. Variables unrelated to mode (such as the trip quality density, or the nontransportation output y) could just be an average weighted to total (rail plus truck) ton-miles.

Regional dummy variables should be one if the demand curve covers that region or zero otherwise. In cases where two or more regions are combined into one "study area," the regional dummy variables should be the percentage of "study area" ton-miles in that region. (Percentages should add up to one.) It is similar for commodity dummy variables where, for instance, bulk goods is a combination of "other" bulk goods and petroleum and petroleum products. Again, the dummy variables should be the percentage of that specific commodity of the general commodity group carried in that region. When seeking the demand curve for manufactured goods, the nondurable manufactures dummy should be set equal to the percentage of nondurable manufactures of total manufactures for that region. The durable manufactures (which is the "base case" and thus has no dummy variable) implicitly will be the remainder of the

Table E.1 Weighted Averages and Sample Means Used in the Manufactures and Bulk Demand Relations in the Official Region

Variable	Units	Value Manufactures	Bulk	Sample mean
q_1	tons/vehicle	14.341900	20.795576	18.016667
q_2	miles	329.42680	146.75698	276.48333
q_3	\$/lb	0.254559	0.044939	0.139419
q_4	tons/car	34.000000	58.489749	44.083333
q_5	miles	353.12873	226.17934	356.00000
y	\$(000,000)	58,191.814	185,133.36	47,463.200
$RDUM_2$	–	0	0	–
$RDUM_3$	–	0	0	–
$CDUM_2$	–	0.519430	0	–
$CDUM_3$	–	0	0.253041	–
$CDUM_4$	–	0	0.746959	–
P_T/P_R	–	–	–	2.863457
Observed conditions				
P_t	¢/ton-mile	6.067632	5.900886	–
P_r	¢/ton-mile	2.404910	2.125411	–
ψ_t	ton-miles (000)	27,512,170	13,372,960	–
ψ_r	ton-miles (000)	83,082,570	57,115,800	–

manufactures. Tables E.1 and E.2 give the variable values used in the model.

According to economic theory, the observed equilibrium should be on the demand curve. Thus, the last step in the construction of industry demand curves will be an adjustment to assure their passing through the observed equilibrium points. Equation (E.14) may be used with the observed equilibrium prices (also given in tables E.1 and E.2) to predict the demanded ton-miles by mode and commodity. Since the equilibrium prices were taken from real-world observations, there was not a single rate for all firms. Therefore, the equilibrium rates were calculated as the total revenue by mode and commodity divided by the total ton-miles by mode and commodity. In each case the predicted ton-miles will not equal exactly the observed ton-miles. This can be corrected by a simple multiplicative adjustment. This may be interpreted as an adjustment of total expenditures by the nontransportation producers E_t. There will be four new E_t's: one for truck manufactures; one for truck bulk; one for rail manufactures; and one for rail bulk.[1]

Table E.2 Weighted Averages and Sample Means Used in the Manufactures and Bulk Demand Relations in the South–West Region

Variable	Units	Value Manufactures	Bulk	Sample mean
q_1	tons/vehicle	14.773176	21.996293	18.016667
q_2	miles	456.31263	218.21319	276.48333
q_3	$/lb	0.231040	0.045966	0.139419
q_4	tons/car	34.127436	60.640528	44.083333
q_5	miles	411.27920	331.68979	356.00000
y	$(000,000)	20,838.032	123,687.95	47,463.200
$RDUM_2$	–	0.231671	0.203162	–
$RDUM_3$	–	0.768329	0.796838	–
$CDUM_2$	–	0.603429	0	–
$CDUM_3$	–	0	0.201691	–
$CDUM_4$	–	0	0.798307	–
P_T/P_R	–	–	–	2.863457
Observed conditions				
P_t	¢/ton-mile	5.453966	3.965199	–
P_r	¢/ton-mile	2.789524	1.663511	–
ψ_t	ton-miles (000)	31,776,709	22,165,783	–
ψ_r	ton-miles (000)	168,830,180[a]	314,080,420[a]	–

a. Because of a large number of "coal roads" contained in the demand, but not in the supply samples, it was felt that the different output mix might represent a technology which the estimated cost function could not adequately handle. For this reason, rail output in this region was taken at the demand sample level, but the mixture of manufactures to bulk was taken from the supply sample.

Equation (E.14) with the corrected values for E_t, may be used to plot the demand curve for each of the four commodity–mode pairs. All variables (except price) should be fixed. One can then vary price and note the change in output demanded for that mode.

E.3 Industry Supply Relations

The supply side of the model is considerably more complex than the demand side. For this reason, this section will describe the elements of supply that are common to both rail and trucking. The subsequent two sections will deal in more detail with the derivation of industry supply for truck (section E.4) and rail (section E.5).

Industry marginal cost relations must be derived from the estimated short-run cost functions. The short-run cost function is used because the firms in an industry may not be in long-run equilibrium. Thus it is the short-run cost curve that may be estimated from observed data.[2] (It is, however, possible to derive long-run costs from a short-run cost function by selecting at each level of output the amount of the fixed factors which minimizes cost. This will be attempted for rail in section E.8).

The estimated short-run cost function is of the form

$$C_m^s = C_m^s(\psi_m, w_m, t_m, q_m), \tag{E.15}$$

where:

C_m^s = the short-run cost for a firm of mode m.

ψ_m = a vector of transportation outputs produced by a firm of mode m.

w_m = a vector of factor prices for mode m.

t_m = a vector of technology variables for mode m.

q_m = a vector of trip qualities for mode m.

By differentiating short-run costs with respect to output type i, one can derive the short-run marginal cost of output i. Thus,

$$\mathrm{MC}_{mi}^s = \frac{\partial C_m^s(\psi_m, w_m, t_m, q_m)}{\partial \psi_{mi}}, \tag{E.16}$$

where ψ_{mi} is output type i by a firm of mode m and MC_{mi}^s is the short-run marginal cost for output i by a firm of mode m.

A competitive firm would expand output of type i until its marginal cost were equal to the prevailing rate for output i in the market. Thus, under competition,

$$\mathrm{MC}_{mi}^s = P_{mi}. \tag{E.17}$$

Economic theory indicates that the industry supply curve for a particular output and mode will be the horizontal summation of the individual firm's marginal cost curves for that output. One can quite easily produce the marginal cost for each of the firms in the sample by using the expression for marginal cost derived from the estimated cost equation. One need only supply the firm-specific outputs, factor prices, technology variables, and trip qualities. In order to approximate the marginal cost *curve* for any firm, one need only vary the output of that firm (holding everything else constant) and note the effect on marginal cost.

This process could be repeated for each of the firms in the sample and then the marginal cost curves could be summed (horizontally) to produce the industry supply curve for output i by mode m.

Unfortunately, in practice a number of practical considerations precluded the use of this method of deriving the industry supply curve. One such consideration was the existence of increasing returns to scale for a number of firms. The horizontal summation methodology only holds when firms exhibit decreasing returns to scale (i.e., when they are producing on the rising portion of their marginal cost curves). Supply curves are only clearly defined for competitive industries that operate with decreasing returns to scale. If one or more of the firms possesses increasing returns to scale over the relevant range of output, a "natural monopoly" will exist. In this case, one or a few of the low-cost firms will dominate the market and the supply functions of these potential monopolists will not be defined. Thus summing the individual marginal cost curves will not yield an industry supply curve.

Another practical problem with the horizontal summation strategy is the existence of discontinuities in the industry supply curves. Many of the translog marginal cost curves for the firms exhibit minima in the relevant range. Because of this, a horizontal summation will exhibit "jumps" in output as each of these minima is encountered.

A third issue with the horizontal summation strategy is the problem of multiple outputs. Because the firms (particularly the rail firms) produce both manufactured and bulk output, it is not always clear how much of each output the firm should produce to maximize profits. This is particularly relevant when the production of one type of output raises the marginal cost of other types of output. Because the relative quantities of each type of output would have to be handled on a firm-by-firm basis (if it could be handled analytically at all), this type of summation strategy would be extremely complex.

For the above reasons, it was decided to calculate the industry supply curve by a different method. The method is based on the marginal cost curve for the "average" firm in the region. Basically, one determines the marginal cost curve for the "average" firm and then scales this up to industry size. Because this method is quite ad hoc in nature, it is not surprising that a number of corrections are required to make it more realistic.

The cost and demand relations were not estimated over the same data. For this reason there are some comparability problems with any supply and demand relations derived. They do not refer to precisely the same ton-miles produced in 1972. This problem was aggravated by eliminating some firms from the cost sample. The difference in the ton-miles is two-fold: the cost and demand samples refer to quantitatively and qualitatively different outputs. To remedy this problem, it was decided to make the derived supply and demand relations resemble as closely as possible the output of the demand sample.

This would imply that the transportation industry, while producing at the 1972 level of marginal costs, should have output roughly equal to that of the demand sample. Furthermore, the output characteristics (such as average load and length of haul) should be the same as those of the demand sample. The exact manner of these adjustments will be described later.

Finally, a note of caution is in order. The truck and rail cost equations were estimated over a sample of firms under regulation. Inasmuch as regulation affects costs through commodity restrictions, backhaul restrictions, etc., it has an effect on the estimated cost equations. This effect will be transferred when industry supply relations are derived. Because of this "regulatory bias," results must be interpreted with care.

E.4 The Generation of Industry Trucking Supply Relations

The final version of the estimated cost function for specialized commodity carriers was

$$
\begin{aligned}
\ln C(\psi, w, t) = \alpha_0 &+ \sum_{i=1}^{3} \alpha_i \ln w_i + \sum_{j=1}^{3} \beta_j \ln t_j + \gamma \ln \psi \\
&+ \frac{1}{2} \sum_{i=1}^{3} \sum_{j=1}^{3} A_{ij} \ln w_i \ln w_j + \sum_{i=1}^{3} \sum_{j=1}^{3} B_{ij} \ln w_i \ln t_j \\
&+ \sum_{i=1}^{3} D_i \ln w_i \ln \psi + \frac{1}{2} \sum_{i=1}^{3} \sum_{j=1}^{3} E_{ij} \ln t_i \ln t_j \\
&+ \sum_{i=1}^{3} F_i \ln t_i \ln \psi + \frac{1}{2} G \ln \psi \ln \psi,
\end{aligned}
\tag{E.18}
$$

where:

C = total cost for the firm.

w_1 = the price of labor.

w_2 = the price of fuel.

w_3 = the price of capital.

w_4 = the price of purchased transportation.

t_1 = average load (tons/truck).

t_2 = average length of haul.

t_3 = insurance per ton-mile.

ψ = output in ton-miles.

Two important points should be made. First, all the independent logged variables have been "normalized" by their mean values. That is, each ψ, w, and t, has been divided by the sample mean for that variable. Second, cost and the first three factor prices have been divided by the fourth factor price to insure linear homogeneity of $C(\psi, w, t)$ in w.[3] For present purposes, it is sufficient to realize that the process has been performed and that it must be "undone" to obtain the observed, unnormalized costs.

The estimation process yields the values of the coefficients in (E.18). These may be found in appendix C. It should be pointed out that the estimated trucking cost equation only has "output" in general and does not differentiate between bulk and manufactured output. This will have to be corrected in order to derive marginal cost relations for both manufactured and bulk output. If, however, we ignore for a moment the problem of two outputs, it is relatively easy to derive a firm's marginal and average costs from (E.18):

$$\frac{\partial C}{\partial \psi} = \frac{\partial \ln C}{\partial \ln \psi} \frac{C}{\psi}.$$
(E.19)

Here

$$C = \exp(\ln C) w_4,^4$$
(E.20)

and

$$\frac{\partial \ln C}{\partial \ln \psi} = \gamma + \sum_{i=1}^{3} D_i \ln w + \sum_{j=1}^{3} F_j \ln t_j + G \ln \psi.$$
(E.21)

exp denotes exponentiation; ln C may, of course, be calculated by means of the estimated cost equation (E.18). Therefore,

$$MC = \frac{\partial C}{\partial \psi} = \frac{\exp(\ln C) w_4}{\psi} \left[\gamma + \sum_{i=1}^{3} D_i \ln w_i \right.$$

$$\left. + \sum_{j=1}^{3} F_j \ln t_j + G \ln \psi \right]$$
(E.22)

and

$$AC = \frac{\exp(\ln C) w_4}{\psi}.$$
(E.23)

From this point, it would be simple to calculate the total, average, and marginal costs for any firm in the sample. All one need do is substitute that firm's output, factor prices, and technology variables into the above equations. In order to obtain the total average, or marginal cost *curves*, one would only have to vary output and create a schedule of the various costs at the different levels of ψ.

One can use this same methodology to find the total, average, or marginal cost curves for the "average" firm. The average firm is defined as a firm that possesses factor prices and technology variables that are the weighted averages of the factor prices and technology variables in the sample. The weighting is the output (in ton-miles) of the firms in the sample. A weighted average was used so that the average firm is more representative of the large output firms, as opposed to being biased by a large number of small firms.

As was discussed in the previous section, a horizontal summation strategy proved impractical in obtaining an industry supply curve. The methodology employed here will (1) generate marginal and total cost curves for the average firm, (2) scale these curves up to industry size, and (3) adjust these curves so that they predict a reasonable profitability. Finally, a method is demonstrated that permits distinction between manufactured and bulk output and allows one to derive independent marginal cost curves for each commodity. These topics will be addressed in order.

As was discussed in the previous section, there are some compatibility problems between the sample used to estimate cost and the sample used to estimate demand. The decision was made to base the model on the demand sample. This will affect the derivation of a trucking industry supply curve in two ways. First, the trip characteristics of the modeled ton-miles should reflect the characteristics of the demand sample. This is important for the three technology variables—average load, average length of haul, and insurance per ton-mile. Second, while producing at the demand sample's level of output, the model should predict a marginal cost that is appropriate for the study year. Both of these conditions prevail in the model to be described.

The first step in creating a trucking industry supply model is the generation of the average firm's total and marginal cost curves. This firm very closely resembles the average firm discussed earlier, except that its traffic's trip characteristics reflect the demand sample as opposed to the supply sample.

The factor prices w used in (E.18) and (E.22) should be the weighted averages of those variables from the supply sample. The weighting is ton-miles.[5] The first two technology variables (average load and average length of haul) were taken as weighted averages from the demand sample. The third technology variable (insurance per ton-mile) had to be taken as a weighted average from the supply sample since insurance was not a variable of the demand sample.

Since the weighted averages for the technology variables should depend on the relative amounts of the two types of traffic, they will be approximated in the following manner.

$$t_i = \frac{t_{im}\psi_{tm} + t_{ib}\psi_{tb}}{\psi_{tm} + \psi_{tb}}, \tag{E.24}$$

where:

t_i = the ith technology variable for output in general.

t_{im} = the ith technology variable for manufactures output.

t_{ib} = the ith technology variable for bulk output.

ψ_{tm} = trucking manufactures output.

ψ_{tb} = trucking bulk output.

The technology variables for bulk and manufactures output are themselves weighted averages from the demand sample. If one wishes general marginal and average cost curves, the observed traffic mix may be used in (E.24). When a competitive equilibrium has been found, that traffic mix may be used. See tables E.3 and E.4 for the values of the weighted averages used in the model, as well as the sample means (used for normalization).

Using these factor prices and technology variables in (E.20) and (E.22) one may generate total and marginal cost curves for this average firm by varying output. The next step is to scale these curves up to industry size.

Now that a schedule of output and marginal and total costs exists for the average firm, multiplying the output figures and the total cost figures by the number of firms in the supply sample would produce a reasonably good model of the trucking industry based on the size of the supply sample. In order to scale to the size of the demand sample, it is necessary to multiply output and total cost by the ratio of the size of the demand trucking sample to the supply trucking sample. It is easy to show that these two scalings can be performed in one step by multiplying output and total cost by an "adjusted number of firms,"

Table E.3 Weighted Averages and Sample Means Used in the Trucking Supply Relations in the Official Region[a]

Variable	Units	Weighted average	Sample mean
w_1^b	\$(000)/man-year[c]	31.868068	30.601300
w_2^b	\$/standardized vehicle-mile[c]	0.064234	0.067913
w_3^b	Index[c]	6.229777	5.125942
w_4	\$/standardized vehicle-mile	0.357404	–
ψ	ton-miles (000)	–	48,632.005
Manufactures output			
t_1	tons/vehicle	14.341900	12.856190
t_2	miles	329.42680	272.41838
t_3	\$(000)/ton-mile	0.000539	0.001115
Bulk output			
t_1	tons/vehicle	20.795576	12.856109
t_2	miles	146.75698	272.41838
t_3	\$(000)/ton-mile	0.000539	0.001115

a. Sample number of firms = 201.
b. Normalized by w_4.
c. Divided by the units of w_4.

Table E.4 Weighted Averages and Sample Means Used in the Trucking Supply Relations in the South–West Region[a]

Variable	Units	Weighted average	Sample mean
w_1^b	\$(000)/man-year[c]	30.956642	27.852870
w_2^b	\$/standardized vehicle-mile[c]	0.116276	0.122363
w_3^b	Index[c]	5.753408	5.564275
w_4	\$/standardized vehicle-mile	0.345916	–
ψ	ton-miles (000)	–	79,118.917
Manufactures output			
t_1	tons/vehicle	14.773176	12.284278
t_2	miles	457.31263	387.86375
t_3	\$(000)/ton-mile	0.000417	0.001302
Bulk output			
t_1	tons/vehicle	21.996293	12.284278
t_2	miles	.218.21319	387.86375
t_3	\$(000)/ton-mile	0.000417	0.001302

a. Sample number of firms = 144.
b. Normalized by w_4.
c. Divided by the units of w_4.

$$N = n\frac{\psi_{td}}{\psi_{ts}},\tag{E.25}$$

where:

N = the adjusted number of firms.

n = the number of firms in the trucking supply sample.

ψ_{td} = the total trucking output in the demand sample.

ψ_{ts} = the total trucking output in the supply sample.

Note that this adjusted number of firms has the interpretation that the average firm is the same for both the demand or the supply sample (except for trip characteristics); but there are a different number of firms in one sample as opposed to the other.[6]

One now has a simple model of industry total and marginal costs. In order that this model be as realistic as possible, one would like to ensure that the supply curve is in the proper relation to the observed market equilibrium. In other words, one wishes the trucking industry model to possess the observed profitability, and we thus make an ad hoc adjustment to the cost curves to ensure this relationship. Although the details of this adjustment are somewhat complex, they should not be allowed to obscure the simple purpose of assuring a reasonable industry profitability with respect to the observed average revenue of the demand sample.

The first step in the adjustment is to determine just what the profitability should be. This type of data was not available in the demand sample, so supply sample figures were used. The ratio of total trucking revenue to total trucking cost was computed to provide an industry profitability figure. This is the total cost the model would predict if it exhibited the 1972 observed profitability. One should find an adjustment factor f so that the model will predict the desired total cost. This factor would simply be the ratio of the desired total cost to the predicted total cost.[7] This factor can be applied to the expression for the average firm's cost. It is easy to show that if this adjusted cost is used, (E.19) still defines the marginal cost.

To summarize, it is desirable that the industry trucking model exhibit profitability commensurate with what has been observed. A factor is devised which may be applied to the average firm's total cost. The relevant costs for the average firm now become

$$C = \exp(\ln C)w_4 f,\tag{E.26}$$

$$MC = \frac{\exp(\ln C)w_4 f}{\psi} \left[\gamma + \sum_{i=1}^{3} D_i \ln w_1 + \sum_{j=1}^{3} F_j \ln t_j + G \ln \psi \right], \quad (E.27)$$

$$AC = \frac{\exp(\ln C)w_4 f}{\psi} \quad (E.28)$$

where all variables are as they appear in (E.20)–(E.23) and f is the computed adjustment factor. These curves may then be scaled up to industry size. This is, in fact, the method used for determining total trucking costs.

The final issue in a trucking supply model is the simulation of distinct industry marginal cost curves for both manufactured and bulk output. The procedure employed is fairly simple. First, output is broken down into a manufactured and a bulk component, or

$$\psi_t = \psi_m + \psi_b, \quad (E.29)$$

where:

ψ_t = total trucking output (in ton-miles).

ψ_m = trucking manufactured output.

ψ_b = trucking bulk output.

Note the simultaneity of this model. While calculating the marginal cost of manufactured output, bulk output is exogenously set and vice versa.

Second, while calculating the marginal cost of manufactured goods, the trip characteristics used reflect those of manufactured goods. Thus, the first two technology variables used for simulating the trucking manufactures supply curve are the weighted averages from the demand sample of those trip characteristics for manufactured goods. The third trip characteristic is not available by manufactures and bulk so the general weighted average from the supply sample must suffice.

The method for obtaining the truck bulk marginal cost curve is analogous. The trip characteristics used reflect bulk commodities.

The scale and profitability adjustments discussed earlier are still in force. All one need do now to obtain the commodity-specific industry truck marginal cost curve is to vary the output of that commodity while holding all else constant and calculate via (E.27) the marginal cost. The schedule created is that commodity's marginal cost curve.[8]

It should be noted that if one tries to compute total costs by this method, they will vary slightly from costs computed by the method described earlier because of the different values of the technology variables. Further-more, this definition of marginal cost with respect to a particular type of output is not exactly equal to the derivative of total cost with respect to output type i. In this sense, the model is slightly internally inconsistent. However, these problems appear minor and unavoidable if one wishes reasonable industry supply functions for both types of output.

E.5 The Generation of Industry Rail Supply Relations

The final version of the rail cost function is considerably more complex than the cost function for trucking operations. There are two outputs— freight ton-miles and passenger-miles (this output is hedonically adjusted). Furthermore, there are several different types of freight output which affect total cost differently. There are five factor prices and five technology variables. The form of the estimated cost equation is

$$
\ln C(\psi, w, t) = \alpha_0 + \sum_{i=1}^{4} \alpha_i \ln w_i + \sum_{j=1}^{5} \beta_j \ln t_j + \sum_{k=1}^{2} \gamma_k \ln \psi_k
$$
$$
+ \frac{1}{2} \sum_{i=1}^{4} \sum_{j=1}^{4} A_{ij} \ln w_i \ln w_j + \sum_{i=1}^{4} \sum_{j=1}^{5} B_{ij} \ln w_i \ln t_j
$$
$$
+ \sum_{i=1}^{4} \sum_{k=1}^{2} D_{ik} \ln w_i \ln \psi_k + F_{11} \ln t_1 \ln \psi_1
$$
$$
+ \sum_{j=1}^{5} F_{j2} \ln t_j \ln \psi_2 + \frac{1}{2} \sum_{j=1}^{2} \sum_{k=1}^{2} G_{jk} \ln \psi_j \ln \psi_k \qquad \text{(E.30)}
$$

(note that many of the possible interaction terms have been constrained to zero), where:

C = the total variable cost of the railroad.

w_1 = the price of equipment capital.

w_2 = a Divisia price index for general labor.

w_3 = a Divisia price index for yard and switching labor.

w_4 = price of on-train labor, defined as wage payments divided by man-hours.

w_5 = the AAR price index for fuel and materials.

t_1 = way-and-structures capital.

t_2 = low-density route-miles.

t_3 = total route-miles.

t_4 = freight average length of haul for the railroad.

t_5 = the ratio of manufactured ton-miles to nonmanufactured ton-miles.

ψ_1 = hedonically adjusted passenger-miles (the adjustment is described below).

ψ_2 = freight output (in ton-miles).

The estimated coefficient values may be found in appendix B.

As in the case of trucks, it should be noted that the independent variables $(w, t, \psi_2 - \psi_1$ will be addressed later) are normalized by their mean values from the sample. Also, the first four factor prices and C have been normalized by the last factor price w_5 to insure linear homogeneity of $C(\psi, w, t)$ in factor prices.

The passenger output ψ_1 has a hedonic quality adjustment.[9] Thus, passenger output may be expressed as

$$\ln \psi_1 = \ln pm + \sum_{i=1}^{2} a_i \ln pq_i + \frac{1}{2} \sum_j \sum_j b_{ij} \ln pq_i \ln pq_j, \tag{E.31}$$

where:

pm = passenger-miles.

pq_1 = average passenger travel length.

pq_2 = passenger-miles divided by passenger route-miles.

The variables pm, pq_1, and pq_2 are all normalized by the means of their respective sample variables.

The technology variables t are relatively straightforward measures of system size, capital, or trip qualities, except for t_5, the last technology variable, which is defined as the ratio of manufactured to nonmanufactured freight output. It provides a method for distinguishing between the two types of freight output—manufactures and bulk.

There are some mild problems with comparability of the supply and demand samples. The nonmanufactures referred to in the fifth technology variable include petroleum and petroleum products; field crops; livestock, fruits, vegetables, and other agricultural commodities; coal; and "other" bulk commodities. The bulk commodities referred to in the demand sample include only petroleum and petroleum products, and "other" bulk commodities. Thus, the bulk goods referred to in the demand relations are only a subset of the nonmanufactures actually carried by the railroad industry. A method to handle this problem will be developed.

As in the case of trucking, the development of rail industry supply requires three steps: calculating marginal and total cost curves for an average railroad; expanding this average firm to industry scale; and adjusting the marginal and total cost curves to yield reasonable costs with respect to revenue.

The first step in the construction of a rail industry supply curve is the derivation of an average firm's total and marginal cost curves. The total variable cost for a firm is

$$C = \exp(\ln C) w_5, \tag{E.32}$$

where w_5 is the last factor price.[10] It is relatively simple to derive expressions for the marginal costs of manufactured and nonmanufactured output. Remembering that the last technology variable is the ratio of manufactured to nonmanufactured output, one may derive expressions for the various marginal costs.

First, for manufactures (by the chain rule),[11]

$$
\begin{aligned}
\frac{\partial C}{\partial \psi_{2m}} &= \frac{\partial C}{\partial \ln C} \frac{\partial \ln C}{\partial \ln \psi_2} \frac{\partial \ln \psi_2}{\partial \psi_2} \frac{\partial \psi_2}{\partial \psi_{2m}} + \frac{\partial C}{\partial \ln C} \frac{\partial \ln C}{\partial \ln t_5} \frac{\partial \ln t_5}{\partial \psi_{2m}} \\
&= \frac{C}{\psi_2} \frac{\partial \ln C}{\partial \ln \psi_2} + \frac{C}{\psi_{2m}} \frac{\partial \ln C}{\partial \ln t_5},
\end{aligned} \tag{E.33}
$$

where:

C = variable costs for the railroad.

ψ_2 = total freight output of the railroad.

ψ_{2m} = manufactured freight output of the railroad.

t_5 = the fifth technology variable (defined as the ratio of manufactured to nonmanufactured output).

Differentiating (E.33) yields

$$\frac{\partial \ln C}{\partial \ln \psi_2} = \gamma_2 + \sum_{i=1}^{4} D_{i2} \ln w_i + \sum_{j=1}^{5} F_{j2} \ln t_j + G_{12} \ln \psi_1 + G_{22} \ln \psi_2 \tag{E.34}$$

and

$$\frac{\partial \ln C}{\partial \ln t_5} = \beta_5 + \sum_{i=1}^{4} B_{i5} \ln w_i + F_{52} \ln \psi_2. \tag{E.35}$$

Therefore, the marginal cost of rail manufactures freight output is

$$
\mathrm{MC}_m = \frac{C}{\psi_2}\left[\gamma_2 + \sum_{i=1}^{4} D_{i2}\ln w_i + \sum_{j=1}^{5} F_{j2}\ln t_j + G_{12}\ln\psi_1 + G_{22}\ln\psi_2\right]
$$
$$
+ \frac{C}{\psi_{2m}}\left[\beta_5 + \sum_{i=1}^{4} B_{i5}\ln w_i + F_{52}\ln\psi_2\right], \tag{E.36}
$$

where C may be calculated via (E.32).

One may derive an expression for the marginal cost of nonmanufactures freight output in a similar manner:

$$
\frac{\partial C}{\partial\psi_{2b}} = \frac{\partial C}{\partial\ln C}\frac{\partial\ln C}{\partial\ln\psi_2}\frac{\partial\ln\psi_2}{\partial\psi_2}\frac{\partial\psi_2}{\partial\psi_{2b}}
$$
$$
+ \frac{\partial C}{\partial\ln C}\frac{\partial\ln C}{\partial\ln t_5}\frac{\partial\ln t_5}{\partial\psi_{2b}}
$$
$$
= \frac{C}{\psi_2}\frac{\partial\ln C}{\partial\ln\psi_2} - \frac{C}{\psi_{2b}}\frac{\partial\ln C}{\partial\ln t_5}, \tag{E.37}
$$

where ψ_{2b} is the nonmanufactures component of rail freight output. Therefore, the marginal cost with respect to nonmanufactures freight output is

$$
\mathrm{MC}_b = \frac{C}{\psi_2}\left[\gamma_2 + \sum_{i=1}^{4} D_{i2}\ln w_i + \sum_{j=1}^{5} F_{j2}\ln t_j + G_{12}\ln\psi_1 + G_{22}\ln\psi_2\right]
$$
$$
- \frac{C}{\psi_{2b}}\left[\beta_5 + \sum_{i=1}^{4} B_{i5}\ln w_i + F_{52}\ln\psi_2\right]. \tag{E.38}
$$

Thus, it is relatively straightforward to calculate total cost or marginal cost with respect to manufactures or nonmanufactures output for any firm in the sample.[12] All one need do is supply (E.32), (E.36), and (E.37) with that firm's factor prices, technology variables, outputs, and passenger trip qualities. In order to obtain the total or marginal cost *curves* with respect to manufactures or nonmanufactures output, one would vary that output. At each level of output, the last technology variable (the ratio of manufactures to nonmanufactures output) would have to be recalculated. A schedule of the effect on total and marginal costs could be created.

It is also easy to find the marginal cost curve for those bulk commodities that correspond to the demand sample's definition of bulk. Nonmanufactures are merely equal to those bulk commodities dealt with in the demand sample *plus* nonincluded bulk commodities (coal, field crops, and agricultural products). In order to get the marginal cost curve for bulk commodities in the demand sense, one should hold the value of nonincluded bulk commodities constant at the level observed for that firm and vary the remaining bulk commodities. Again, the last technology variable t_5 would have to be computed at each level of output. At each level, the marginal cost for these (and, in fact, all) bulk goods can be found through (E.37).[13] This marginal cost curve for demand-relevant bulk commodities is what we shall refer to as the bulk marginal cost or bulk supply curve.

The process to find the average firm's total and marginal costs is similar. All one need do is supply the expressions for total and marginal cost with the weighted[14] averages for factor prices, technology variables 1 through 4,[15] passenger-miles, and passenger trip qualities.[16] These values may be found in table E.5. One must also supply nonmanufactures output if one desires a manufactures marginal cost curve, or supply manufactures and nonincluded bulk outputs in determining a bulk supply curve. These supplied figures may be set arbitrarily, but are usually set to a meaningful level such as the sample average or a weighted average. One can then vary the desired freight output, calculate t_5 at each increment, and plot the total and marginal costs.

The next step in the development of an industry rail supply curve is scaling up the average firm's cost curves to industry size. The process is a bit more complex than for the trucking industry.

Before attempting this scaling, a theoretical aside is in order. Some firms in the rail sample are markedly larger than others. This is true, for example, of the Penn Central in the Official Region. This is going to give some trouble when an attempt is made to scale the model to industry size. Suppose, for pedagogical purposes, that there are six railroads in a region, each with an identical marginal cost function. Further suppose that five of the firms produce 10 billion ton-miles at a marginal cost of 2¢/ton-mile and the remaining firm carries 50 billion ton-miles at a marginal cost of 4¢/ton-mile. Since half of the output (in ton-miles) is produced at a marginal cost of 2¢ and half at 4¢, one might like an industry model to predict a marginal cost of 3¢/ton-mile at the industry output of 100 billion ton-miles. If, however, one merely scales up the marginal cost curve of each firm by a factor of six (because there are six firms), a marginal cost of approximately 2.4¢/ton-mile will be predicted. The problem appears to be that not enough emphasis was placed on the dominant firm. What one would like is a measure of concentration in the market and an adjustment that would reflect the percentage of ton-miles produced by the large firms.

This can be accomplished by dividing the demand industry output by

Table E.5 Weighted Averages and Sample Means Used in the Rail Supply Relations[a]

Variable	Units	Official Region	South–West Region	Sample mean
w_1^b	¢/unit asset[c]	0.00113464	0.00107830	0.00103495
w_2^b	Index[c]	0.01018172	0.01005622	0.00832172
w_3^b	Index[c]	0.01080657	0.01097135	0.00860830
w_4^b	$/man-hour[c]	0.07248802	0.08311375	0.06152379
w_5	Index	118.1	118.1	–
t_1	$	6,465,418,600	2,259,162,000	1,570,102,500
t_2	Route-miles	5,717.7127	3,227.6276	1,860.1295
t_3	Route-miles	15,967.256	11,917.034	6,760.4286
t_4	Miles	303.74255	469.40623	326.89619
t_5	–	–	–	1.2227694
pm	Passenger-miles	–	–	454,405,730
pq_1	Miles	23.734239	287.75706	209.28418
pq_2	Passenger miles/route-miles	1,648,084.6	148,976.26	257,565.24
ψ_2	Ton-miles (000)	–	–	24,085,983

a. Sample number of firms: 6 (Official); 13 (South–West).
b. Normalized by w_5.
c. Divided by the w_5 index.

a weighted average of the outputs by firm. (The weighting is ton-miles.) This statistic indicates how many weighted average firms are needed to make up the industry when the firms are viewed in light of which ones actually carry the traffic. Note that it need not be an integer.

In our sample, this adjusted number of firms would be calculated as follows:

$$N = \frac{\text{observed ton-miles}}{\text{weighted average of ton-miles}}$$

$$= \frac{100}{\dfrac{10.10 + 10.10 + 10.10 + 10.10 + 10.10 + 50.50}{10 + 10 + 10 + 10 + 10 + 50}} = 3.33. \quad (E.39)$$

Let us interpret this to mean that 3.33 weighted average firms would be needed to comprise the industry. If we scale the "typical" marginal cost curve by a factor of 3.33, we have improved the predicted industry marginal cost, which now equals 3.3. For this reason, the concentration adjustment will be incorporated into the industry rail model.[17]

We now return to the problem of scaling up the average firm to industry size. The weighted average for factor prices, technology variables 1 through 4, and passenger trip qualities will be used. One can then allocate the various types of output to the weighted average firms by dividing the observed[18] manufactures, bulk, nonincluded bulk, and passenger outputs by the adjusted number of firms for the sample. One may then use the method outlined earlier to derive the total and marginal cost curves for any of the weighted average firms. (Costs are, of course, the same for each of these firms.) This could be scaled to industry size by multiplying output and total cost by the weighted average of firms. Industry size in this case would be that defined by the supply sample.

As in the case of the trucking analysis, the industry size we wish to simulate is that defined by the demand sample. However, since the manufactured–bulk mix was substantially different for the supply and demand samples, the industry model will be calibrated using the supply data (i.e., it will be adjusted to yield the proper cost at the observed level of output). Then the model will be adjusted to the demand sample size.

Because of data limitations, it was decided that the best way to calibrate the model would be to assure that the rail model predicted the observed total cost (from the supply sample), while producing at the observed levels of output. To assure this, a multiplicative adjustment factor was attached to the expression for the total cost of a firm. Thus,

$$C = \exp(\ln C)w_5 f \qquad \text{(E.40)}$$

when the adjustment factor[19] f may be calculated as

$$f = \frac{\text{observed total variable cost}}{\text{predicted total variable cost}}. \qquad \text{(E.41)}$$

It is easy to show that the expressions for marginal cost are still correct, provided that the new expression for total cost (E.40) is used.

The final step in the creation of an industry rail model is to adjust the model so that it reflects the demand sample. For various reasons (firms being deleted, etc.) the rail supply sample and the demand sample are not exactly comparable. Because we have decided to define the industry model on the basis of the demand sample, we must adjust our model to that size.[20]

There are numerous ways to accomplish this. Due to data limitations, to make the analysis tractable, a (relatively) simple methodology was chosen. The ratio of total rail output from the demand sample to the comparable rail output from the supply sample was calculated:

$$f_2 = \frac{\text{manufactures + bulk from the demand sample}}{\begin{array}{c}\text{manufactures + bulk (not including coal, field crops,} \\ \text{or agricultural products) from the supply sample}\end{array}}. \qquad \text{(E.42)}$$

This factor was applied to the weighted average number of firms.[21]

$$N' = N f_2, \qquad \text{(E.43)}$$

where:

N' = the adjusted number of firms used in the model.

N = the weighted average number of firms based on concentration, calculated as the observed ton-miles from the supply sample divided by the weighted average of ton-miles.

f_2 = the ratio of rail output from the demand sample to the comparable supply rail output.

This serves two purposes. First, when demand-sized output is divided by the adjusted number of firms including this factor, it scales the output so that it is on the proper portion of the supply curve. Second, when scaling the average firm up to industry size, the size is representative of the demand sample.

Because no demand statistics were available on passenger output and nonincluded bulk commodity output, their *total* levels were defined as the supply sample values[22] times f_2.

The methodology is a bit confusing. It might be worthwhile at this point to review briefly the process by which one would generate industry rail supply and total cost curves.

The basic methodology entails the scaling up of an average railroad's total and marginal cost curves to industry size. This average railroad faces factor prices, technology variables 1 through 4, and passenger trip qualities which are weighted averages from the supply sample. The outputs which this average firm produces are the total outputs for the region divided by the adjusted number of firms [see (E.43)]. Total manufactures and bulk outputs are taken from the demand sample. Total passenger output and nonincluded bulk output are defined as the supply sample values times f_2 [see (E.42)].

One may derive total cost for the average firm by means of (E.30) and (E.40). By varying the desired output, one may derive the marginal cost curves for manufactured and bulk by means of (E.36) and (E.38). (At each level of output a new value for t_5, the fifth technology variable, must be calculated.)

These average firm marginal and total cost curves may be scaled up to industry size by multiplying output and total cost by the adjusted number of firms.

E.6 Modeling the Status Quo

Now that the capability exists to produce supply and demand curves for both modes and both commodities, one is interested in knowing how these different curves interact. More specifically, one would like to know how they relate to one another in the observed equilibrium and what a competitive equilibrium would look like. We already have the tools available for examining the initial condition. To obtain a competitive equilibrium we need a method of solving the nonlinear system of equations. This will be addressed in the next section.

The system of supply and demand equations takes the general form

$$\text{MC}_{tm} = S_{tm}(\psi_{tm}, \psi_{tb}, w_t, t_{tm}), \tag{E.44}$$

$$\text{MC}_{tb} = S_{tb}(\psi_{tb}, \psi_{tm}, w_t, t_{tb}), \tag{E.45}$$

$$\text{MC}_{rm} = S_{rm}(\psi_{rm}, \psi_{rb}, \psi_{ro}, w_r, t_r, pq_r), \tag{E.46}$$

$$\text{MC}_{rb} = S_{rb}(\psi_{rb}, \psi_{rm}, \psi_{ro}, w_r, t_r, pq_r), \tag{E.47}$$

$$\psi_{tm} = D_{tm}(P_{tm}, P_{rm}, q_{tm}, q_{rm}, X_m), \tag{E.48}$$

$$\psi_{tb} = D_{tb}(P_{tb}, P_{rb}, q_{tb}, q_{rb}, X_b), \tag{E.49}$$

$$\psi_{rm} = D_{rm}(P_{rm}, P_{tm}, q_{rm}, q_{tm}, X_m), \tag{E.50}$$

$$\psi_{rb} = D_{rb}(P_{rb}, P_{tb}, q_{rb}, q_{tb}, X_b), \tag{E.51}$$

where:

$$MC = \text{marginal cost.}$$
$$\psi = \text{output.}$$
$$w = \text{factor prices.}$$
$$t = \text{technology variables.}$$
$$pq = \text{passenger trip qualities.}$$
$$q = \text{freight trip qualities.}$$
$$X = \text{other nontransportation variables.}$$
$$S, D = \text{supply and demand, respectively.}$$
$$t, r \text{ subscripts} = \text{truck and rail, respectively.}$$
$$m, b, o \text{ subscripts} = \text{manufactures, bulk, and "other" output.}$$

As was discussed in the opening section of this appendix, this system of equations is not solvable per se. However, by fixing the values of the factor prices, technology variables, passenger trip qualities, freight trip qualities, "other" output, and other nontransportation variables (by the methods described in the preceding sections), the problem becomes somewhat more tractable. The system now reduces to 8 equations in 12 unknowns (4 MC, 4 ψ, and 4 P). As we shall see in the next section, when firms operate under competition, they equate their marginal costs to the market prices. This reduces the number of variables to 8, and the system of equations is, in general, solvable. There is no guarantee, however, that the industry was in a competitive equilibrium in the study year. In this section we shall develop a methodology for examining the status quo.

Figure E.1 depicts a typical "observed equilibrium." There is an industry marginal cost and demand curve for each of the four commodity–mode pairs. The point on each graph represents the observed market output and rate for that particular mode and commodity. The demand curves are constrained to go through these observed equilibria. The marginal cost curves do not necessarily intersect these points. Some firms may be making monopoly profits, others (for whatever reasons) may be losing money.

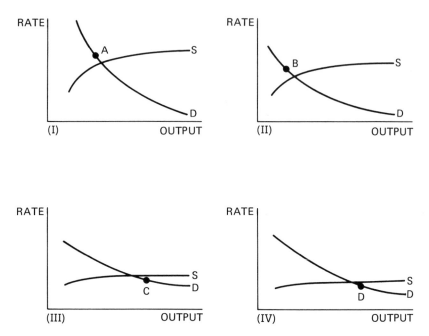

Figure E.1   A hypothetical "observed equilibrium." (I) Trucking manufactures, (II) trucking bulk, (III) rail manufactures, (IV) rail bulk.

The methodology for producing this status quo model is simple enough. It merely requires the plotting of the industry supply and demand curves as described earlier. Perhaps it would be worthwhile to put the whole process into brief perspective.

The first step in producing the initial equilibrium is to determine the actual points of production (points A, B, C, and D in figure E.1). There are four points, each representing the observed output and rate for one commodity group by a particular mode. These points may be derived for the study year from the demand sample. Output is simply the total output for each commodity–mode pair. The rate may be computed as total transportation revenue (by commodity–mode pair) divided by the relevant output.

The next step is to produce the demand curves for both commodity groups by truck and rail. We thus apply the methodology described in section E.2. One must supply the study year's observed trip qualities, modal rates, regional and commodity dummy variables, nontransportation output, and transportation expenditures. Transportation expenditures must be corrected to ensure that the demand curve goes through

the observed equilibrium point. To derive the demand curve for a particular commodity–mode pair, one should vary that mode's rate, while
holding everything else constant, and plot the effect on output.

Truck and rail industry marginal cost curves may be derived via the
methodologies outlined in sections E.4 and E.5. Supply curves are not
defined in noncompetitive situations, but one would like to know the
relationship between the observed equilibria and the marginal cost curves.
For each mode–commodity pair, one must supply the expression for
marginal cost with the study year's observed factor prices, technology
variables, trip qualities, and outputs. The marginal cost expressions
should be "corrected" in both the output and cost axes, so that at the
output levels of the demand sample the expressions produce realistic
total and marginal costs. To derive the marginal cost curve, one need
only vary the relevant output (holding all else constant)[23] and note the
effect on marginal cost.

This process produces a realistic model of the observed equilibrium
for the study year.

E.7 Modeling the Competitive Equilibrium

Modeling the joint competitive equilibrium is a bit more complicated
than modeling the observed equilibrium. Rather than duplicating the
conditions that exist (but are not readily observable), one wishes to see
how the equilibrium would look if firms equated their marginal costs
to the rates for transportation decided in the market.

While the mathematical forms of the supply and demand curves are
identical under competition, there are now eight variables which must
be simultaneously determined, namely, the competitive rate and output
for each of the four commodity–mode pairs. By equating the various
marginal costs to the market rate, we obtain eight equations in eight
unknowns. The system should have a solution, but because of the simultaneity and nonlinearity, the solution can not be found by analytical
methods. For this reason one must turn to a computer simulation. The
technique used to solve the system is known as Newton's method.[24]
Basically, one starts by guessing a solution to the nonlinear system. The
computer program[25] then approximates the nonlinear equations by
linear approximations at the guessed solution. This new system of linear
equations is then solved and the solution is taken as the next point of
approximation for the nonlinear equations.

The program iterates in this manner until eight error functions equal (within a tolerance) zero. The error functions compute the difference between supply and demand and the difference between price and marginal cost for each of the commodity–mode pairs.

This method can be shown to converge, provided that the initial guess is "sufficiently" close to the true solution and the Jacobian (the matrix of the differentials of the error functions) is "well behaved" in the area of the true solution. The program aborts if the Jacobian is ill conditioned.

The computer program must be supplied with expressions for marginal cost and the output demanded for both commodity groups for truck and rail. It must also be supplied with the Jacobian—analytical expressions for the differentials of the error functions with respect to each of the eight variables.

The demand expressions are similar to the ones presented in section E.2. One must supply the appropriate trip qualities, regional and commodity dummy variables, nontransportation output, and transportation expenditures. (Transportation expenditures should still be corrected so that the demand curve goes through the observed equilibrium at the observed rates.) The rate variables (i.e., the rates for each commodity–mode pair) will be simultaneously determined.

The supply relations are similarly specified. By sections E.4 and E.5, one must supply the expressions for marginal cost with the appropriate factor prices, technology variables, and trip qualities. The marginal cost expressions are "corrected" both in terms of output and cost. (One must supply the "observed" values for rail passenger output and rail "other bulk" output.) Truck and rail outputs for manufactured and bulk commodities are also simultaneously determined by the computer program.

The values for the elements of the Jacobian must be determined by differentiating the 8 error functions with respect to each of the rate and output variables. Since there are 8 variables, the Jacobian contains 64 (or 8×8) elements. Most of these elements degenerate to zero or unity. The remainder are fairly complicated. All of the elements of the Jacobian will not be derived here, but are available in the program. Here, however, one element will be derived for illustrative purposes.

The solution methodology works on the differences between supply and demand and between transportation rates and marginal costs. For example, the trucking manufactures supply relation uses approximate values of trucking manufactures and bulk outputs (and other inputs) to determine the marginal cost of trucking manufactures. This is then compared to the rate for manufactures by truck. In equilibrium the difference goes to zero (or becomes very small). This relationship can be seen in the error function

$$f(1) = MC_{tm} - P_{tm}, \tag{E.52}$$

where:

$f(1) =$ a measure of the discrepancy.

$MC_{tm} =$ the industry marginal cost of manufactures by truck.

$P_{tm} =$ the industry rate for manufactures by truck.

The Jacobian requires the differential of this error function with respect to each of the eight rate and output variables. As an example, we will derive the differential with respect to industry trucking manufactures output ψ_{tm}. The industry marginal cost is, of course, a function of this variable:

$$\frac{\partial f(1)}{\partial \psi_{tm}} = \frac{\partial}{\partial \psi_{tm}} [MC_{tm} - P_{tm}] = \frac{\partial MC_{tm}}{\partial \psi_{tm}}. \tag{E.53}$$

This, of course, is the differential of industry marginal cost for trucking manufactures with respect to *industry* trucking manufactures output. The expression for marginal cost in section E.4 [see (E.26)] is the marginal cost of trucking output with respect to the *average* firm's output. Fortunately, we can relate the two.

$$\psi_{tm}^f = \frac{\psi_{tm}^i}{N}, \tag{E.54}$$

where:

$\psi_{tm}^i =$ industry trucking manufactures output.

$\psi_{tm}^f =$ the average trucking firm's manufactures output.

$N =$ the adjusted number of firms.

Thus, by the chain rule

$$\frac{\partial MC_{tm}}{\partial \psi_{tm}^i} = \frac{\partial MC_{tm}}{\partial \psi_{tm}^f} \frac{\partial \psi_{tm}^f}{\partial \psi_{tm}^i} = \frac{MC_{tm}}{\partial \psi_{tm}^f} \frac{1}{N}. \tag{E.55}$$

We can now find $\partial MC_{tm}/\partial \psi_{tm}^f$ by differentiating (E.26):

$$MC_{tm} = \frac{\exp(\ln C) w_4 f}{\psi_{tm}^f} \left[\gamma + \sum_{i=1}^{3} D_i \ln w_i + \sum_{j=1}^{3} F_j \ln t_j + G \ln \psi_t^f \right], \tag{E.56}$$

where ψ_t^f equals total output for the firm and all C, w, and t terms are for the average trucking firm producing manufactured output. Differentiating,

$$\frac{\partial MC_{tm}}{\partial \psi_{tm}^f} = \frac{\exp(\ln C)w_4 f}{(\psi_t^f)^2} \left[\left[\gamma + \sum_{i=1}^{3} D_i \ln w_i + \sum_{j=1}^{3} F_j \ln t_j + G \ln \psi_t^f \right] \right.$$
$$\left. + \left[\gamma + \sum_{i=1}^{3} D_i \ln w_i + \sum_{j=1}^{3} F_j \ln t_j + G \ln \psi_t^f \right] + G \right], \quad \text{(E.57)}$$

and the differential for the industry is

$$\frac{\partial MC_{tm}}{\partial \psi_{tm}^i} = \frac{1}{N} \frac{\partial MC_{tm}}{\partial \psi_{tm}^f}. \tag{E.58}$$

The differential with respect to bulk output is the same. The differential with respect to the industry rate for trucking manufactures is -1. The remaining five differentials for this error function are 0.

Once the computer program is supplied with the proper relations for supply, demand, and the Jacobian, all one need do is guess an approximate solution and invoke the computer program. Convergence is generally rapid and computing time short.

For the case of competitive equilibrium, one might be interested in performing various comparative static experiments—predicting how the equilibrium would look under a number of different conditions concerning the exogenous variables. Experiments might include a calculation of the equilibrium for different factor prices, trip characteristics, or numbers of firms in the market.

Perhaps the simplest example might be if one wanted the factor price for truck fuel to increase by, say, 10 percent. In each place the truck fuel factor price is employed, one would want to increase the figure by 10 percent.[26] The program would then be used to calculate the new equilibrium.

Changes which affect both supply and demand are, of course, more complicated. Take, for example, a change in the trip characteristic—average load size for truck. This would have to be changed in the marginal cost functions for truck manufactures and bulk output, the total trucking cost function, the two trucking demand relations, *and* the two rail demand relations, because demand for rail is a function of the trip attributes of its competition—truck. In the demand relations, the trip characteristic should be changed *after* the adjusted value of expenditures $\hat{E}_t$ is calculated.

A final type of static experiment involves changing the number of firms in the market. Trucking in the Official Region appears to exhibit increasing returns to scale. Thus, one might be interested in the savings possible by having a severely limited number of firms which were compelled to price at marginal cost. This could be accomplished by keeping the average firm's marginal cost curve the same, but scaling this curve up by a lesser amount to represent fewer firms in the industry.

This is done most easily by simply changing the adjusted number of firms in the industry. Thus, when the program chooses an industry output, it is divided among fewer firms, so that each firm produces further along its marginal cost curve. When these firms are expanded to industry size, the multiplication is by a smaller number, reflecting the smaller number of firms in the market.

E.8 The Long-Run Industry Rail Supply Relations

The industry rail supply relations of the previous sections were based on short-run cost functions. Since there was no guarantee that the observed rail firms were in long-run equilibrium, only short-run cost functions could be estimated. As was suggested in section E.3, it should be possible to derive a long-run cost relation from the estimated short-run function by selecting, at each level of output, the quantity of the fixed factor that minimizes cost.

The estimated short-run rail cost function (described in section E.5) was of the form (ψ, w, t). The t represented a vector of technology variables. The first of these variables, t_1, was the fixed factor—the capital cost of way and structures. By choosing at each level of output the value for t_1 that minimizes cost, one should be able to generate the long-run industry supply curve for rail. The relationship can be seen to be

$$C^l(\psi, w, t) = C^s(\psi, x_F^*, w_V, t) + w_F x_F^*, \tag{E.59}$$

where:

C^l = total long-run cost of the railroad.

C^s = total variable cost of the railroad.

ψ = a vector of output.

w = a vector of factor prices.

t = a vector of technology variables.

x_F^* = the optimal value of the fixed factor (the first technology variable).

The subscripts F and V denote fixed and variable factors, respectively, and $w = w_V, w_F$.

Now, holding output ψ constant at any value,

$$\frac{\partial C^l}{\partial x_F^*} = \frac{\partial C^s}{\partial x_F^*} + w_f. \tag{E.60}$$

To minimize cost, this partial derivative must equal zero, or

$$0 \equiv \frac{\partial C^s}{\partial x_F^*} + w_f, \tag{E.61}$$

$$\frac{\partial C^s}{\partial x_F^*} = -w_F. \tag{E.62}$$

This agrees with economic intuition. It says simply that to minimize cost at a particular level of output, the marginal cost savings with respect to the fixed factor must equal the gross rate of return. Furthermore, it can be shown that at a long-run equilibrium,

$$\frac{\partial C^s}{\partial \psi} = \frac{\partial C^l}{\partial \psi}. \tag{E.63}$$

This should make it simple to calculate the long-run supply curve. All one need do is choose the value of the fixed factor that satisfies $\partial C^s / \partial x_F^* = w_F$ and calculate the marginal cost. Unfortunately, it seems impossible to isolate an analytical expression for the value of x as a function of output. For this reason, one must turn to simulation.

The methodology described herein varies the value of the fixed factor until (E.62) is satisfied. Then, it calculates marginal cost.

The partial derivative of short-run cost with respect to the fixed factor is easy to calculate:

$$\begin{aligned}
\frac{\partial C^s}{\partial x_F^*} &= \frac{\partial C^s}{\partial \ln C^s} \frac{\partial \ln C^s}{\partial \ln x_F^*} \frac{\partial \ln x_F^*}{\partial x_F^*} \\
&= \frac{C^s}{x_F^*} \frac{\partial \ln C^s}{\partial \ln x_F^*},
\end{aligned} \tag{E.64}$$

where $\partial \ln C^s / \partial \ln x_F^*$ is easily calculable from the estimated short-run cost expression.

The solution methodology also makes use of the fact that $\partial C^s / \partial x_F^*$ is monotonic in t_1 and in output over the relevant range. (This fact should be tested under different conditions.) The methodology finds the level of the fixed factor appropriate for the weighted average firm and expands this level to industry size. For this reason, comparisons to the existing level of the fixed factor should be made with extreme caution. A value of 12.2 percent was chosen for the gross rate of return (see chapter 4).

Basically, the algorithm used to obtain the long-run competitive equilibrium starts with a low[27] value of t_1, the fixed factor. Short-run costs and $\partial C^s / \partial x_F^*$ are calculated for the approximate outputs for the weighted average firm. If $-\partial C^s / \partial x_F^*$ is greater than 12.2 percent, t_1 is incremented. The process iterates until $-\partial C^s / \partial x_F^*$ is equal to 12.2 percent. This is taken as the optimal level of the fixed factor. Short-run marginal costs (which are equal to long-run marginal costs) are calculated. The level of t_1 is scaled up to industry size.

As was discussed in section E.7, Newton's method requires the partial derivative of marginal cost with respect to manufactures and bulk output. For the same reasons that an analytical expression is not possible for the level of the fixed factor, expressions for these partial derivatives are not possible. However, it was found that setting these partial derivatives to zero was sufficient to allow Newton's method to converge and find a long-run competitive equilibrium. In order to generate a long-run rail supply *curve* for manufactures or bulk, one would have to find for each level of output the optimal level of the fixed factor and then calculate marginal cost.

Notes

1. In practice, the four different corrected values of E_t can cause predicted total expenditures on transportation to vary with the mode share. This should cause no major problems.

2. The trucking supply functions were estimated from a long-run cost function. Since, however, the short-run cost function is somewhat more general, we present it here.

3. For a more complete discussion of the reasons behind this process, see appendix A.

4. The factor w_4 must be included to reverse the effect of normalization by w_4.

5. In this case the weighted averages were taken after the first three factor prices had been normalized (divided) by the fourth factor price.

6. The ratio ψ_{td} / ψ_{ts} is equal to 4.179539 for the Official Region, and 4.734653 for the South–West Region.

7. The adjustment factor is 1.2435 in the Official Region, and 1.163279 for the South–West Region.

8. The use of (E.27) implies that both commodities at any level of output have the same marginal cost. It is the different trip characteristics for manufactures and bulk which cause the two commodities to have qualitatively different marginal costs.

9. See appendix B for a further description of hedonic quality adjustments.

10. This factor price must enter as a factor in the expression for total cost because of the initial normalization by it in the estimation process.

11. Some quick mathematical reminders may prove helpful for the simplification:

$$\frac{\partial \ln \psi_2}{\partial \psi_2} = \frac{1}{\psi_2}; \qquad \frac{\partial C}{\partial \ln C} = C;$$

since $\psi_2 = \psi_{2m} + \psi_{2b}$,

$$\frac{\partial \psi_2}{\partial \psi_{2m}} = 1;$$

and finally,

since $t_5 = (\psi_{2m}/\psi_{2b})/(\widehat{\psi_{2m}/\psi_{2b}})$, where the hat denotes the sample mean for that statistic, $\ln t_5 = \ln \psi_{2m} - \ln \psi_{2b} - \ln(\widehat{\psi_{2m}/\psi_{2b}})$, and so

$$\frac{\partial \ln t_5}{\partial \psi_{2m}} = \frac{\partial \ln \psi_{2m}}{\partial \psi_{2m}} = \frac{1}{\psi_{2m}}.$$

12. Since this is a joint production function, it is impossible to speak in terms of average cost. A certain mix of outputs is produced for a certain cost, but allocation of the cost by output is not possible.

13. ψ_{2b} would still equal *all* of the nonmanufactures output. This construction only implies that from the point of view of technology, the demand bulk commodities are no different from the other nonincluded bulk commodities.

14. Weightings, again, are by ton-miles.

15. Unlike trucking, the estimated rail cost equation has no trip quality variables that may be taken from the demand sample for compatability purposes.

16. It should be noted that 1972, the study year, was a transition year in terms of passenger operations. As such, some of the firms reported zero or unusual values for their passenger-miles and passenger trip characteristics. For this reason, the 1971 or even 1970 values of these variables had to be used for some firms.

17. There are 1.5523197 weighted average rail firms in the Official Region and 8.619337 in the South–West Region.

18. Observed in the supply sample.

19. The value of the adjustment factor is 1.137276 for the Official Region and 0.956239 for the South–West Region.

20. The South–West Region contains a relatively large number of "coal roads" which were eliminated from the supply sample. The data for these firms, however, remained in the demand sample. The ratio of manufactures to bulk was significantly different from one sample to another. It was felt that this different output mix might represent a technology that could not be handled adequately by the estimated cost function. For this reason rail output (manufactures plus demand-relevant bulk) for the South–West Region was taken at the demand sample level, but the initial mixture of manufactures to bulk was taken from the supply sample.

21. The factor f_2 is 1.793245 for the Official Region, and 0.975725 for the South–West Region.

22. For the Official Region, these values are 2.076122×10^9 passenger-miles, and $26{,}965{,}699 \times 10^3$ ton-miles. For the South–West Region, the values were 1.194829×10^9 passenger-miles and $86{,}464{,}300 \times 10^3$ ton-miles.

23. Except, of course, for the fifth rail technology variable. See section E.5 for details.

24. A description of the algorithm may be found in Dahlquist et al. (1974, pp. 249–251).

25. The program employed is a modification of one written June 1975 at the University of

Toronto, Department of Computer Science. The original program provided a general solution to an N-dimensional system of equations via Newton's method. A copy of the program used to solve the equilibrium will be made available upon request.

26. The increase should, of course, be performed before the factor price is normalized by the last factor price.

27. The starting value of capital for the weighted average firm for the Official Region was $3 billion and for the South–West $1. For the generation of supply curves, a somewhat lower initial value of capital was used. A value of $500 million was used for both the Official and South–West Regions.

References and Bibliography

Adams, F. G., C. G. Brooking, and N. J. Glickman (1975). On the specification and simulation of a regional econometric model: A model of the Mississippi, *Review of Economics and Statistics* 57: 286–298.

Allen, R. G. D. (1956). *Mathematical Analysis for Economists*. New York: Macmillan.

Barten, A. P. (1969). Maximum likelihood estimation of a complete system of demand equations, *European Economic Review* 1: 7–73.

Baumol, W. J. (1965). Models of the estimation of freight demand, *Mathematica*.

Baumol, W. J. (1979). Quasi optimality: The price we must pay for a price system, *Journal of Political Economy* 87: 578–599.

Bell, F. W. (1967). An econometric forecasting model for a region, *Journal of Regional Science* 7: 109–127.

Benson, L. (1955). *Merchants, Farms, and Railroads: Railroad Regulation and New York Politics, 1850–1887*. Cambridge, Massachusetts: Harvard University Press.

Berndt, E., and L. Christensen (1973a). The internal structure of functional relationships: Separability, substitution, and aggregation, *Review of Economic Studies* 40: 403–410.

Berndt, E., and L. Christensen (1973b). The translog function and the substitution of equipment, structures and labor in U.S. manufacturing, 1929–68, *Journal of Econometrics* 1: 81–113.

Berndt, E., and L. Christensen (1974). Testing for the existence of a consistent aggregate index of labor inputs, *American Economic Review* 64: 391–404.

Berndt, E., and N. E. Savin (1975). Estimation and hypothesis testing in singular equation systems with autoregressive disturbances, *Econometrica* 43: 937–958.

Berndt, E., and D. O. Wood (1975). Technology, prices and the derived demand for energy, *Review of Economics and Statistics* 57: 259–268.

Berndt, E., B. Hall, R. Hall, and J. Hausman (1974). Estimation and inference in nonlinear structural models, *Annals of Social and Economic Measurement* 3–4: 653–665.

Bitros, G. C. (1976). A statistical theory of expenditures in capital maintenance and repair, *Journal of Political Economy* 84: 917–936.

Blackorby, C., D. Primont, and R. R. Russell (1977). On testing separability restrictions with flexible functional forms, *Journal of Econometrics* 5: 195–209.

Borts, G. H. (1952). Production relations in the railway industry, *Econometrica* 20: 71–79.

Borts, G. H. (1960). The estimation of rail cost functions, *Econometrica* 28: 108–131.

Boyer, K. D. (1977). Minimum rate regulation, modal split sensitivities and the railroad problem, *Journal of Political Economy* 85: 493–512.

Brown, R., D. Caves, and L. Christensen (1979). Modelling the structure of costs and production for multiproduct firms, *Southern Economic Journal* 46:256–273.

Buck, S. J. (1965). *The Granger Movement, 1870–1880*. Cambridge, Massachusetts: Harvard University Press.

Burgess, D. F. (1975). Duality theory and pitfalls in the specification of technologies, *Journal of Econometrics* 3: 105–121.

Caves, D., and L. Christensen (1976). Modeling the structure of production in the U.S. railroad industry. University of Wisconsin: Mimeo.

Caves, D., L. Christensen, and J. Swanson (1980a). Productivity growth, scale economies, and capacity utilization in U.S. railroads, 1955–1974. University of Wisconsin, Social Systems Research Institute: Paper 8002, January.

Caves, D., L. Christensen, and J. Swanson (1980b). Productivity in U.S. railroads, 1951–1974. *Bell Journal of Economics* 11:166–181.

Chiang, Shaw-er Judy Wang (1979). The structure of cost and technology of regulated common carriers of general commodities. Massachusetts Institute of Technology, Department of Civil Engineering: MS Thesis.

Chow, G. (1978). *The Economics of the Motor Freight Industries.* Bloomington: Indiana University, Division of Research, School of Business.

Christensen, L., and W. H. Greene (1976). Economies of scale in U.S. electric power generation, *Journal of Political Economy* 84: 655–676.

Christensen, L., D. Jorgenson, and L. Lau (1973). Transcendental logarithmic production functions, *Review of Economics and Statistics* 55: 28–45.

Crow, R. T., (1973). A nationally linked regional econometric model, *Journal of Regional Science* 13: 187–204.

Dahlquist, G., A. Bjorck, and N. Anderson (1974). *Numerical Methods.* Englewood Cliffs: Prentice-Hall.

Daugherty, A. F., and F. S. Inaba (1977). Empirical aspects of service differentiation and transportation demand. Northwestern University, The Transportation Center: Working Paper 601–7711.

Denny, M. (1974). The relationship between functional forms for the production system, *Canadian Journal of Economics* 7: 21–31.

Denny, M., and M. Fuss (1977). The use of approximation analysis to test for separability and the existence of consistent aggregates, *American Economic Review* 67: 404–418.

Diamond, P. A., and J. Mirrlees (1971). Optimal taxation and public production, I and II, *American Economic Review* 61: 8–27, 261–278.

Diewert, W. E. (1971). An application of Shephard duality theorem: A generalized Leontief production function, *Journal of Political Economy* 79: 481–507.

Diewert, W. E. (1974). Functional forms for revenue and factor requirements functions, *International Economic Review* 15: 119–130.

Diewert, W. E. (1976). Exact and superlative index numbers, *Journal of Econometrics* 4: 115–146.

Douglas, G. W., and J. C. Miller (1975). *Economic Regulation of Domestic Transport: Theory and Policy.* Washington, DC: Brookings Institution.

Eads, G. (1972). *The Local Service Airline Experiment.* Washington, DC: Brookings Institution.

Eads, G., M. Nerlove, and W. Raduchel (1969). A long-run cost function for the local service airline industry, *Review of Economics and Statistics* 51: 258–270.

Emery, P. W. (1965). An empirical approach to the motor carrier scale economies controversy, *Land Economics* 41: 285–289.

Engle, R. F. (1976). Supply and demand for metropolitan manufacturing employment and output. Massachusetts Institute of Technology, Department of Economics: Mimeo.

Federal Railway Association (1978). A prospectus for change in the railroad industry. Preliminary Report to the Secretary of Transportation (October).

Fisher, F. M., and K. Shell (1972). *The Economic Theory of Price Indices.* New York: Academic Press.

Friedlaender, A. F. (1969). *The Dilemma of Freight Transport Regulation.* Washington, DC: Brookings Institution.

Friedlaender, A. F. (1978a). Alternative scenarios for federal transportation policy: Second year report, Vol. I. Washington, DC: US Department of Transportation Report DOT-RSPA-DPB-50-78-31.

Friedlaender, A. F. (1978b). Hedonic costs and economies of scale in the regulated trucking industry, in *Motor Carrier Economic Regulation.* Washington, DC: National Research Council.

Friedlaender, A. F., and R. de Neufville (1979). The political rationale of federal transportation policy, *Research in Law and Economics* 1: 97–114.

Friedlaender, A. F., and J. Hammer (1976). Interindustry relations and the surface freight transportation industries. Massachusetts Institute of Technology, Center for Transportation Studies: Mimeo.

Friedlaender, A. F., and R. H. Spady (1980). A derived demand function for freight transportation, *Review of Economics and Statistics* 62: 432–441.

Friedlaender, A. F., J. Halpern, and A. Rodrigues (1977). Freight rates, commodity flows, and regional income. Massachusetts Institute of Technology, Center for Transportation Studies: Mimeo.

Friedlaender, A. F., G. Treyz, and R. Tresch (1975). A quarterly econometric model of Massachusetts and its fiscal structure. Report prepared for the Massachusetts Senate Ways and Means Committee (July).

Friedman, M. (1955). *Business Concentration and Price Policy.* Princeton: Princeton University Press, National Bureau of Economic Research.

Fulda, C. (1961). *Competition in the Regulated Industries: Transportation.* Boston, Massachusetts: Little, Brown & Co.

Furchtgott, H. (1978). A comparison of technology within the regulated trucking industry between carriers of general freight and carriers of other specialized commodities. Massachusetts Institute of Technology, Department of Economics: BS Thesis.

Gellman, A. (1971). Surface freight transportation, in W. Capron (ed.), *Technological Change in Regulated Industries.* Washington, DC: Brookings Institution.

Glickman, N. J. (1971). An econometric forecasting model for the Philadelphia region, *Journal of Regional Science* 11: 15–32.

Griliches, Z. (1972). Cost allocation in railroad regulation, *Bell Journal of Economics and Management Science* 3: 26–41.

Hall, R. E. (1973). The specification of technology with several kinds of output, *Journal of Political Economy* 31: 878–892.

Harbeson, R. W. (1969). Toward better resource allocation in transport, *Journal of Law and Economics* 12: 321–338.

Harris, R. G. (1977a). Rationalizing the rail freight industry: A case study in institutional failure and proposal for reform. University of California, Berkeley, Department of Economics: Working Paper SL-7705.

Harris, R. G. (1977b). Economies of traffic density in the rail freight industry, *Bell Journal of Economics* 8: 556–564.

Hasenkamp, G. (1976a). *Specification and Estimation of Multiple Output Production Functions.* New York: Springer-Verlag.

Hasenkamp, G. (1976b). A study of multiple-output production functions: Klein's railroad study revisited, *Journal of Econometrics* 4: 253–262.

Hausman, J. A. (1974). Full information instrumental variable estimation of simultaneous equation models, *Annals of Economic and Social Measurement* 3: 641–652.

Hausman, J. A. (1975). An instrumental variable approach to full information estimators for linear and certain nonlinear econometric models, *Econometrica* 43: 727–738.

Hudson, E., and D. W. Jorgenson (1974). U.S. Energy Policy and Economic Growth: 1975–2000, *Bell Journal of Economics and Management Science* 2.

Interstate Commerce Commission (1887). *First Annual Report.* Washington, DC: Government Printing Office.

Interstate Commerce Commission (1963). Elements of value of property used in common carrier service as of December 31, 1962, class I line haul railways. Bureau of Accounts: Mimeo.

Interstate Commerce Commission (1976). *The Costs and Benefits of Transport Regulation.* Washington, DC: Government Printing office.

Isard, W. (1960). *Methods of Regional Analysis: An Introduction to Regional Science.* Cambridge, Massachusetts, and New York: MIT Press and John Wiley.

Johansen, L. (1972). *Production Functions.* New York: North-Holland Press.

Jordan, W. A. (1970). *Airline Regulation in America: Effects and Imperfections.* Baltimore: Johns Hopkins Press.

Jorgenson, D. W., and L. Lau (1974). The duality of technology and economic behavior, *Review of Economic Studies.* 41: 181–200.

Keeler, T. E. (1972). Airline regulation and market performance, *Bell Journal of Economics and Management Science* 3: 399–425.

Keeler, T. E. (1974). Railroad costs, returns to scale, and excess capacity, *Review of Economics and Statistics* 56: 201–208.

Klein, L. R. (1947). The use of cross section data in econometrics with application to a study of production of railroad services in the United States. National Bureau of Economic Research: Mimeo.

Klein, L. R. (1953). *A Textbook of Econometrics.* Evanston: Row, Peterson.

Klein, L. R. (1969). The specification of regional econometric models, *Regional Science Association Papers and Proceedings* 23: 105–116.

Kneafsey, J. T. (1975). Costing in railroad operations: A proposed methodology. Massachusetts Institute of Technology, Department of Civil Engineering: Studies in Railroad Operations and Economics, Vol. 13.

Kolko, G. (1965). *Railroads and Regulation.* Princeton: Princeton University Press.

Lau, L. (1974a). Comments on Diewert's "Applications of Duality Theory", in M. D. Intriligators and D. A. Kendrick (eds.), *Frontiers of Quantitative Economics*, Vol. II. New York: North-Holland.

Lau, L. (1974b). Econometrics of monotonicity, convexity, and quasiconvexity. Stanford University, IMSSS: Technical Report 123.

Lau, L. (1976). A characterization of the normalized restricted profit function, *Journal of Economic Theory* 12: 131–163.

Lawrence, M. L. (1976). Economies of scale in the general freight motor common carrier industry: Additional evidence, *Proceedings of the Transportation Research Forum*, Oxford, Indiana: Richard B. Cross Co.

Leontief, W. W. (1947). Introduction to a theory of the internal structure of functional relationships, *Econometrica* 15: 361–373.

Levin, R. C. (1978). Allocation in surface freight transportation: Does rate regulation matter?, *Bell Journal of Economics* 9: 18–45.

Lipsey, R. G., and K. Lancaster (1956). The general theory of the second best, *Review of Economic Studies* 24: 11–32.

Lucas, R. E. B. (1975). Hedonic price functions, *Economic Inquiry* 2: 157–178.

MacAvoy, P. W. (1965). *The Economic Effects of Regulation: The Trunk-Line Railroad Cartels and the Interstate Commerce Commission before 1900.* Cambridge, Massachusetts: MIT Press.

McFadden, D. (1963). Further results on CES production functions, *Review of Economics and Statistics* 30: 73–83.

McFadden, D. (1978). Cost, revenue, and profit functions, in M. Fuss and D. McFadden (eds.), *Production Economics.* Amsterdam: North-Holland Press.

Meyer, J. R., M. J. Peck, J. Stenason, and C. Zwick (1959). *The Economics of Competition in the Transportation Industries.* Cambridge, Massachusetts: Harvard University Press.

Michaels, L. P. (1978). A competitive equilibrium in the rail and trucking industries: A simulation study. Massachusetts Institute of Technology. Department of Civil Engineering: MS Thesis.

Miernyk, W. H. (1965). *The Elements of Input-Output Analysis.* New York: Random House.

Moore, T. G. (1972). *Freight Transportation Regulation.* Washington, DC: American Enterprise Institute.

Moore, T. G. (1975). Deregulating surface freight transportation, in A. Phillips (ed.), *Promoting Competition in Regulated Markets.* Washington, DC: Brookings Institution.

Moore, T. G. (1976). The beneficiaries of trucking regulation. Stanford, California, Hoover Institution on War, Revolution and Peace: Mimeo.

Morton, A. (1969). A statistical sketch of intercity freight demand. Washington, DC: Transportation Research Board, Highway Research Record 296.

National Highway Carriers Directory, Inc. (1973). *National Highway and Airway Carriers and Routes.* Buffalo Grove, Illinois: National Highway Carriers Directory, Inc.

National Research Council (1978). Motor carrier regulation. Northwestern University, Transportation Center: Proceedings of a Workshop conducted by the NRC, Committee on Transportation, in Cooperation with the Transportation Center, Northwestern University.

Nelson, J. C. (1965). The effects of entry control in surface transport, in *Transportation Economics.* Introduction by J. R. Meyer. New York: Columbia University Press.

Nelson, R. A. (1956). The economic structure of the highway carrier industry in New England. New England Governors' Committee on Public Transportation.

Nelson, R. A. (1974). Values of U.S. class I railroads. AAR Staff Studies Group Consultant Report 73–3.

Nelson, R. A., and W. R. Greiner (1965). The relevance of the common carrier under modern economic conditions, in *Transportation Economics.* Introduction by J. R. Meyer. New York: Columbia University Press.

Nerlove, M. (1963). Returns to scale in electric supply, in C. Christ (ed.), *Measurement in Economics: Studies in Mathematical Economics and Econometrics, in Memory of Yehuda Grunfeld.* Stanford: Stanford University Press.

Oi, W. Y., and A. P. Hurter Jr. (1965). *Economics of Private Truck Transportation*. Evanston: Northwestern University Press.

Oramas, U.A. (1975). The cost structure of regulated trucking. Massachusetts Institute of Technology, Department of Civil Engineering: PhD Thesis.

Oum, T. H. (1977). Derived demand for freight transportation and substitutabilities among modes in Canada. University of British Columbia, Center for Transportation Studies: Report.

Panzar, J., and R. Willig (1977). Economies of scale in multi-output production, *Quarterly Journal of Economics* 91: 481–493.

Polenske, K. (1974). *State Estimates of Technology*. Lexington Books, Lexington: D. C. Health & Co.

Ratajczak, D. (1972). A quarterly econometric model of California. Paper presented before the Western Economic Association, American Economic Association.

Roberts, B. F. (1972). Econometric modeling of regions under data constraints. University of California, Berkeley: Mimeo.

Roberts, B. F., G. Wittels, and M. H. Jorgensen (1972). The CEFP/CAL4 econometric model of California. University of California, Berkeley: Mimeo.

Roberts, M. J. (1956). Some aspects of motor carrier costs: Firm size, efficiency and financial health, *Land Economics* 32: 228–238.

Roberts, P. O. (1976). Factors influencing the demand for goods movement. Paper presented at the Annual Meeting of the Transportation Research Board, Washington, DC.

Roberts, P. O. (1977). Some aspects of regulatory reform of the U.S. trucking industry. Massachusetts Institute of Technology, Center for Transportation Studies: Report 77–1.

Rodrigues, A. P. (1977). Manufacturing employment in nine regions in the United States. Massachusetts Institute of Technology Department of Economics: BS Thesis.

Rosen, S. (1974). Hedonic prices and implicit markets: Product differentiation in pure competition, *Journal of Political Economy* 82: 34–55.

Samuelson, P. A., and S. Swamy (1974). Invariant economic index numbers and canonical duality: Survey and synthesis, *American Economic Review* 46: 566–593.

Shephard, R. W. (1953). *Cost and Production Functions*. Princeton: Princeton University Press.

Shephard, R. W. (1970). *Theory of Cost and Production Functions*. Princeton: Princeton University Press.

Sloss, J., and I. E. Harrington (1978). Some observations on domestic freight forwarding in Canada and the United States—an hitherto neglected component of the transportation universe. *Proceedings of the 19th Annual Meeting of the Transportation Research Forum in New York (October)*. Oxford, Indiana: Richard B. Cross.

Spady, R. H. (1979). *Econometric Estimation for the Regulated Transportation Industries*. New York: Garland Publishing.

Spady, R. H., and A. F. Friedlaender (1976). Econometric estimation of cost functions for the transportation industries. Massachusetts Institute of Technology, Center for Transportation Studies: Report 76–13.

Spady, R. H., and A. F. Friedlaender (1978). Hedonic cost functions for the regulated trucking industry, *Bell Journal of Economics* 9: 159–179.

Taff, C. A. (1976a). Classifying interstate motor carriers. University of Maryland: Working Paper.

Taff, C. A. (1976b), A study of A-17 irregular route motor common carriers of freight: The expansion and scope of their operating rights since 1970. University of Maryland: Working Paper.

Tarbell, I. (1904). *The History of the Standard Oil Company*. New York: Macmillan & Co.

Terziev, M. N. (1976). Modeling the demand for freight transportation. Massachusetts Institute of Technology, Department of Civil Engineering: MS Thesis.

Theil, H. (1971). *Principles of Econometrics*. New York: John Wiley.

Trinc's Blue Book of the Trucking Industry, 1967–1977 editions. Washington, DC: Trinc Transportation Consultants.

Uzawa, H. (1962). Production functions with constant elasticities of substitution, *Review of Economic Studies* 44: 291–299.

Uzawa, H. (1964). Duality principles in the theory of cost and production, *International Economic Review* 5: 216–220.

Varian, H. (1978). *Microeconomic Analysis*. New York: W. W. Norton and Co.

Wales, T. (1977). The flexibility of flexible functional forms: An empirical approach, *Journal of Econometrics* 5: 183–193.

Warner, S. (1965). Cost models, measurement errors and economies of scale in trucking, in M. Burstein (ed.), *The Cost of Trucking: An Econometric Analysis*. Evanston: Northwestern University Press.

Wyckoff, D. D. (1974). *Organizational Formality and Performance in the Motor Carrier Industry*, Lexington: D. C. Health & Co.

Wyckoff, D. D., and D. Maister (1975). *The Owner-Operator: Independent Trucker*. Lexington: D. C. Heath & Co.

Wyckoff, D. D., and D. Maister (1977). *The Motor Carrier Industry*. Lexington: D. C. Heath & Co.

Index